MODERN TRANSFORMATIONS OF MOENKOPI PUEBLO

Shuichi Nagata

 ILLINOIS STUDIES IN ANTHROPOLOGY NO. 6

Board of Editors: JULIAN H. STEWARD AND EDWARD M. BRUNER

© 1970 by the Board of Trustees of the University of Illinois. Manufactured in the United States of America. Library of Congress Catalog Card No. 70–76829.

252 00031 5

To my parents and my wife

Foreword

In this case-study of the transformation of Moenkopi pueblo over the course of a century, from a summer farming colony of Oraibi to an independent Hopi community with multiple ties to the outside world, Dr. Shuichi Nagata has made an important contribution to our understanding of the processes of modernization in the Pueblo world. The Hopi Indians, along with their Pueblo neighbors, view their world as a "steady state" with a predestined course, and their relative isolation up to the 1930's kept the influence of external factors at a low level. But World War II had a profound effect, and in the last two decades there have been important changes in all aspects of Hopi life.

These changes have affected even the conservative villages on Second Mesa, as Edward A. Kennard's report on "Post-War Economic Changes among the Hopi" (1965) demonstrates. But nowhere among the Hopi has the exposure to the external forces of the outside world been greater than in Moenkopi. Dr. Nagata concludes his account with the statement that "Moenkopi today emerges as the most profoundly transformed of all the Hopi villages." As such it offers us a "preview" of what is happening throughout the Hopi world, and more generally to the other American Indian groups in the Southwest as well.

The author is a Japanese anthropologist who brings new and somewhat different perspectives to bear on the study of the Hopi villages. The assumption that anthropologists are "culture free" became questionable with the work of Li An-che at Zuni in the 1930's, and more recently other anthropologists from abroad have become interested in the American Indian, with important results. In addition we are beginning to get an inside view of Pueblo life from American Indians themselves.

Dr. Nagata attended the University of Tokyo and later Tokyo Metropolitan University where he studied social anthropology under Professor Toichi Mabuchi. Here he met Professor Julian Steward and joined his project, "Studies of Cross-Cultural Regularities," later coming to the University of Illinois for further graduate work. His field research on Moenkopi pueblo was primarily carried out in the period from June, 1962, to November, 1963, with brief visits later, amounting to almost two years in the field.

This study is the first full-length monograph on a Hopi village since Mischa Titiev's *Old Oraibi* (1944), which provides the essential social, cultural, and historical background for a full understanding of Moenkopi. In addition, Dr. Nagata has made excellent use of the documentary sources, particularly the "letterbooks" kept at the various agencies and the documents collected for the Claims cases and other court hearings. These have enabled the author to present a detailed chronological account of the crucial events involved in the major social, political, and economic changes which have taken place, and also to identify the particular individuals involved and their placement in the society and culture. During his residence in Moenkopi, Dr. Nagata was also able to get considerable information on the major factions, always a difficult problem, as well as on relations with the Navajo, other Hopi villages, and the multitude of government agencies.

The history of the development of Moenkopi over the last century is a fascinating account in itself. Here an oasis in the desert, which had been intermittently occupied for a considerable period, became of critical importance in the 1870's and 1880's with the Mormon expansion and colonization and the growing dissention in Old Oraibi. The Mormons introduced large-scale irrigation systems and other innovations, but before their influence became strong they were forced to sell their holdings to the U.S. government, which established an agency to look after the new reservation and its Hopi and Navajo wards.

During the reservation period the agricultural lands in Moenkopi Wash were allotted, and a policy of assimilation into the larger American society was emphasized through off-reservation schooling and work projects. But progress was slow, and it wasn't until the Indian Reorganization Act in the 1930's, with its emphasis on Indian self-government, reservation schools, and reservation development, that the relative isolation of the Hopi villages was broken. During this period Moenkopi gradually loosened her ties with Old Oraibi as new problems arose that had to be solved locally. Within Moenkopi factions gradually developed which ultimately led to the separation of the community into Upper Moenkopi and Lower Moenkopi, but with cross-cutting ties of kinship and common interests.

World War II had a profound effect, both by reducing government expenditures on the reservation and by encouraging off-reservation employment by whole family groups, in addition to the effects of the draft and military service. Subsistence farming was reduced and ceremonial activities were curtailed. Moenkopi was now a nearly independent community and the separation from Oraibi was almost complete.

The post-war period has shown an intensification of these developments. The Long-Range Program for the Navajo-Hopi Reservation emphasized physical improvements on the reservations, including schools, roads, housing, range improvement, electricity, and water, and an increasing number of government agencies are currently operating in both Tuba City and Keams Canyon.

The long-range trends involve integration into the national economy, the emergence of the nuclear family household, and the suburbanization of the village community to Tuba City. Integration is still only partial, since land and resources are marginal, but there has been an almost complete shift from a subsistence to a cash economy. Wage work is the mainstay of the village economy and agriculture has declined in importance. Dr. Nagata notes that the Hopi have not taken any advantage of the possibilities inherent in the irrigation systems left by the Mormons and maintained by the government. With allotment of agricultural lands and the control of inheritance by white law, the matrilineage and clan organization have become less important and the nuclear family has emerged as the basic unit. The husband, as the major wage earner, has a more dominant role and has largely absorbed the authority position of the mother's brother. Cooperation between families is still important but is on the basis of bilateral relationships rather than lineage relationships. When households are extended, they are variable in composition rather than matrilocal. In many respects Moenkopi has become a wage labor reservoir for the agencies in Tuba City or for Flagstaff and other communities. This has led to a declining interest in community problems and community cooperation. Today the factional split is almost complete, but the two factions parallel one another in interesting ways, rather than continuing to diverge. Both still define themselves as "Hopi" but their alliances and interests remain separate, and neither Upper nor Lower Moenkopi is quite sure just where it is headed.

Modernization is a complex process which involves economic, social, and political transformations, but also includes new perspectives, new values, and new ideas. Moenkopi has largely managed the first set of changes but has not yet developed a modern world view. The young educated Hopis, who initially set up a "village council" to consider local problems, now find themselves in close alliance with the traditionalists of Hotevilla, who are anti-white and against governmental aid and interference, rather than developing a future-oriented and forward-looking viewpoint. Here the Hopi elites have not taken advantage of the opportunity to make the processes of modernization relevant to Hopi culture. Until there is both political and intellectual leadership, the quest for modernity will be only partially realized.

December 15, 1967   FRED EGGAN
University of Chicago

Acknowledgments

The research for this monograph was supported by "Studies of Cross-Cultural Regularities" of the Department of Anthropology of the University of Illinois from June, 1962, to August, 1966. I express my sincere gratitude to Professor Julian H. Steward of the Department of Anthropology, who directed the "Studies," for making this support available to me and for supervising all phases of my work within the larger framework of his research. Without his assistance, this investigation could not have been completed.

The monograph was originally submitted to the Graduate College of the University of Illinois in partial fulfillment of the requirements for a Ph.D. degree in anthropology. I would like to extend my thanks to the members of my thesis committee—J. H. Steward, J. B. Casagrande, Oscar Lewis, E. M. Bruner, and Luis Schneider. I also wish to thank the following members of the department for help in various phases of my work: F. K. Lehman, A. H. Jacobs, the late Betty Starr, P. D. Young, and Patricia J. O'Brien.

In the course of my field work, I relied on the help of innumerable individuals and institutions. My special thanks are due to Dr. H. S. Colton, Dr. E. B. Danson, Mr. B. A. Wright, and Miss Kathleen Bartlett of the Museum of Northern Arizona, Mr. Ray Eicher of the Western Navajo Subagency, Bureau of Indian Affairs, Mr. D. M. Brugge of the Navajo Tribe, Professor E. A. Kennard of the University of Pittsburgh, Professor Fred Eggan of the University of Chicago, Professors R. B. and M. F. S. Woodbury, then of the University of Arizona, and especially Jerrold E. Levy, then of the Tuba City Indian Hospital, Public Health Service, and

Arlette Frigout of the Centre National des Recherches Scientifiques.

Professor Fred Eggan has kindly read my original dissertation and suggested certain revisions, most of which I hope to have incorporated in the present work. I am most grateful for his help and especially his foreword.

Finally, I will forever be in debt to the people of Moenkopi who endured my sojourn in their village. It is my sincere wish that the present work will contribute to an understanding of their problems and to their greater prosperity in the future.

Preface

The present research was carried out between June, 1962, and May, 1966, while I was a research associate of Professor Julian H. Steward of the Department of Anthropology, University of Illinois. Professor Steward offered me this position in order to study the process of modernization among the Hopi Indians as part of his larger program, "Studies of Cross-Cultural Regularities," which has been conducting research on contemporary changes among traditional societies in various parts of the world. A study of the Hopi that followed the general objectives and employed the basic concepts of the larger program would provide data that are comparable to those of previous studies in Nigeria, Kenya, Tanganyika, Burma, Malaya, Japan, Mexico, and Peru (Steward, 1967). At the same time, research on the Hopi would require modifications of the methodology owing to the distinctive cultural tradition or heritage of the Hopi and to their distinctive national context.

I accepted Professor Steward's offer and left for Arizona in June, 1962. Although I had become aware of something ethnographically extraordinary about the Hopi village of Moenkopi in the summer of 1960 on an archaeological field trip in Arizona under Professor John C. McGregor, it was only through the initial suggestion of Professor E. A. Kennard of the University of Pittsburgh and Professor Steward's subsequent insistence that I more or less unwillingly decided to stay in Moenkopi and concentrate on this village alone. Looking back, I am only grateful to their insight.

A total of 23 months were spent in the field—June, 1962, to

November, 1963, July, 1964, to October, 1964, and May, 1965. The following year was devoted to preparation of this work.

It has long been recognized by anthropologists that field work is exceptionally difficult among the Pueblo Indians because of their long contacts with such outside groups as the Spaniards, the Mexicans, and the people of the United States and because of recurrent factionalism among the Indians. Researching among the Hopi, one encounters many delicate situations, and the Indians have learned to mistrust outsiders through experiences, some of which border on the grotesque. Thus, during my study a Chinese Buddhist priest accompanied by a Japanese interpreter visited the village of Hotevilla on World Peace Day at the invitation of an Eskimo Bahaist who resided in Moenkopi, to proselitize for Bahaism and also to denounce the United States government and the Hopi Tribal Council. Some of the older Hopi accepted the Chinese priest as a genuine messiah who had come to deliver them from the control of their Tribal Council, but many of the Hopi are wary of any outsiders who have no lasting commitments to the Indians and who "cause nothing but troubles." Anthropologists, too, are at first regarded with suspicion and mistrust.

The attitude of the Hopi creates serious problems for a fieldworker. It is very difficult simply to enter a pueblo and remain there long enough to conduct research as a participating observer. Even after rapport is established, it must be maintained through constant vigilance. The fieldworker must be sensitive to innumerable possible misunderstandings, and he must preserve neutrality in the face of pressures that might align him with one or another faction and thereby bias his data.

Prior to beginning research in Moenkopi, I spent three summer months of 1962 at the Research Center of the Museum of Northern Arizona, which kindly placed background material on the Hopi at my disposal. After several attempts to find a place to stay in Moenkopi, in late August I obtained lodging with a family in Upper Moenkopi and remained there until the following Easter. Although the two Moenkopi village segments represent opposing factions, I was able to establish rapport with the people of Lower Moenkopi and with their allies in Upper Moenkopi. During this period, I maintained friendly relations by various means extraneous to research. I made my automobile available, even for driving the Indians to Flagstaff, helped in the farming, and assisted in such matters as obtaining a lawyer for a man involved in a suit following an automobile accident. My role with respect to the villagers was, in effect, that of the traditional, helpful son-in-law. In addition, as a Japanese, I aroused friendly curiosity among many persons, although others viewed me with misgivings.

My fairly intense interactions with the people of Lower Moenkopi and their relatives in Upper Moenkopi, however, deprived me of the opportunity to establish rapport with the people and the Council of Upper Moenkopi. My role of helpful boarder in the "traditional" Upper Moenkopi home became so solid that I was regarded as belonging to this household and hence not available to those who did not get along with this family. This led to a situation in which I could not contact the Upper Moenkopi people and Council without jeopardizing my relations with Lower Moenkopi. Eventually, a crisis with the Upper Moenkopi Council facilitated the formation of a tenuous rapport with the village but also resulted in my leaving the village temporarily.

In early May of 1963, I moved to a house trailer in Tuba City. From then on to October, 1963, I could arrange contacts with my informants on my own terms, thanks mainly to the privacy of my trailer. It was during this period that I collected some of the critical information regarding the political process of Moenkopi through interviews with the members of both Lower and Upper Moenkopi. During my stay in the trailer court, I also came to know many Tuba City residents and something of the social structure of this agency town.

Back in Flagstaff, I worked at the library of the Research Center of the Museum to collect information regarding the history of the area. In November, 1963, I returned to the University of Illinois campus.

In July, 1964, I revisited Arizona. The main objective of this second trip was to collect further historical data from the records of the offices of the Bureau of Indian Affairs at Tuba City and Window Rock and the Coconino County office in Flagstaff. During this second period of field work, the staff of the Museum in Flagstaff was preparing a display on the history of Moenkopi under the direction of Barton A. Wright, the curator. The collection of materials for this exhibit was extremely informative. I returned to Illinois in October, 1964.

Shortly before Christmas in 1964, I located a Hopi resident in Chicago and contacted him for the translation of some tape recordings in Hopi. At the same time, I asked Professor Fred Eggan of the University of Chicago to loan me the microfilm records of the letters issued from Keams Canyon Agency during the period between 1899 and 1916. He kindly honored my request and included other films of great relevance to my study.

For the third and last time, I visited Arizona in May, 1965, and stayed a month in a motel at Window Rock. This time I studied volumes of the copies of letters issued from Tuba City Agency from 1902 to 1916. The final preparation of this work began during the summer of 1965, and it incorporates data from the sources described above.

HISTORICAL SOURCES

The information used for the reconstruction of the history of the village of Moenkopi can be divided into four classes.

1. Direct interviews with elderly residents of Moenkopi and other villages. During these interviews I made extensive tape recordings, which were later translated by younger Hopi and others almost verbatim during my second field trip.

2. Letterbooks. I consulted copies of the letters written by various superintendents of Tuba City, Keams Canyon, and Fort Defiance Agencies, which are respectively referred to as Tuba City Letterbooks, Keams Canyon Letterbooks, and Fort Defiance Letterbooks. These are subsequently abbreviated as TCL, KCL, and FDL.

The existence of the letters issued from Fort Defiance Agency has long been known and the collection is usually referred to as Fort Defiance Letterbooks. The letters cover the period between 1880 and 1899, and Robert W. Young of the Navajo Agency made detailed card files of those between 1880 and 1894, which are today preserved at the agency in Window Rock, Arizona. Recently, a major portion of the collection was microfilmed by the Pioneer Historical Society in Tucson. I have studied not only the files and microfilms but the original letterbooks as well.

I refer to the collection of letters issued from Keams Canyon Agency between 1899 and 1916 as Keams Canyon Letterbooks. I have not seen the original letterbooks, but microfilms of the letters in the possession of Professor Fred Eggan were made available to me. Professor Eggan's collection also includes films of the letters by an allotment agent from 1892 to 1893, which I included in the KCL.

Copies of the letters from Tuba City Agency, which I call here Tuba City Letterbooks, are stored in a warehouse of the Navajo Agency in Window Rock. These as well as those from Fort Defiance Agency are all bound in book form (hence "letterbooks").

It appears that these were originally collected by Richard Van Valkenburgh during the 1930's or perhaps earlier. In any event, the TCL cover the period between 1902 and 1917 and are not microfilmed. Hence I studied the original copies and made excerpts, copies of which are now kept at the Research Center of the Museum of Northern Arizona. The inventory of these letterbooks and their locations is also available at the Center.

Because there are so many dates and authors of these letters, it was decided that reference to them should indicate the sources but not specific dates or writers. Particular letters are identified only when comparatively lengthy quotations are made from them.

3. Court exhibits for the *Healing* vs. *Jones* case. At the time of my field work, litigation was going on between the Hopi and Navajo tribal councils over the disposal of the 1882 Executive Order Hopi Reservation. In connection with this case, both councils compiled extensive exhibit materials to be presented to the court. These exhibits were mainly concerned with the history of the two tribes after the U.S. government took over the administration of the area. HvJ, referred to in the text, indicates this source.

4. Thanks to the Museum display on Moenkopi, I was able to collect further information on the Mormon period, which was gathered through interviews by the Museum staff of former Mormon settlers in Tuba City. I interviewed Dr. H. S. Colton of the Museum and Mr. and Mrs. Walter Runke of Flagstaff for this purpose.

The above four sources of information make up the main body of data for historical reconstruction.

PSEUDONYMS

Apart from persons already deceased, the names of the individual villagers that appear in the present work are my own creation. A reader who attempts to identify them with any existing personalities shall only be disappointed.

Contents

1	Introduction	1
2	Social Characteristics of a Colony Village	7
3	Natural Environment	16
4	Federal and Local Contexts: The Reservation	23
5	The Background to Change: Pre-Modernization	30
6	History of Political Change	42
7	Process of Economic Change	98
8	Process of Kinship Transformation	223
9	Contemporary Moenkopi	288
10	Summary and Conclusion	301
	Bibliography	316
	Index	327

1

Introduction

Moenkopi is a Hopi colony on the present Navajo Reservation of northern Arizona, about 40 miles west of its parent village, Oraibi. It is the only Hopi community that lies outside the Hopi Reservation. As compared with the Hopi villages of First, Second, and Third Mesas, the impact of external influences has wrought profound changes in Moenkopi. It is the purpose of this study to describe these changes and assess the factors and processes that have brought them about.

Moenkopi today consists of about 600 residents who are divided between the upper and lower segments. Moenkopi adjoins Tuba City, which has a population of approximately 1,500 persons and is the site of the Western Navajo Subagency. A majority of the Tuba City population is employed in governmental services and in operation of stores, restaurants, service stations, and other private enterprises.

A perennial stream in Moenkopi Wash and a plentiful supply of underground water must have attracted the various Indian populations to this locality from prehistoric times. Numerous Hopi clan legends are recounted about the ruins and prominent natural features in the vicinity (Mindeleff, 1891:28, 33). A survey of the pueblo sites around Moenkopi in the files of the Museum of Northern Arizona shows that the occupation of the area was already in evidence in the thirteenth century.

More or less continuous settlement at the present Moenkopi site as a colony of Oraibi began about a century ago. The processes evident in the subsequent transformations of Moenkopi are similar to those which have operated elsewhere in the world, and they are discernible even among more conservative Hopi villages. Ceremonialism has declined and ceremonial ties between kinship and other social segments have lost much of their former importance. The nuclear family has acquired increased importance as extended matrilineal kinship ties have been weakened by economic and religious changes. A cash orientation that followed the introduction of wage labor and involvement in a money economy has undermined the system of clan and lineage land holdings and cooperative subsistence activities. Territorial, occupational, and social mobility have become possible. As these processes became effective in Moenkopi, factionalism developed, especially between the younger and older generations and between the early settlers and later comers. It continued between those oriented toward the larger society, with its new opportunities and alternatives for the individual, and the others still attempting to adhere to the traditional social and ceremonial structure.

The processes of change are interrelated and mutually reinforcing. They were initiated mainly by factors external to Hopi society. These factors of change ultimately originated in American political, economic, and other institutions, and the United States government attempted to impose some of them directly through its Bureau of Indian Affairs (BIA hereafter). Other factors were mediated by state institutions, missionaries, and private businessmen. In recent years, the people of Moenkopi have had increasing face-to-face interactions with whites and other Indians on and off the reservation and further factors of change were introduced through these contacts.

Hopi culture differs sharply from that of neighboring Indians. The Navajo, who moved into Hopi country in increasing numbers in historic times, were dispersed pastoralists and had become predators on their neighbors. The Southern Paiute, who occasionally drifted down from the north, were scattered in family clusters of simple hunters and food collectors who were engaged in only a minor amount of farming. The Walapai and Yavapai to the west were culturally as simple as the Southern Paiute. The Havasupai, on the other hand, practiced irrigation farming during the summer and hunting and gathering during the winter; they were active traders to the neighboring Indians, including the Hopi from whom they borrowed numerous cultural traits.

On the other hand, the traditional Hopi culture share many basic traits with the other Western Pueblos, including Zuni, Acoma, and Laguna. These communities all possess complexly interrelated matrilineal clans, kivas, initiation rites, and men's and women's societies with special functions in curing, hunting, warfare, fertility, and other purposes. They occupy permanent villages which were supported in the past by intensive farming. The majority of the Hopi live principally on three mesas at altitudes of about 6,000 feet and depend upon flood-water and sand dune farming.

The complex structure and integration of Pueblo culture as a whole are understandable as the result of more than a millenium and a half of history. The Pueblo culture spread during many centuries through northern Arizona, New Mexico, Colorado, Utah, Wyoming, and eastern Nevada until territorial retraction began around 1300 A.D. as a result of the great drought and pressure from the nomadic invaders. The greater concentration of the population in the larger sites occurred in the subsequent period, and distinct features of the Western Pueblo social organization appear to have developed to accommodate the influx of alien groups into the pueblos during this period. Territorial retraction and amalgamation of the diverse groups in Pueblo communities continued under Spanish sovereignty as exemplified in Hopiland by the destruction of Awatobi shortly after the Pueblo Revolt of 1680 and establishment of Hano by a group of Tewa refugees on First Mesa around 1700. When the United States acquired supremacy over the Southwest in 1848, all of the Western Pueblo villages remained highly nucleated in protected localities, such as mesa tops, and their population has become reduced in number by almost chronic famines and diseases.

Of all the Indians north of Mexico, the Pueblos of the Southwest were subjected to both Spanish and American policies. Following the general pattern of administration in the Spanish colonies elsewhere in the New World, the Spaniards directed their policies to the Indians mainly for the exploitation of natural resources and the conversion of native populations to Catholicism. Expropriation of lands, resettlement of the native population as a labor force, and missionization dominated their dealings with the Indians, who were left with a modicum of subsistence lands for themselves. In the Southwest, attraction of the fertile lands of the Rio Grande Valley and the mineral resources of the neighboring mountains in New Mexico induced the Spaniards to force so many Indians into hard labor that, in some instances, entire villages became extinct or were abandoned, while others were strongly Hispanicized. On the other hand, in Southern California, another area under Spanish rule north of Mexico, mission control was more important than economic exploitation; because of this and the aggravating effect of diseases, the Indian population sharply decreased.

Due to the isolation by the deserts and mesas and absence of easily exploitable mineral and agricultural wealth, the Western Pueblos were largely cut off from effects of Spanish control. However, Spanish missionaries, aided by the soldiers, managed to reach these villages where they were instrumental in population decline, abandonment of certain villages, and consolidation of others.

American policies contrasted with the Spanish in important ways. North America, with the exception of Spanish colonialism in the Southwest, was settled directly by pioneering families who worked the land themselves. The Indian population was too sparse and too loosely attached to localities to be utilized as laborers and the areas of plantation development had to depend on imported Negro labor. As the American frontier extended westward, however, lands were forcibly expropriated from the Indians, who either moved farther west, or, when frontier lands no longer existed, were allotted reservations, usually consisting of restricted areas of marginal land. The original policy on these reservations was a strongly authoritarian if somewhat paternalistic treatment of the tribal remnants as wards of the government, with an ultimate aim of remaking them in the Anglo-American pattern. The superintendent of the reservation, assisted by teachers, policemen, doctors, and farm specialists, undertook to implement this policy. Because so many reservations had a scattered population, scant resources, and entrenched traditionalism, these policies enjoyed only minor success. Even children, who were taken from their families and communities and sent to distant boarding schools, usually came home to resume tribal life. The economic plight of the Indians was intensified by the allotment of land in fee simple with disposal rights, which resulted in the loss of much fertile land to the whites. There was a chronic need and hope for government economic help.

This initial phase of the American policy toward the Indians, however, affected the Hopi much less than most tribes. The Hopi villages retained their lands and continued subsistence farming by their own distinctive methods. The carrying capacity of the high mesas and plateaus for livestock was too limited to be a major factor. The sandstone mesas of northern Arizona had no easily extractable mineral wealth, except for a few seams of coal. Even when the whites began to settle northern Arizona, the Hopi remained too isolated to be drawn into the economic system of the whites or to sustain face-to-face relations with them. While these circumstances resulted in limiting external influences on the Hopi to those principally from the federal government, one of the notable consequences during this period was decentralization of communities which followed the pacification of the area and protection of the Hopi from such predators as the Navajo. A number of Hopi moved from their mesas to be closer to their farm lands and sources of water. Oraibi, which had been the only community on Third Mesa since at least 1150 A.D., split in 1906 and subsequently gave rise to Hotevilla, Bacabi, and New Oraibi on the same mesa. Stabilization of Moenkopi as Oraibi's colony also belongs to this period.

As the United States itself changed, especially after World War I and the depression of the 1930's, its Indian policies were also altered. The New Deal for the Indians reversed the previous policy of assimilation, undertook a program of stock reduction, attempted restoration of native economic bases, stopped the sale of lands to whites, installed day schools, and encouraged the formation of tribal governments. At the same time, improved transportation and communication increased contacts between whites and Indians. In the Southwest, private business and missions on the reservations encouraged the change toward greater comprehension of the workings of the larger society and, in many cases, involvement in cash economy.

These trends were further accelerated after World War II and there are now profound internal changes on the reservations as well as a strong drift of the Indians away from their reservations. Traditionalism, lack of education, isolation, and racial segregation, which had retarded change, have been reduced, although by no means eliminated.

Most of the Hopi villages, however, still remain fairly isolated and unchanged. Their complex institutional structures, especially those related to the native religion, tend to perpetuate older patterns. For this reason, anthropological studies have leaned toward focussing on the complexity of aboriginal socio-religious institutions and Moenkopi, the most modern of all Hopi villages, has been largely ignored.

For the study of social change, however, Moenkopi illustrates an interesting case in which highly distinctive institutions are being affected by the processes common to many other parts of the world. Moenkopi exemplifies in broad terms a category of cases in which a segment of a native community has moved to a new locality for economic reasons but at first constituted an exclave of its parent community. Later, it became an ethnic enclave in its new situation and its dependence upon the parent community was greatly weakened. Its social and economic ties shifted toward institutions and social segments of the larger society.

Subsequent chapters will assess the different sets of factors that brought about the transformation of Moenkopi. Analysis of the specific processes of change will deal with the interaction of the distinctive and complex features of aboriginal Hopi society with the particular agencies and mechanisms by which external influences were mediated to Moenkopi. After delineating the general characteristics of Moenkopi as one type of Hopi village community, the features of the natural environment of Moenkopi that attracted the Hopi, Mormons, and later the Navajo Agency will be described. Further it will be shown that the location of Moenkopi on the same reservation as their traditional enemies, the Navajo, and the growth of Tuba City as the seat of what was formerly the Western Navajo Agency, enabled the people of Moenkopi to take advantage of external political controls and created a situation where they could find far superior economic opportunities than was possible in Oraibi. Processes of transformation of Moenkopi will finally be related to modifications of federal Indian policies in each period and to changes in the total national context which contributed to the eventual decrease in the isolation of the Hopi from the larger society.

Main social changes in Moenkopi followed the shift of emphasis from subsistence farming and the system of clans and lineages to wage work economy and bilateral family household at the expense of extended matrilineal kinship ties. Further discussion will show how the changed economy and weakened kinship ties, so intricately related to ceremonial roles and religious performances, caused Moenkopi to reduce its participation in ceremonialism at Oraibi.

Finally, contemporary Moenkopi will be seen as a community in which the nuclear family household is the basic social and economic unit and where this unit relates itself to the national society through the mediation of not only the reservation institutions but, more important, the off-reservation economic and educational institutions of the northern Arizona region and the state of Arizona. Moenkopi has not entirely severed its bonds with Oraibi nor lost the sense of being Hopi, but the decreasing importance of these bonds has created internal factional segments based on the pull of traditionalism and the goal of modernization as they are represented in the residential segments of the village.

2

Social Characteristics of a Colony Village

Prior to the analysis of the modernization process in Moenkopi, it is necessary to indicate a number of characteristic traits which set our community apart from other villages of Hopiland proper. These traits appear to have already been in existence at Moenkopi as a basic orientation of the community when Moenkopi came in contact with the Mormons and the governmental agents of modernization in the last century.

The purpose of this chapter is twofold. First, it indicates that Moenkopi was *not* a representative Hopi community; it was at most a subtype of a Hopi village. Second, it presents these traits as what may be termed a *charter* of Moenkopi for its legitimate existence within the Hopi social system and as an implicit social matrix which contained the constraints and potentials for change throughout the period in question. As such a matrix, they emerge only after an analytical abstraction of the contemporary descriptive materials of Hopi society; their historical origin, on the other hand, is submerged in a larger time perspective than the one presently adopted. As the subsequent chapters will show, however, their relevance to the modernization of Moenkopi has been more than apparent.

THE IDEAL VILLAGE COMMUNITY

A Hopi village, in its ideal form, is a corporate group in Radcliffe-Brown's sense (1950:41). First a chief (*kikwimongwi* or "chief of houses") represents the village community. Second, villagers of both sexes organize and perform ceremonies, but none of these is given as a joint undertaking of more than one village. Finally, the village controls its own territory, including individually occupied residential lots on the village site, farm land owned by clan segments, and communal hunting and gathering "outland."

The village is also a closed group. A person is born into his mother's village and is ascribed membership in that village. This entitles him to be initiated into the Kachina and other religious societies of the village. Membership in religious societies is not transferable from one village to another except by reinitiation. Since political roles among the Hopi are often associated with the religious societies, the outsiders, who do not belong to the societies of their villages, are excluded from participation in village political affairs; in contrast, they are relieved from such responsibilities as would arise from membership.

Matrilineal clanship and matrilocal residence provide the village with a mechanism of continuity. The women, who remain in their village of birth, form the core population. Children fathered by men of different villages, tribes, or even races are incorporated without difficulty into Hopi society through affiliation with their mothers' villages. Men may leave their villages of birth on marriage but return there to perform the ritual duties to their natal households and villages.

Village farm land is divided among the component clans and each clanwoman possesses the land which furnishes basic subsistence. The village hunting and gathering area, however, is utilized by all members of the village. Use of certain tracts of land for hunting rabbits and gathering yucca leaves, fire wood, or clay does not give exclusive rights to the users; these tracts are open to all the residents of the village. Certain localities are accorded religious significance and controlled by the clans concerned with the village ceremonies involving the use of products from these localities. Beyond the realm of the village territory, there exist a number of places of pan-Hopi significance, including the Grand Canyon and San Francisco Peaks.

Harmony through cooperation within a village is the ideal of daily social intercourse. Anyone who disrupts the normal course of life is strongly censured as a nonconformist (*aiyave*). In practice, however, there is a great deal of covert competition among the villagers, and considerable jealousy and suspicion exist between the households in regard to material wealth and economic welfare. Such competition, derived mainly from the limited natural resources and almost entire absence of division of labor, is counteracted only by mystical means of ritual cooperation.

Any village-wide decision ideally depends on unanimous agreement. One of the functions of the village chief is symbolically to seal agreements as unanimous. The requirement of unanimous agreement in decision-making has been a serious obstacle to introducing government-sponsored community projects and has contributed to the formation of factions.

Harmony within the village is also threatened by the development of special economic interests among lineages and nuclear families. Whereas kinship among the Hopi is sanctified in a series of rituals, it also involves joint production and consumption by kinsmen. These activities contribute to the cohesiveness of kin groups, which is enhanced by the absence of economic division of labor within the village. Ideally, this tendency of kin group solidarity to increase at the expense of village solidarity is kept in check by the reshuffling of members of kin groups into numerous ceremonial societies and kiva groups. The ceremonial organization itself, however, is highly complicated and subject to constant criticism and disorganization. Moreover, although each society includes members of diverse clans, the ceremonial prerogatives of the societies are controlled by specific clans in the village. Even in the organization of the kiva groups, kinship is by no means irrelevant because one's affiliation to any kiva is usually determined by one's "ceremonial parent," whose selection is often based on the consideration by one's real parents of the private interests of their family and lineage. Kinship thus permeates the ceremonial societies and kiva groups and subverts their independent existence. The solidarity of a Hopi local community is, therefore, maintained on the precarious balance of the mutual interests between the kinship and religious organization. When the religious cooperations are disrupted, it is usually the kin-based groups that develop as potent political units within the village. On the other hand, the religious organization can further the solidarity of the village when it is powerful enough to conduct ceremonies, uphold the value of village harmony, and check the growth of kin-based interests. The interrelatedness of local, kinship, and religious institutions has often made it very difficult for one aspect of Hopi society to change without affecting the others.

Although the representation of a village is explicitly formulated in the position of the village chieftainship, the chief lacks power to enforce decision. The war chief (*kalé:taqa*), who policed the village and led the war parties in the days of native warfare, had the duty of maintaining peace and order in the village with the help of disciplinary kachina impersonators, and yet his power was limited to the affairs connected directly with warfare. After the abandonment of war, therefore, the role of the war chief was curtailed to ceremonial spheres alone.

The Hopi village chief, however, does not lack authority nor fail to command the respect of his people. The chief of Oraibi was relieved of the burden of cultivating his own fields by his villagers (Titiev, 1944:65). In theory, no village-wide action should be initiated without his approval. If the people accuse each other of negligence in religious duties and of indulging in social dances and debauchery, the chief must remain detached from such unruly subjects and concentrate on prayers and rituals. He is their "father" and they his "children." Like a Hopi father, he is indulgent and seldom reprimands his people. Hopi folktales frequently describe the distress of a chief because of the misdemeanors of his people. Even if a chief rebukes the people, he does through his personal sacrifice, revealing to them how "sad" he is. The chief avoids involvement and partiality by seldom making his will explicit.

In recent years, when factional disputes have become endemic and persistent, such passive leadership can hardly cope effectively with the swiftly changing situation. This is frustrating not only to those in his charge but also to the outsiders, especially governmental agents who are often willing to support chiefly authority. In the contemporary context, therefore, the passivity of chiefly leadership emerges as a virtual threat to the institution of chieftainship itself.

Another threat to village autonomy arises from matrilocal residence. Matrilocality ensures continuity of the component clans of a village and hence the village itself. But a village may come to contain a considerable number of men who move there from other villages upon marriage. These men can be a menace to the solidarity of the village. It is important to note here that traditionally "public" affairs among the Hopi are chiefly men's business. Although women may privately influence their men in specific matters, they rarely have an effective say in discussions and decisions concerning matters of the village as a whole, such as organizing and carrying out ceremonies. Recently, however, an increasing number of issues have come to involve more secular matters that vitally concern members of the households. Under these circumstances, women, who have been managing the practical affairs of the households, insist on participating in decision-making processes. If the husband comes from another village, however, the woman may appeal to her kinsmen in the village for support, but these male relatives are already committed to their marital households in the village and may not wish to become involved. There results a cleavage of interests within the village between those of local and outside birth.

Finally, men from outside the village tend to have little regard for the mores and idiosyncracies of the village into which they marry; their roles there are restricted to domestic spheres while their politico-religious duties are tied to the villages of their birth. If outside economic opportunities arise, therefore, they rarely hesitate to take advantage of them while giving up dependence on the productive resources provided in the village of their wives. The village, on the other hand, cannot prevent this tendency. Many men thus become "free" of the village, while continuing to fulfill marital obligations. Here again is the Hopi village susceptible to division.

INTERACTION BETWEEN MAJOR VILLAGES

In contrast to the other Western Pueblo societies, the Hopi live divided into numerous villages on three mesas. Disregarding the sprawling residential areas at the foot of the mesas for the moment, these villages today consist of Walpi, Shichomovi, and the Tewa-speaking Hano on First Mesa, Shongopavi, Mishongnovi, and Shipaulovi on Second Mesa, and Oraibi, Hotevilla, Bacabi, and New Oraibi (or Kikochomovi) on Third Mesa, with Moenkopi historically derived from Oraibi. Two types of interaction differentiate these communities into three clusters according to their mesa affiliation. The first type is characteristic between the villages on different mesas, especially between those that have been conducting major ceremonies, and is indicative of the mesa-level of integration within Hopi society.

First to be noted between these major villages are mutual independence and lack of cooperation. Politically, Hopi society is stateless (Titiev, 1944:68). Second, competition often characterizes the interactions between them. In a diffuse context of daily life, for instance, one frequently hears the remarks by the Third Mesa Hopi about the people of First Mesa or "Polacca" that disparage their appearance, dress, or devotion to Hopi tradition. Kachina dances and ceremonial races during the basket and snake dances provide another context for implicit inter-village competition through remarks and reputations of different villages regarding the excellence of their dances and physical prowess of the young men.

In addition to competition, Hopi villages are brought into mutual interaction through the recognition by the people of pronounced dialect (Ives, 1861:127; Voegelin, 1959) and craft differentiations among the three mesas. One of the more salient phenomena of inter-village interaction, however, can be seen in the articulation of ceremonial cycles among the major villages of Hopiland. Along with the colorful kachina dances and the famed snake dance, the cycle includes such ceremonies as Wuwuchim, Soyal, and Powamu and the Oaqöl, Marau, and Lakon dances of women's societies. At present, it is difficult to observe the complete cycles of ceremonies in any single village. Some villages no longer perform certain ceremonies, whereas Walpi is apparently resuming ceremonies once suspended. Yet one can detect a certain order in the way these dances are given in different villages. Most of the dances during my stay, for example, started in Mishongnovi, then moved to Walpi, Shongopavi, and finally to Hotevilla and occasionally to Oraibi. An old man at Shichomovi said the order in 1963 somehow changed into Mishongnovi and Hotevilla first and then First Mesa, Shongopavi, and Shipaulovi. In determining this sequence, there does not seem to be any conscious effort for coordination of the dates between different villages. Many factors are involved in deciding dates, and, recently, a dance announced for a particular date may be shifted to another.

Calendrical coordination of ceremonies between the major villages of the three mesas is still clearly observable in the case of the annual alternation of the snake and flute dances. Thus Walpi and Mishongnovi give the snake dance in one year, when Shongopavi gives the flute ceremony, but in the following year, Shongopavi and Hotevilla give the snake dance and Walpi and Mishongnovi the flute ceremony. The orderliness in arranging dances and ceremonies in the villages of Hopiland, though now extremely incomplete, is enough to arouse a feeling that the entire country of the Hopi is throbbing and respiring with an organic rhythm. Thus, while each major village is relatively autonomous and self-sufficient in political and economic organization, all the villages are closely knit into the mesh of the Hopi social system through articulation of ceremonial activities.

COLONY AND MOTHER VILLAGES

The second type of interaction between village communities is limited to those on the same mesa. John Connelly, who first systematically studied this phenomenon on the basis of his Second Mesa data (1956), argued that there exists a persistent tendency toward lineage and community differentiation among the Hopi and that the societal model of the Hopi allocates "social locations" of "prime," "reserve," "marginal" or "mother," "guard," and "colony" roles to the respectively established lineage segments and local communities on a mesa. This pattern of differentiation is partly a result of adjustment to a precarious environment with severely limited technology and allows the Hopi cultural complex to survive by sloughing off the excess population (Eggan, 1964). At the same time, these "locations" structure the relationships between the villages on the mesa with important bearings on social change. Thus, previous to Connelly's study, Dozier showed the "guard" role of Hano of First Mesa in bringing about the social integration of the First Mesa community (1954, 1966b). In the present work on Moenkopi, on the other hand, it is the "colonial" position that is of particular concern.

On each mesa, there is a pair of villages that fall in the category of "mother" and "colony" villages. They are Walpi and Shichomovi of First Mesa, Shongopavi and Shipaulovi of Second Mesa, and Oraibi and Moenkopi of Third Mesa. Of the first pair, Parsons mentions that Shichomovi "should be described as a suburb of Walpi. Not having its own winter solstice ceremony [Soyal], it is not an independent town" (1931:233). Spicer says of Shipaulovi that the village was built during the Spanish period to store the ceremonial goods of Shongopavi in a safe and inaccessible place on Second Mesa (1962:192). Eggan speaks of the same village as Shongopavi's "semicolony" (1950:17, 343). Thompson and Joseph describe such a differentiation of the Hopi communities in terms of "mother" and "daughter pueblos" (1944:47). As these designations suggest, the relationships between the villages of a pair are not like those between relatively independent major villages of different mesas. More specifically, one of the pair is historically derived from and, for performance of certain ceremonies, dependent on the other.

The situation emerges most clearly in the case of Moenkopi and Oraibi. The former community was variously known in the literature as "colony" (Thompson, 1950:37; Dozier, 1966b:20), "summer colony" (Eggan, 1950:18), and "permanent colony" (Titiev, 1944:201). Although the settlement started in the last century, most of the population of Moenkopi came from Oraibi in the early part of the present century. Even after a permanent settlement was created,

3

Natural Environment

The physical setting of Moenkopi can be best described by comparison with that of Hopiland proper. Topographically, both belong to the Colorado Plateau. Surrounded by the Rocky Mountains to the northeast and the Painted Desert to the southwest, the country of the Hopi and Navajo forms a geographical enclave, marginally placed within the United States as a whole. Although existence of such landmarks as Grand Canyon, Monument Valley, and the San Francisco Mountains provided the basis for an active tourist industry in the vicinity and brought the Indians in contact with the general American public, the region was by and large left undisturbed until quite recently.

Similarity of the environments of Moenkopi and Hopiland proper ends here, and remarkable features in the microgeography of Moenkopi set the village apart from all the other Hopi communities. First to be noted in Map 1 is spatial isolation of Moenkopi from Hopiland proper. In the south, Moenkopi Plateau, about 6,000 feet above sea level, removes Moenkopi from the nearest Hopi village by about 40 miles. This distance is greater than that between the most widely separated villages of Hopiland proper, Hotevilla and Hano. In the north and west, the southern escarpment of Kaibito Plateau and the belt of Painted Desert, respectively, bound the arid and inhospitable landscape. Finally, in the east, Black Mesa and Shato Plateau present a further obstacle to access from Hopiland proper.

Second, the climate of Moenkopi is generally warmer and drier than that of Hopiland. Perhaps due to lower altitude (4,500 feet above sea level) and its proximity to the lowland river valley of the Painted Desert, the average temperature of the Tuba-Moenkopi area is 55.0° as against 50.0°F in Keams Canyon (Hack, 1942:9). Temperatures rarely rise above 100.0°F in summer and only occasionally dip below 0°F in winter. According to Hack, our area lies outside the belt of less than 150 frost-free days that covers Hopiland proper (1942:8).

On the other hand, the average annual rainfall in the area amounts to 6.72 inches (U.S. Weather Bureau, 1960), only about two-thirds of what Hopiland receives at 6,000 feet altitude. Of this rainfall, more than half occurs between July and December, leaving April, May, and June as the driest months. Of 55 years of precipitation records (1897–1959), 10 showed no rainfall for May, while there was only one rainless August out of 51 years of the same records. On the average, the dry season accounts for only about 15 per cent of the yearly precipitation. The remainder of rain is confined to the three summer months of July, August, and September. Forty per cent of the winter precipitation falls as snow, which seldom stays on the ground more than a few days. Gregory gives about six inches as an average annual snowfall (1915:112). Feeble spring rain starts at the same time that a certain amount of this snow seeps into the ground to be stored there under the sands. With these two sources of water, native corn seeds manage to germinate and send shoots above ground. Later in its growth, the crop demands water to reach maturity (Forde, 1931:361). The May and especially June rains, therefore, assume a critical role for success of the crop (Gregory, 1915:112). But these are dry season months. June, in fact, is the second driest month (0.30 average inches) with 13 rainless Junes in the 56 years' record (1897–1959).

Annual variations in rainfall are also considerable. The total precipitation was 5.08 inches in 1945, only 3.95 inches in 1946, but in 1947 it reached 6.92 inches, surpassing the 44-year average by 0.20 inches. For the entire Navajo country, Gregory mentions that the variation "ranges between half the normal and twice the normal, measured through a period of years" (1916:60).

The effect of precipitation on farming is severely limited by the character of the rainfall. Best described as rainstorms or thunder showers, a month's precipitation not infrequently occurs within a few hours. Gregory cites an instance of the April rain for 1913, 0.12 inches, which fell within the single day of April 2 (1915:110). Each shower covers only a small area and can be easily detected from a distance by the presence of dark columns of rain against a clear sky. Most rainfall does not seep into the ground but runs off in torrential streams into the lowlands. The destructive power of rainstorms is considerable not only to the crops (Forde, 1931:163) but to human lives as well.

If the rainstorms are not very conducive to farming, rapid evaporation of the surface water during the hot, dry months only aggravates the problem. One frequently observes shriveled young leaves turned yellow. Some farmers cover their corn shoots with tin cans to protect them from dessication during the early months of their growth. Young shoots of the Japanese seedless melons I persuaded a Hopi to plant wilted shortly after they broke ground.

To conclude, agricultural problems implied in the above climatic factors of the Moenkopi area are the exact antithesis of those of Hopiland proper. In the latter, they derive from the "moist region [with] a very short growing season" (Hack, 1942:8), while in our area the problems are of the very dry region with a comparatively long growing season. Dry farming, one of the most predominant forms of farming in Hopiland, is, therefore, precluded from Moenkopi agriculture.

Third, the drainage system of the Moenkopi area eliminates the possibility of practicing the other type of Hopi traditional agriculture, flood-water farming (Forde, 1931:361; Hack, 1942:26ff.). In Hopiland proper, numerous washes, each relatively shallow and long, provide extensive flood plains on which to practice agriculture. In our area, the only wash comparable in its length to those of Hopiland is Moenkopi Wash, which begins at Black Mesa and courses a distance of about 75 miles to drain finally into the Little Colorado. However, erosion of the Wash floor has reached such a stage now that even at times of increase in the flow, the stream never spreads itself over the wide, alluvial floor.

Arroyo cutting of Moenkopi Wash appears to have been in progress since the last century (Gregory, 1915:115). Hack suspects changes in the course of the Wash for an unknown period of time (1942:80). While all this indicates the possibility of flood-water farming in the past, I was unable to obtain confirmation of the practice from the present residents of Moenkopi or from the available literature. Apart from the evidence of construction of a diversion dam on a point near *Tuviktsyala* (see Map 4) during the Mormon settlement period in Tuba City, it appears certain that direct flood-water farming has never been practiced in this area. Utilization of the perennial stream in Moenkopi Wash around Moenkopi has, on the other hand, been incorporated into the general framework of irrigation farming.

If the geography of the Moenkopi area precludes the possibility of traditional Hopi agriculture, its geology provides an excellent opportunity for irrigation, a minor form of farming in Hopiland proper. The geological structure of Kaibito Plateau, on which Tuba City and Moenkopi stand, is crucial here. The surface rock of the plateau consists of highly porous Navajo sandstone, which, due to intensive wind action, contains numerous depressions on top. Sand dunes exist in abundance on its northern slope. Consequently, the huge surface area of the plateau works as an effective intake of rainwater. Further, the shale, which lies beneath the surface sandstone and retains the ground water, slopes down south and southwestward to Moenkopi Wash, which, in turn, exposes the water-bearing level by cutting the fill and canyon bed (Gregory, 1916: 145–60). Finally, the surface sandstone, worn through weathering and aeolian abrasion, brings the water level closer to the surface (Gregory, 1915:114). Thus the underground water becomes available either in the form of natural springs or of artificial wells. Tuba City, Moenkopi, Moenave, and Willow Spring are locations of the innumerable natural springs of various sizes, which enabled verdant growth of cottonwoods and induced Gregory to call them the oases of the Navajo country (see Map 1).

With the water supply secure in the geological structure of the area, wind loses the significance it has in sand dune farming in Hopiland proper (Hack, 1942:32ff.). However, severe sand storms are quite frequent in our area, especially during the spring. The direction of these storms, as well as the milder winds in other seasons, is uniformly southwest. To the north of Tuba City, one observes fresh sand dunes and outcrops of denuded rock, including Castle Butte. This area is mostly arid and unoccupied even by the Navajo. These dunes have been travelling farther to the northeast to cover the upper portion of Reservoir Canyon[1] (Gregory, 1916: Plate XXIV B) and have buried a few springs there (1915:101). On the wall of Moenkopi Wash, opposite the village, three such sand dunes formed and apparently stabilized two or three decades ago. Since dry farming is a remote possibility, no effort has been made by the villagers to retain aeolian sands on farms by laying

---

[1] It is now called Pasture Canyon. Throughout the present work, I use the older name, "Reservoir Canyon."

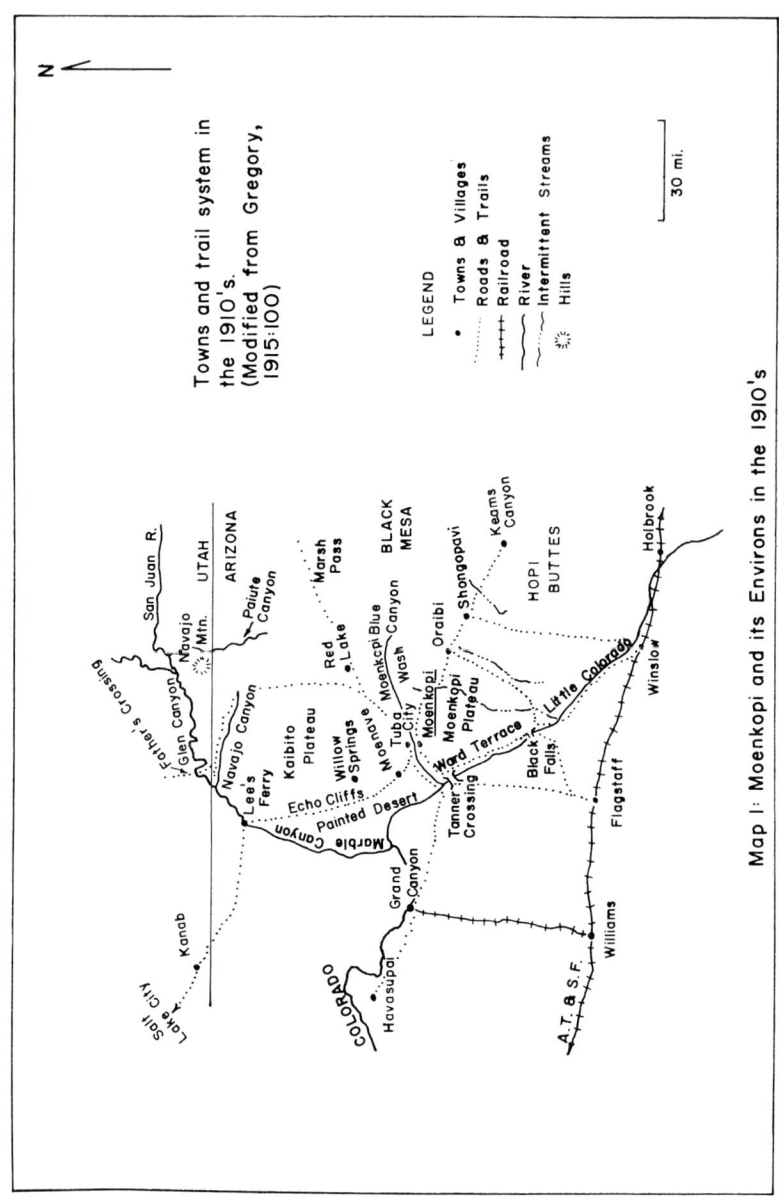

Map 1: Moenkopi and its Environs in the 1910's

down windbreaks of brushwood. However, the winds carry various extraneous objects into the irrigation canals and ditches, and the need for their constant removal, in addition to the general repair work of the water course, emerges as an important task for the community of Moenkopi.

The forage type of the Tuba-Moenkopi area falls in the "browse" category of the barren Painted Desert rather than the "grassland" that characterizes Hopiland proper (Humphrey, 1955). A grove of cottonwoods in Moenave, seven miles west of Tuba, appears as a surprise to a traveller approaching the area through the desert. In Reservoir Canyon, cattails (*wipo*) and reeds are lush and the Hopi have been collecting them for ceremonial purposes in Third Mesa. Cedar and willow dot various parts of Moenkopi and Tuba City. A mile or so beyond these settlements, however, the vegetation is suddenly reduced to such hardy desert plants as sagebrush, rabbitbrush, wheatgrass, snakeweed, and Mormon tea. Wild onions (*si:wi*), saltbrush (*ongatoki*), wild spinach (*homina*), and other grasses, which the Hopi use in their cuisine, sprout in this surrounding area in springtime. Piñons and junipers, important as firewood, are found only in the remote localities of Black Mesa, Shato Plateau, or the Coconino National Forest to the west across the Painted Desert. Gregory mentions that "the nearest piñons were 15 to 20 miles distant [from Tuba City]" (1915:112). For timber, the Indians have looked mainly to the San Francisco Mountain range.

Finally, Moenkopi Plateau presents an interesting case in regard to mineral resources. A canyon issuing northeast of the plateau exposed a vein of coal in the past and some efforts have been made by the Tuba City Agency to develop a coal mine there. The Hopi and Navajo Indians have been extracting it for pottery manufacture. The wind-swept, sand-free rocks to the north of Tuba City have also been important as building materials.

Since the exploitation of oil and natural gas resources by the Navajo Tribal Council, the rich mineral deposits in the Navajo country have been attracting the attention of outside interests. The Tuba-Moenkopi area is not an exception and and a uranium mill was constructed about 10 miles east of Tuba City about five years ago (Young, 1957:92). The implication of these latent resources for the social change of Moenkopi will be discussed in subsequent chapters.

To summarize, the Tuba-Moenkopi area is an oasis in the desert. The environmental complex of Moenkopi sharply separates our village from Hopiland proper. In addition to its colonial position in the traditional social system, the physical setting of Moenkopi gave another set of unique conditions which influenced the developmental course of the village as they came to be exploited in the framework of the Indian reservation system.

4

Federal and Local Contexts: The Reservation

In the framework of the national legal system, the majority of the Indians of the United States are placed under the direct supervision of the federal government through their respective reservations. State-level institutions become relevant to the life of the Indians only through the mediation of the federal government. This juxtaposition of the two integrative levels of administrative institutions and the degree of their reciprocal transactions constitute a measure of assimilation and integration of the Indians into the main stream of American society.

RESERVATION SYSTEM

Based on the assumption that "assimilation of the American Indians into the normal stream of American life is inevitable" (Provinse et al., 1954:388) or "desirable" (Spicer, 1954:890; also see Kelly, 1954:710; 1957:72; Dozier et al., 1957:161–62; Fontana, 1963:176; Dunning, 1962:209–32), the federal government implemented various policies designed to bring about assimilation and entailing eventual withdrawal of direct federal supervision of the Indian reservations.

Federal Supervision

The Indian reservation, according to Spicer, is "built on political and economic linkage, coercive roles, and structural reorganization" (1962, ed.:526). Politically, the reservation system places the Indians in a "colonial setting" (Shepardson, 1963). The locus of sovereign responsibility in dealings with the surrounding populations shifts from the Indians themselves to the U.S. government. They become the latter's "wards." In the past, the Indians manipulated the balance of power between such groups as the government, Mormons, white traders and missionaries, and other Indian tribes to protect their own interests, but with the imposition of the system, room for such independent maneuvers was drastically curtailed and opportunities to employ skillful diplomacy disappeared rapidly.

The imposition of the reservation system also meant the incorporation of the Indians into the national legal system. State laws seldom applied to them directly, but the uniform application of reservation principles made American Indians a homogeneous legal category under federal law. The basis of the present pan-Indianism was thus laid out. Though innumerable complications ensued from this separation of the state and federal governments, the mutual adjustment of the two legal systems was gradually effected. The legal status of the Indians in the federal code of law as well as the application of state law in specific areas have been changing as the involvement of the Indians in the larger society off the reservations proceeds.

As Spicer pointed out (1962:343-44), one characteristic of the Indian reservations is that they were treated as a framework within which to execute economic policies for development of the reservations and to promote the material welfare of the resident Indians. To the Hopi, this meant considerable improvement in their chances for survival over the pre-reservation period. On the other hand, the role of the Bureau of Indian Affairs, especially during the initial period when it issued rations of food and other provisions, came to be tinged with paternalism and its image as a benefactor of the Indians appeared to be fixed in the minds of many Indians.

Institutional and territorial separation of the Indians on the reservations resulted in their relative isolation from the outside society. Their interaction with non-Indians or Indians of alien tribal affiliations became highly restricted. In fact, as Vogt and others have argued (1951:94-98; Adams, 1963:90-91), the most important sources of modernization (boarding schools, wage work, and military service) to the Indians existed outside the reservations, which tended to maintain the traditional pattern of life in isolation from the larger American society. Added to the economic marginality of many reservation lands, the reservation system tended to create socio-cultural enclaves (Spicer, 1962:2) of the Indians lagging behind the march of the national society. Changes that occurred in many reservation societies, therefore, often took divergent courses from those in American society at large.

The federal supervision of Indian affairs on the reservations is broadly differentiated into two periods by the passage of the Indian Reorganization Act of 1934 (IRA hereafter). The major aim of this act consisted of restoring to the Indians the land bases on which to rebuild a self-sufficient reservation economy and, second, of providing a form of self-government with Indian leadership to manage the internal affairs of the respective tribes. On the Navajo and Hopi reservations, the former aspect of the new law resulted in the stock reduction programs and establishment of land management units. The general orientation of economic development was further pursued in the post-war period through the initiative of the BIA and, in the case of the Navajo tribe, from the Tribal Council itself. At the same time, the government renewed its efforts in numerous service projects, including land management, schooling, and medical services. Recently, the BIA also came to handle relief projects for destitute Indian families and individuals (Brophy and Aberle, 1966:71).

In short, the Indian reservations provided boundaries within which the government performed a dominant role in its comprehensive "programs for civilization" (Spicer, 1962). This also applies to the recent introduction of medical services to the Indians through the Public Health Service. Through the Indian administration, the government in Washington maintained an autonomous tie with the Indians, which was only occasionally challenged by such other groups as Congress, the Indian Rights Association, business interests, missionaries, anthropologists, and others. Thus, though the autonomy of federally supervised reservations was not absolute, the over-all BIA policy served to prolong relative isolation of the Indian groups.

The policies the Indians were submitted to were certainly never consistent during the entire period of American rule, and often a new policy reversed an earlier one. But the reservation system, by minimizing opportunities for direct contact with the dominant American populations, contributed greatly to the protection of individual Indians and the preservation of their societies and cultures. The termination of federal assistance and supervision through the reservation system, a law enacted during the Eisenhower administration, amply demonstrated the disruptive consequences following dissolution of the Indian reservations (La Farge, 1957:41–55; Stern, 1961–62:172–80; *Indian Voices,* 1965).

Tribal Self-Government

Since the IRA in 1934, tribal councils have been an integral part of the reservation system. The general objective behind the creation of councils was to restore the rights of the Indians to govern their own affairs as a transitional stage to eventual assimilation into the American social system; as such, they represented a shift in policy of the Indian administration from the preceding, paternalistic "superintendent system" (Spicer, 1962:351). In Spicer's terms, tribal councils are "without control of their external relations but with control over their own internal affairs" (Spicer, 1962:353).

Establishment of the tribal councils resulted in a degree of tribalization among Indians who were traditionally bereft of formal tribal organizations. Recently the councils have come to assume an important economic function within reservations and have induced many outside business concerns to operate on the reservation land. In some cases, the councils themselves offered a significant amount of employment to the Indians on the reservations.

One of the important tasks that the councils perform at present is to provide a channel between the BIA and individual communities for the introduction of community projects. Partly because of lack of participation in some villages, this role of the tribal government has not been effectively played out among the Hopi. However, the basis for this role is there and as the government has launched an increasing number of projects, the function of the tribal council as a mediator has also been gaining importance.

Councils maintain tribal courts and police corps. These institutions have been comparatively successful in controlling minor violations committed by the Indians on the reservations (see Thompson, 1950:86). As yet, however, federal courts and the FBI handle 10, and on the Navajo Reservation, 11 major crimes, including homicide and robbery, committed on the reservations by the Indians (Brophy and Aberle, 1966:49; Shepardson, 1963:119).

STATE SYSTEM

In the pre-war years, the relationship between the state and federal governments in regard to the administration of Indian affairs on the reservations was characterized by mutual antagonism, and the federal government was preoccupied with the task of protecting the rights of the Indians from the encroachment of state interests by maintaining intact the isolation of the reservations. The state, on the other hand, countered the government by disfranchising the

Indians in its political elections and refusing to extend its services to them.

After World War II the hostile atmosphere between them was considerably mitigated, and, though in theory the jurisdictional separation is still maintained, several accomodative changes have been made to increase the participation of Indians in the affairs of their states (Spicer, 1962:352). In 1948 their right to vote in state elections was recognized in New Mexico and Arizona (Shepardson, 1963:60). Since 1950 public school instruction has been carried out on the Navajo Reservation (Young, 1957:11). At about the same time, the state of Arizona extended its Employment Service facilities to strategic points on the reservation for recruitment of forest fire fighters and construction laborers. The state of Arizona also handles public welfare programs for the Indians (Young, 1961:297-98). This participation by the Indians in state institutions should not be regarded as a unilateral concession by the state. While the reservation land remains tax free (Spicer, 1962:353; La Farge, 1957:42; Shepardson, 1963:61), the Indians are subject to "federal income, excise, and other taxes, and all state levies on their salaries, off-reservation earnings, purchases, and property" (Brophy and Aberle, 1966:16). Federal assistance earmarked for Indian welfare is extended to the state of Arizona in the form of percentile return of the federal taxes, collected from the state, back to the state (Young, 1961:295).

FEDERAL AND LOCAL CONTEXTS OF MOENKOPI

As an Indian community, Moenkopi comes under these systems in the general terms described previously. Once again, however, details of their relevance to our community entail a significant twist which sets Moenkopi apart from other villages of Hopiland proper.

First, its location on a reservation mainly occupied by the Navajo marks one distinction. Moenkopi certainly is not the only Indian settlement whose reservation contains tribally heterogeneous populations. A number of Indian reservations in the United States are composed of tribally and culturally different groups of Indians that are lumped together in a single reservation framework. In order to take these situations into consideration, numerous executive orders include a clause to secure the rights of other Indians than those designated in the names of the newly established reservations (see the Executive Order of December 10, 1882).

In spite of this legal precaution, the status of Moenkopi on the Navajo Reservation has had serious consequences in the course of transformation of the village. To begin with, the Navajo Indians are the traditional enemy of the Hopi and, as shall be shown later, one of the main preoccupations of the early Moenkopi settlers was to form an effective alliance with outsiders in order to defend the village from attacks by the Navajo. The enmity between the Navajo and the Moenkopi Hopi has not been resolved by the inclusion of the village on a reservation where the Navajo dominate. For various reasons, some of which have already been mentioned, Moenkopi maintained a close tie with the Hopi in Hopiland proper, but since the latter were allotted their own reservation and agency, the position of Moenkopi has been supported in a similar reservation system framework that bases itself in Keams Canyon. There is, therefore, a serious discrepancy between the location of Moenkopi and its administrative linkage, and one cannot take the former as indicating the latter. More succinctly stated, the minority status of Moenkopi on the Navajo Reservation has been made secure through retaining an administrative tie with the Hopi Agency. Had there not been such a source of support, Moenkopi would have had no choice but to be assimilated in the single administration of the Navajo Agency. The problem of jurisdictional ambiguity as a result of the location of Moenkopi seems to have become more acute since World War II, when the tribal governments of the Navajo and Hopi came to assume greater importance to the lives of the Moenkopi residents.

A similar jurisdictional separation of Moenkopi from Hopiland proper exists within the state system as well: Moenkopi belongs to Coconino County of Arizona while Hopiland proper is in Apache County. Because of the strength of the federal context so far, this difference in county affiliation has not been significant enough to call for detailed analysis. Yet its future implications are more than apparent, since local and national politics, education, and taxation are all organized on the basis of county divisions. Already the state welfare payment comes to Moenkopi through the Coconino County Office at Flagstaff.

In addition to the jurisdictional affiliation of Moenkopi but perhaps more important to its modernization is its geographical proximity to Tuba City, the site of present Western Navajo Subagency. Spicer has already discussed the importance of such an agency community in the socio-cultural change of the Indians (1962:353ff.). Just as the missions of the Spaniards and garrison posts of the American federal troops, the agency towns formed a contact community in which the Indians interacted face to face with the messengers of the civilization; the schools and hospitals were built around the agency office and trading posts drew the Indians into the orbit of national economy. The agency towns were, and in many reservations still are, a place for Indian wage earning activities as the government hired Indians capable of performing various jobs.

All these features of an agency community applied to Moenkopi with greater cogency than any other villages in Hopiland proper. While the distance between the Hopi Agency in Keams Canyon and its closest Hopi community, Polacca, is about 10 miles, Moenkopi is only about two miles from Tuba City, the distance easily covered on foot for daily commuting. To the agency in Tuba City, on the other hand, Moenkopi turned out to be the most stable and reliable source of Indian labor in contrast to the relatively mobile Navajo. For a period, when the agency was engaged in commercial crop production, therefore, Moenkopi maintained a very intensive contact with the whites in Tuba City. To varying extents, Moenkopi has been an integral part of the agency community that centered in Tuba City. Economically, the Hopi of Moenkopi have been more dependent on Tuba City than the Navajo, of whose administration the Tuba City Agency has been in charge.

In addition to its colonial position and unique natural environment, then, the minority status of Moenkopi on a reservation dominated by the Navajo, the traditional enemy of the Hopi, and its geographical proximity to the agency community of Tuba City constitute the final characteristics of Moenkopi to be taken into account in the analysis of its modernization.

5

The Background to Change: Pre-Modernization

PRE-MORMON PERIOD (prior to 1875)

To date little is known of the prehistory of the area. There are several pueblo ruins in the vicinity of Moenkopi, but they have not yet been subjected to intensive archaeological analysis. Posiolelena ruin, located just north of the present village of Moenkopi, has, on the basis of a surface collection of pottery, been tentatively dated at post-1300 A.D. (see Map 3). Other sites in the area have also been listed in the Museum of Northern Arizona files as dating from 1200 to 1300 A.D. At present there is no information on the possible relationship of these ruins to present-day Moenkopi, though some Hopi clan legends mention former occupation of these sites during their easterly migration to Oraibi (Mindelef, 1891:28, 33; Titiev, 1944:74).

A brief description of the area during the eighteenth century is provided by two Spanish explorers, Escalante and Garces.[1] Both traversed the northern Arizona region, but only Garces appears to have encountered evidence of recent Hopi occupation in the Moenkopi area (Coues, 1900:357–59, 393, 401–2). Escalante bypassed the Moenkopi area on the west (Auerbach, 1943:106–7; Bolton, 1950:231). However, both explorers reported Havasupai, Yavapai,

---

[1] Gregory identifies "Rancheria de los Gandules," described in the account of the Oñate expedition of 1596–98 from New Spain to New Mexico, with one of the ruins in the Moenkopi area (1915:115). K. Bartlett of the Museum of Northern Arizona says this identification is incorrect (cf. Hammon and Rey, 1953:V, 328).

Ute, and Paiute camps and fields in the vicinity of present Moenkopi (Coues, 1900:356–57; Auerbach, 1943:103; I. Kelly, 1934:549–50).

The Hopi appear to have already been farming in the environs of Moenkopi in the latter part of the eighteenth century. Garces' account of July 1, 1776, gives some indication of the pattern of land utilization around Moenkopi:

> I went one league and a half east southeast, and found a river that seemed to me to be the Rio de San Pedro Jaquesila [Moenkopi Wash?], and on a mesa contiguous thereto a half-ruined pueblo. I asked what that was, and they [Yavapai guides] answered me that it had been a pueblo of the Moqui [Hopi], and that some crops which were near to a spring [Moenkopi spring?] were theirs, they coming to cultivate them from the same Moqui pueblo [Oraibi] that is today so large (Coues, 1900:357–58).

Escalante reported "a little field and the farm of the Cosninas [Havasupai]," planted with corn, beans, squash, watermelons, and muskmelons, probably in the Blue Canyon area (Auerbach, 1943:106). During this period the Hopi also traded with the Utes in the Moenkopi area (Coues, 1900:356).

Thus, during the latter half of the eighteenth and the first half of the nineteenth centuries, the area was occupied by numerous small Indian bands engaged in subsistence activities; and there was apparently little conflict between these bands. The comparatively peaceful co-existence of the different ethnic groups appears to have been disrupted by the arrival of the Navajo from the east and northeast in the middle of the last century. The marauding Navajo made Hopi farming in Moenkopi extremely precarious. Under these circumstances the Hopi had to enlist the help of a third power strong enough to check the Navajo advance. While the U.S. government performed such a function for the eastern Hopi, the western Hopi looked to the Mormons who were moving into Arizona from the north.

MORMON MISSION PERIOD (ca. 1875–ca. 1885)

More detailed historical documents relevant to Moenkopi are available for the period after the Civil War. During the 1850's and 1860's, the Mormons were colonizing the fringes of Kaibito Plateau, which had been the territory of the Utes and Paiutes. During the 1860's and the early part of the 1870's, the Navajo were a serious threat to the outlying Mormon communities in southern Utah and to the Moenkopi area. Although the campaign of Kit Carson,

1863–64, appeared to halt the ravages of the Navajo on the Hopi villages, it had little effect in the Moenkopi area, where the small Hopi colony was left at the mercy of the Navajo raids.

Mainly because of these dangers, the Hopi remained in Moenkopi only during the farming seasons and did not form a permanent settlement. They stayed in Oraibi for the remainder of the year and took part in village religious activities. Even this seasonal residence in Moenkopi was sometimes so threatening that a Hopi named Tuba induced the Mormons to settle in the area in return for protection from the Navajo. The Mormons, who had been preparing to extend their colonization into Arizona and even farther south, were glad to conclude the agreement.

The first successful colonization of the Little Colorado region by the Mormons was carried out in 1875. The Moenkopi area, which had frequently been visited by the Mormon explorers previously, was colonized at the same time. The purpose of their settlement in this oasis was to construct a liaison station between the settlements in southern Utah and new colonies along the Little Colorado and to secure a mission post for proselytization of the Mormon faith among the Indians in the area. Thus Tuba City came into existence in 1878.

Following the general pattern of Mormon colonization in the Southwest, the pioneers succeeded in improving the land by building an extensive irrigation system, including a series of reservoirs, rock and earthen dams, and canals, along Reservoir Canyon and Moenkopi Wash. The crops they grew consisted of a variety of corn, wheat, barley, oats, beans, potatoes, sweet potatoes, melons, cotton, and even "sugar cane" (sorghum?) for molasses. The pioneers also planted several kinds of vegetables, numerous apple, pear, peach, apricot, and prune trees, and grape vines. Although the sale of farm produce outside the area was not recorded, quantities of surplus fruit appear to have been sold in Flagstaff.

The livestock business was introduced by two Mormons to Tuba City, one of whom came to be known widely in northern Arizona as one of the largest cattle operators in the region. While no Mormon sheep were mentioned in the literature for this period, chickens and hogs were raised by individual households for domestic consumption.

The Mormons also engaged in limited commercial activities. Apart from a general merchandise store for dealing with the Indians, the settlement of Tuba City contained a blacksmith shop, two mills, and a short-lived woolen mill which attempted to process Navajo wool. One of the major occupations of the Mormons during this period was freightage. Navajo wool was frequently shipped to Utah and to Winslow and Sunset, Arizona, and Mormon piñon nuts and dried peaches were hauled to Flagstaff. From Utah and from Winslow, Holbrook, and Flagstaff, Arizona, flour, lard, and lumber were brought back to the settlement.

The presence of the Mormons in the area obviously eased the minds of the Hopi, who moved down to Moenkopi in increasing numbers and built permanent homes. Although the Hopi settlement thus became stable and expanded, the tranquility of the colony was not to last very long. Mormon exploitation and development of the land around Tuba City and Moenkopi was spectacular and not infrequently aggressive. Their appropriation of the land resources proceeded quickly, and soon they began to invade the territory that the Hopi regarded as theirs. The Hopi farmers were relegated to the position of sharecroppers by the Mormons (TCL). Conflicts with the advancing Navajo over range land were also present and occasionally resulted in killings on both sides. Toward the end of the last century the Mormons were entangled in a competition with the Protestant missionaries and the Indian Rights Association, both of which entered the area with the aim of wooing the Indians from their faith and removing the Mormons. The latter, on the other hand, attempted to retain the fruits of their endeavors by allying themselves with the gentile interests of the state of Arizona and Coconino County.

EARLY RESERVATION PERIOD (ca. 1885–ca. 1900)

In Hopiland proper, the Navajo, who had once been contained on the eight million acre reservation of 1880, kept pouring out and trespassing "upon Hopi gardens and grazing lands, seized and carried away livestock and committed physical violence" (U.S. District Court for the District of Arizona, 1962:12). During this period, the Santa Fe Railway was in the process of construction along the Little Colorado, and such railroad towns as Holbrook and Winslow grew in the immediate neighborhoods of the Mormon towns of St. Joseph, Sunset, and Snowflake. In order to eliminate the Navajo menace as well as to avoid further encroachment of the Mormon and gentile settlers in Hopi territory, the government issued an Executive Order demarcating the Hopi Reservation in 1882 (Jones, 1950). However, the new reservation did not include the Moenkopi area, which was left to the mercy of Navajo and

Mormon exploitation. In part to secure this area from the mounting conflicts between the Mormons and Indians and in part to answer the wish of the local Indians for a government school, a spot was chosen in Blue Canyon at the western end of the 1882 Hopi Reservation for a new boarding school in 1899.

These measures by the government, however, did not ameliorate the gravity of the situation in Moenkopi and Tuba City. Agitations by private individuals of the Indian Rights Association and the Protestant missionaries continued and a series of court struggles ensued. Finally the government acted on the fact that the Mormon right in the Tuba City area was only a squatter's right and on January 8, 1900, William McKinley signed an Executive Order which closed this part of the public domain as the Western Navajo Reservation. In 1902 the government purchased the Mormon improvements in the area for $45,000, and the school in Blue Canyon was moved to Tuba City in the spring of 1903.

During the final decade of conflict between the Mormons and the government, the latter sent out a party of inspectors, who surveyed the land on the alluvial floor of Moenkopi Wash and allotted it among the Hopi and Navajo Indians on the basis of claims made prior to the Mormon colonization. Though this action was based on the General Allotment Act of 1887 and aimed at adjusting the difference between the Indians and Mormon settlers, the actual awarding of the allotments had to wait until after Mormon withdrawal from the area in 1903. All the rest of the improvements by the Mormon settlers, including a complex of irrigation systems in both Reservoir Canyon and Moenkopi Wash, came under the management of the Indian Agency in Tuba City (see Map 2).

BEGINNING OF MODERNIZATION (ca. 1903)

Reservation Status

In the administrative framework of the Indian reservation system, Moenkopi posed a serious problem. Tribally, the people of Moenkopi belonged to the Hopi Reservation, while regionally, they lived on a reservation set up for the Navajo Indians. Though probably out of bureaucratic rivalry, a superintendent of the Hopi Agency at Keams Canyon wrote as early as 1900: "Many of them [Hopi of Moenkopi] owning or claiming land are residents of this reservation and are exceedingly anxious that they be brought under the control of this Superintendent" (KCL). This dual administra-

PRE-MODERNIZATION 35

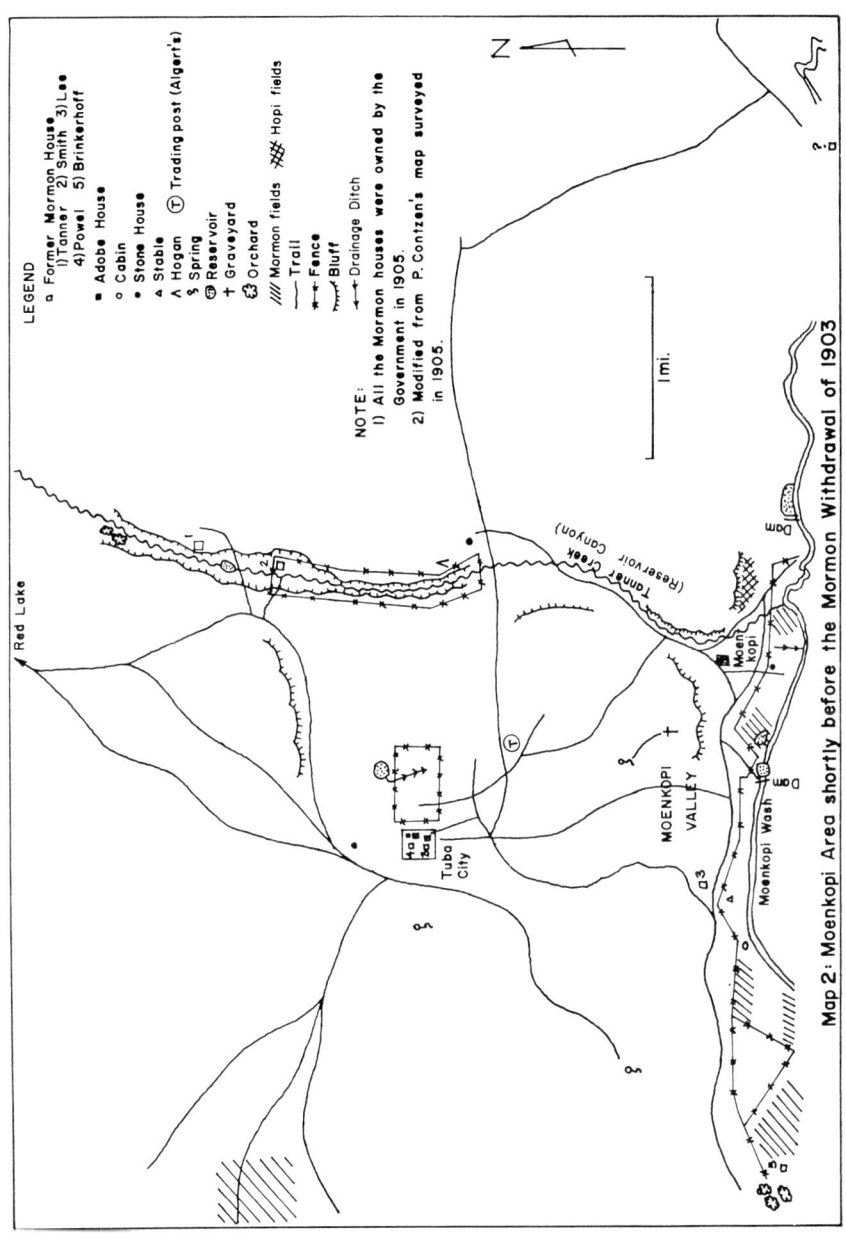

Map 2: Moenkopi Area shortly before the Mormon Withdrawal of 1903

tive affiliation of Moenkopi was to plague the BIA for the entire period to follow. It was only recently that some serious consideration was given to improving the situation.

The inclusion of the Moenkopi Hopi into a reservation of their traditional enemy, the Navajo, caused considerable anxiety among the villagers, who were afraid of discrimination and unfair treatment from the government. On the other hand, they attempted to divert the pressures of governmental programs by taking advantage of this fact whenever opportunities were presented.

Agency Community

The shift of dominant power in the area from the Mormon pioneers to the government meant the transfer of the direct burden of areal development from the Mormons to the Indians. While the Mormons personally took hoes and shovels in their hands, the government personnel simply instructed the Indians. The Mormon settlers were committed to the land, and their dealings with the local Indian population tended to be based on considerations of their own survival: ". . . government officials are, however, under no obligation to support themselves from the yield of local fields, and if occasion demanded it all food for man and beast could be obtained from outside sources. The government at Tuba is a dispenser of charity rather than a commercial enterprise, and agriculture is practiced for the benefit of the Indians, not as a means of self-support" (Gregory, 1915:117). Though the agency at Tuba City was charged with the task of improving the general lot of the Indians, its major concern was limited to the management of the boarding school, transferred from Blue Canyon. The government continued to maintain the agricultural improvements made on the land by the Mormons, but these efforts were subordinated to those of preserving law and order on the reservation as a whole and, especially, protecting the land resources for the welfare of the Indians as the latter exploited them by their traditional modes of subsistence activities. Thus Gregory rightly pointed out, "From the standpoint of agriculture the change in ownership has resulted in loss" (1915:118).

The establishments that moved into Tuba City soon after the Mormon withdrawal consisted of the following. First came the government boarding school, which enrolled the Hopi children from Moenkopi and Navajo children from the reservation. The superintendent of this school was to assume administrative duties of local Indian affairs on the Western Navajo Reservation. The boarding school included a mess hall, laundry, and living quarters for school personnel. The vacated Mormon buildings were used for these purposes. More important, the government inherited the farms and orchards from the Mormons and continued their operation mainly for the provision of school children. Finally, the government maintained a hog farm and kept milk cows and calves. The agency personnel formed a majority of the white population in Tuba City, which could not have been larger than 50 persons.

In addition to the governmental establishments, three Protestant missions and four trading posts were being operated in Moenkopi, Tuba City, Moenave, Willow Spring, and Red Lake. These stations formed satellites of Tuba City and maintained close contacts with the Indians in the area, who were mainly Navajo, with a small number of Paiute in Willow Spring and Hopi in Moenkopi.

The reservation community of Tuba City and its satellite posts provided a number of economic alternatives to the Indians. Though the basis of the Indian economy was traditionally subsistence agriculture, contact with a cash economy came to be maintained with considerable regularity through the existence of these outposts of American civilization. Of all the Indians in the area, however, the Hopi of Moenkopi were in the most advantageous position to benefit from these alternatives.

Off-Reservation Town

The significance of Flagstaff to the Indians on the Western Navajo Reservation was highly limited. After the removal of the school from Blue Canyon to Tuba City, Flagstaff took over the position of supply center from Holbrook and many Indian freighters visited the town to haul agency supplies or deliver mail. Apart from this, the Indians did not remain in the town for any prolonged period of time. None worked in Flagstaff even as temporary wage laborers. Some white sheep drovers, coal miners, and traders from Flagstaff frequently visited Tuba City.

Community Structure

The residents of Moenkopi, numbering about 100, were people who had little or no farm land resources in their original village of Oraibi. They were "transplanted" (*kupiwa*) from Oraibi in order to preserve this area as a part of Oraibi territory. The political dependence of Moenkopi on its "mother" village of Oraibi is well expressed in the following statement by an older resident of contemporary Moenkopi: "Lololoma [chief of Oraibi during the second half of the last century] sent these people out here to live. It was the people who didn't own farming land in Oraibi, were the ones he sent out. . . . He told them to stay out here and take care of it for Oraibi. He said *Mongwi* [chief] of Oraibi holds on to it. . . . He said for them to take care of this place and look after it for him." Being a colony, Moenkopi did not have "clan houses." The Hopi residents spent a great amount of time in Oraibi for ceremonies, and the one kiva in Moenkopi was utilized only for kachina and social dances. Initiations and other "religious" ceremonies were held in Oraibi, whence the residents of Moenkopi returned.

Though the Moenkopi Hopi resented their inclusion on a Navajo reservation, the mutual relationship between the Moenkopi and the government was tinged with indifference tending toward amiable tolerance. Even before the Oraibi split, the government regarded Moenkopi as a "friendly" village and the latter looked upon the former as a protector from the Navajo.

Primarily to lead the residents in dealings with this government, a woman from the Pi:kyas clan, Nashileowi, assumed the position of chief of Moenkopi.[2] There are two accounts regarding the choice of this woman as the chief. One states that in order to evade the Navajo attacks, a woman was selected by Tuba for the Navajo were thought not to kill women. Another insists that she was chosen through the people's consent. The latter account states that in the course of selection, some people suggested Lololoma's daughter but Lololoma declined the offer.[3]

Whatever the actual process of selection might have been, the chiefly position of Moenkopi was secular in nature. Its authority was derived mainly from the position of the Pi:kyas clan in the Oraibi Soyal ceremony, while its power was based on the virtual

---

[2] Nashileowi was known in several ways to the Mormons as well as other white people then resident in Tuba City. All the terms of reference to this woman chief are derived from *mö:wi* or female in-law (Voegelin and Voegelin, 1957:D1.7.3). Thus the Mormons called her "May Way," while the other whites "Mary" or "Queen Mary." In terms of the extension of kin terms to political positions among the Hopi, this produces the following chain of contrasts: chief/female chief/chief's sister: : father/female in-law/mother (see Eggan, 1950:104; 1964:179–80; Connelly, 1955:19). I was not able to determine, however, if the term, *mö:wi*, was derived chiefly from the political position or from other circumstances. The Water Coyote clan of Moenkopi, to which Nashileowi was *mö:wi*, was known, on the other hand, as the supporting clan of the Pi:kyas.

[3] His daughter's husband eventually obtained an allotment in Moenkopi, however.

monopoly of strategic resources in the traditional economy, i.e., farm land and irrigation water. However, the constitution of this power contained two serious flaws. First, it was limited to the traditional sector of the economy and hence susceptible to economic change. Second, the ultimate sanction of the power lay with the government that granted these resources for the Indians to use, while retaining the final right of control to itself. In addition to the structural ambiguity of Moenkopi as a colony, this separation of authority and power of the Moenkopi chieftainship between Oraibi and the Tuba City Agency provided Moenkopi with another source of ambiguity.

Basis of Village Economy

Immediately after the transfer of the location of the agency to Tuba City, the most important economic alternatives available to the residents of Moenkopi consisted of subsistence agriculture and wage labor for the government and other white establishments.

Moenkopi agriculture was based on irrigation of allotment lands from the reservoirs, originally constructed by the Mormons on Reservoir Canyon. Of the 16 tracts of land allotted to the Navajo and Hopi, the latter obtained 11, two of which contained the site of the Moenkopi village. In theory, each of the Hopi allotments was 20 acres, while four of five Navajo allotments were 40 acres each. In reality, however, the cultivable size of an allotment varied.

The clan affiliations of the original 11 allottees and their cultivable acreage are shown in Figure 1. The distribution of allotments shows the Pi:kyas clan as a majority among the allottees. Their advantage is further enhanced by the fact that four other allottees were affinally related to the Pi:kyas clan. For example, Allotment No. 45 was being used by a member of the Water Coyote clan on behalf of the Pi:kyas. Thus, as far as agricultural resources were concerned, the Pi:kyas retained a dominant position, which was further reinforced by the location of their allotments in regard to accessibility to irrigation water.

It appears that at the beginning of the BIA administration in Tuba City, most of the irrigation facilities left by the Mormons were applied to the school farms and orchards. Only the surplus water from the reservoirs, after joining the canyon, was utilized for irrigation of the Moenkopi allotment fields in its course to Moenkopi Wash. Significantly, the allotment located closest to the mouth of Reservoir Canyon and hence most advantageous, belonged to Nashileowi (see Map 4). Another Pi:kyas allotment was

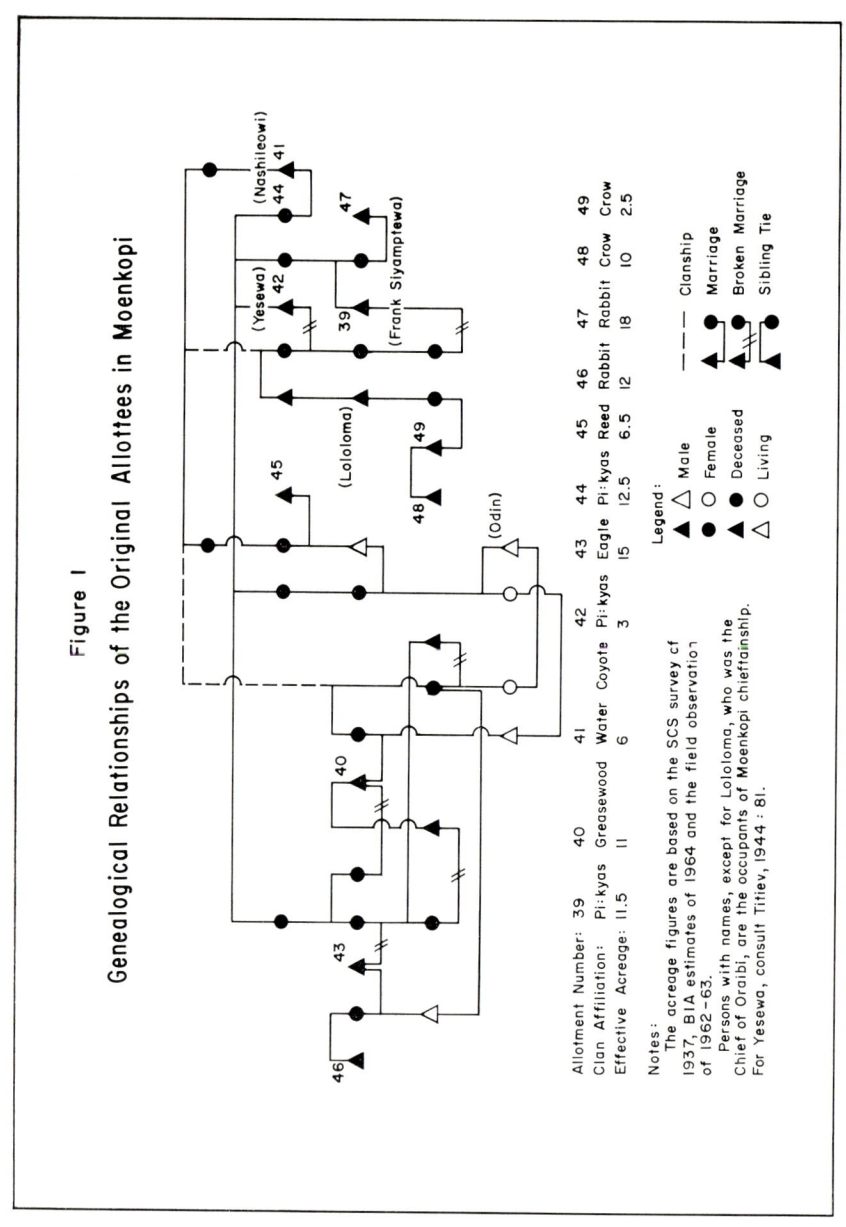

Figure 1
Genealogical Relationships of the Original Allottees in Moenkopi

situated next closest to the mouth. Nashileowi's allotment also collected the water from Moenkopi spring, which was used to irrigate a communal vegetable garden on her allotment. Finally, a major portion of the village site lay on her allotment as well. This somewhat unusual dominance of the Pi:kyas clan in subsistence economy is acknowledged by the other residents of Moenkopi today, who claim that Nashileowi was a greedy person.

Wage work in the white establishments in Tuba City formed the second most important economic alternative. Since farming was strictly limited to the nonmoney subsistence sector, the only contact with cash economy was maintained through wage income from mainly governmental employment and the cash purchase of market products available at the trading posts in Tuba City. Indian wage labor was restricted to Tuba City and its mobility was virtually nonexistent outside this small agency town. The strong limitation of wage earning power of the Indians corresponded to their low need for cash. Thus the subsistence sector assumed a dominant position relative to the money sector. Livestock operation was almost nonexistent at this early period, although some possessed saddle horses.

Household Organization

As previously mentioned, the majority of the Moenkopi population consisted of the indigent families who left Oraibi for better economic prospects and yet who still retained religious ties with their mother village. They were the members of the lineages "sloughed off" the "core household-lineage" that stayed in Oraibi to preserve and uphold clan ceremonial traditions (Connelly, 1956:19). They belonged to marginal, peripheral lineage groups (Eggan, 1964:178). While they were relieved of the immediate responsibilities of sustaining clan houses, ceremonies, and accompanying paraphernalia, it appears they were expected to contribute economically to the original home of Oraibi. Land appropriated by individuals in Moenkopi was often transmitted to their lineage relatives from Oraibi for further cultivation. Portions of the field produce were taken from Moenkopi to Oraibi and occasional labor was furnished by lineage members of Oraibi to Moenkopi. Individual homes in Moenkopi were thus closely tied to those in Oraibi through participation in ceremonies, use of land, allocation of agricultural labor, and distribution of field crops.

6

History of Political Change

DEVELOPMENT OF VILLAGE FACTIONALISM (1903–34)

Traditional Leadership

The political organization of Moenkopi at the time of its establishment already deviated from the ideal pattern of a Hopi village, and its deviation partly conditioned the future course of change. The Moenkopi leadership was created by consent of the people of Oraibi. The U.S. government was represented in Tuba City as the administrative power in the area. The people, mainly settlers in Moenkopi, chose Nashileowi, a Pi:kyas clan woman, as their chief in order to cope with this novel situation. The chieftainship thus arose out of the local political need and assumed a nontraditional, secular character.

The office was, however, invested with a myth that sanctifies the position in the native theory of chieftainship. The tradition of the Pi:kyas clan claims that the clan originated in Tewa, came to help the Bear clan of Oraibi, and, with the latter, settled in the Moenkopi area as one of the original group of settlers. In evidence of this, the present chief points to the existence of house ruins in two spots nearby, one of which he claims belongs to the Bear clan. The clan's position in the Oraibi ceremonial hierarchy gives another indication of its close association with the Bear clan.

In the organization of the Oraibi Soyal ceremony, from which "everything branches out" (Titiev, 1944:142; Eggan, 1950:97), the village chief "acts as chief priest" (Eggan, 1950:97), while "the Pi:kyas chief . . . impersonates the Aholi kachinas" (Titiev, 1944: 142). On the ninth day of the initiation ceremony, the pair of kachinas, Eototo and Aholi, perform a distinct segment of the rite in the village (Earle and Kennard, 1938:23; Titiev, 1944:117). Of the two kachinas, Titiev mentions:

Eototo is the spiritual counterpart of the Village Chief who has charge of the Eototo mask and who, alone, may impersonate this Kachina. It is said that the Eototo was first brought to Oraibi by its traditional founder, Matcito. The Aholi kachina is second in importance at Oraibi and is portrayed by the Pi:kyas chief, who is first assistant to the Bear clan leader in the performance of the Soyal (1944:114–15; Earle and Kennard, 1938:Pls. IV, V).

Both kachinas are regarded as *wuya* (eponyms) of the Bear and Pi:kyas clans, respectively (Titiev, 1944:114). While these two ceremonies were, at the time of my field work, only imperfectly given, the present chief of Moenkopi still goes back to Oraibi to take part in the esoteric part of the rituals.

The Pi:kyas clan thus ranks below the Bear clan, and its ceremonial position is closely dependent upon that of the Oraibi chief. Politically, then, the Moenkopi chief stands in submission to the Oraibi chief, and no discord is supposed to arise between the two. The chief of Moenkopi is expected to assist the Oraibi chief without antagonizing him.

Within Moenkopi itself, the Pi:kyas clan has been supported by the Water Coyote clan through marriage alliance. As shown in Figure 1, four chiefs, from Nashileowi to the present chief, Odin, have been married to the men and women of the Water Coyote clan. Such marriages between the two clans have also been frequent outside the chieftainship itself and, as shall be shown later, a Water Coyote clansman married to a Pi:kyas woman had been recognized not only by the villagers but by the government as the leader and representative of Lower Moenkopi during a period of vacant chieftainship after World War II. Economic cooperation in the use of land has been prominent between the members of the two clans.

Structural factors behind this alliance still remain obscure to me. While the protector role of the Water Coyote clan appears well recognized by the people, the present chief rationalized it by saying that the Water Coyote clan possesses no important ceremony,[1] and hence is able to take over the chieftainship in the event of extinc-

---

[1] A cursory examination of the officers in the Oraibi "Chief's Talk" as well as in the various ceremonies of Oraibi at the turn of the century has not produced the Water Coyote clan except for a questionable one in the Soyal (see Titiev, 1944:59–60, 81–82, 242–43).

tion of the Pi:kyas clan. Further, the unit of alliance does not seem to be genealogically traceable lineage but, as much as I could determine, three lineages of the Water Coyote clan appear involved in the chiefly alliance. Finally, though this phenomenon of alliance has been noted in the past (see Brandt, 1954:25), my information in this respect is not conclusive.[2]

In spite of these obscurities, it seems fairly certain that the two clans have been closely united for defense of Moenkopi, and it was under their protection and control that the people of marginal lineages from Oraibi settled in Moenkopi.

The Moenkopi chief had a more solid economic basis than any other village chief in Hopiland. I have already indicated the content of this basis. The comparative concentration of strategic resources in the hands of the chief inevitably secured and enhanced her influence over village politics. The BIA, however, placed a serious limitation upon her power. She was more vulnerable to the government than the chiefs of other villages. Furthermore, her wealth was mainly in the agricultural sector of the village economy, and her power was seriously curtailed in such other productive activities as livestock operation and wage work. Even in the matter of residence, one could, if he chose, live outside the tiny village site of Moenkopi and thus out of her direct interference. Thus, within the Moenkopi area, the chief's position was solid only in a restricted sphere of life. However, this solidity was more prominent and specific than in any other chiefly position in Hopiland. The subsequent changes in the surrounding social and economic conditions gradually revealed the vulnerability of the Moenkopi chieftainship.

General Condition of Third Mesa

Soon after the Moenkopi allotment, an incident of major significance in Hopi political history occurred. In 1906 the Hostiles of Oraibi seceded from the village and moved up the mesa to settle by a spring. The spot had already been in use as a vegetable

---

[2] The Hopi term, *pavansinom*, seems important here. *Pavan* means force, strength, and perhaps supernatural power (Voegelin and Voegelin, 1957: C4.4), and *pavansinom* is contrasted to *shikabunsinom* or "ordinary people." The former refers to the clans owning ceremonies or members of such secret societies as Momchit. The people using *poaka* or witchcraft are also called *pavansinom* and now the Tribal Council is so called because of its power. One informant mentioned that the *pavansinom* tended to marry each other for fear of clan secrets being stolen by nonimportant people.

garden by some Hopi of Oraibi, and, when the faction settled there, it grew up as the village of Hotevilla. From 1906 to 1910 Bacabi and New Oraibi were also founded by the seceding group of Oraibi (Titiev, 1944:94–95). These communities later developed varying degrees of pro- or anti-government attitudes and displayed corresponding degrees of acculturation. Their position with respect to Oraibi also differed, although the latter was the parent village to all of them.

The exact role Moenkopi played in the Oraibi split is not clear. A Mennonite church was being constructed in Moenkopi at the time, and those who were engaged in the work were unable to be present when the split occurred. A large number of Moenkopi residents, however, actively took part in what some Hopi now call the "Revolution" and sided with the Oraibi Friendlies in defending Chief Tawaquaptewa and expelling the Hostiles and their leader, Yokioma, from Oraibi (TCL). The subsequent development of the three villages and the differentiation in their relationships with the parent village and the U.S. government inevitably more clearly defined Moenkopi's position relative to Oraibi and increased its commitment to the latter. This was not without a grave consequence in the later process of political changes at Moenkopi, because Oraibi was rather a mercurial community in its relationship to the outside world, especially to the government, and soon after the split, it became antagonistic toward the government. This consequently presented Moenkopi with the difficult choice of loyalty to the parent village or to the government.

With the Oraibi split, a large group of people migrated to Moenkopi (TCL). Some took their wives with them, and others came down alone and married into the village. Partly because of their late arrival in the community, they had to content themselves with poor land or else supplement their income through government employment. Some of these later entered the cattle business. Since Moenkopi was a colony village, it could not bar the newcomers from participation in village politics and soon a Greasewood clansman, who settled at Moenkopi after the split, built the third kiva, *Ka'waikiva* (Titiev's *Kawaieva*, 1944:95; see Map 3).

Relationships with the Government

The image of the government as a protector of Moenkopi and provider of wage work developed early in the minds of the residents, and Tuba City and Moenkopi maintained fairly amicable relationships as long as each abstained from serious interference in the affairs of the other. For the administration, however, the village's location on a Navajo reservation posed a vexing problem and an Indian agent proposed the inclusion of Moenkopi in the Moqui (Hopi) Reservation as early as 1900 (KCL; TCL).

The villagers, on the other hand, did not hesitate to take advantage of any conflict that arose between the two agencies. Thus, many children avoided attending school at Blue Canyon by saying that they were from Oraibi and hence expected to attend Keams Canyon school. The Oraibi children sometimes claimed Moenkopi as their residence and Blue Canyon as their school. This exasperated the superintendents of the two reservations, who accused each other of smuggling children (KCL; FDL; TCL). One superintendent at Keams Canyon wrote in 1904: "Nearly all of the Hostile children came back promptly. Four ran away to Moenkopi under charge of Supt. Needham and I respectfully request that they be returned to this reservation by Mr. Needham. I respectfully protest against Moenkopi being made a 'City of Refuge' for Oraibi children who do not want to go to school as it has been for the last four years" (KCL, September 12, 1904). When the hair-cutting order was issued on the Hopi Reservation in the early part of the 1900's, "many of the Oraibi families took refuge at Moenkopi" (TCL, February 4, 1905). In 1914 a Hopi student from Bacabi escaped from the Phoenix Indian school and hid himself in Moenkopi (KCL). Thus Moenkopi's unique position as a Hopi village outside the Hopi Reservation served to accommodate the Hopi from other villages who rebelled at certain of the BIA policies, which were often not coordinated from one jurisdiction to another.

Relationships with the Navajo

The Navajo threats to the stability of Moenkopi have already been indicated. While all the Hopi villages had been menaced by the Navajo since the Spanish period in the seventeenth century, the Navajo in the Moenkopi area presented a unique situation within the administrative framework of the BIA. Though the Navajo directly around Moenkopi were yet few in number (KCL) and dispersed widely on the Western Navajo Reservation, they caused enough trouble to force the resignation of a superintendent (Brown, 1952; Crane, 1925:139–41) in 1919. In 1916 the same superintendent had written an irate letter to Washington requesting stronger authority to protect Hopi livestock more effectively (TCL).

During the period when the government was not regarded as trustworthy and the Hopi villages were all too distant to recruit ready help, Moenkopi, in self-defense, cultivated friendly relationships with the numerically superior Navajo. In this earlier period, moreover, the difference in the modes of subsistence helped to create a symbiotic relationship between Moenkopi and the Navajo and to lessen the opportunities for actual competition. In the absence of superordinate, tribal bureaucracies in both groups, their contacts occurred mainly in face-to-face interactions. The common experience in the Blue Canyon and later Tuba City boarding schools and in off-reservation schools not only encouraged many Moenkopi Hopi children to learn Navajo but also contributed to creating personal friendships between them.

At the same time, however, the Hopi attempted to reinforce their social boundary from the Navajo. This was indicated in the petition they filed at the Tuba City Agency in 1905 regarding the construction of their own day school near the village "in preference to sending them [children] to other schools with Navajo children" (TCL, January 14, 1905). Day schools had already been built for the Hopi in Polacca, Oraibi, and Toreva by 1899. Hence Moenkopi's similar petition may be regarded as following the same trend. Yet the Moenkopi petition was motivated by the desire for separation from the Navajo under the tutelage of the government. This ethnic exclusiveness of Moenkopi was manifest more explicitly in the subsequent development of tribal relationships in the area.

Relationships with the Missionaries

Three Protestant missions replaced the Mormons in the area immediately after the latter's withdrawal. These were the Episcopalians in Tuba City, the Gospel Union on Lyond's Ranch, and the Mennonites in Moenkopi. The first and second confined their work to the Navajo, while the Mennonites limited their activity to the Hopi of Moenkopi (TCL). The Gospel Mission, initially stationed in the old woolen mill in the village, left the Tuba-Moenkopi area by the early 1930's. Its influence on the Navajo in the vicinity of Moenave is now difficult to detect except for two stone buildings, at present in use as quarters for the BIA employees.

Hopi contact with the Mennonite mission started early, and the first station was established in Oraibi in 1893 (Thompson, 1950: 137) with H. R. Voth as the missionary. J. B. Frey and his family came to Moenkopi from Goessel, Kansas, shortly after the Mormons left the Tuba City area. With the help of local Indian labor, he began the construction of a church on a bluff east of the village and completed it in 1905. By 1915 he had a terraced vegetable garden and farms on the south side of the church building. Coal was provided by the government from a nearby mine, and the church offered a small amount of irregular employment to Indians of the village. Economically, the Mennonite church was supplying its own needs from the immediate vicinity of the village and it soon began vigorous missionary work among the Hopi.

Even discounting some of the tales told by older residents of Moenkopi today, it appears quite likely that mission activity in Moenkopi was quite aggressive. Frey himself took every opportunity to preach whenever he could find a group of people, irrespective of their attention.

His Sunday schools were, however, never very successful, and in 1906 he requested the government require a one-hour daily session of Bible teachings at the Moenkopi Day School (TCL). By 1916 his religious instruction at the school so irritated the villagers that they petitioned the government to halt it (TCL). He continued, however, until 1918. Then, one day, a number of village ruffians waylaid Frey on his way to school and one of them attempted to rope him. Superintendent Walter Runke, hearing of the trouble, drove to the village to rescue Frey, but the incensed crowd stopped the car and forced Runke to turn and speed away. The lariat thrower was later apprehended by the agency police but, with Frey's intercession, was released without a trial (Carlson, 1964:82).

Moenkopi was also chosen as a meeting place of Mennonite converts from different Hopi villages, who met for several days once a year. Sometime between 1922 and 1925, the dispute about the church reached a crisis when Frey led a party of Christians to one of the stores by the plaza. A group of villagers, who had already gathered expecting trouble, was led by the Moenkopi chief, Siyamptewa, and his close associates of the Water Coyote clan. As Frey started to preach, Siyamptewa called out to the crowd, "We are going to decide once and for all which one of us you are going to have as a leader. All who want to follow me come over here, and all who want to follow him, go over there." After a great commotion among the people, everybody, except for a Hopi assistant chaplain from New Oraibi and his wife and child, joined Siyamptewa. Since the assistant chaplain's wife was from Moenkopi, some of her relatives, including her sister, were undecided, but the wife told them that she did not expect them to be forced to join her. Thus assured, they joined the majority. Siyamptewa then gave Frey an ultimatum to stop further mission work in the village and soon thereafter, Frey left Moenkopi for Oak Creek Canyon. The Hopi assistant and his family returned to New Oraibi in 1925.

The Mennonite mission was also encountering similar difficulties in Old Oraibi, which the missionaries left by 1930. It may be that the church's troubles in Moenkopi were related to similar occurrences in Old Oraibi or even coordinated with them. In any event, the influence of the Mennonites in Moenkopi was reduced to simple Sunday schools for village children, since no serious convert had been obtained during the subsequent period of the church's presence in the village.

Discussing the disruptive effects of the Mennonites on Hopi society and culture (1950:139–41), Thompson points out, in particular, the "separatist, nonorganic, antiesthetic nature of the implicit assumptions [of the Mennonites] . . . regarding man and nature, compared to those of the traditional Hopi" (1950:139). In the Moenkopi disputes it is difficult to determine how these doctrinal aspects of the church influenced the actual process of contact. One might argue that the Mennonite tendency to discredit the government (Thompson, 1950:140–41) was strongly resisted by the village men, to whom the government offered indispensable economic and social security. Moreover, the mission's emphasis on household autonomy which discouraged kinship and ceremonial interactions (Thompson, 1950:140) was probably frustrating. Whatever the reasons, the church was expelled by the united front of the villagers, and no factional splits were brought about. Indeed, the people were united in opposition to the common enemy.

It is also noteworthy that as far as Moenkopi is concerned, the issue of a Christian mission has never caused serious factional disputes. The minority of Christianized Hopi have never been strong enough to influence political issues. The structure of the factionalism that was developing during this period involved the more powerful and constant agency of change, the federal government.

Development of Factionalism

Though Moenkopi finally acted as a group vis-à-vis the missionary Frey, the leaders of the preceding incidents constituted a potentially divisive element, which had temporarily chosen to ally itself with the traditional power of the village. This element consisted of persons who had made good in the few available government positions. One was an interpreter at the Tuba City Agency, and another a regular employee of the Tuba City boarding school (TCL). A few had opened general stores. The educated Indians, and some recent arrivals who brought a deeper orientation to the cash economy and less dependence on the traditional pattern of subsistence farming and sheep herding, also challenged the traditional power structure of the village, which was based on allotment lands and sanctioned by the parent village of Oraibi. On the other hand, most of Siyamptewa's followers worked as freighters or temporary government farmers and had no lasting contacts with the white personnel of the agency. The challengers were similar to what Kluckhohn described as "Agency Indians" (Kluckhohn and Leighton, 1948:106).

The cleavage between the two groups involved large phases of life and covered differences in age, education, economic interests, political outlook, and period of settlement in Moenkopi. Young people moved to a new village site that had been in the process of construction since 1913 on a large level tract immediately joining on the west their present (lower) segment (TCL). The appropriation of the new site was made through the efforts of a superintendent, who saw the solution to crowded conditions in the pueblo in the establishment of a "new town" and even supplied building materials for house construction (TCL).

Although the differences are diverse and all-pervasive, the affiliation of the villagers to each of the groups was neither clear nor stable and, apart from a small number of actives, the majority of the villagers appeared little concerned with the struggle soon to develop. Further, the village still retained important assets in the irrigation system, the kivas, and the common plaza. The chiefly position had majority support and cooperation in agriculture was organized on a village-wide basis, as joyously recounted by the Sun Chief for the early 1910's (Simmons, 1963:150-52). In short, the village during this period was unified, and lines of difference were only vaguely and tentatively drawn over a number of issues.

To the emerging discontents, however, the control of corporate wealth in addition to such peripheral matters as maintenance of the village roads and springs provided the very issues to be fought over later, and the competition between the two groups was phrased in terms of who should take over the general village administration. Eventual secession or fission into two distinct political units was not raised as an issue. In this sense, the dispute was within a single corporate group. I define this phase of the political process in Moenkopi as *factionalism*, following Boissevain (1964: 1275-76).

Toward the end of the 1920's, the rift between the groups became overt within the village. It appeared in the lack of ceremonial cooperation and squabbles over the distribution of irrigation water. A small number of older residents refused to take part in the dances or go through the required preparatory rites that included the young antagonists. Many who were involved in the ceremonial disputes held responsible positions in the Oraibi rituals.

One of the disputes is related to a kachina dance and concerned Guy Talas of the Water Coyote clan and Tony Wepo of the Reed clan, both of whom were early settlers from Oraibi and belonged to the Wuwuchim society there. Tony used to play the lead man in the kachina dances but he had heard a rumor that Guy was neglecting the four-day abstinence before the public dance in the plaza. During the preparation for a particular kachina dance, he found out that the rumor was true. Outraged, he decided to withdraw from Moenkopi ceremonies forever. The loss of the leading dancer generated ill feeling between young and old factions of the village and eventually, in the late 1930's, led to separate performance of the dances.

The casual system of irrigation maintenance functioned when all households depended on farming as their sole means of subsistence. However, within 10 years after the establishment of the Tuba City administration, money economy was making a gradual inroad into the community and a considerable number of individuals were receiving wages from the government.

Opposed to the young people, who were adjusting to reservation life, were the older residents, who still accepted the authority of Old Oraibi and who brought any serious dispute in Moenkopi before the Oraibi chief for arbitration (see Titiev, 1944:201-2). This frustrated the younger residents, who wished to decide village affairs themselves. Thus, the divisive effect of the village economy, together with disagreement about the locus of ultimate authority, prevented reconciliation of the two factions.

A Compromise

By the summer of 1930, the situation reached a critical stage. The frequency of kachina dances in the village dropped drastically and cooperative labor on irrigation maintenance was seldom organized. When a group of graduates from the Sherman Institute returned to Moenkopi, they were dismayed at the deterioration of cooperative effort in the village. One of this group, Kenneth Loma of the Coyote clan (whose father belonged to the Patki, an important clan of Moenkopi) decided, with the zeal acquired at school, to restore harmony in the community. With the young "educated" people of the village, he attempted to form a group to improve community relationships. He tried to influence both old and young residents of the old and new village sites. His recruitment, however, was successful mostly among the young, while the older people merely regarded the project with suspicion and refused to participate. Significantly, he failed to obtain the support of Chief Siyamptewa, and this led his followers to antagonize those of the chief. The first meeting, held at the house of one of the supporters, attracted about 40 people, among whom the future core of the Moenkopi branch of the Hopi Tribal Council was preponderant. Some who attended the first meeting, however, later dropped out and either remained neutral or returned to the fold of Siyamptewa.

This group, that came to be called "Village Council" by Kenneth and others, initiated several community projects: improvement of roads and irrigation ditches, assistance in expanding the day school and encouraging the children, and holding sports events, such as basketball and football games or track races. Small dues were collected from the members and a tool shed was constructed, but no financial support was sought from the government, although they wanted the agent's recognition. The group gave small feasts and village "banquets" and it appears to have performed a police function in protection of the livestock from Navajo thieves.

While the need for such a group as the "Village Council" continued to exist in the village, it did not survive the growing conditions of both internal and external worlds. Internally, the small success that the group achieved was to be utilized as a weapon against the traditional authority. Its accomplishments were taken as evidence of the ineptness of the traditional leadership. Its avowed aim of village harmony and integration resulted in the further alienation of the older sympathizers. Rapport deteriorated after the organizer, Kenneth, left for Bacone College, Oklahoma, as a scholarship student at the end of the summer of 1930. When he came home two years later, the "Council" was entirely controlled by the younger people of the upper village segment.

The attempt of the "Village Council," though a failure, was a spontaneous effort of the perceptive young elites to meet local needs. It had been intended to mitigate the factional differences by providing a group "which did not discriminate by religion and . . . which everybody in the village could join." No effort was made to spread the organization to other villages, although there was a similar self-governing group in New Oraibi at that time and the Moenkopi Council possibly had some connection with it. The council did not presume to be the village governing body itself. It wished to serve "not as leaders but as a group of people who could take any problems to the leaders." Despite these modest claims, its success was short-lived and the schism only deepened in the following periods, because any increase in village autonomy through the council placed in jeopardy Moenkopi's tie with the mother village of Oraibi and thus inevitably alienated the traditional power the council tried to incorporate.

INTENSIFICATION OF TRIBAL FACTIONALISM (1934–45)

Territorial Framework of Factionalism

Broad differentiation of the two factions into two geographically distinct residential areas provided the framework in which the interplay of political and economic forces was to unfold in the future. The population movement to the new site appears to have been complete in its present form by the end of the 1930's. It numbered about 50 homes. While expansion of the population to the upper village site has continued, its present rate appears to be much lower than during the 1920's or 1930's. Three streets, originally named after the important figures of Moenkopi (*Mö:wi, Ma'atsya,* and *Letokshi*), were taking a visible form, and in 1943 about one-half of the Moenkopi population was living in the upper village site (Long Range Program, 1944).

Since many of those who built homes on the new site had been raised in the lower village segment, they all had close ties of kinship with the residents of the latter. The factions are, therefore, associated more closely with residential territory than with kinship. The new site, set apart from the lower village and planned on an entirely different pattern from that of the traditional pueblo, was also free from the control of the traditional power based on the allotments covering the lower segment site. Thus the upper segment faction began concentrating its efforts on the new site.

Yet the division between the lower and upper segments of Moenkopi was sufficiently vague to allow a degree of fluidity in affiliation between the two factions, and there remained, in each segment, a body of people who simply "watched" how one or the other group might move, or who affiliated themselves with the other groups outside Moenkopi. Exact characterization of the "uncommitted" body of people in the respective areas is difficult and their significance in the politics of Moenkopi only became prominent much later. The subsequent political developments can better be characterized as a process of incorporation of each segment, or more specifically, of the upper one into an independent decision-making unit.

Ceremonial Division

The first incident of any significance in this process occurred in the ceremonial life of Moenkopi. Sometime during the 1930's and perhaps simultaneously with the question of establishing the Tribal Council (see below), the upper Moenkopi group decided to give its own initiation ceremony to the Kachina society. The implication of this action was serious. Until then, the upper group had been giving ceremonies in Moenkopi under the leadership of the lower group, but now it chose to defy the religious prerogatives of the latter. The participants in the ceremony included only the sympathizers of the upper segment, and no adherents of the lower group joined.

The ceremonial disturbance on this occasion first brought about the differentiation of kivas between the upper and lower segments. *Letaiovi* of the Coyote clan, the oldest kiva in the village, and *Ka'waikiva* of the Greasewood clan were eventually brought under the control of the upper group, while the lower group managed to retain only *Iskiva* belonging to the Water Coyote clan.[3] In 1942 the lower group constructed another kiva, *Ta:vankiva* ("West Kiva"), for themselves (see Map 3). Its first owner was Teddy Honyumptewa of the Coyote clan. Each group now had two kivas.

The second consequence was the establishment of a spatial boundary partially dividing the two groups. This incident was recounted by a present member of the upper segment. During the parade of kachinas, on the second day of the Kachina society initiation, members of the lower group attempted to drive the kachina dancers out of their site, telling them that the upper segment people no longer belonged to their village and that they should stay on their new site above the bluff. The upper group thus claims today that this boundary was forced upon them and they accepted it, but the lower group refuses to admit that such a boundary exists (see Map 3). However, it is taken as the boundary by some political actives of Hotevilla, even though they are sympathetic to the lower group.

---

[3] *Letaiovi* is Titiev's *Kuwanovi,* and *Iskiva* is his *Istiya* (1944:95).

The boundary did not clarify rights to all geographical features. The sacred spring and the road going by it were regarded as common resources. The roads going through the upper segment had to be used by the lower people to leave the village, and these were regarded as open to both groups. The graveyard, located on the rim of the upper knoll, was also jointly held and used by both segments. While the upper group conceded these rights, it retained the rights to the two kivas and the village plaza on the lower group site.

Tribal Council

The impact of depression and subsequent advent of the Indian New Deal placed further pressure on the schisms of Moenkopi. John Collier, who visited Moenkopi while commissioner, introduced the Hopi to the idea of tribal self-government. Its general form and role were formulated into the present constitution of the council, which included Moenkopi as a unit community with two representatives allocated to it. The draft of the constitution and by-laws was voted on by the Hopi and subsequently adopted in 1936. A man from First Mesa was then "elected" as the first chairman of the council.

All through the process of the establishment of the council, Moenkopi manifested its factional split ever more clearly. Kenneth and others, who tried to be a unifying element in Moenkopi through the "Village Council," could not maintain the mediating position in this all-too-clear choice between the BIA-inspired tribal organization and the village, which admitted to no higher authority than Oraibi. With the entire tribe as a group of higher authority than Oraibi, the unique tie of Moenkopi with Oraibi was endangered. The "tribe," as represented in the tribal council, thus emerged as another divisive factor in Moenkopi. The "Village Council" could have continued to exist as long as its actives affected only their own village of Moenkopi. Now this condition disappeared.

The change brought about through the adoption of the tribal council constitution, however, served merely to formalize the division of the upper and lower segments into "Lower and Upper Districts of Moenkopi," from each of which one representative was to be selected. Otherwise the council was inactive because of the lack of cooperation of component villages. The stock reduction program was imposed by the BIA during this period of infancy of the council.

Relationships with the Government

The Hopi Tribal Council did not play a significant role in the ponderous task of reduction of the number of livestock. As one of the Upper Moenkopi Village Council officers related in 1955: "[The] only solution to the stock reduction at that time was that a committee should be formed in each individual village. Each individual village set up committees, and those who cooperated could set up or determine for themselves the carrying capacity of that particular sub-unit" (Hopi Hearings, 1955:310). Thus the execution of the program through which the Navajo Tribal Council gained in experience (Shepardson, 1963:80–81) only made more difficult the development of Hopi self-government.

For Moenkopi, the stock reduction program renewed the question of its dual administrative affiliation. Though the establishment of the land management units "took into consideration all of the major factors involved in the Reservation range use . . . including political and economic considerations" (Young, 1961:155), Moenkopi came to be included in District 3 and was separated from the Hopi District 6. Its relationship with the BIA during this period is well summarized in the following statement by the General Superintendent of the Navajo Reservation: "As a part of the Hopi tribe, they are responsible to the Hopi superintendent. On the other hand, they are responsible to us [Navajo Agency] for the management of their livestock and for other things which made it impossible for us to be completely divorced from their administration" (HvJ, Def. Ex. 483). While Collier encouraged the development of a tribal organization among the Hopi, he was recommending the administration of Moenkopi from Tuba City (HvJ, Def. Ex., III, 846). The same proposal was made in the Rachford Report of 1940 (HvJ, Def. Ex., III, 821). Since the New Deal funds for the reservation development were channelled by the local BIA, those that were to be processed at Keams Canyon did not reach Moenkopi and this caused considerable anxiety among the officials of the Upper Moenkopi District (HvJ, Def. Ex. 477a). At the very moment when the upper segment thought they could strengthen their stand in Moenkopi as well as their minority position in the Tuba City area through their own tribal organization, the latter appeared to abandon them. Their "step-child" status (Hopi Hearings, 1955) did not seem to improve.

Under these circumstances, Tuba City loomed large as the only effective fulcrum to lever their position. Thus Moenkopi came to take an active part in the stock reduction program through the

Tuba City Agency. As previously mentioned, a number of the core members in the upper group were successful in the cattle operation, which itself was free from the intervention of the traditional power. On the other hand, the number engaged in livestock raising in the lower group was comparatively small and sheep were more important than cattle.

The cattle owners in the upper group, then, came to be employed by the Soil Conservation Service to carry out stock reduction in District 3, where all livestock from Moenkopi grazed. They not only helped the Service carry out the reduction program among the Navajo and Hopi herders but also took part in the economic survey of the area. The experience helped to familiarize them with the administrative work of the BIA but, more important, enabled them to secure a lasting liaison through employment in the local agency.

When the tribal council was still impotent and the Keams Canyon office indifferent to Moenkopi affairs, it was the Tuba City office, although primarily charged with the administration of the local Navajo, to which the upper group turned to strengthen their position in Moenkopi itself. They justified their role of mediator of village affairs on the theory that the village chief was not expected to deal with outsiders and that such dealings had to be in the hands of people who did not hold important positions in the native ceremonial hierarchy. They were also more competent in English and had a greater knowledge of, as well as personal connections with, the outside world. The BIA, in urgent need of local cooperation, did not hesitate to enlist their support. The lower group sheepherders, who had to submit to the orders of the BIA, however, came to resent strongly the government as well as its upper group helpers.

The participation of the upper group in the wide range of the program also contributed to their establishment as an important political factor in the local administration of the Indians in general. Moenkopi, which had been left to deal with the Navajo and a few other groups of Indians by itself, had now to be incorporated into an ever more complicated local administration. The war years, however, temporarily halted BIA administrative changes in the Tuba City–Moenkopi area.

World War II and General Tribal Conditions

A sizeable number of young men from Moenkopi were either drafted or enlisted in the armed services during World War II, and a few servicemen were killed in action. While individual participation in the war was thus quite prominent in Moenkopi, there was no patterned community reaction.

The Hopi Tribal Council was still suffering from general inaction through this period and the ceremonial activities in Hopi villages were also at a low ebb (Hopi Hearings, 1955:310). One notes, however, the emergence of Hotevilla as active in upholding the traditional ideology during this period. The "chief" of Hotevilla, supported by the son of the former chief, Yokioma, raised a voice of protest against compulsory draft of the Hopi youth and this was widely publicized in an Arizona newspaper. Yokioma's son also hailed Hitler as the legendary savior of the Hopi (Simmons, 1963:379). Several young men from Hotevilla refused to answer the draft and eventually served jail terms. Kenneth Loma, who by now was settled in New Oraibi through marriage, also joined this group, which was hailed as "conscientious objectors" in some quarters of the nation. Though it focussed national attention on the Hopi, it was obvious that Hotevilla was now waving the old flag against the U.S. government as well as a new one against the latter's "puppet," the Hopi Tribal Council. Kenneth now found in Hotevilla vent for his political ambitions, which provided some residents of Moenkopi, notably Kenneth's kinsmen, with an area of possible improvement in their political position in the village. Thus, during the war years, three components of political orientations were initially given in Moenkopi: Oraibi for the lower group, whose power was focussed in the lower village site of Moenkopi; Moenkopi itself for the upper group, whose power was based upon its connection with the Tuba City Agency; and Hotevilla for some of those dissatisfied with both of the above.

TRENDS IN THE POST-WAR ERA (1945–58)

Growth of Tribal Self-Government

As one of the leaders of the upper group remarked in 1955 (Hopi Hearings, 1955:312), the development of the tribal government among the Navajo marked the early post-war years of the Navajo and Hopi reservations. To further this trend, the Navajo BIA transferred some of its functions to the Navajo tribe. One such action was the establishment of the grazing committees in 1940, which replaced the district supervision of the BIA (Adams, 1963: 48). Each grazing committee was assigned the task of maintaining the prescribed sheep units within a land management district as well as issuing new permits for livestock operation and probating their inheritance in that district. This threatened the Hopi of Moenkopi, especially its upper group, which was to come under the administration of the grazing committee of District 3. The threat was temporarily ameliorated, however, when the committee agreed to have one representative from the upper group.

About the same time (1948), the upper group succeeded in sending one of its members to the Navajo police corps in Tuba City. The infiltration of the upper group into the Tuba City administration proceeded further through employment in such critical areas of policy-planning of the local BIA as land management and supply and provisions. In the face of the ineffectiveness of its own tribal council, the upper group attempted to secure its position within the framework of the growing Navajo tribal institutions and the BIA in order to gain control over the entire village of Moenkopi.

The rapport of the upper group with the local Navajo tribal organization, however, soon ended when the Navajo decided to place the committee members on the tribal payroll in 1953 (Young, 1961:158), and the Hopi representative to the grazing committee was dropped. In 1950 the Hopi policeman was involved in a land dispute with a fellow villager, with whom most of the upper group actives appear to have sided, presumably because of their own interests in the disputed area, and this disillusioned him and his family. At the same time, the family had been a target of jealousies of the upper group residents because of favoritism shown by the principal of the day school. Finally, the policeman was more attracted by a remunerative job in the construction of Route 3. These involvements induced him to quit his job as policeman.

A brief period of upper group participation in the Navajo tribe ensued in 1955, when the Land Board (see p. 101) was organized and the Moenkopi Hopi were again represented by an active member of the upper group. But by 1961 he too had dropped out. Thus the tenuous rapport between the two groups totally disappeared at the level of tribal organization.

Belatedly, however, the Hopi Tribal Council was recalled into action in 1948 (Hopi Hearings, 1955:312), and in 1951 the council hired John Boyden as tribal lawyer to protect tribal interests, especially from the Navajo (Hopi Hearings, 1955:313–14). The upper group of Moenkopi now turned to New Oraibi and Keams Canyon, where most of the council activities were planned and executed. Matters regarding the two tribes were being taken up through the two tribal councils and their respective lawyers.

The extensive "tribalization" of the Hopi and Navajo thus decreased the significance of local-level interactions between them. Schematically, in the Tuba-Moenkopi area the Navajo were organized into the Tuba City and Coal Mine chapters, which are directly connected to the tribal council at Window Rock. The upper group of Moenkopi looked to New Oraibi and Keams Canyon. But while the upper group reinforced its tie with the Hopi Council at the expense of the traditional, personalized relationship with the local Navajo individuals, the lower group of Moenkopi maintained the pattern of face-to-face interrelations with them.

Outside Individuals in Village Politics

The period between the adoption of the tribal council constitution and its reorganization also helped clarify the issue of "sob sisters" or outside sympathizers to the upper group. Since the time of the Keams Canyon school in the 1900's, the local BIA had been a target of criticism by various outside groups, including missionaries and anthropologists (see Golden, 1951). Some superintendents tried to limit the entry of these "self-imposed people" to the reservation by issuing permits (Crane, 1925; KCL). On the other hand, when their government seemed fluctuating and inconsistent to them, the Indians took even a slight sign of assistance from an outside group or individual as a firm commitment to their cause. They occasionally singled out individual government employees as either their allies or enemies. One example is a devoted school principal of Moenkopi.

The principal, who had served the community about 25 years since 1925, was then charged with the responsibility for not only the education of six grades of children, but also such community affairs as sewing classes for women, health inspection of the villagers by doctors from Keams Canyon, giving showers to the villagers in the school's shower room, and holding Moenkopi fairs. In addition, he took it upon himself to enlighten the villagers in the American way of life and to induce them to participate in the newly introduced national institutions. He helped some to file applications for retirement payments. When a water storage tank and sewer system was installed at the school during the 1950's, some householders in the upper segment individually obtained consent from him to connect their plumbing to the school's, thus giving them running water and in some cases, flush toilets and bath tubs. Since the village was without formalized channels of communication, his contact with the people was mainly on the basis of individuals who came voluntarily to ask assistance. Some upper group actives resented his actions, regarding them as deliberate and biased interference in the management of village affairs (Hopi Hearings, 1955). The resentment was probably exaggerated because of the greater function that the school had then to play in the community. Eventually, he had to be transferred from Moenkopi to Oklahoma.

In 1955 comprehensive hearings were held between the BIA officials from Washington and the Hopi of major villages (except Oraibi), and a wide gamut of grievances was brought into the open. Among other accomplishments of the hearings, it was impressed on the minds of the Hopi that: 1) the government was indeed committed to the promotion of Indian welfare; and 2) the Hopi Tribal Council was the government's sole recognized organ for the Hopi. Thus, from 1955 on the ties between the tribal council and Washington, and the Moenkopi upper group and Keams Canyon, became immune from outside meddling.

Decentralization of Regional Administration

The development of tribal self-government among both the Navajo and Hopi tended to retard regional integration under a unified administration. While the Tuba City Agency, prior to the Indian Reorganization Act, was the sole office which served both Moenkopi and local Navajo settlements, decentralization (see Adams, 1963: 253) and dichotomization of the local Indian administration between the BIA and tribe, between the Tuba City and Keams Canyon agencies, and finally between the Navajo and Hopi tribal councils, were frequently a source of curious political merry-go-rounds in the small areal framework of Tuba City and Moenkopi. A peak was reached when the medical services for the Indians were transferred from the BIA to the Public Health Service of the Department of Health, Education, and Welfare (PHS hereafter) in 1956.

It proceeded further when the state of Arizona finally granted to the Indians voting rights for state and national officials in 1948 (Shepardson, 1963:60; Spicer, 1962:351). In 1953 the state initiated several services for the Indians, which included public school education, welfare, and employment services. In Tuba City there are now three public schools, covering all grades (since 1956), and a state employment agency.

The effect on Moenkopi of this decentralization of local affairs was varied. Among other things, it offered an unprecedented number of economic opportunities to the villagers. However, increasing economic opportunities outside the village and the fact that participation by daily commuting was possible only frustrated the upper group's attempt to control the community, whose strategic resources (land and water) were not in its hands. Prior to 1955 a remark that those against the government could not hold jobs in the BIA appeared to influence some people (Hopi Hearings, 1955), who made a point of avoiding employment by the BIA. This type of threat lost much force after 1953. Occupational diversity in Moenkopi was on the increase and there appeared less need for the self-governing organization within the village. Specifically, the hope of solidifying the two segments under the control of the upper group appeared totally crushed. The topic of the tribal council remained for awhile entirely abstract, particularly to the people of the lower segment, and the land dispute between the Hopi and Navajo filed in 1962 had only an academic significance to many villagers. Thus, from 1955 to 1960 the Upper Moenkopi District appeared to be only an appendage to the tribal council, while there seemed to prevail relative apathy to the problems of the community and tribe among the majority of the residents in Moenkopi.

ACCOMMODATIONS TO EXTERNAL INSTITUTIONS (1958–64)

Further Segmentation

The separation of the upper group has proceeded in recent years to a stage where the two segments have become *almost* autonomous as political units. In 1959 the upper group adopted its own constitution, which was approved by the Keams Canyon superintendent, and declared itself as Upper Moenkopi Village Council. The constitution has several features that define the political autonomy of the upper village segment. One is the membership requirement, which states that the voting privilege is confined to adults with two years' residence in the segment. Next it defines the residential area as demarcated by the partial boundary already mentioned and others "traditionally" claimed. No precise description of these boundaries was given, however.

Also in 1959, following joint instructions from the Tuba City and Keams Canyon agencies, two sets of keys were made for each of the two headgates of the reservoir and each group was entrusted with one pair, to be controlled by the watermaster of the upper group and Guy Talas of the lower group.

In 1963 the upper group was notified by the lower group that its use rights to the plaza and two kivas in the lower segment were being revoked because they were located in the chiefly allotment. The upper group began construction of its own kiva and dancing ground on its own site in 1963. At least one kachina dance from New Oraibi was performed in the upper segment in 1964 (see Map 3).

Thus, by the end of 1964 the political division of the two groups was nearly completed and formalization of the sharing procedure on the once communally held resources had been accomplished. At present, no item is held by the two groups without some stipulation about its use. Even the school shower room is used on alternate days by them.

The incorporation process of the upper group advanced further when they installed the water-sewer system in the community in the spring of 1964. Along with this project, the three major streets in the upper segment were paved with concrete. The pavement ends at the boundary between the two groups.

The two groups now represent formally independent political units. In theory no common problems will arise to be solved through their cooperation. Dichotomization is also reflected in the maintenance of the irrigation ditches, each group scrupulously making sure that there will be no chance meeting with the other.

Relationships with Outside Groups

The differentiation of the two segments into mutually exclusive decision-making units was accompanied by independent articulation of each to outside groups. The Upper Moenkopi Council has a close connection with the Keams Canyon Agency through its participation in the tribal council. Employment in informational posts of the Tuba City Agency also gave the Upper Moenkopi Council a privileged position in the area in comparison with the lower segment. The Upper Moenkopi Council relates itself to the Navajo tribe through the Hopi Council, and recently, as the local Navajo were integrated into their own tribal organizations, an increasing number of local problems were taken up jointly by the two tribal governments. This has tended to impersonalize daily interactions between the Navajo and Upper Moenkopi Hopi.

Lower Moenkopi, on the other hand, seldom deals with these agencies or tribal councils. It comes into contact with the Navajo Tribal Council only in crisis situations, and formal dealings of any constancy are absent. In short, Lower Moenkopi does not possess a formal organ for dealings with outside agencies, but *ad hoc*

64 MODERN TRANSFORMATIONS OF MOENKOPI PUEBLO

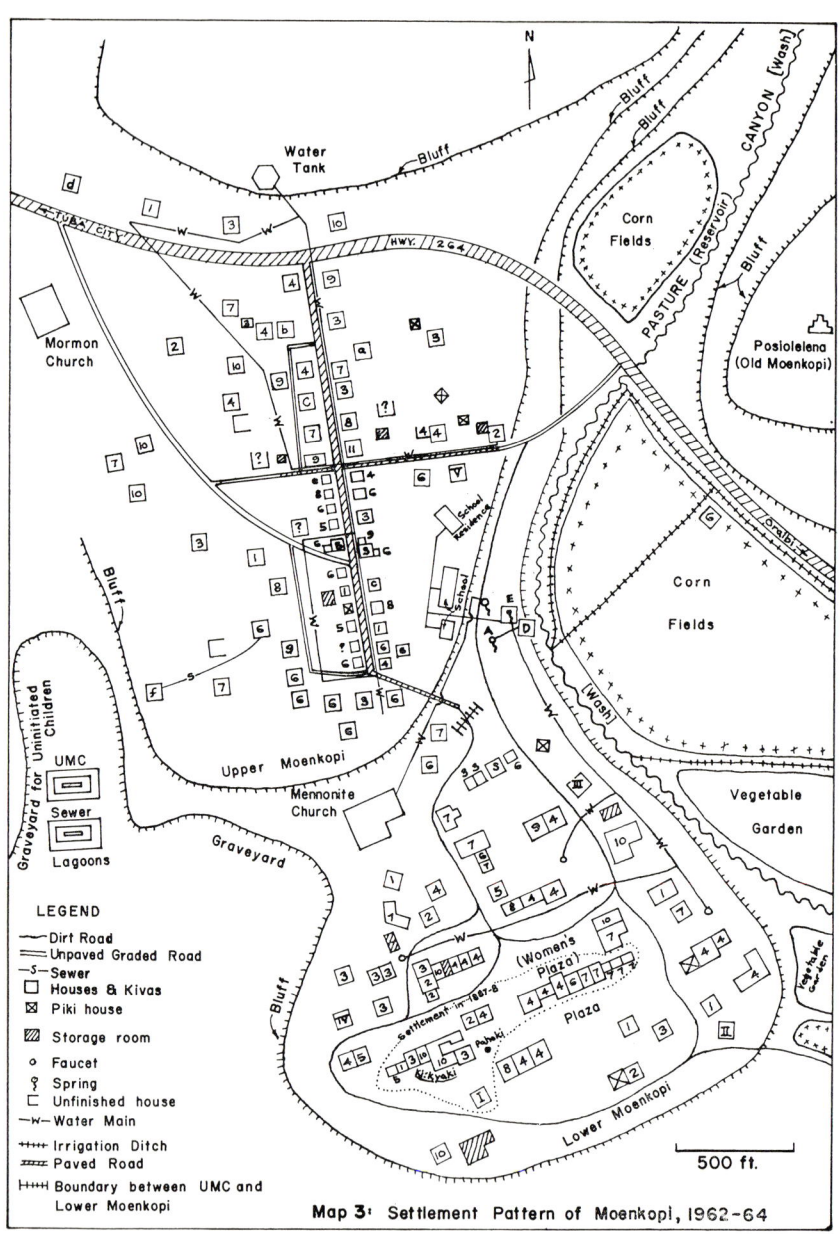

Map 3: Settlement Pattern of Moenkopi, 1962-64

Additional Legend to Map 3

1) Clan affiliation of houses: 1 = Rabbit; 2 = Snake; 3 = Sun's Forehead; 4 = Reed; 5 = Greasewood; 6 = Coyote; 7 = Water Coyote; 8 = Ma'asau; 9 = Badger; 10 = Pi:kyas; 11 = Bluebird.

groups are organized whenever a problem arises between them. The people of Lower Moenkopi appear to maintain more personalized, individualistic relationships with the local Navajo through trade, sheep herding partnerships, visits to medicine men, and mutual attendance at dances.

Within the village the Mennonite church and the Hopi Day School exert only a minimal influence over community affairs. The church still provides the children of the village with Christmas programs and Sunday schools. On Sunday afternoon, when most of the Hopi are in other villages watching dances or in Flagstaff shopping, the church loudspeaker broadcasts hymns to the almost vacant village. The church has only two elderly female converts, who attend Sunday services with some regularity. The church maintains friendly relationships with a few families of the upper segment and can enlist their assistance on occasion.

The attitude of the people toward the church is largely exploitative. They reject its teachings but accept its yuletide charity. Though many households in the lower segment are indifferent to Christmas, families in the upper segment now decorate Christmas trees, exchange gifts, and eat turkeys. However, these activities are seldom associated with Christianity as a religion or with the birth of Christ. "We don't teach our children what Christmas is about. We leave it to the church," said an elderly Hopi woman, when she was told that her daughter did not know Jesus was born on Christmas Day. Children are also exposed to Christianity in school. These experiences are compartmentalized. Adults do not openly challenge the religious teachings. Children are left to resolve conflicts of religious and secular values by themselves, their parents preferring not

---

2) Kivas: I = *Letaiovi,* of the Coyote clan; II = *Iskiva,* of the Water Coyote clan; III = *Ka'waikiva,* of the Greasewood clan; IV = *Ta:vankiva,* of the Coyote clan; V = new kiva belonging to the Upper Moenkopi Council (in construction in 1964).

3) Other houses and structures: a = a Zuni wife's; b = a Choctaw wife's; c = a San Juan wife's; d = a Navajo wife's; e = auto repair shop; f = sewer tank; g = shoe repair shop.

4) Other features: A = Moenkopi spring; B = Upper Moenkopi Council room ("Old Cafe"); C = Upper Moenkopi Council warehouse; D = pump house; E = sump; S = store.

Note: 1) *Ki:kyaki* is where the first chief of Moenkopi, Nashileowi, lived. In other villages, it is the clan house of the chiefly lineage. The Moenkopi *ki:kyaki* once stored kachina masks of the people of Moenkopi. Later, they were moved to the Kiva II.

2) *Pahoki* is where prayer feathers (*paho*) are placed for kachina dances (Voegelin and Voegelin, 1957:C4.1).

to become involved. Thus individual religious conflicts are devoid of social context and do not develop into a serious problem.

There are two other circumstances that limit the Mennonite church's influence over the village. First, missionaries no longer give daily or weekly sermons to school children. Second, the church does not sanction marriage as it once did. The segregation of church activities from the BIA enterprise have deprived it of any significant community function.

The Mormon church, built at a corner of the upper segment site, is more active in community programs than the Mennonites. Its rapport with the village, however, is also limited to recreation and charity. It does not enjoy wide support among the villagers, and it is politically alienated from households antagonistic to the Upper Moenkopi Council. The Upper Moenkopi Council is said to have been instrumental in inviting the Mormons to the present site. The political association of the Mormon church with the Upper Moenkopi Council, however, has been consistently weakened because of the church's inability to intervene in the ever recurring strife in the village without endangering its missionary activities. Consequently, the Mormon church has recruited a larger part of its congregation from among the local Navajo.[4] Both Mennonites and Mormons are regarded by a majority of the villagers with indifference or impartiality, although they receive more sympathy and help from some members of the Upper Moenkopi Council.

Since 1956 the Moenkopi Day School has had only four grades in addition to a beginner's class, all the higher grades having been transferred to the Tuba City public schools. Enrollment was made optional, but, partly because of the free lunches (see Brophy and Aberle, 1966:196) and other savings, a majority of the village children still attend the day school. As the homes in Upper Moenkopi were improved, the use of the school shower rooms decreased drastically, and the people of Lower Moenkopi have been going up to the homes of their relatives in Upper Moenkopi or in Tuba City, or to the community center in Tuba City. Sewing classes and motion picture showings have ceased to be day school functions. Since 1950 the school has been staffed by a white couple and a Hopi man from Moenkopi. The latter obtained his teaching license after training subsidized by the World War II GI Bill. Since he is

---

[4] Gibbons mentions that an estimate of the combined membership of the Moenkopi and Polacca Mormon branches is about 460 (1963:990). The number of Moenkopi Mormons was not obtained but does not seem very large (Johnson, 1964).

identified as a Lower Moenkopi sympathizer, the people of Upper Moenkopi hesitate to bring the day school into politics for their own cause.

The school is now much less significant to the community than in the past. At the present time, with the factional split becoming more acute, the new school principal maintains an attitude of neutrality in order to secure the smooth operation of the school.

The relationships of Upper and Lower Moenkopi with other villages of Hopiland are difficult to characterize. As Titiev and others noted, politics among the Hopi merge with ceremonial activities and kinship relationships, and the diverse ties that an individual has with different villages assume various meanings and functions depending on situational factors.

Regarding ceremonial activities, many children from Upper Moenkopi are now initiated in New Oraibi, while Old Oraibi performs the Kachina and Powamu initiations for children from Lower Moenkopi. Some children from the "uncommitted" group of families have been initiated in Hotevilla. The exchange of dancers and dance troupes is most frequent between Upper Moenkopi, New Oraibi, and Bacabi on the one hand, and between Lower Moenkopi and Oraibi on the other. No dance troupes from Hotevilla have ever visited either Moenkopi segment, although some "uncommitted" members from Moenkopi have joined dances in Hotevilla.

In terms of kinship ties, it is likely that the people of Upper Moenkopi have more frequent relationships with the people of New Oraibi and Bacabi than with others, while those of Lower Moenkopi are with Old Oraibi. The extension of kinship through clanship and initiatory ceremonies defies any attempt to substantiate this suggestion. However, if one confined observations to actual daily interactions, some differentiation appears to emerge. Many families of the upper group visit relatives in New Oraibi and Bacabi, while lower group families interact more frequently with residents of Old Oraibi.

The political ties of the respective segments with Third Mesa villages are most explicit. The Upper Moenkopi Council's political actions are often coordinated with New Oraibi and Bacabi as exemplified by the simultaneous execution of the road paving project. The lower group takes its stand in line with Old Oraibi and still regards the Oraibi chieftainship as the ultimate locus of authority, despite the absence of its incumbent at present. Thus, in the land dispute with the Navajo tribe and reintroduction of the Mennonite church to Oraibi, it stood with Oraibi in opposition to both actions, while the Upper Moenkopi Council did not. In theory, both Old Oraibi and Lower Moenkopi refuse to recognize the tribal council as the representative of their interests. Finally, a section of the "noncommitted" people aligned themselves with Yokioma's son and the latter's Hotevilla actives to strengthen their position in Moenkopi. Since 1958, when the Upper Moenkopi Council adopted its constitution, the conflicting positions of minority and colony have been accommodated in the following pattern of alliance: its minority position is secured through the Upper Moenkopi Council by its affiliation with the Hopi Agency and Tribal Council, and its colonial tie with Old Oraibi through Lower Moenkopi by its lukewarm and unsure participation in the "traditional" tribal politics.

Moenkopi as a whole is now subject to federal law for the 11 major crimes, national income taxation, and draft calls and holds voting rights in national elections. Participation at the state level is through payment of income taxes, voting, and receipt of welfare benefits and public school education. The village is also under the jurisdiction of the Navajo Tribal Police for minor offenses, the Navajo Land Board for land assignments, and the Navajo Grazing Committee for grazing activities. Thus, if the "triple system of government" (Spicer, 1962:417) of the Hopi, consisting of the Hopi Tribal Council, the so-called conservatives, and state-national political organizations, is "the most complicated . . . of the [Southwestern] region" (Spicer, 1962:417–18), Moenkopi contains the most complicated form of political ties of all the Hopi villages.

Leadership Structure

The leadership of the Upper Moenkopi Council is collective, a condition partly deriving from the lack of concentration of such strategic wealth as land and water in the hands of any particular individual or family. However, the collective leadership of the Upper Moenkopi Council is far from representative and its present officials were recruited mainly from among members of the upper group who were active during the period of the "Village Council." The occupational background of most still includes government service. Further, close kinship ties prevail among those who form the "Board of Directors," the decision-making body of the Upper Moenkopi Council. In 1962–63, the son of the village representative to the tribal council was a lieutenant governor, his father's brother's son, another lieutenant governor, and his brother's son, governor. These officials also tend to rotate the positions among themselves, althought an "election" is held every two years.

Collective leadership gives the Upper Moenkopi Council an advantage over the monolithic leadership of Lower Moenkopi. Criticisms of and abusive comments about the Upper Moenkopi Council cannot be directed against any specific official, so the Hopi technique of social sanction through gossip is far less effective than when directed toward the chief of Lower Moenkopi. While the absence of popular support of the Lower Moenkopi chief results in inactivity, the Upper Moenkopi Council has managed to carry out several community projects despite the rampant criticisms of many residents.

Though Lower Moenkopi has retained the traditional form of leadership, hereditary chieftainship, the chiefly position deviates considerably from the native ideal. Succession to the position has so far been limited to the Pi:kyas lineage of Moenkopi. After the death of the second chief, Frank Siyamptewa, in 1945, the position was vacant until 1960. During this period, Guy Talas, a respected man of the Water Coyote clan, represented the "village down below," i.e., the lower group.

Guy Talas' assumption of the leadership of Lower Moenkopi was aided by the following factors. First, he was married to a woman of the Pi:kyas clan, who died in the late fall of 1962. Second, he was a renowned medicine man of the village. Finally, he was supported by his four siblings, one of whom was a village crier, a position that has since lapsed. As a medicine man, he enjoyed the patronage of many Navajo not only from near the village, but from Utah, Colorado, and New Mexico as well. His wealth, in the form of pawned jewelry and ready cash, had long been a source of loans to the residents of Lower Moenkopi and his bank savings in Flagstaff were said to amount to $50,000. His brothers belonged to the oldest lineage of the Water Coyote clan in the village, which has been closely associated with the chiefly lineage of the Pi:kyas through marriage since the allotment period. They were mainly occupied in the traditional farming and sheep herding, and none had kept cattle until quite recently. Except for the youngest, none had been employed by the government for any significant amount of time. Because of his clan affiliation, Guy Talas did not assume any office in the Soyal ceremony of Oraibi, but he was a member of both the Wuwuchim and the Powamu. Thus, although he did not command English well, nor was his knowledge of the BIA administration and the tribal governments extensive, he was regarded as a representative of Lower Moenkopi by his people and by government agencies.

In 1960 Odin Talas, one of Guy's sons, succeeded Frank Siyamptewa to the position of Lower Moenkopi chief. Born in 1912, he was initiated to the Kachina society in Moenkopi and then to the Powamu in Old Oraibi. Because the Wuwuchim ceremony had long since lapsed in Old Oraibi, he was never initiated to this society. After the death of Chief Tawaquaptewa of Oraibi in 1960, he was finally installed in one of the offices in the Soyal ceremony of Oraibi and this appeared to validate his claim to the chieftainship in Moenkopi.

There are many in Lower Moenkopi who refuse to recognize Odin Talas as a valid chief and who insist that Guy "pushed" him in. Though the youngest of the family, Odin seems to have enjoyed Guy's indulgence. He was instructed in the art of medicine by his father. The oldest of the sons has long resided in Flagstaff and does not have a house in Moenkopi. The second son, though married to a woman of Lower Moenkopi, moved up to the upper village segment and built a house there. Guy gave all his grazing permits to this second son.

While his brothers were thus disposed of, there was yet another pretender to the chieftainship: Ted Talas, whose mother's mother's brothers were Frank Siyamptewa and Qooyama. The latter are Odin's mother's sister's sons. Qooyama was an important religious leader in Moenkopi as well as Oraibi. Ted's father, Teddy Honyumptewa of the Coyote clan, apparently tried to push his own son to be the Moenkopi chief and enlisted the support of Charlie Talasmenewa, Ted's mother's father and an original allottee. Qooyama appears to have been more or less neutral. However, Guy had all of his four Water Coyote brothers on his side and along with his own experience as the village representative after Siyamptewa's death, easily managed to steer Odin into the chiefly position. This manipulation by Guy, however, left a considerable amount of discredit on Odin's chieftainship, and Ted's sister claims that Guy actually got rid of Talasmenewa with his medicine. Many Lower Moenkopi residents, as mentioned, flatly deny that Odin is their chief. In spite of all this, it is he who is consulted in crises in Lower Moenkopi and he, in turn, willingly represents the people.

Odin's leadership in Lower Moenkopi, however, is not based entirely on his ceremonial position in the Soyal and his clan membership. Two other factors, both a result of the contact condition of his community, appear more significant.

The first is Odin's occupational experience and the knowledge he acquired from it. As a young man, he worked outside the village in Page, Window Rock, Chinle, and Flagstaff. He now belongs to a Flagstaff local of the construction laborers' union. Through these experiences, he acquired enough knowledge of English to at least make himself understood by outsiders. At the same time, with his father, he had dealt with the government agencies on past occasions. These qualities, while they could disqualify him as a chief in other villages, are perceived as desirable in Moenkopi. For example, a claim was once made by a man of the Ma'asau clan to the chieftainship. Apart from his genealogical relationship to the late chief of Oraibi, Lololoma, he based his claim on his knowledge of government regulations. Odin himself refuses to use interpreters in meetings between government officials and his people.

The second is his "accommodative" ideas regarding the relationship between his village on the one hand and the government and the white man's world on the other. His attitude toward the government is much less hostile than the current "traditional" view and he does not hesitate to say that "you cannot get rid of the government." The same applies to the cash economy and, quoting the late Tawaquaptewa, he frankly admits the village's need of money. His ideas on education are also enlightened, and he not only sends all his children to school but has managed to make a practical nurse out of one daughter. The latter once told me that her father was willing to pay for her college education if she wished to attend.

Leadership in Action

In order to view the effectiveness of leadership in both groups, let us examine the execution of the water-sewer project in the upper village.

The Upper Moenkopi project was carried out under Public Law 86–121 (73 Stat. 267), known as the Indian Sanitation Facilities Act (Brophy and Aberle, 1966:222), and several Indian tribes had already drawn benefits from it. The application by the Upper Moenkopi Council was accepted, according to one of the project workers of the PHS, because the water supply in Moenkopi was sufficient for installation of the system. Lower Moenkopi, which was also approached by the PHS officials, refused to apply for the project. The factors leading up to the Upper Moenkopi Council's application and Lower Moenkopi's refusal are not known to me at present. However, it is significant that the PHS concerned was the one stationed at Keams Canyon and not the one at Tuba City. A preparatory study for the same project had been carried out previously in South Tuba by the Tuba City PHS (Levy, 1962b) and though the main was installed there, no hook-up from individuals has been made so far.

The project, as promulgated in the law, required a division of labor between the recipient of the benefits and the PHS. The former was to provide labor and the right of way to the project workers from the PHS, while the latter was to offer technical assistance as well as necessary equipment. Finally, the Upper Moenkopi Council was also to provide a site for two sewer lagoons for an open sewer system. In the actual operation of the project, therefore, recruitment of labor emerged as a major task imposed on the Upper Moenkopi leadership.

In order to meet these conditions, the Upper Moenkopi Council assigned each "individual householder . . . to donate 88 hours of labor in the digging and covering of trenches, or pay a sum of $110.00. This amount was to be paid on installment basis if so desired" (*Navajo Times*, July 22, 1965). This assignment rule, as well as others in regard to the actual construction, were adopted after a series of meetings and were distributed to constituent households in a printed form letter. The form also included an application sheet for the project itself. About five of 60 households in the upper segment refused to join the project for political or economic reasons or for both. Some others reluctantly joined after prolonged persuasion by a project worker herself and Upper Moenkopi Council members. A few of the initial applicants dropped out.

The construction work began in the fall of 1962; its major aspect was completed and the system put into operation in the early spring of 1964. During this period, the greatest difficulty of the Upper Moenkopi leaders lay in recruiting labor. For about a year of my stay in the village during the construction period, there was hardly a day when more than 10 villagers worked for the project. Characteristically, a few Upper Moenkopi Council leaders, who are all of retirement age, contributed a considerable portion of the daily labor. One or two unmarried young men, who were unemployed at the time and whose parents are staunch supporters of the Upper Moenkopi Council, also worked regularly.

Otherwise, however, the labor contribution was very irregular and progress frequently lagged behind schedule. The deadline date was postponed twice during my observation period of 1962–64. A project worker told me that it had taken more time than was spent in other reservations for the same scale of work.

Lack of cooperation was evident not only in the households antagonistic to the Upper Moenkopi Council but also in some of the supporter households. It is thus incorrect to assume that political antagonism was the sole reason for lack of community cooperation.

More important is the fact that most of the householders in Moenkopi were engaged in wage work in Tuba City and its environs and, tied to a 40-hour work schedule, many of them simply could not afford to give time to the project. Apparently, a considerable number of households chose to pay cash in lieu of labor. A few households, who could not afford it, had their relatives who happened to be out of work contribute labor on their behalf. Some householders worked on weekends. Others had their older relatives, still living in the lower village, come up and work for them. Sons-in-law worked for their parents-in-law and fathers worked for the households of their children. A number of men also worked for more households than merely their own.

As shown above, the Upper Moenkopi Council leadership is not simply the decision-making body but also the group that actually executes decisions which have been made. They monopolize initiative in community improvement programs and often leave the upper group residents with an image of being pushed around in total passivity. The lacuna remains unfilled, mainly because the public is apathetic to the problems of the community; in addition, the community leadership feels threatened by the tribal factionalism of the Hopi and its minority position in the area and thus places itself in a competitive position vis-à-vis the leadership of the lower village segment, others in Hopiland, the Navajo tribe, and the latter's local leadership. These situations tend to tinge the Upper Moenkopi Council with aggressiveness and political power play, and to induce severe criticisms from the village public.

It might appear that the lower group leadership is in a much stronger position through concentration of such strategic resources as the residential site, Moenkopi spring, choice allotment farms, a communal vegetable garden, and the chiefly household's custody of the reservoir keys. This is not the case, however. With the increased dependence on wage work, the strategic significance of farm land and irrigation water resources has drastically declined. Second, possible control over the village through such remaining wealth as the residential site is severely limited by governmental sanctions. Finally, and perhaps most important, the emergence of the aggressive Upper Moenkopi Council and the maintenance of Lower Moenkopi's colonial tie with Oraibi has deprived the lower group leadership of incentive for independent actions. Hence the contexts in which the leadership is required to act have been limited to crisis situations which demand defense of the traditional village structure. The nature of Lower Moenkopi leadership was thus primarily passive; it became active only at the demand of the people.

When the chief did occasionally initiate an action, his amorphous constituents usually abandoned him. Thus, when Odin procured $400 from a road construction company as compensation for the use of irrigation water, his suggestion to utilize the funds in raising the dike at the reservoir in order to increase its capacity did not arouse enough response from the villagers, and the money, originally a share with the Upper Moenkopi Council, had to be given up to the latter to avoid suspicions among his people, who had no need for the community funds. In another case, it was discovered in the course of the project that the water main leading to the communal faucets of the lower village segment from a well by Moenkopi spring (see Map 3) was corroded and was in urgent need of replacement. The chief was informed of this by a PHS worker from Keams Canyon and accordingly obtained an agreement for installation of the new pipes with village labor. His subsequent consultation with the people in this regard, however, was futile. Thus, although the people of Lower Moenkopi were similarly apathetic to community affairs, the economic isolation of the leadership from the individual interests in the community, its concentration in a single person, and its traditional character prevented it from taking positive actions for the community.

The shift of the economic basis from village-based agriculture to wage work outside the village and the resulting high mobility of the resident population thus brought about wide-spread indifference to community affairs among the residents of Moenkopi. In addition, extensive kin ties between the residents of the two groups made it difficult for the leadership of each to act on the assumption of political autonomy. The Upper Moenkopi Council leadership came to be characterized by aggressiveness, that of the lower village by withdrawal. What a former tribal council chairman once said to me appeared to well sum up the predicament of the leaders: "Damned if I do, damned if I don't."

The high residential instability and the existence of outside residents from Moenkopi gave rise to more serious problems in the Upper Moenkopi Council, where the decision-making process is collective and diffuse, than in Lower Moenkopi, where the process is mainly confined to a small number of older residents and the chief and where decisions usually involve passive acceptance. As previously mentioned, the Upper Moenkopi Council constitution includes a clause limiting membership to those with two years' continuous residence on the site. However, it does not specify terms for revocation of membership. Hence many off-reservation residents, originally from Moenkopi, carry a vague status in regard to village politics. The incorporation process of the Hopi into a tribe and possibility of tribal funds through oil lease and other sources further make tribal membership into a tangible right to the off-reservation Hopi in general. The membership question was seriously debated in the Hopi Hearings at Moenkopi. Finally, many Hopi still regard the village of their origin as their homeland and a place to which they can retire. These factors contribute to continuing interest in Moenkopi among the outside residents. For example, for some time it has been a custom in the upper segment to hold social dances in cooperation with former residents who now live in Flagstaff.

Political participation of former residents in the affairs of the upper segment has not been negligible either. When the lower group refused to permit the upper group to use the plaza and two kivas in 1963, some residents in Flagstaff, who were originally from Moenkopi, joined with the upper group leaders to decide where to hold the dances to be given by a visiting troupe of New Oraibi performers. One of them suggested that they go ahead and use the village plaza and in the event of a disturbance, call in the Hopi Police. Partly because they do not live in uncomfortable daily interaction with members of the lower village segment, their proposals and suggestions often assume a radical tone as illustrated in this case. Generally their participation is appreciated by the Upper Moenkopi Council and attention is given to their views. However, though they seldom play any crucial role in final decisions, their existence often delays and occasionally cripples the efficiency of the operations of the Upper Moenkopi Council.

Social Control

Social control in Moenkopi has undergone a serious change in the post-war era. The rumors and gossip that commanded conformity and cooperation from the people (Aberle, 1951:122–23; Brandt, 1954:47, 73, 327), and still do in some villages of Hopiland, have lost much of their effectiveness in Moenkopi along with the decrease of community solidarity and increasing economic opportunities outside. The changes in family organization, reduction in ceremonial activities, and extensive school education have deprived the household of its traditional role of socialization, including the inculcation of fear (D. Eggan, 1943:370f.) and corresponding conformity to the public opinion by internal control. Rumor and gossip are still rampant in the village, and clowns in the kachina dances occasionally present piquant plays about the quaint behavior of fellow villagers. Sometimes the clowns ridicule a man of more than average wealth as *nouveaux riches* and expose his acquisitive actions to the entire audience of the village. Increasingly, however, lack of solidarity in village life makes these measures less and less effective. This is illustrated in the following case material.

Around 1956 the Arizona Power Company drew lines to the then established Rare Metals, a uranium mill about 10 miles east of Tuba City. The company also drew lines to the upper segment of Moenkopi, where the households belonging to the Upper Moenkopi Council desired it. Once the lines were drawn, however, the subsequent drawing of lines to homes which did not necessarily go along with the Upper Moenkopi Council was also done in the form of individual subscription to the company. The Upper Moenkopi Council could not refuse them the opportunity to take advantage of the already existing lines on their site, although this action did arouse snide comments among the members of the Upper Moenkopi Council that their antagonists who drew lines were inconsistent, for they availed themselves of the white man's way. Utilization of propane gas for cooking as well as heating, which began in 1948, also occurred as individual innovations (see below) outside the control of the Upper Moenkopi Council.

A trend now exists from internal to external forms of social control as the surrender of extensive community functions led Moenkopi to depend on outside agencies to police the community. Thus, importation of liquor and violation of curfew laws and traffic regulations have been under the surveillance of the Navajo Tribal Police, and offenders are tried by the Navajo Trial Court in Tuba City. It is not unusual for one or two Navajo police cars to park by the lower segment plaza on the occasion of kachina dances.

Recently, however, the Upper Moenkopi Council requested that the Hopi Tribal Police enforce its policies and maintain order in the upper segment site. I have already mentioned the suggestion by a Flagstaff resident from Moenkopi to call the Hopi Tribal Police in for the kachina dance of the upper village to be given at the lower segment plaza. In my own case, it was the Hopi Police from Keams Canyon who came to the upper segment to arrest me as a politically

Plate 1. Partial view of Upper Moenkopi; note electric cables and a water tower.

undesirable outsider. After the completion of the water-sewer project, the Upper Moenkopi Council asked a Polacca policeman from Keams Canyon to shut off the water to the three households in the upper segment that refused to pay the $3 monthly dues for the maintenance of the system as defined in new Upper Moenkopi Council regulations regarding the use of the system (*Navajo Times*, July 22, 1965).

As easily surmised, the reliance of the Upper Moenkopi Council on the Hopi Tribal Police developed after the Navajo tribal institutions in the area, including the police, barred the Hopi from participation. To the Upper Moenkopi Council, it was thus a logical course of action. However, because of the ambiguity in jurisdiction between the two police forces, the recourse of the Upper Moenkopi Council to the Hopi Police was limited to affairs of a political nature, which, in turn, strengthened the impression among the people that the police were the machine of the Upper Moenkopi Council and that the council was acting behind the veil of the Hopi Police. This resulted in alienation of the police from the households antagonistic to the Upper Moenkopi Council and in general reticence on the part of the Hopi policemen who are asked to intervene by the council. The policeman who accompanied the Upper Moenkopi Council members in turning the water off attempted to excuse himself by telling the womenfolk present on the spot that he did not know what he was called in for.

The position of the households antagonistic to the Upper Moenkopi Council, on the other hand, is not that of mere alienation from their tribal police. In fact, it would have been an intolerable one, had they not had support for their position within the village. Rather, their support consists of an ever present possibility of resorting to the off-reservation establishments or to that faction antagonistic to the tribal council, of receiving help from the kin in their own village, and finally, of manipulating the two existing political divisions of Moenkopi. The first possibility has already been commented upon in connection with increased mobility of the resident population. The second means is more particularly employed by a small group of households opposed to both the Upper Moenkopi and Lower Moenkopi leadership. On the basis of individual relationships through kinship and ceremonial participation, they have aligned themselves with the political orientation of Hotevilla. Thus, when the water of one of these households was shut off by the Upper Moenkopi Council, the first reaction for the woman of the household was to contact leading "traditionals" at Hotevilla and Kenneth Loma at New Oraibi through her brother at Tuba City. They arrived at her home on the evening of the day when the water was stopped and kept a vigil there to wait for the PHS officials from Keams Canyon, who had also been contacted by phone at the day school for intercession.

As so often happened, however, the opposition was ineffectual; for though the meeting was held on the next day and the PHS explained that it was no longer responsible for the action of the Upper Moenkopi Council and suggested that the "traditionals" meet directly with the council, this was never carried out and the households remained without water for some time. Though the Upper Moenkopi Council appeared to crush this opposition successfully, its success was not a lasting one and did not bring about the desired end of forcing the antagonists to recognize their authority. On the contrary, it revealed a lack of power in their control of the upper segment. Before going into this matter, however, I shall comment on another measure that the Upper Moenkopi Council adopted for community control.

One of the main difficulties in the attempt of the Upper Moenkopi Council to administer the affairs of the upper segment is that, within the site, the residents form *ad hoc* cooperative groups for diverse purposes on the basis of kinship and thus create groups within a group, making united administration difficult. The problem was explicitly perceived by the officials of the Upper Moenkopi Council, one of whom mentioned that already a certain row of the three streets had been dominated by so-and-so's "outfit." Thus, shortly before the water-sewer system was put into operation, the Upper Moenkopi Council adopted a set of regulations which included, in addition to the monthly dues, a clause prohibiting the lending and borrowing of water between "neighbors," viz., kinsmen. This rule as well as others in the set was debated heatedly among the residents prior to their adoption. Its purpose was to isolate households and bring them into utter dependence on the Upper Moenkopi Council. This challenge to one of the fundamental values of Hopi society, namely kinship solidarity, which was firmly maintained among the staunch actives of the Upper Moenkopi Council themselves, invited strong criticism from the people. In practice the rule was not followed. When the above households were deprived of community water, their first reaction was to borrow water from neighboring households, many of which were related to them. For example, one of the households connected a plastic pipe to an outside faucet of its neighbor household, the two being related by a brother-sister sibling bond. Despite its prohibition, the Upper Moenkopi Council could not indict the violators because of the lack of policing powers within the group itself and because to do so would have precipitated a dispute with the helping households, some of which were supporters of the Upper Moenkopi Council.

In addition to kinship, Moenkopi's division itself provides another avenue of evasion. When the Tuba City and Keams Canyon agencies jointly issued a notice to establish watermasters in the respective segments who should control the keys to the irrigation reservoirs and thus better maintain the system, it was intended that the new rule bring the farmers in both groups under the authority of the two groups, a program which the BIA has been attempting without success. However, the policy was not as effective as expected. Apart from the decentralized feature of irrigation farming in Moenkopi, those dependent on the water from the reservoirs were well aware that once the use of the keys was refused to them in one group, they could always borrow from the other through the channels of kinship or friendship. Since each group contains dissidents, many of whom ostensibly go along with the other group, and since each is eager to acquire more followers, ambiguity in political affiliation gives room to exploit the division to advantage. Neither leadership is able to curb such evasions.

The village itself did not provide an effective means of social control for either group. The site of the lower segment that was originally contained in the chiefly allotment soon spread out to a section of an adjoining allotment even before the present upper village site was allocated for residence in 1914. Hence, when the power lines were drawn to the upper village, several people residing in this section of the lower segment took the opportunity to draw electricity to their homes. They were the supporters of the Upper Moenkopi Council, in which they had many close kin as actives. Since this southwestern portion of the lower segment (see Map 3) belonged to the allotment whose heirs in the village were opposed to the lower segment leadership, the chief was unable to stop the spread of electricity within the site. However, those households in this section which remained loyal to the chief refused the service and, as a result, homes with electricity in this section were checker-boarded by those without it. Though Odin, the present chief of Lower Moenkopi, attempted to excuse himself by stating that the incident happened during his absence from the village, many villagers were aware that the above situations were undermining chiefly control. Thus, after Upper Moenkopi was denied the use of the two kivas in Lower Moenkopi, one was left unused by Lower Moenkopi, supposedly because it was located outside the chiefly allotment.[5]

The probation of the allotment land in 1960 undermined the traditional control on the basis of the chiefly allotment. In a meeting which was presided over by the Navajo tribal representatives and which demanded the presence of the officials of the Upper Moenkopi Council as well as the Lower Moenkopi chief and his aides, the members of the Upper Moenkopi Council challenged the chief's qualification as Lower Moenkopi representative on the basis of his still unprobated heirship to the allotment. As the meeting was held soon after his mother's death, the theory behind the opposition by the Upper Moenkopi Council was that his claim had to be

---

[5] This explanation was given by the chief himself and a few of his close associates. There are, however, others who maintain that it was abandoned because of "witchcraft" in the kiva. I was unable to ascertain the nature of the witchcraft, although this particular kiva has a long history of personal struggles in regard to its use. One informant, whose father used to be one of the chief members of the kiva and who recounted the history, denied the witchcraft accusation.

approved by the government through another probation on the inheritance of the mother's share in the chiefly allotment. This point was, however, overruled by the Navajo representatives, who were only eager to find a solution to the problem in the meeting. Though it was brushed aside for the moment, it became obvious that chiefly control based on the ownership of the village site is seriously undermined through probation, for now each heir to the allotment can theoretically claim his share of inheritance to the site. The chief once mentioned to me the possibility of charging land rent to the residents, but he is also aware that this might further weaken his own control, which is now precariously based on the political solidarity of the heirs, consisting not only of the members of the chiefly lineage but, due to bilateral inheritance, of those outside it. It is with such tenuously based control that Odin, following the lead of Oraibi, still denies electricity to his residents despite the intense wish of some, which occasionally flares up under the influence of liquor.

A rather dissimilar situation prevails in the control by the Upper Moenkopi Council of its residential site. Here the land is not individually divided into allotments. On the other hand, the action of the superintendent at Tuba City in 1914 had never been recognized by the Washington authority, and hence, theoretically, the major portion of the area still belongs to the Navajo Reservation. It is, in the words of the Upper Moenkopi constitution, only "traditionally" delimited. Thus, when it was found out that some horses kept roaming into the upper segment site and destroying fences and crops of home gardens, all the Upper Moenkopi Council did was to put up signs in the Tuba City Post Office and supermarket, requesting possible owners to keep them under control. Characteristically, no countermeasure was suggested in the notice.

The allocation of house sites has been made by the members of the Upper Moenkopi Council and, more recently, through formal permission granted by the Board of Directors. The status of each house site, however, remains as ambiguous as the status of the upper village site itself, and the question was immediately raised when some households which refused to join the water project of the Upper Moenkopi Council, as well as those whose water was shut off from the system, decided to provide their own water. One individual reportedly wrote to Senator Goldwater to inquire about the feasibility of digging a well on his house lot. The inquiry was said to have been referred to the superintendent at Keams Canyon, who confirmed its legality. Thus assured, he hired a well-digging outfit from Flagstaff and had a well dug on the lot. Two other households, both opposed to the Upper Moenkopi Council, did the same. In so doing, one household had to sell several head of cattle to pay for the cost, about $650, considerably more than the cost of subscription to the Upper Moenkopi system (*Navajo Times*, July 22, 1965). These households, that had either been obtaining water from their neighbors or daily carrying it in milk cans from Tuba City and the Moenkopi spring for about two months since the incident, now equipped themselves with their own water supply. One of them, at least, now even has its own sewer tank, thus indicating a trend toward greater household autonomy.

The case illustrates a characteristic weakness of social control by the Upper Moenkopi Council. Through the administrative interpretation of house sites by the Hopi Agency, they slipped out of the ultimate control by the community itself. The antagonistic households, in turn, resorted to an off-reservation agency to solve their problem.

Pattern of Political Interactions between Upper and Lower Moenkopi

So far we have mainly dealt with the political aspects of each group independently. Reference to the mode of interactions between the two groups has been slight. I shall now deal with the latter and show how their political relationships are ordered in terms of Moenkopi's contextual position.

The discussion in the present section is based on direct field observations. However, the detail in this section is due to the relevance of the problem to the entire political history of Moenkopi as well.

POLITICS WITHOUT CONFRONTATION. As previously mentioned, the separation of Moenkopi into the lower and upper groups as two independent decision-making units has been complete merely in formal terms. There yet remain such important community assets as the irrigation reservoirs and ditches, whose use and maintenance are equally but separately assigned to the two groups. As new community projects were introduced into the upper segment, the matters that once had been left without explicit division were brought up anew and called for negotiations, agreements, or compromises between these groups. Finally, their intensive participation in the institutions of the greater Tuba region brought about many problems whose solutions demanded their representation. Despite these circumstances, the mode of interaction between them, when faced with a common problem, revealed an unusual and, to an outsider, often irritating pattern of political processes.

(1) *Irrigation Complex.* The lack of explicit social control and the extensive involvement in a cash economy induced further deterioration of the cooperative labor necessary for the maintenance of the irrigation reservoirs and ditches. The decline in farming activities and, finally, decentralization of irrigation systems in the area further devalued the system of reservoir irrigation. The lower group leadership found it impossible to recruit labor and organize the maintenance work on a wider basis. Although persons in its leadership group were most dependent on the water from this system, their concern with the maintenance itself had long been lukewarm and haphazard. A different situation prevailed in Upper Moenkopi. In default of particular community wealth significant enough to exert control over the residents by withholding it from defiants and recalcitrants, the Upper Moenkopi Council long had been trying to achieve control of the reservoir facilities. The Upper Moenkopi Council took advantage of the "sloppy" administration of the reservoirs by Lower Moenkopi and attempted to rectify it by turning the reservoir water into a saleable commodity and charging fees to irrigate fields. The plan was put into effect in 1957. This upset Lower Moenkopi and Guy, Odin's father, immediately took it up with his son who was employed outside Moenkopi at the time. They returned to the lower segment, held a meeting, and decided to take the matter to Phoenix, capital of Arizona.

The decision is characteristic of the way the lower group operates in disputes with the upper group. First, the lower group scrupulously avoided bringing the matter up with the Tuba City or Keams Canyon agencies, whom they distrust. Direct negotiations with the upper group had already been ruled out. On the other hand, the decision to appeal to Phoenix was not intended as going over the head of the Keams Canyon office. In fact, while Phoenix was brought up as a possibility, there was no definite organ to whom the chosen people knew to make an appeal. Their first contact in Phoenix was a voluntary organization of the local Indians in that area, in which Odin had a few personal acquaintances. The organization referred them to a private Indian rights organization in town, which, in turn, referred them to the Phoenix Area Office of the BIA. There they met a Land Operations officer, who subsequently notified the local offices in Tuba City as well as in Keams

Canyon, and the matter of charging for irrigation water was dropped.

The second dispute between the two groups regarding the use of irrigation water occurred shortly after 1959. When the BIA notice was issued on the establishment of the watermasters and headgate keys, the Upper Moenkopi Council, without any previous consultation with Lower Moenkopi, set the padlocks at the gates and kept the keys to themselves. They then started selling the water to a road construction company from Albuquerque, New Mexico, which was building the present State Highway 64. The sale soon came to the attention of Lower Moenkopi, which held another meeting and decided to send the same group of people again to the Phoenix Land Operations officer. The latter, by now apparently fed up with the business, bluntly told them to see the Upper Moenkopi Council directly. Odin Talas brought this message to his people.

The news left the people dismayed, for now they were confronted with a direct clash with the Upper Moenkopi Council. A few older people in positions of influence backed down from the required confrontation. Odin told the people that he would do the "talking" all by himself and went up to see a long-time representative to the tribal council from Moenkopi. According to Odin, the representative told him that "he wasn't living on farms; he wasn't eating things from the farm but he was making money,"[6] and yet "he was the one who always went out to clean the ditches." Odin then replied to the representative by saying that in that case, he should simply withdraw and stop meddling with the reservoirs. This appeared to settle the matter. Shortly thereafter Odin brought a couple of sets of padlocks, one of which was given to the Upper Moenkopi Council. The road construction company later paid $800 to be divided between the two groups.[7]

The two cases show that Lower Moenkopi always attempts to avoid direct confrontation with the upper group by asking a third party of superior position to bring pressure to bear on the Upper Moenkopi Council. It should also be noted that the course of actions Upper Moenkopi follows is similar to that of Lower Moenkopi, for they also consolidate their position by first contacting the

---

[6] The representative is a long established cattleman.

[7] Odin mentioned to me that the company had already made a payment of $1,350 to the Upper Moenkopi Council, which did not share any portion of it with Lower Moenkopi.

HISTORY OF POLITICAL CHANGE 85

Plate 2. Irrigation gate of Hopi reservoir.

local BIA in order to forestall any possible objections of Lower Moenkopi.

Avoidance of direct encounters is also shown in the manner in which the two groups send out separate ditch repairing parties in the spring. This has been the custom in Moenkopi since their split. Each group, especially Lower Moenkopi, scrupulously avoids working on the same day, and since Upper Moenkopi has been more aggressive, Lower Moenkopi tends to labor on whatever is left by the Upper Moenkopi party. Recently, the repair work by Lower Moenkopi took on an entirely random character and not more than 10 members or less than five families of close chiefly association have been seen on the work. This is because, apart from reasons mentioned earlier, of the small amount of work left after Upper Moenkopi took care of the major portion of the cleaning, and of the fact that except for these families, most of the serious farmers in Lower Moenkopi are no longer dependent on the reservoir water for irrigation. Yet the token participation by Lower Moenkopi is significant as an expression of its material claim over the reservoir complex.

(2) *Moenkopi Sewer Lagoon.* The two groups, as shown above, attempt to avoid direct political contacts. When communication is necessary, it is accomplished by contacting outside allies or sym-

pathetic parties of each group, who, in general, do not have a particular stake in the village politics.

In 1960, when the application was accepted for the water-sewer project, the Upper Moenkopi Council was required to furnish a site for a community sewer lagoon within the village site. Through a consultation with the project engineer, one of the original allotments was chosen for the lagoon site. Apart from the technical considerations, the choice of this allotment land was based on the following circumstances. Because of its location at the mouth of an arroyo, the land had been gullied deeply in many spots and the vicinity of the land used as a dump area by some people of Upper Moenkopi. It had long been out of cultivation and its appraised value at the time of probation in 1962 was only $1,410. Finally, one of the heirs was a long-time resident in Flagstaff. These factors obviously contributed to lessening the curiosity and antagonism of the people and left only a small number of them aware of the plan.

In order to secure the land for the project, all the heirs to the allotment were contacted by a project worker as well as by the officials of the Upper Moenkopi Council and their signatures were obtained. The circumstances under which the signatures were collected cast some doubt upon their validity. The people involved

Plate 3. Newly constructed sewer lagoon for Upper Moenkopi.

appeared to have divergent views on the exact purpose of signature; some were willing to sign because of their political affiliations. The husband of one of the signers was the watermaster for Upper Moenkopi. Others were more or less talked into it without a full understanding of the implication of their action, or signed from disinterest in the already devalued allotment.

Theoretically, however, all the allotment lands are held in trust by the government and their final disposal needs to be approved by the BIA as in the case of inheritance. The Keams Canyon PHS apparently did not duly appreciate this and, through a tacit understanding with the tribal lawyer that community interests take precedence over individual interests (principle of eminent domain), satisfied itself with receiving signatures from respective heirs.

Thus there was an irregularity beyond the framework of village politics. It was a matter to be taken up by the BIA and related legal agents and not by the village. In fact, the entire issue would have passed without incident had there not been agitation instigated by an active "traditional," Kenneth Loma. He had already taken it upon himself to inform the people of such conservative villages at Hotevilla and Shongopavi about the Moenkopi project. On the basis of his affiliation with Moenkopi through birth and his political convictions, he urged the Lower Moenkopi chief to take action against this allotment affair as well as against a plan to enlarge the capacity of the sacred spring by digging another well nearby. As for the latter, however, the project itself decided to do a minimum of work, leaving the entire access to the spring open to the villagers as it had been. Thus the opposition could only make an issue out of the allotment problem.

The manner in which this was handled by Lower Moenkopi was indicative of the way it generally operated. Apart from the limitations set to the opposition by the legal framework, it was also known to its leaders that the individuals approached for signature cared less about Lower Moenkopi. Thus, instead of marshalling their support to the opposition, they immediately contacted the probation officer from the Gallup area office who was responsible for the inheritance. Then, one night in the winter of 1962, a large meeting was held by the chief at his house. The officer expressed his "private" opinions regarding possible irregularities involved in the transfer of the allotment to the project. Nothing of any consequence, however, developed from this long-awaited meeting and, as mentioned, the project proceeded without much difficulty.

The case shows, if incompletely, that affairs in Moenkopi do not stand isolated but they immediately evoke the tie that it has with other villages of Hopiland, and their handling is done in cooperation with the people from these villages. In the case of Upper Moenkopi, such a tie extends to Bacabi, New Oraibi, and other council villages of Second and First Mesas. If the political confrontations are absent between Upper and Lower Moenkopi directly, they occur in mediation through the associated groups of Hopiland. It also indicates the involvement of the superordinate power in forming the opposition.

(3) *Navajo Sewer Lagoon.* Sometime between 1959 and 1961, the Navajo tribe constructed open sewer lagoons for Tuba City with the help of their PHS. A system of the present four-stepped lagoons was completed in 1962. The construction plan of the system itself became a matter of dispute between Upper and Lower Moenkopi. The site chosen for the lagoons was to the east of Tuba City, close by a section of the Hopi irrigation canal which runs parallel to Reservoir Canyon. In theory, the oxidated sewer flows into the canyon but, in reality, the distance between the canal and canyon in this section is only a few yards and there is a danger that the Tuba City sewer will contaminate the irrigation water.

Upper as well as Lower Moenkopi were contacted by the Navajo tribe and PHS for the discussion of the plan and, on that occasion, both groups strongly objected to the idea. Lower Moenkopi even filed a petition to the Keams Canyon office with signatures of the residents in opposition to the 1959 plan. Nevertheless, the plan was carried out and the lagoons were made in the above-mentioned area.

The form of opposition by the two groups again displays the characteristics mentioned above. First, as expected, there was no consultation between them nor any attempt to organize a concerted opposition. Further, it was the Upper Moenkopi Council that tended to monopolize the dealings with the outside agents. Lower Moenkopi, on the other hand, could not handle the task by itself and awaited Kenneth Loma's help as an articulator at the meeting. There the representatives from Lower Moenkopi, consisting of Odin, his mother's mother's sister's daughter's daughter's daughter (as an interpreter), and Kenneth, appeared too late to be heard and they interpreted this as manipulation of the meeting by the Upper Moenkopi Council; hence the petition, which included a proposal to locate the lagoon on a spot southwest of Tuba City.

In the winter of 1963 the Navajo tribe was employing several local Navajo to blast the ice formed on the surface of the lagoons.

The operation resulted in the accidental destruction of two sections of the dikes. The sewer started flowing into the canyon and then, gullying its wall, into the canal itself with considerable pressure. In the middle of the night, a man from Lower Moenkopi was alarmed by the unusual noise from the canal and reported it to the chief. Having confirmed that the situation in the reservoirs was normal, the chief discovered the accident in the lagoons and took the matter to the Navajo Police station in Tuba City. The policeman on duty refused to take his report seriously and no action appeared to be coming. So the chief went up to the PHS hospital, where the nurse on night shift neglected to relay his news to the doctor on the spot. It was only on the next day that the accident came to the attention of the police as well as the PHS.

Immediately, two problems were presented: 1) fear of contamination of drinking water; and 2) contamination and destruction of some Hopi fields. The first question was competently tackled by the Tuba City PHS, which gave typhoid shots to all the residents in Moenkopi, while prohibiting the use of water from the sources in the village except after sufficient boiling. Their speedy response was later acknowledged by the Keams Canyon PHS. By nature, the second took a prolonged time for solution.

Despite detailed precautions by the PHS to secure the maximum response from the villagers to the preventive measures, they failed to appreciate an aspect of the political situation in the village and gave permission to the Upper Moenkopi Council to take signatures for a petition to the Navajo tribe and other related agencies for the removal of the lagoons from the present location.

Collection of signatures was done at the day school on the occasion of the first injection. The day school represented neutral ground between the two groups. The signers of the petition in its final form included some sympathizers to Lower Moenkopi who understood that it was for the good of Moenkopi as a whole. However, later a rumor spread that Lower Moenkopi signers were now joined with the Upper Moenkopi Council in a suit against the Navajo tribe as well as the government and that they partook in a political activity while assuming federal employment. Consequently, the Lower Moenkopi people urged the chief to draw up a counter petition to withdraw signatures from the petition of the Upper Moenkopi Council and emphasized their preference for direct negotiations with the tribe over a legal suit.

This incident sheds further light on the pattern of competition between the two groups. Again the Upper Moenkopi Council took the initiative in dealing with outside groups. Second, the political affiliation of a number of residents was yet ambiguous and uncommitted. Hence the leaderships of the two groups were constantly vying for larger followings and stable constituents. When the signatures were collected by the two groups, information was clandestinely exchanged between them about the size of their respective petitions and eagerly debated.

On another occasion the chief mentioned to me that he was willing to accept government programs and assistance so long as the government recognizes and respects the difference between his followers and those of the Upper Moenkopi Council. During 1964, when some households in Upper Moenkopi were in trouble with the Upper Moenkopi Council regarding the water system, he even suggested another program of the same nature from the government for his own people and collected applications from his constituents, although nothing came of it. This competitive aspect of the two groups led a woman of Lower Moenkopi to an inadvertent remark, *Itam hapi pelangaihoyam* ("We are now legendary echo boys"). The people, on the other hand, exploit this competitive situation to their advantage by soliciting either leadership. These situations, in turn, force outside agents to deal with both political groups instead of just one of them and result in more labor and difficulty and often disgusted abandonment of projects.

The question of the compensation for damaged fields was also complicated by political antagonisms. The Upper Moenkopi Council proposed to have a joint meeting with Lower Moenkopi prior to a session with the representative from outside. In communicating this plan, the Upper Moenkopi Council typically avoided sending any of its men to Lower Moenkopi as messengers, but asked a Hopi sanitarian from Second Mesa who had been working for the water-sewer project in the village at the time. Utilizing his neutral position, he discreetly approached the chief. One day the chief happened to pass by the road connecting the two segments where the sanitarian was working, and the latter told the chief of the Upper Moenkopi Council plan, which was flatly refused on the spot. Thus no meeting came about between the two groups.

In March, 1963, i.e., two months after the accident, the Navajo tribe held a meeting on the compensations with both Upper and Lower Moenkopi at the community center in Tuba City. The news of the meeting was transmitted by the Navajo tribe to the Tuba City BIA, where some of the actives of the Upper Moenkopi Council were employed. Thus the Upper Moenkopi Council immediately got ready for it. Lower Moenkopi had one woman working in the Tuba BIA office, who also gave the tidings to the chief. The Upper Moenkopi Council informed the Keams Canyon Agency of the slated meeting and asked for attendance of some officials. The Lower Moenkopi chief, on the other hand, managed to persuade two PHS officials from Tuba City to attend it on their behalf. The latter move was derived from the brief association between Lower Moenkopi and the Tuba City PHS, when a representative from the latter took part in a meeting with the lower group for the explanation of the PHS measures at the time of the lagoon incident. The objections by the Upper Moenkopi Council to Odin's attendance and the reaction of the Navajo tribal representatives at this meeting have already been mentioned. An agreement reached then among the attendants was that the Navajo tribe assume full responsibility for cleaning the damaged fields with heavy equipment. No monetary compensation was contracted, however.

The repair work was accordingly done under the supervision of a member of the Upper Moenkopi Council and no Lower Moenkopi people were involved in the actual operation, although most of the fields belonged to the latter.

The above case shows an already enumerated complex of patterned interactions between the two groups in the problem-solving process. To sum up, they do not behave as one unit vis-à-vis outside groups, but whenever dealings with the latter are necessary, each separately enlists its allied agencies for support. Avoidance of mutual interaction is meticulously observed by the respective groups. Politics are played not between the two groups directly, but between the superordinate groups with which the respective groups are in association.

From the viewpoint of the village, elimination of political confrontations within it means not only ridding itself of psychological embarrassment among the residents, who live in close daily contact with each other, but, perhaps more important, enables the community to impress the outside world and to further confound it with the problem of authentic representation and thus ensure its political boundary. The reality of the first element is shown in a practice once prevalent in the lower segment. When the upper group was still giving the dances in the original plaza, it was usual for the houses adjoining it to pull down the window curtains so as not to see the dances outside (Hopi Hearings, 1955). Needless to say, these houses went along with the Lower Moenkopi leadership.

"Politics without confrontation" of the leaders of Moenkopi does not mean that they never confront each other. Though very seldom, there are occasions when they meet to discuss and negotiate problems. The question of charging for irrigation water is a case in point already discussed. As this illustrates, however, the leaders generally attempt to avoid such confrontations and look for other agents of mediation to do the necessary work of politics. When the mediators are not available, they reluctantly and secretively meet each other. Thus, when the Upper Moenkopi Council was given an ultimatum denying it use rights to the plaza and kivas, all the officials, instead of a single representative, barged into the chief's father's house through its back door in the middle of the night as if to avoid public detection.

FACTIONALISM, INDIVIDUAL FREEDOM, AND COMMUNITY SEGMENTATION. In spite of the peculiar pattern of political interaction between the two groups, it seems difficult to regard the present cleavage of the community as either schismatic or pervasive factionalism (Siegel and Beals, 1960; Friedl, 1963:283–84). Through a process of differentiation, the division of the communal property is now *almost* complete, and when there is a residual item to be shared, duties of its maintenance and rights to its use are minutely prescribed and observed. In particular, the territorial separation, though yet incomplete, has provided a most stable criterion by which to articulate political differences in the village: hence the designation of the upper and lower segments as in the present discussion. The leadership of the two groups is also sharply demarcated along this line of cleavage and the Lower Moenkopi chief has not claimed to be the chief of Moenkopi at large. At the same time, the Upper Moenkopi Council has limited itself to the upper village segment. Interaction within each group regarding particular issues occurs more regularly in the Upper Moenkopi Council than in the leadership group of Lower Moenkopi. The former, in particular, has weekly meetings with agenda, and the Board of Directors forms an inner and stable core of the decision-making and problem-solving organ. Though formally less explicit, the lower group is also equipped with the chief and a small number of his associates who meet as issues arise. On occasions, open meetings are given. These characteristics appear to better qualify the two groups as *parties* than as *factions*, as noted by Lasswell and others (Lasswell, 1931:49; Boissevain, 1964:1275, 1285).

With regard to membership and recruitment, however, the division has not yet reached the stage of stability and permanence.

First to be noted is the ambiguity in the terms designating the two divisions. In the daily native parlance, the term most frequently used to call the Upper Moenkopi Council is *kansul* or, with a slight derogatory connotation, *kansulhoyam* ("little council people"), while that for Lower Moenkopi is simply *aiyave* ("non-conformists," Voegelin and Voegelin, 1957:D1.4). Both terms are most frequently used by the antagonists. Although I was once introduced to a group of anti-council people of Shongopavi by an anti-council woman as *aiyave*, the people who are against the council, either of Upper Moenkopi or tribal, appear to resent being called by this term and only rarely designate themselves with it.

An attempt to elicit Hopi equivalents for the terms "traditional" and "progressive" was futile. Of the numerous terms that represented the attempts of various informants, none had the right connotations. Furthermore, the Hopi terms[8] are only infrequently, if at all, used by the members of one group in referring to the members of the other, and the contrast they provide is between Hopi and whites and not between "traditional" and "progressive."

In English the term "progressive" appears to be specifically avoided. I have not heard the anti-council actives of the tribe speak of their antagonists as "progressives" but always as "council." Some of them explicitly denied that their antagonists are in any way "progressive." In Moenkopi even the term "traditional" is infrequently used to designate the people antagonistic to the Upper Moenkopi Council. While the two groups call the Upper Moenkopi Council "council," its antagonists are called by the people of the Upper Moenkopi Council "lower village people," "Hotevilla," and sometimes simply "down below." The latter, however, seldom employ these to designate themselves nor do they have an alternative term.

Criteria for membership in either division are also ambiguous. While the cleavage is expressed and concretized through the territorial separation of residential sites, each contains a considerable number of families who are either uncommitted or go along with the opposite group. Though a frequently adopted criterion of membership has been ceremonial participation, irrespective of the area of his residence, many are left unclassified mainly because the

---

[8] For "traditional" I was given the terms *hisat sinom* ("ancient people") and *hopivitsukani* ("those who observe the Hopi way"). For "progressive," referring to the Upper Moenkopi Council, *tsotsivalhoyam* ("those who meet"), *pahanvinaguti* ("those who live white man's way"), and *pensilhoyam* ("little pencil people").

ceremonies do not involve all the population any longer. Some take part in the ceremonies of other villages, and others do not take part at all.

Another factor leading to fluctuation in membership is the increasing lack of lineage solidarity. As the nuclear family household came to assume the functions of a lineage and became more central, the continuity in political orientation either matrilineally or otherwise broke down and each household made its own decisions on the basis of diverse factors. Titiev has already pointed out the absence of matrilineal orientation as a determining factor in the Oraibi split (1944:88–89). On the other hand, it now appears that affinal relationships are often employed to rationalize political affiliation in Moenkopi. Several men gave as the reason for going with the lower group their marriage to women of the village Pi:kyas clan. The father of one of these men was once a staunch supporter of the Upper Moenkopi Council. It is generally regarded as preferable to solidify a household with the same political orientation and marital unions between the two groups are disapproved. A man whose father was an active supporter of Lower Moenkopi once complained to me about the domination of his household by his wife, whose father was the representative of Upper Moenkopi to the tribal council.

The last factor in the ambiguity of membership is deeply rooted in the context of contemporary Moenkopi. In addition to those who look to Hotevilla for the leverage of their position in Moenkopi, there are those to whom village politics have little relevance in their daily lives. Through experience in such off-reservation institutions as schools and military service or through off-reservation employment, these people base their economy entirely outside the village, which is only the place of residence for them. Their value orientation is individualistic and rarely directed toward the collective efforts of the village community. The context of Moenkopi, on the other hand, allows such households to exist by providing social and economic opportunities in nearby Tuba City. They have little stake in the village and form a core of the uncommitted people in village politics (see Fox, 1961). Fluctuations in the membership of Upper and Lower Moenkopi thus occur around this collection of people who manage to enjoy the fruits of the white man's civilization without much interference from the leadership of either segment.

It is questionable how much loyalty is involved in the political affiliation of a household. One household was once a strong supporter of the Upper Moenkopi actives. However, through its involvement in land disputes with other members of the group, it withdrew from it and chose to align itself with Hotevilla, the husband's village. Consequently, its alliance with Lower Moenkopi is usually regarded with some suspicion and its actual association with them has been occasional and sporadic.

The ambiguity in membership of each group has its advantage as well in the contemporary life of Moenkopi. The internal division is kept constantly alive and in competition. The two leadership groups vie for uncommitted constituents. Further, by restricting the sphere of social control through the existence of the body of uncommitted households and through the division itself, the rest of the households can take part in the outside institutions and groups at their own discretion and choice. A large area of individual freedom is thus provided in the very fact of ambiguity in competitive division. By manipulating such ambiguity, a few households of Upper Moenkopi managed to install their own wells as mentioned previously. For an individual household, which has at present much to incorporate from the outside world and which gains comparatively little from the community, this freedom is highly meaningful and hence seldom surrendered except in cases of close kinship relationships with the leadership groups.

One consequence of individual freedom, when one is faced with such an opportunity in the outside world and protected by the political structure of Moenkopi, is to increase the atmosphere of competition among individual households. A woman of Upper Moenkopi mentioned that when she first purchased a gas cooking range through a personal acquaintance in Flagstaff in 1948, her house was frequented by both upper and lower group women who came to see it. Her innovation erased most of the people's fear of gas and immediately other houses equipped themselves with cooking ranges.

The competition among the individual households tends to weaken the traditional *vs.* progressive dichotomy in regard to material equipment in the village homes. A young woman of the lower village, a close relative to the chief, once irately denied the charge that the lower village homes are more "backward," giving an example that a wooden stove is still used in the home of one official of the Upper Moenkopi Council, while many in Lower Moenkopi now have propane gas stoves. In general, it is misleading to associate the dichotomy based on the political orientation with that based on the degree of acculturation of individual homes.

The existence of opponent households in one and the same site often makes it difficult for the leaders to execute any program without provoking the antagonist group. Much in the manner of affines in a camp among the Nuer (Gluckman, 1956), the opponent households help to curb aggressive innovations by the leadership groups. This again partly accounts for the tendency of both groups to take their political questions outside the village with the aim of reducing direct conflicts within it.

To conclude, the factionalism in Moenkopi at present reveals both schismatic and pervasive aspects (Siegel and Beals, 1960). It is an important mechanism, enabling the community to articulate its ties with two factional segments of the tribe and other alien groups and institutions, including the government and Navajo tribal organizations. At the same time, the present factional situation admits a great deal of leeway for individual households to exploit the opportunities provided in the context and, especially, participate in the economy of the larger society. To be sure, the development of factionalism resulted in progressive deterioration of cooperative labor (Siegel and Beals, 1960; Friedl, 1963:283–84), disintegration of traditional internal control, and incomplete replacement of external control by the tribal police. However, it also provided room for constituent households to take part individually in the wage economy and to adopt alien goods in increasing frequency. Though Moenkopi factionalism was dysfunctional in maintaining solidarity in the community, it was, nevertheless, eufunctional in the acculturation of individual households.

Cushing *et al.* (1922:283) and others (Parsons, 1931:14; Thompson and Joseph, 1944; Thompson, 1950; Spicer, 1962:500) have suggested the prevalence of internal discord among the Pueblo Indians and its eventual resolution through the process of community segmentation. This process as a mechanism of conflict resolution appears to have been more pronounced after the pacification of the Southwest by the U.S. government, when the threat of outside enemies was eliminated. The Oraibi split of 1906 represents an example of such a process (Titiev, 1944; Siegel and Beals, 1960:394). The development of the two decision-making units in Moenkopi generally conforms to this pattern of conflict resolution. It is important to note here that the tribal council movement among the Hopi has been most successful in those villages that are comparatively late in origin and that were not provided with the traditional chieftainship. In addition to Upper Moenkopi, they include New Oraibi and Bacabi of Third Mesa, Polacca of First

Mesa, and probably Shipaulovi of Second Mesa. The movement thus failed to replace the traditional political structure with a component organization of the tribal council. In fact, as has been shown by Dozier (1954), the articulation of the First Mesa villages into the system of the tribal council was only possible by retaining the villages on the mesa top in the traditional pattern but adding the dispersed settlement of Polacca below the mesa. As expected, Polacca became a community which took innovations in from outside. This case, along with the political history of Moenkopi, well compares with the Navajo, among whom the tribal council became a successful as well as now an indispensable organ. Steward has already shown the relevance of levels of socio-cultural integration in the process of social change (1951:385–86; Gouldner, 1959:261), and Shepardson argued that the absence of corporate groups was one of the conducive factors in the success of the Navajo tribal council (1963:117). The Hopi case, in reverse, shows that one of the difficulties of the tribal council movement was the existence of corporate village structure.

A considerable scale of recent migration by individuals and families from the Hopi villages has also contributed to the reduction of conflicts within respective communities. Their motives for migration are naturally diverse and often based on individual considerations. Frequently migration to off-reservation towns is inspired not only by the availability of wage work but also to flee from the restrictions imposed by the leaders of the community on adoption of the white man's way of life. Migration based on the latter motive appears to occur most frequently among those to whom the alternative of deserting the traditional leadership for the sake of acculturation on the reservation is blocked, either because of close kinship relationships to the leaders or of ideological commitments. As a result, it is not infrequent that some migrants, who are seemingly well adjusted to the life in off-reservation towns, turn out to be staunch adherents to the conservative ideology and politics on the reservation. Migration from their own communities thus provides a compromise to them. There are also those who migrate because of their dissatisfaction with the political situations in their own villages (see Dozier, 1966a). Whatever the motive for migration may be, it eliminates from the communities a possible strain which otherwise might lead to segmentation (Spicer, 1962: 558). The present decentralizing tendency of the Hopi population, either in the form of community segmentation or of individual migration, helps to reduce the conflicts within a particular community in the process of change.

7

Process of Economic Change

INTRODUCTION

In the following analysis of the economic history of Moenkopi, we shall pay particular attention to the dichotomy of Hopi subsistence and American money economies. Each of the two economies reveals changes through time in its own institutional set-ups, volume of activities, and interactions with the other. Our problem in this chapter is to present these changes and analyze the process and structure of articulation and integration of the two economies in Moenkopi, which were brought into contact through the reservation system.

Subsistence economy shall be roughly defined as the economy in which production and consumption are geared to survival of certain sub-groups within a community; each group produces for its own consumption. In particular, it is characterized by the absence of outside markets to which the "surplus" products may be directed (Wolf, 1966:3–4). In this economy no universal medium of exchange exists, but exchanges, including barter, of different goods often occur on relatively discrete levels (Firth, 1939:340ff.). The means of production are controlled by the community and unalienable to outside groups. The Hopi economy is of this type, that is, "primitive" and not "peasant" (Firth, 1939:353ff.; Wolf, 1966).

On the other hand, the American economy is a highly developed capitalistic economy which is, in essence, characterized by a universal medium of exchange, capital accounting, free labor, market competition, profit incentives, and, lately, "government."

The dichotomy of Moenkopi economy has thus been on an entirely different plane from what presumably led to the creation of a "peasantry" in the world. In a majority of the "peasant" societies, the dichotomy had already been in existence between a local community and a feudal kingdom, to which the former contributed its produce as taxes or levies. The subsequent dichotomy was established, as Wolf has described (1955, 1957), between such "peasant" communities and colonial powers, the economic structure of the latter being appreciably "backward" in comparison to the modern developed capitalism and hence leading to various forms of exploitation in labor or production (see Wolf, 1959). None of these processes occurred in Moenkopi. To recapitulate, the dichotomy in our problem is unique in regard not only to the condition of contact (reservation system) but the entities in contact (primitive and developed capitalistic economies) as well.

RESERVATION LAND RESOURCES

Traditional Land Use Pattern of the Hopi

Ideally considered, the subsistence economy of a Hopi village community is based on the following four categories of land: 1) village site, in which each house is allotted a lot; 2) common vegetable garden, "just outside of the pueblo"; 3) clan and society lands for farming; 4) "outland," outside the clan lands, originally for hunting but later for grazing (Colton, 1934:22). The last category of land included shrines and quarries of rocks, firewood, timber, coal, and other resources.

In theory all the above categories of land are controlled by the village chief. Though not clearly stated in the available literature, even the clan lands of Third Mesa were thought to have been originally allocated by the chief of the Bear clan, which first settled in Oraibi (Titiev, 1944:61). Each category of land is held by a corresponding rule of tenure. Thus, an individual woman holds use rights over a house site and vegetable patch in the communal garden, and a clan or society over farm land. In this regard it is misleading to speak of clan "ownership" of farm land because land "ownership" in the sense of transferable title never existed in the Hopi theory of land tenure.

All the land in the Moenkopi area was "outland," and the development of farm land tenure by colonists to Moenkopi since 1903 was highly conditioned by the native patterns of use of this type of land. I shall discuss the implications of this in the following sections. It is sufficient to mention here that even during the period of farm expansion in Moenkopi, the land around the village was frequently visited by the people of Third Mesa for hunting and gathering purposes. It was regarded as the territory of Oraibi, of which Moenkopi was a colony.

Even after the separation of Moenkopi from Oraibi by a reservation boundary, the Hopi from Third Mesa continued to visit *Shalako* spring and *Patu:pa* pool in Reservoir Canyon for the water used in the Shalako ceremonies and for reed and cattails for the Soyal ceremony in Oraibi. Third Mesa Hopi also went to Moenave for cottonwood fruit, *Pikyaingkolu* (Wildcat Peak) for firewood and timber (TCL), *Pikino* in Reservoir Canyon for rocks, and *Oako* on Coal Mine Mesa for coal.

It was in this general milieu of the Oraibi "outland" that farms were opened by the colonists of Moenkopi. However, the agriculture in Moenkopi did not develop simply as another Hopi economic activity in unrestrained village "outland." The reservation system, which alienated the village from its parental community in the administrative superstructure, emerged as a constant factor to reckon with. In addition, this system was originally designed for the Navajo in the area, who were later integrated into their own tribal government. In the BIA theory the land on which Moenkopi developed its subsistence economy was no longer in Oraibi's territorial domain. It was the government on which Moenkopi had to depend for the ultimate sanction of the productive resources in the traditional economy.

Reservation Control of Land Resources

Perhaps the most critical element in the Indian reservation system is the status accorded to the reservation land. As Oliver La Farge so succinctly stated: "Indian special status consists mainly in the ownership of land—reservations and grants—and income therefrom held in trust for them and tax exempt" (1957:42). The land policies adopted so far naturally varied from one reservation to another and even their general tenets, as maintained by the federal government, did not remain constant. In the present section, I discuss only those features of the policies that have been relevant to Moenkopi.

Apart from the establishment of the reservation in this area, the first policy of great importance to Moenkopi is the General Allotment Act (Dawes Act) of 1887, through which land allotments of 400 acres were made on the alluvial floor of Moenkopi Wash (TCL). The spirit of this act was derived from the then current policy of assimilation of the American Indian. The general mechanism of the act, on the other hand, was to divide up the reservation land into individual allotments, whose patents were held in trust by the Indian Service for 25 years, and the "surplus" from the allotment was to be opened for homesteading (Haas, 1957:13).

In Moenkopi, however, the allotment lands were surrounded by the reservation that was established almost simultaneously with the allotment. The existence of the reservation and allotment lands contributed to the repeated confusion of the earlier superintendents on both the Western Navajo and Hopi reservations (FDL; KCL). In any event, all categories of land were thus denied to public entry and remain so at the present time.

A serious modification, indeed, a reversal of this policy was brought about with John Collier's Indian New Deal and its cornerstone legislation, the Indian Reorganization Act of 1934, which formally repealed the Dawes Act (Haas, 1957:19–20). This act intended to restore the land basis of the Indian communities in the country and to promote Indian self-determination on the basis of restored land resources.

On the local level of Moenkopi and Tuba City, the new act later led to the transfer of managerial functions of land resources to the Navajo tribe from their BIA, which retained an ultimate veto power. Generally, this resulted in a more stringent control of the resources with the help of the tribal court and police. Thus the quarries the Hopi used to visit as a part of the Oraibi "outland" were closed. The Hopi were denied access to the rock quarry in Reservoir Canyon during the 1950's. Firewood and coal collection have been conducted since then only by evading the watchful eyes of the Navajo. Some Navajo took advantage of this situation and have been selling firewood and coal to the Hopi of Moenkopi. Hunting and fishing activities came under the tribal game regulations and permit system as well. Cutting piñon pines around Shonto for Christmas trees has to be carried out only in the absence of Navajo policemen in the vicinity.

More serious in its effects on the Moenkopi economy was the establishment of the Land Board and grazing committee as local land controlling organizations of the Navajo Tribal Council. Since they are the organs of the Navajo tribe, the Hopi community of Moenkopi is excluded from formal participation. I shall discuss the grazing committee and its relevance to Moenkopi later. The implications of the Land Board to Moenkopi are just as serious. While the allotment lands remained exempt from the supervision of the board and continued to be held in direct trusteeship of the BIA, all the remainder of farm land in the area came under the authority and power of the board, which includes assignment of land, settlement of disputes over land and water distribution, and supervision of transfers of assigned land.

In the framework of Moenkopi agriculture, therefore, two kinds of land rights exist at the present time. First, the farm land in the allotment area is held by the allottees or their heirs irrespective of actual cultivation, and the transfer of farming right itself is arranged without intervention of either the Navajo tribe or the government. Mismanagement of the allotment lands is not sanctioned by either of the two groups. Apart from the governmental sanctions on sale, it is the category of land on the reservation for which the right comes closest to "ownership."

Assignment land, on the other hand, is subject to several additional restrictions imposed by the Land Board. The assignment "may be cancelled" in the case of two years' nonuse, failure to pay water use assessments (this clause is inapplicable to the Moenkopi area), or more generally, if "beneficiary use is not being made of" the land (Navajo Tribal Council, 1954). The land whose assignment is revoked or relinquished returns to the Land Board for future assignment. Thus the right derived from assignment is, in essence, usufruct. The tribal court probates inheritance of assignment at the death of an assignee. In this action the court is advised to keep the assignment as an intact "economic unit."

Both allotment and assignment lands are under the ultimate trusteeship of the U.S. government, whose representative on the Indian reservations, BIA, deals with, in the case of the Navajo, "the sale, exchange, partition, patenting and leasing" of land (Young, 1961:263) through the Branch of Realty and with probation of inheritance of allotments by an examiner of inheritance (Young, 1961:264).

AGRICULTURE

Expansion and Contraction of Farm Acreage

The basis of Moenkopi agriculture was founded on a complex of 11 allotments. Soon, however, the reduction in arable land acreage in Third Mesa and general political unrest induced migration of the Third Mesa Hopi to fill the land vacancy left by the Mormon withdrawal (TCL). In 1907 the land under Hopi cultivation reached 385 acres for the population of 150, giving 2.5 acres per person

(TCL). Less than 10 years after the establishment of the reservation, the village population had doubled in size (Gregory, 1915: 119). The appropriation of land for farming by these immigrants first occurred along Moenkopi Wash, formerly in cultivation by the Mormons. In the early part of the 1910's, Moenave, another spot of Mormon irrigation farming, and an area around *Pa:latuika* (dry farming) came under Hopi use (see Map 4). Competition with the Navajo over the farm land resources was not serious in this early period. In fact, the transfer of the Moenave farms to the Hopi was made by the Navajo settlers, who were not interested in small, intensive irrigation farming then. Later, one of the Navajo allotments, 40 acres in size, was sold to a Hopi for an alleged sum of $500 and "groceries to be delivered in [his] convenience."

The period between the 1920's and 1930's is characterized by further expansion of farm acreage in Moenkopi. It proceeded on the basis of individual reclamation. Two conditions for this process can be noted.

First, the appropriation proceeded to the area where irrigation was possible. The alloted tracts of about 70 acres, adjacent to allotments A 47, A 48, and A 49 (see Map 4), came under cultivation almost simultaneously with the original allotment lands (between 1904 and 1907). These farms depended on the same irrigation system as the allotment fields.[1] The fields in the *Ma'asau* area (approximately 120 acres; 200 acres according to HvJ, Def. Ex. 106) were turned to Hopi use about 1920. They have been irrigated from the Wash.

The second type of reclaimed area depended on "flood-water farming" (Hack, 1942:26).[2] Another large Akchin field was constructed to the west of the *Ma'asau* area. The second group of this type of field used the flood plains of Reservoir Canyon and another unnamed wash by an old bridge across Moenkopi Wash farther south.

The last type of field includes a small number of dry farms around *Pa:latuika*, which must have been in cultivation prior to 1912 (Gregory, 1916:144; see Map 4). The farms built around the cattle corrals in Red Lake and Coal Mine Mesa and those by

---

[1] Before merging with the allotment irrigation, these tracts may have been watered by an arroyo that drains to *Tuviktsyala* (see Map 4).

[2] Of these, the farms at *Wikopsi* represent a typical Akchin field. They are located at the mouth of two small arroyos, which forms a comparatively wide, level plain.

104 MODERN TRANSFORMATIONS OF MOENKOPI PUEBLO

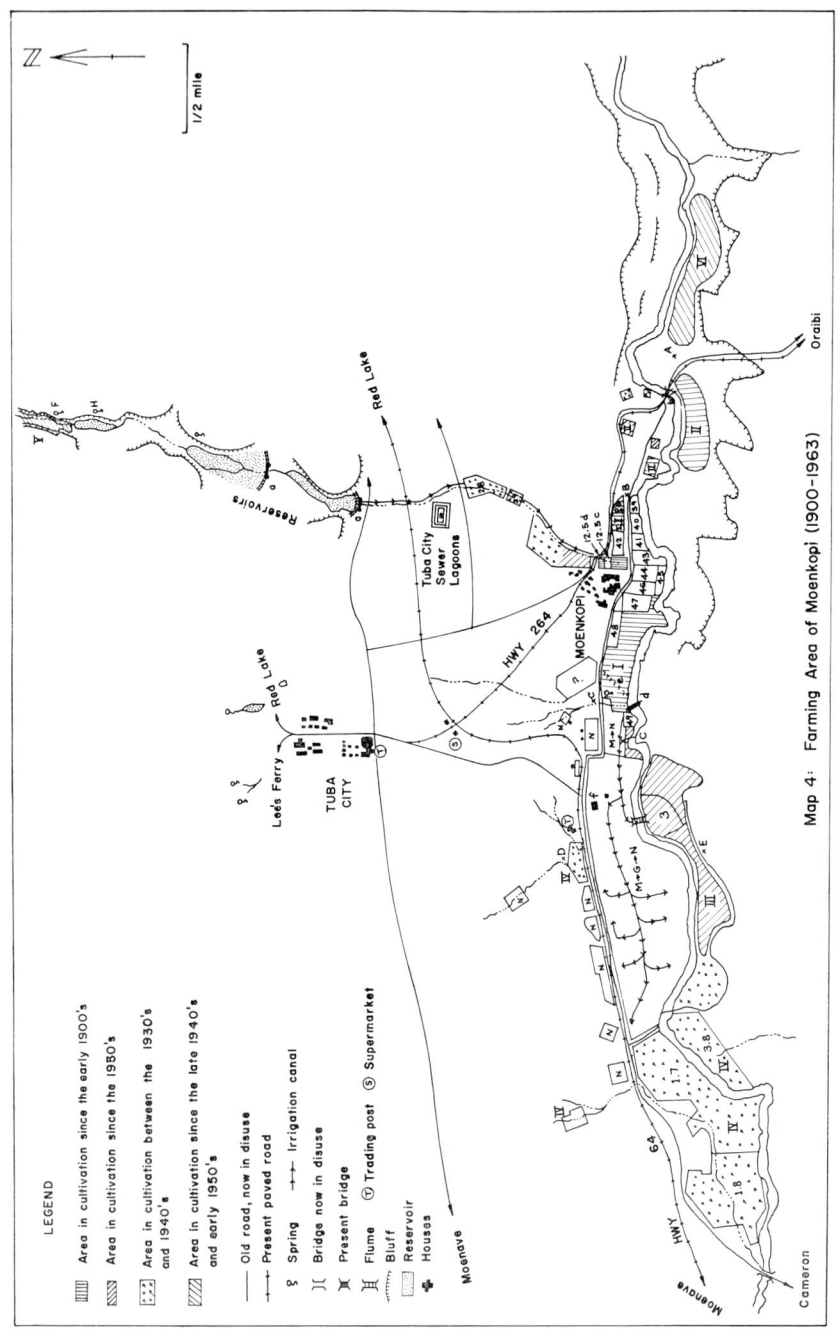

Map 4: Farming Area of Moenkopi (1900-1963)

Plate 4. Moenkopi Wash near the fields in Ma'asau.

Dinnebito Wash that belong to one Upper Moenkopi household are all of this type.

By 1937 a major portion of the ecological niche of the area around Moenkopi was thus being exploited by the Hopi farmers. The total amount of acreage rose to about 800 acres, four times as large as

---

Additional Legend to Map 4

1) Numerals 39 to 48 are allotment numbers. Other numerals indicate the plot numbers in assignment lands.

2) I = irrigated area from the reservoirs; II = dry farming area; III = irrigated area from the Wash through the diversion dam; IV = Akchin fields; V = individually irrigated area from the Wash; VI = area irrigated by springs.

3) A = *Hu:yankikyö*; B = *Pa:latuika*; C = *Tuviktsyala*; D = *Wikopsi*; E = *Ma'asau*; F = *Shalako*; G = *Ma:tsya*; H = *Patu:pa*; I = *Pavaukyaoki*.

4) a = dam and headgate, originally constructed by the Mormons; b = dam first constructed by the Mormons but fallen into disuse after their withdrawal (it was proposed to rebuild it during the 1910's); c = dam constructed by the Mormons but fallen into disuse since the late 1900's; d = diversion dam, originally constructed by the Mormons; e = old diversion dam in the Mormon period; f = government dairy in use until around 1935.

5) M = former Mormon farms; G = former government farms; N = Navajo farms.

Sources: Blout, 1911; Gregory, 1915:118; 1916:Pl. XXVII; Page and Lavantu, 1937; U.S. Geological Survey, 1957; field work, 1962–63.

the initial allotments. The increase in acreage corresponded to the continuing growth of the population through immigration and natural growth. Per capita acreage in 1937 was about two acres.[3]

Several factors are involved in this process of farm land expansion. First, the political stability brought about by the BIA made possible the Hopi migration and agricultural exploitation of land resources. Second, rapid adoption of wagons and draft animals during this period facilitated transportation between the distant farms and the village (Forde, 1931:365; Watson, 1945:67–71). Finally, the villagers were yet only marginally involved in money economy through occasional wage work at the local agency and sale of farm and livestock produce. Since the village economy for this period was based chiefly on subsistence agriculture, the increase in farm acreage corresponded in the main to the growth of the village population.

A significant change in Moenkopi economy began with the advent of World War II. While the population continued to increase, the total farm acreage appeared to reach a peak by 1940, when the period of decline set in. Thus the fields at *Wikopsi* were abandoned to the Navajo. The fields in such outlying spots as Red Lake and Coal Mine Canyon were also given up to Navajo herders toward the end of the 1950's. Two areas of flood-water farming were abandoned because of deep arroyo cutting, which decreased the cultivable area of level land. The remainder of the flood-water farms were left out of operation because of a shortage of labor.

On the other hand, new fields were opened during the 1940's and '50's. In 1940 the Tuba City BIA, which had been operating farms for the Navajo Boarding School, released them for the use of the Hopi farmers. They are about two miles upstream from the reservoirs and well watered by a series of springs, including *Shalako* (see Map 4). The farms around *Hu:yankikyö* were individually opened in the post-war period and have not been legally recognized by the government nor by the Navajo Land Board. These are located about two miles northeast of the village and irrigated from the Wash (see Map 4).

At present, about 550 acres constitute the farm acreage of Moenkopi (1962–63), with an average of 0.95 acres per person. However, many plots within this complex of farms have been out of operation for several years, though retained as Hopi farms (see Map 5).

---

[3] This figure corresponds to the per capita "cultivated" acreage in the Hopi District in 1936 (Human Dependency Survey, 1939).

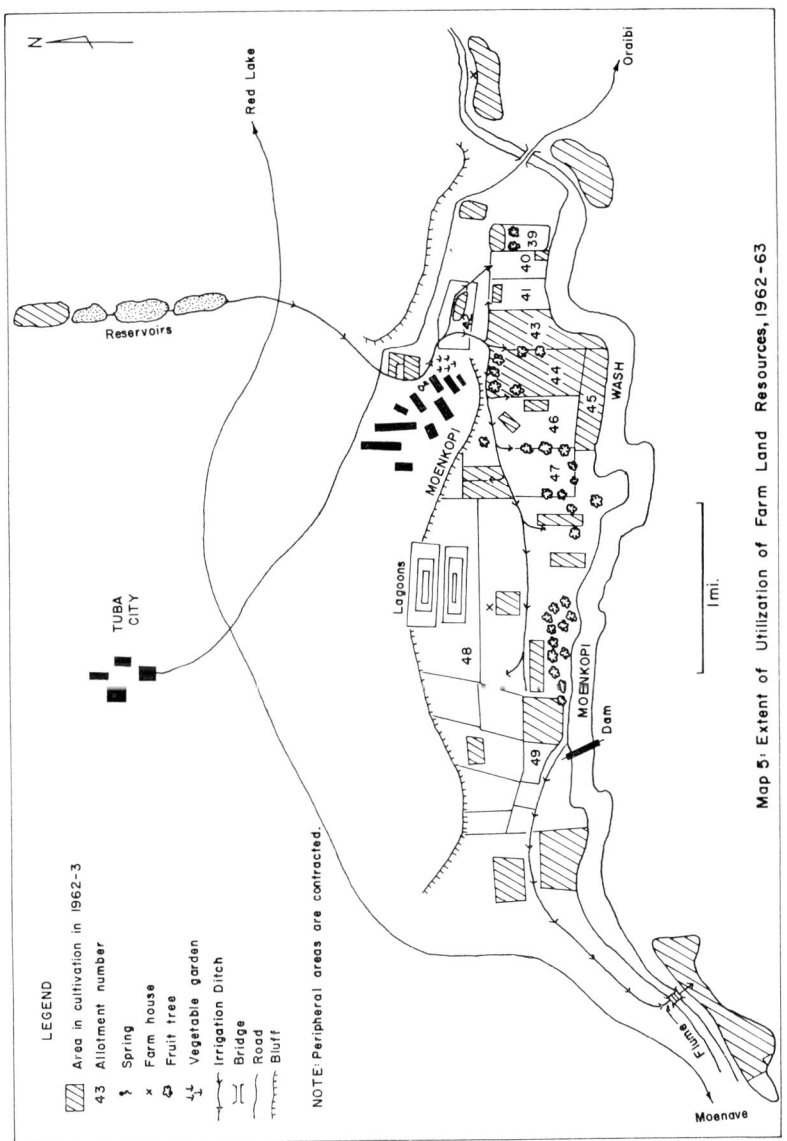

Map 5: Extent of Utilization of Farm Land Resources, 1962-63

More recently, some farms were taken out of cultivation for nonagricultural purposes. Thus Allotment No. 48 was turned into two sewer lagoons for the sewage system of the upper segment in 1963. A portion of the farm by the Moenkopi Day School was used for a house site in the same year.

The decline in farm acreage, the movement of the farms closer to the village despite improvement in transportation by popular adoption of automobiles and construction of paved highways, and the conversion of farm land to nonfarming use all represent the dislocation of subsistence economy to the increasing pressure of money economy, which had not only attracted the Navajo to this area since the stock reduction program (Levy, 1962a:796), thus creating competition for land in the immediate environs of Tuba City, but also has extracted a great amount of labor for wage work, thus causing a shortage of farm labor in Moenkopi.

Tenure and Distribution of Farm Land

The discussion of tenure of agricultural land in Moenkopi is complicated by the fact that the native system of land tenure, which was in the process of radical change at the time of allotment in Moenkopi, was superimposed by the reservation system of land control. I shall first deal with the change in land tenure that spread in Third Mesa at the turn of this century.

EMERGENCE OF RIGHT OF INDIVIDUAL DISPOSAL ON THIRD MESA. It has already been pointed out that the Moenkopi area, in which the Hopi opened farms, was Oraibi "outland." In regard to the cultivation right in this section of the village territory, the literature indicates "male individual ownership" as a prevalent form of customary right. For Second Mesa during the 1930's, Beaglehole mentions as follows: "Apart from the clan control of land there exists individual ownership of land by the male. This occurs when a man breaks in land from the waste and plants it with fruit trees or cultivates squash or beans on it. The waste land is usually part of the village land, rarely part of the clan lands" (1937:16). For Third Mesa, Eggan remarked that "there were probably always a certain number of fields owned by Hopi men outside clan areas" (Watson, 1945:67–68). Page made the following quote from Stephen's rather cryptic observation for Oraibi: ". . . during the late 1880's . . . 'of the land properties there are still traces that it once was divided on a communal basis for use of families composing the clans and not as individual holdings'" (1954:9). This appears to indicate that individual holdings were already prevalent in the last century.

On rights over farm land in this area, Beaglehole further states:

With the death of the owner, the land relapses to village waste, or is taken over by clan relatives or by the son of the deceased. If the land goes out of cultivation during the owner's lifetime, another interested in the field may take it over, usually by mutual agreement. Should the owner wish to renew his rights he may secure the return of the land without question. If no attempt is ever made to resume ownership the land is, by tacit understanding, considered the property of him who has taken it over to cultivate (1937:16).

This statement points out that the farming right in the "outland" is essentially usufruct and contingent on continued cultivation. Forde (1931:379) and Colton (1934:22) further believe that male control of reclaimed fields in the "outland" emerged under the influence of the reservation system, while Beaglehole (1937:17) suspects the same for the inheritance by a reclaimer's own children of this type of field. This, however, does not appear to be the case.

My arguments for aboriginality of usufruct by individual males in the outland and its inheritance by their children are based on the following considerations. First, as Colton mentions (1934:22), the outland was primarily used for grazing. From this, Watson suspects that individual "ownership" was partly derived from individual appropriation of grazing ranges (1945:68-71). However, as shall be mentioned, the appropriation of ranges in Hopiland proper is often made by a group of Hopi herders and not by individuals. It appears more reasonable to assume that the farming right in the form of usufruct by an individual was established through an act of reclamation and protected by the village as such for the duration of cultivation even by his descendants (see ter Haar, 1950:85). The fact that such a piece of land was invariably held by men appears to have derived from the traditional division of labor, which excluded women from farming activities. The ultimate sanction of the use right in this section of the village territory resided in the village and its representative, the village chief. Inheritance by the children and not by the matrilineal descendants appears to be due to the fact that the former, especially sons, start working on their parents' land before and stay there even after marriage and that subsequently they inherit at their fathers' deaths the usufruct of the fields the latter opened through continuous cultivation.

What is unique in the land tenure of Third Mesa is the absence of a clan land system as described by Forde (1931) and others. The relevance of the reservation system appears more direct in this respect than in the existence of the right of individual disposal itself. During the survey in the 1930's by the Soil Conservation Service, Page discovered the absence of clan lands in Third Mesa. All the farms there were held in the form of "individual ownership" (Page, 1954:11).

The process through which the right of individual disposal of farm land was established in Third Mesa involves three factors: population, available farm land, and sanction structure. First, the population of Oraibi, the sole village on Third Mesa at the time, reached 900 in 1898 (Page, 1940), almost equal to the total of First and Second Mesa populations. At the same time, the land basis of Oraibi agriculture was in the process of rapid deterioration because of the erosion of the Oraibi Wash, on which most of the Oraibi farms were located (Hack, 1942:34; Titiev, 1944:62). The pressure on the land, then, resulted in increased reclamation of the outland, including the Moenkopi and Dinnebito areas.[4] The decrease in available farm land through population increase and erosion cycles must have been a common occurrence in the history of other Hopi communities. The uniqueness of the Oraibi experience is the very context in which the process went on.

Briefly stated, the imposition of the reservation system and consequent restriction of movement, along with the censure of religious practices, were undermining the village authority, which could not control developing factionalism (Eggan, 1964:182). As the clan lands were gradually abandoned, the individual control of farms in the outland became a predominant form of land use. In the face of weakened village authority, the same procedure must have been adopted in the use of the remaining farms in the clan blocks. Confinement on a reservation further made it difficult for Oraibi to shift the location of the community through migration or segmentation. The physical basis of clan solidarity was thus deteriorating long before factionalism precipitated the Oraibi split (Titiev, 1944). The final result was a replacement of the clan land system with individual land right. As the latter became the sole form of right over farm land, its transmission was now executed without reference to clan organization. Since the land right ceased to be sanctioned by any particular village after the disorganization of Oraibi, the right over a piece of land did not revert to the latter as an ultimate possessor of domain but remained as the original reclaimer's. The disputes over the land that ensued were now resolved not by village

---

[4] Since the Dinnebito fields mostly depend on sand dune farming (Hack, 1942:33), irrigation farming in Moenkopi is irrelevant to the development of right of individual disposal in Third Mesa.

authority but by the BIA, which held final control over the land. More often, however, individual negotiations took the place of formal adjudication by the BIA. Thus all the Third Mesa farms came to be individually held as they are at present.

As this reconstruction of the process (see Eggan, 1950:107) shows, the relevance of the reservation system was crucial, and yet the government, which instituted the system, did not dictate such a change. This is indicated by the fact that in contemporary First and Second Mesas clan lands still exist in juxtaposition to individually held lands (Page, 1954:11).

Through trusteeship of "individual land ownership," the government replaced a Hopi local community as a final sanctioning body of land resources. On the one hand, this provided protection from the encroachment of outside interests. Yet, on the other hand, it did away with the context for further development of the concept of "individual ownership" by choking the process that had been in progress in Third Mesa. The trusteeship was thus a legal fiat thrust into the indigenous movement of changes in land right, which, given market economy and commercial agriculture, could well have resulted in genuine "individual ownership." This did not materialize in Moenkopi, however.

What happened or has been happening in the village is a complicated pattern of adjustment in farm distribution among the kin whose subsistence needs for land are meted out on the basis of an amorphous concept of individual "control" within the framework of overriding supervision by the government.

FARM LAND TENURE AND INHERITANCE. The general process of breakdown of clan "ownership" of farm land also affected the land tenure pattern in Moenkopi. All information regarding land rights in the area prior to Mormon control of the Moenkopi valley indicates individual appropriation of farm land. The allotment subsequently froze this type of individual tenure into law. However, as already indicated, the distribution of the allotments clearly reveals a mode of farm land appropriation that must have been extensively employed in this early period. A tract of land was delimited by a group of matrilineally related men and their male in-laws. Within the land demarcated by this group, each member acquired a piece for his own cultivation, claimed it as his, and disposed of it as he saw fit. The group itself was formed for reclamation and probably for defense of the reclaimed territory.

Prevalence of this mode of land appropriation for farming purposes is also indicated by the fact that the two men of the Patki clan, resident in Oraibi then, demanded an allotment in Moenave during the second allotment project in 1910 (KCL; TCL). They claimed they represented their clan "of seven families and forty-six persons" and expressed a wish to return to Moenave, where they farmed "for four or five years previous to 1907" (KCL, October 1, 1910). Their request was not approved, however, on the ground that they already belonged to the Hopi Reservation (TCL).

It may be speculated that had the mode of reclamation by a group of matrilineally related men and their male in-laws continued, it could have led to the establishment of clan lands. This did not develop in Moenkopi, because the government insisted on the principle of land distribution on the basis of individuals' residence in Moenkopi. This principle came into direct conflict with the colonial position of Moenkopi, which was characterized by fluidity of residence in the component population. No longer could a Hopi live in Oraibi while holding land in Moenkopi. It resulted in the abandonment of a number of farms to relatives living in Moenkopi and, often, to the matrilineage members by the original reclaimers, who decided to settle on Third Mesa after having opened the fields in Moenkopi.

An illustrative example is a Coyote clansman who opened fields with his friends in the Moenkopi valley in the early 1910's. On his marriage to a woman from Bacabi, he gave his Moenkopi fields to his sister's daughter and her husband (see p. 249). The latter, in turn, later divided the fields among their children.

Close association in native theory between a claimant and his right of disposal in the outland resulted in the assumption of this right mostly by men who brought women from other villages through marriage. These women did not possess the land in the area where no clan claim was recognized in farming.

With the disposal right in the hands of the original claimants, their children were frequently heirs, irrespective of sex. Though members of the claimants' matrilineages did inherit farm land, the incidence seems much lower. Two factors appear relevant in the predominance of inheritance by children.

First, the colonial character of the village resulted in distortion in genealogical composition of the resident population. The early settlers in the village brought their wives more frequently than their sisters or more distant relatives. There existed differential availability in possible heirs, and one's children became more likely heirs simply because they were easily available.

Second, the fact that the right over a piece of land in the outland is contingent on actual cultivation prompted the process of land transmission to one's children, for the land could not be left idle if it was to remain his farm. Given an equal claim by his children as well as by his matrilineal relatives, a man chose whoever immediately needed the land. In Moenkopi those with immediate needs for land were more often the children than the matrilineal relations, since the former, especially the sons, began farming on their fathers' land before marriage. Upon marriage, they often took women from other villages and hence without farms in Moenkopi. Thus they chose to work on their fathers' land even after marriage. On the other hand, women came to seek permission from their fathers or brothers to let their husbands cultivate a piece of land.

Corollary to the second aspect, it frequently happened that as cultivation was continued over years on a piece of land, the cultivator came to assume this disposal right without regard to its original holder. Though my informants often claimed that a certain piece of land belonged to someone and that he was going to get it back from the present cultivator in the near future, this has seldom been done and only one case has been recorded so far. This possibility of establishing the disposal right through the act of cultivation in default of an immediate arbitrator results in overlapping of land rights and consequent obscuring of land claims.

At the present time, an important characteristic of the land right in Moenkopi is this disposal aspect by an individual. The possessor of the disposal right can be either male or female. Though the government as well as the Navajo Land Board formally registers the cultivators as the title holders (allottees and assignees), there is a wide discrepancy between the actual holders of disposal right and registered land holders.

The prevailing flexibility in rights to agricultural land in present-day Moenkopi still persists chiefly due to the governmental sanction on the sale of the farm land and to the position of Moenkopi agriculture in the total economic context.

FARM LAND USE AND DISTRIBUTION. The right of individual disposal, when set in the context of the reservation "dual" economy, produced several interesting features in the pattern of agricultural land use in Moenkopi. The first of the notable tendencies is *frequent entries into a piece of land and withdrawals therefrom by blood and affinal relatives,* one of whom is usually regarded as the "owner" of the land and whose permission is sought at entry. I shall examine this in two of the allotments.

The boundaries of the allotment lands were already obscured by

1914 (TCL), and those meted out during the period of cultivation subsequent to the allotment were maintained until 1937, when a survey crew from the Soil Conservation Service plotted the entire allotment area. Since then, no mapping had been conducted until for the recent probation of inheritance (1962), appraisal of the value of each allotment was done on the basis of a survey of areas in actual cultivation and improvements laid thereon. In the case of Allotment No. 44, its cultivable acreage is reduced by a portion of the land that covers the present lower village site.

This allotment was originally granted to Nashileowi, the first chief of Moenkopi. She was regarded as the "owner" of this tract. Her husband, Letokshi, had his own allotment in *A 41*, where he farmed and the produce from which he apparently contributed to his marital household. Nashileowi was childless (see Figure 2).

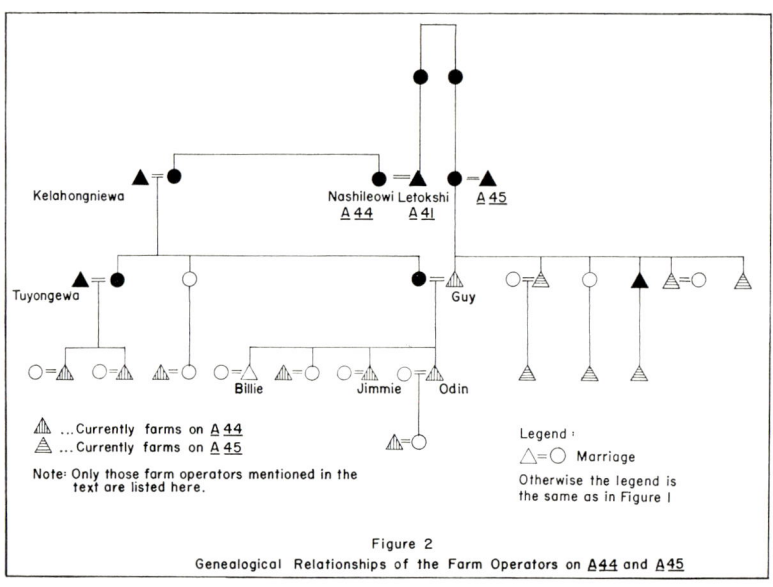

Figure 2
Genealogical Relationships of the Farm Operators on A44 and A45

Thus the actual operators of her allotment consisted of her sister's husband and the husbands of the latter's two daughters. One of the latter two husbands, Guy Talas, also worked on *A 41*, whose allottee, Letokshi, is his mother's mother's sister's son (see Figure 2). Guy never worked on his father's allotment, *A 45* (see Map 4), apparently because too many operators crowded the land and it was already reduced by the gullying of the Wash. A major portion of this allotment lay on the other side of the Wash where irrigation was impossible. The remaining operators did not have allotments nor did their near relatives.

Nashileowi died "a few years" (TCL) before 1912. It is reported that "By a sort of tacit agreement the oldest of these [three] daughters has been regarded as the present owner . . . although her claim is disputed by one Frank Siyamptewa who is the Chief of the Hopis [of Moenkopi] and nephew of the original allottee" (TCL, December 16, 1912). The daughters are, in reality, Nashileowi's sister's daughters. Further, the "ownership" by the oldest daughter is misleading in this context for it was a fiction convenient for dealings with such outsiders as the government. In any event, with the deaths of Nashileowi's husband and the husband of one of her sister's daughters, the cultivation was undertaken by the latter's two sons. Guy, on the other hand, had two of his sons working for him now in Nashileowi's allotment. The three also worked in *A 41*.

By 1937 Nashileowi, Letokshi, Kelahongniewa, and Tuyongewa (see Figure 2) had all died and Guy took over the control of the allotment. One of Guy's two sons, Billie, was then married to a daughter of the allottee of *A 48*, but he did not move there partly because its land was limited in size by accumulation of silt from a small wash and partly because it had four operators already. Soon, however, Billie found wage work in Flagstaff and left his field in *A 41* unoperated. His plots in *A 44* were soon taken over by his other brother, Jimmie, who had previously worked in Belmont. Jimmie's wife's father gave a portion of the field opened by him to Jimmie at his marriage and thus Jimmie had two plots to work on.

Odin, Billie's other brother, who had been working with his father, Guy, before Jimmie came in, married a woman whose father's father was the allottee to *A 43* and whose step-father's mother's brother was the allottee to *A 46*. Neither of these allotments was entered by Odin because of congestion. There was, however, another aspect to this situation. Odin and his father were politically antagonistic to these allottees and Odin obviously avoided asking for their permission. Odin's sister, who married a man from Hotevilla and who had been away to Belmont for wage work with her husband, came back at the recent death of her mother and obtained a piece in *A 44* from her father, Guy. Her return to the village was only for the purpose of farming; otherwise, she and her husband still stayed at Belmont. Odin gave a piece to his daughter, who married a man from Shongopavi and who now lives in the upper segment site with him.

Another man, who had been working on his father's allotment,

A 40, acquired a piece in A 44 at his marriage to Nashileowi's sister's daughter's daughter before 1937, through Guy's permission. He claims the soil in A 44 is better than A 40, but he continued to work on A 40 as well.

All in all, there are at present eight workers in Allotment No. 44 alone, each holding a little more than an acre. They consist of the members of the chiefly lineage of the Pi:kyas clan and their male in-laws. A sort of compromise pattern was thus created between the traditional mode of land use and that of "individual" tenure.

Though the position of the "owner" of the allotment has been indicated for the entire period, it carried little weight in the actual control of the land. Once an "owner" permits an entry, he seldom evicts an entrant. Such an entrant often establishes the right of disposal in his plot, which becomes an object of inheritance through continuous cultivation.

The cultivation history of Allotment No. 44 has revealed to some extent the solidarity of matrilineal relatives within the chiefly lineage. This trend, however, does not prevail in the history of other allotment or assignment lands. Allotment No. 45, for instance, shows remarkable solidarity of the patrilineal relatives of the original allottee.

The irrigable land in A 45 amounts to only about five acres. The remainder is on the other side of the Wash and unirrigable. Recently, sand dunes have been drifting down from the bluff on the southern edge of this part of the allotment and have covered a major portion of the level land there.

The original allottee, of the Reed clan, is said to have come from First Mesa and hence he was without close relatives in the village. He married a mother's sister's daughter of the allottee to A 41. No entry was made by his wife's people, however. Three of his five sons initially joined their father in cultivation of A 45. The wife of one of the three was from Oraibi and so her husband had no choice but to seek a piece of his father's land. The family of another son's wife, though from Moenkopi, was similarly landless. These two sons, however, later built their own fields elsewhere to supplement their small holdings in A 45. The third son meanwhile obtained a piece in A 39 on his marriage to its allottee's sister's daughter (through the allottee's permission). Later three other operators joined in the cultivation of A 45. Their genealogical relationships to the original allottee are indicated in Figure 2. At the present time, of the six operators of A 45, all but one are patrilineal relatives of the original allottee. The exception belongs to the same Water Coyote clan as the initial three operators. His entry was made through his mother because his father was from Oraibi and without farms, primarily being engaged in sheep herding, while his wife is from Mishongnovi and also without farms in Moenkopi.

As the above two cases indicate, farming in Moenkopi has been characterized by fluidity in the composition of the operators on a given tract of land. This corresponds mainly to the fluid population resident in the village, which divided its economic activities between Moenkopi and Oraibi in the earlier days and between Moenkopi and on- and off-reservation towns in the recent period. It should also be noted that the shift of land rights from the control of clans to that of individuals provided a greater number of choices in acquisition of farm land and thus accomodated the instability of postmarital residence because of the high incidence of inter-village marriages in Moenkopi.

The relationships sought for entry are extremely diversified. However, it is important to note the dominance of kinship. They include, apart from the parental ones (father to son, father to daughter, mother to son, mother to daughter), sibling, affinal, and, with several degrees' removal, patri- or matrilineal relationships. Though infrequently, clan relationships are resorted to as well. A man may give his farms to an adopted son. A common procedure is for a man to obtain the farm belonging to a person he interred.

On the other hand, relationships devoid of kinship correlates are based on political and friendship relationships. These are, however, often spoken of in terms of distant kinship. Dissociation of kinship in entry to land presents an interesting question in regard to the development of "rent" relationship and shall be discussed below.

The above pattern of entries into the land already shows significant deviations from "the [Hopi] theory of land distribution" (Forde, 1931:377). Male members of a matrilineage now work on the land of one of the lineage members, either male or female, and often do not move to their wives' lands. Moreover, an entry to a wife's land is often regarded as a secondary alternative to a parent's and when it is made, one usually does not abandon the piece of the parent's land. Forde already reported cases of men working on their own as well as wives' clan lands on First Mesa (1931:378, 380). In these cases, however, the men's fields on their clan lands are claimed to revert to the clan at their death (1931:378). In Moenkopi a man's holdings on his "parental" land are most frequently taken over by his children, both male and female.

As previously mentioned, land assignment is an assignment of usufruct to a farm within the theoretical framework of reservation land tenure. Each transfer of this usufruct requires approval from the local Land Board. In actuality, however, numerous transfers occur without awaiting such actions from the board. Inheritance of assignment lands has been made as frequently without probation by the Navajo Tribal Court in Tuba City. In one of such inheritance cases, a man "gave" a piece of the land he obtained from his adopting father to his brother. In another, a young man gave "permission" to his mother's brother for entry to the land he inherited from his father, the original reclaimer and assignee. This occurred when the young man was incapacitated by drunkenness. However, the mother's brother continued to work there even after he recovered and eventually brought one of his sons onto this land to work with him. As these cases show, the patrilineal transmission of land rights is not a result of imposition of government regulations, which do not, in fact, specify the mode of inheritance of assignment lands.

As already noted, frequent entries and withdrawals on the farm land and the process of establishment of the disposal right through continuous cultivation may lead to overlapping land rights of several individuals on a single piece of land and consequent confusion in regard to its ultimate possessor. Such is the case of a plot near the Moenkopi spring by the present Moenkopi Day School.

This land was originally utilized by the school as a small-scale demonstration farm. It appears that during the 1920's it was released for Hopi use and a man of the Patki clan from Oraibi became its holder. The farm land itself is a tiny two acres but direct irrigation from the spring and the proximity of the village site made the land comparatively more valuable than the outlying farms with greater acreage. The Patki man first gave a portion of the land to a friend in Moenkopi. When the Patki man died sometime before 1937, his son took it over. Through the son's wife, her male clan relative from Hotevilla obtained a portion in the land. Further, through the original Patki man's wife, her male clan relative obtained another piece there. When the Patki man's friend died, his portion went to his daughter and her husband. By 1948 the son had died. As a result three men have been working on this narrow strip of land up to the present time. The son's wife as well as his brother now claim "ownership" of the land but no actual attempt has been made to regain it. In fact, the present operators are political antagonists to the son's brother and it appears unlikely that he will dare to assert his claim, which would inevitably conflict with that of his sister-in-law.

The second feature of agricultural land use in Moenkopi is *frag-*

mentation and scattering of farm land holdings (see Brophy and Aberle, 1966:73–74, 76). The land holdings of many individual farmers were already diverse when a survey by the Soil Conservation Service was conducted in 1937. The original allottees and their immediate relatives, who held small plots in the allotment area, soon opened fields in other areas. The later arrivals, on the other hand, sought through kinship relationships the use of fields in areas already reclaimed and supplemented these with land they themselves reclaimed. At present, it is not unusual for one farmer to work on a piece in the allotment area dependent on reservoir irrigation, on another piece in the *Ma'asau* area dependent on Wash irrigation, and on a last piece of land in the dry farming area.

Several factors are involved in this seemingly "uneconomic" combination of land and labor. First, the trust ownership of land by the government formed an effective barrier which protected the basis of Moenkopi subsistence economy from the national competitive market. Second, participation of the villagers in the money economy mainly through wage work *dislocated* the subsistence economy to a residual activity within the total economic complex.[5] All through the period in question, no trend for accumulation of land in the hands of any individual has been observed. Third, individualization of economic activities through the above-described land tenure and participation in wage work eliminated the community and its component groups as possible production corporations oriented toward commercial economy. Finally, and perhaps most important of all, in spite of the general advocacy of land reform policies, the peculiar character of right of individual disposal inhibited movement of land capital along channels of demand and supply. This is most clearly seen in the *poorly developed contractual land relationship.*

I have already pointed out the significance of kinship in the disposal right over farm land. Conversely, it is rare to observe "renting" relationships between a possessor of the disposal right and his non-kin user. Such "renting" appears to be on the increase in recent years among families who migrate out of the village for off-reservation employment. However, all these relationships I observed are characterized, in addition to the absence of direct kinship between the parties concerned, by lack of specific terms of "rent" and its duration. The only term involved consists of maintenance of the

---

[5] Incentives for economic employment of farm land capital, e.g., for commercial production, were thus no longer seriously considered in the allocation of productive labor. The surplus land that resulted from this process has been left idle.

fields in a cultivable condition, or "keeping the field clean of weeds." Though it is sometimes stated that a portion of the produce from the rented fields is to be given to the possessor of the land, exact specification of the portion was never clearly mentioned to me. More often no reciprocation in kind is made by the "renter," who, in fact, appears to obligate the possessor of the right over the field by his maintenance labor. Thus it seems more appropriate to speak of these relationships as borrowing of land rather than "renting."

As previously mentioned, the present pattern of land use is seemingly "uneconomic." This observation can be derived from the viewpoint of either subsistence or money economies; the acreage is insufficient for subsistence on farming alone, while the cost of production is noncompetitive in terms of production for a national agricultural market. Agriculture in Moenkopi has not been either an isolated, closed form of subsistence economy or a fully integrated segment of the national money economy. Since the founding of the community, it has been in contact with money economy through wage work, sale of farm produce, and cash purchase of a few grocery items. This contact was accompanied by governmental control of basic agricultural capital, which was originally meant to insure the subsistence of the Indians. In this condition of dual economy, it is meaningless to define the "minimum land requirement" in the agricultural sector as a former superintendent once did: "If the average Indian family numbers five, forty acres of good land, with water would be ample, for agricultural purposes" (TCL, October 8, 1907).[6] In short, the boundary of the two economies has been flexible and the subsistence activities have been easily reduced or augmented to accomodate the variable pressures derived from contact with the money economy without serious alterations in the land rights. In the dual economic framework of Moenkopi, then, present land use cannot be discounted as simply "uneconomic."

In summarizing Hopi land tenure more than 30 years ago, Forde mentioned that ". . . the Hopi system of land tenure, while in theory one of clan ownership with inheritance of usufruct by females in the female line, is, in practice, subject to considerable modification . . . [partly] due to the dwindling of numbers and the emigration of individuals to the Agency workshops and to the American towns to the south" (1931:378–79). A significant change in the land tenure system of Moenkopi from Forde's Hopi system

---

[6] Brophy and Aberle mention the 80-acre unit as the minimum capable of profitable cultivation at present (1966:79).

exists in the above-described right of individual disposal, which itself was a result of expansion of farming in the outland under the reservation system.

The pattern of farm land distribution based on the right of individual disposal quite recently underwent a serious change in the allotment area. In 1962, with a notice from the Hopi Agency at Keams Canyon, the Western Navajo Subagency at Tuba City invited an examiner of inheritance from the Department of Interior to probate the inheritance of allotment lands, the original grantees of which had been dead for more than 20 years. Pursuant to Title 25, Code of Federal Regulations, Part 15, each allotment was appraised on the basis of acreage, topographical features, farming improvements, number of dwellings, and so on (Young, 1961:264; Andre, personal communication). Hearings were held in Tuba City and Moenkopi. In order to identify legal heirs, genealogies were compiled. Curiously, however, the probation did not take into due account the actual operators in each allotment at the time. The genealogical information collected for this purpose was frequently incomplete, and a considerable number of descendants who otherwise would have obtained shares were left out. On the other hand, the blood relatives of the original allottees who had never worked on these lands were included. Not only these but those who left for other villages after marriage and settled there now obtained shares. Cases of remarriage and adoption were often neglected or they alone were considered. It amounted, in short, to imposing an entirely alien rule of inheritance, based on bilateral kinship of the American society, upon the Hopi farmers, who had wrought out a mode of adjustment over half a century of time.

The consequences of the probation were diverse and often disastrous. In some allotments farming operations were brought to an abrupt end. From *A 41*, for instance, two operators, Guy and Odin, withdrew. Guy is the original allottee's mother's mother's sister's daughter's son and this was too distant a relationship to entitle him to a share in the land. On the other hand, only one out of eight inheriting families of *A 41* lived in Moenkopi but no member of this family has farmed the land since probation. This land is still idle.

A 39 was taken away from the matrilineal relatives of the original allottee, who were farming the land at the time, and given to the latter's children, none of whom lived in the village at the time of probation. The operators of *A 39* moved to *A 47*, in which some of them received shares and which had been out of cultivation for some years already. In moving, one of the *A 39* operators removed the fence wires and posts from this allotment, while leaving fruit trees planted by the original allottee. Of the original allottee's three children, to whom the allotment was probated, only one started working on a small portion of the land in 1963. Since her family lived in Flagstaff, they came back to the village only for planting.

Through diverse kinship relationships, some of the heirs obtained shares in more than one allotment. Frequently, however, they took the largest share and let those in other allotments rest as they had been. Some heirs with shares in a single allotment refrained from working the land because it was already overcrowded. The extent of each share also fluctuated extensively and in the case of heirs to *A 48*, some received only one-twentieth of the 10-acre tract, which had a total assessed valuation of only $1,410! There were also heirs who had settled in other villages long ago and who, as a result, declared surrender of their shares to the other heirs who had been working on the probated allotments. Finally, some others who were unable to activate their rights because of their residence outside of the village arranged to have their village acquaintances work their shares on condition that they "keep their fields clean."

All in all, an immediate consequence of the probation was to appreciably discourage actual operation in the allotment area, and in 1963, a year after the probation, only four out of 11 allotments were cultivated to any significant degree (see Map 5).

The impact of this action on the concept of land rights was just as serious. Though the ultimate right of supervision still rested with the government, the villagers clearly perceived the changed status in land rights. Now the act of cultivation did not guarantee rights over the land. Conversely, "owners" no longer needed to be actual operators on the land. With this awareness, several political actions were initiated by the two groups of the village (see p. 80–81). It even involved the question of legitimacy of the residential area, and the young chief of the lower segment wondered about collecting rents from the residents upon it.

The brief process of these adjustments to the introduction of a new land right concept through the probation clearly was possible because of greater reliance on wage work in recent years. If the change in the combination of land and labor had been carried out in the sole context of subsistence economy, its effect could have been disastrous, since it would presuppose a comparatively rigid correlation of the two factors of production (land and labor) on the basis of the subsistence needs of each household. In Moenkopi, however, this change was brought about without many deleterious effects on economic activity as a whole, partly because the area affected was limited to the allotment lands, but more important because the economic structure of Moenkopi itself was dual and the number of wage work opportunities was, at the time, on the increase. It meant a further displacement of subsistence agriculture and greater commitment to money economy.

Farm Labor Organization and Supply

The changing conditions of the dual economy brought about a new pattern of labor recruitment and organization for farming purposes. In the olden days, when the labor was concentrated on the subsistence economy, the entire male population of the village took part in farming activities. Further, it appears to have been common during the early period of the 1910's and 1920's for relatives from Oraibi and other Third Mesa villages to come down to Moenkopi to help with the farming there (see Simmons, 1963:208). With a more rigid administrative separation of Moenkopi from Hopiland and with differing degrees of involvement of all the Hopi villages in wage economy, the labor recruitment from the other villages for farming ceased to exist.

In this early period the villagers cooperated in the harvest of the chief's fields to relieve the chief and his family of this labor (Simmons, 1963:150–52.) At present, no labor contribution is made to the chief's family in its farming activity by the villagers.

At the present time, farm labor on a tract of land is mainly provided by the household to which that tract belongs. The only occasions for the traditional type of cooperation of kin in farming are limited to the first day of planting and harvesting phases, when the women of the household give feasts for the helpers. Usually, however, neither of the activities is finished in one day, and the male members of the household continue the work to completion without the help of nonhousehold kinsmen.

One of the characteristics of the dual economy is for an individual or a household to divide its labor force between subsistence agriculture and wage work. The division involves a decision-making process based on diverse factors, economic as well as noneconomic. The optimality question involved in the division in a particular household may be difficult to determine. Yet it appears certain that many households in Moenkopi are now short of farm labor, obviously because of the absorption of the labor into the wage work sector. A majority of the villagers do not have time to collect completely the ripened fruit of their trees during the fall season. Much fruit is left strewn on the ground and often rots there. Middle-aged men of the village attribute the cause of inefficient employment of farm land in Moenkopi at present to the growing laziness of the young people (see Rubin, 1961:126–27), although a majority of the latter are employed in wage work and hence have no great interest in farming. While the constraint on the transfer of land imposed by kinship and reservation regulations creates an impression of land shortage, the shortage in farm labor is responsible for another picture that the land in Moenkopi is, in fact, in surplus. The two impressions are shared by many village farmers, with some confusion.

The following modes of accommodation in the households also indicate the intensity of involvement in money economy in Moenkopi. First, many male wage earners return to their farms during after-work hours on weekdays or on weekends. Since the engagement in wage work is no longer seasonal (see Adams, 1963:141), they take days off from their regular wage work for farming during the busy planting and harvesting periods. Second, if old and "retired" males are available at home, the burden of farming often falls on their shoulders. Often a young household leaves the farming of its own fields to the old men of a parental household. The sharing of labor between brother households has also been frequently observed. These labor arrangements usually include such other reciprocations as feeding the old fathers at the home of their children and giving a portion of the field produce to them.

Another type of farm labor recruitment is from the unemployed young men, who return to farming for the period of unemployment. Since the engagement in wage work at present is mostly year-long, the context for seasonal adjustment of farming and wage work activities does not exist in Moenkopi. Although construction labor is now the only occupation that retains seasonality, its season overlaps with that of farming and hence no significant labor contribution to farming can be made by these people.

The shortage of farm labor has also resulted in relative relaxation of the sexual division of labor in farming. Traditionally, women seldom took part in the cultivation of fields. Though shelling of beans and corn from the stalks collected by men in the fields had been women's responsibility and though women had been gathering fruit, they had had no part in any phase of the cultivation of the main crops in the fields. Nowadays, however, a few young women do not hesitate to go out to the fields and help their menfolk harvest corn or thin corn stalks. A young divorcee of the lower segment has frequently been seen driving a pickup truck to haul her father's corn from the fields; it was also her task at home to chop firewood every afternoon.

On the other hand, with the wide use of grinding machines, the village women have been released from the toilsome work of daily corn grinding and no longer does a tranquil atmosphere of grinding songs exist in Moenkopi. Further, men frequently take the place of women in grinding corn by machine. The release of women from heavy household chores, however, has only infrequently led to their increased contribution to the subsistence economy across the traditional division of labor, primarily because a goodly portion of their released labor time has been absorbed in wage work, in which women have occupied an important position since the very early days of the Tuba City Agency.

It is important to note at this juncture that all these modes of labor recruitment in farming are based on kinship relationship, bilateral or otherwise. The premium placed on kinship for farming has apparently prevented the development of "contractual" labor organizations (Fitchen, 1961:114-15). Although the Sun Chief mentioned working for the Hopi in the fields for wages as early as the 1910's (Simmons, 1963:203), no significant attempt to introduce wage labor in farming has been made in the village so far. Though there are cases of hiring fellow villagers or Navajo farmers on the basis of cash wages, their number is yet extremely limited and has only slightly affected the position of Moenkopi agriculture as subsistence economy.

Commercial agricultural production is only slightly in evidence. Two old farmers from Moenkopi have been conducting full-time cultivation of the crops primarily directed to the local market for sale. Specialization of their agricultural production for sale purposes, however, is severely restricted by the kinds of crops, which consist entirely of traditional subsistence crops. What demarcates them from other village farmers is merely their relative emphasis on salability. They have made no attempt to expand the basis of their operation either by acquiring more land, or by hiring more laborers, or by raising nontraditional crops.

Technology of Farming

The technological aspects of Moenkopi agriculture represent the area of the greatest outside influence. It was the Mormon settlers and later the government that bequeathed a huge complex of irrigation canals to the Moenkopi farmers. Nevertheless, a characteristic feature of agriculture in Moenkopi is a peculiar lack of integration between irrigation, on which farming has been dependent since the beginning of the village, and the traditional Hopi techniques of dry or flood farming.

IRRIGATION. Though the Hopi always practiced a small scale of irrigation from contact springs on the mesa walls in terraced vegetable gardens near the villages (Forde, 1931:365–66), it never reached the extent and intensity of Moenkopi irrigation. I have already mentioned the traditional type of irrigation adopted in Moenkopi prior to the withdrawal of the Mormons from the area. However, this was immediately replaced by the reservoir irrigation system that the Mormons originally developed. At the same time, a great number of local Indians were employed for labor on the government irrigation farms and must have been acquainted with the principal aspects of irrigation agriculture. At any rate, irrigation in Moenkopi remained highly dependent on government supervision. This still holds true in the irrigation from Moenkopi Wash.

Of the two major irrigation systems that the Mormons developed, the first consisted of three small reservoirs in Reservoir Canyon and a ditch leading to the fields on the alluvial floor of Moenkopi Wash. Gregory observed a dam built by the Mormons in this set of reservoirs in 1912: "The waters of the lower 'lake' or reservoir, with an area of about 15 acres, [are] retained by a dam 350 feet long and 5 feet high. About 75 acre-feet is drawn off during the growing season" (1916:109). Since the government took over the administration of the area in 1903, another dam was constructed for the middle "lake" in order to prevent seepage in the lower "lake," and in 1908 the two dams were raised to the capacity of 350 acre-feet (Long Range Program, 1944:19). Each of the two dams was equipped with an independent gate. During the 1930's "drifting sand threatened to choke the [irrigation] channel, and a stone culvert was built and later extended with corrugated pipe. A new feeder canal was built in 1937" (Long Range Program, 1944:19). Sometime later the culvert was rebuilt with cement. The feeder canal, though improved in spots later, runs its course without a major change since the time of its construction; the course is parallel to Reservoir Canyon and merges with it only by the village, again to prevent seepage. In 1962 a new canal was laid out to connect the "middle" and "lower" reservoirs with stone slabs and cement; it runs on higher ground than the older one.

Another item of the Mormon legacy is a diversion dam on Moenkopi Wash, about a mile west of the village, where a small arroyo joins the Wash through *Tuviktsyala* (see Map 4). The water was diverted from the dam through a canal to the fields north of the Wash, to which it was brought back after a mile's run. The dam and canal were first used for the government farms of about 250 acres. During the time of this school farm operation, a diverse system of canals was added to the main ditch. Between 1915 (Gregory, 1916: map facing p. 144) and 1937 a flume was constructed to lead the water across to the fields in the *Ma'asau* area. The main canal from the diversion dam was paved with cement in 1960.

A trace of a long earthen dam still remains by the present diversion dam on Moenkopi Wash. This may have been built by the Mormons prior to the present one and used to innundate the adjoining fields. There is no evidence, however, that this dam was made use of by the government after the Mormon withdrawal.

Presumably first the Indians (FDL) and then the government attempted to build another diversion dam near *Pa:latuika*, but this project was not completed (Gregory, 1916: map facing p. 144). During the 1910's the government at Tuba City also constructed a series of small reservoirs to impound spring water for the cultivation of the 60-acre school orchards in Tuba City. They were never applied to Indian farming. Only one of these reservoirs still exists in Tuba City, while the others were desiccated.

(1) *Reservoir Irrigation.* Of the above two major irrigation systems, that of Reservoir Canyon was the first turned over to the use of the Hopi allotment fields. The Hopi farmers were entrusted further with its maintenance, which included clearing the ditch or canal and repairing the dam.

It is difficult to know how the Hopi performed these tasks in the early period. In addition to the two tasks of maintenance, it also included that of constantly keeping the water level of the reservoir below the danger of overflow. Whoever noticed this danger was to open the gate to drain the surplus water. These tasks required cooperation among the farmers, and the village chief was to direct the entire work. In theory, cooperative labor on the irrigation system was carried out in the spring and occasionally in the fall after the crier announced the date for work. No rule was established, however, as to the amount of labor each household or any other unit group within the village was to contribute. The work itself continued only for two days.

This organization of cooperative labor, however, was unsuccessful for the following reasons. First, the village contained households whose farming did not depend on this system of irrigation. Second, some of those whose farms were irrigated from the reservoir simply refused to contribute their labor because of personal differences with others. Instead, they went out to work on their own accord. On the other hand, some others who did not depend on the reservoir irrigation came out and helped the work to cull a favor from the chief. Still others sent out small boys, who went simply for the fun of it. Consequently, it appears the work that started out as a village undertaking soon ended up as a private enterprise of the chiefly lineage and its associate households, all of whom were dependent on this system of irrigation.

A similar difficulty became evident in the irrigation of individual farms. This was again a matter of unstated, unspecified understanding or agreement. Individual irrigators opened the gate and let the water to their fields whenever they were ready to do so. This started soon after the repair of the ditch from April to May. Before drawing water to the field, it was ploughed by a mule plough only once. Earthen ridges surrounding a plot were raised and repaired to prevent leakages. Then the plots were inundated "brim full" (five to 10 inches deep). Planting began only after the water seeped into the soil and the ground sufficiently dried up. Depending on the growth of the corn shoots, the second or third irrigation

Plate 5. Irrigated fields of Moenkopi in winter.

was done in June or July. On the other hand, irrigation was entirely skipped for a year when the fields were considered to be sufficiently wet.

This mode of irrigation of individual fields continues at the present time without significant change. It should also be noted that the entire procedure is strongly reminiscent of flood-water farming as practiced in Hopiland proper (Hack, 1942:26ff.). Further, the technique prompts salinization of the soil by letting the alkaline-impregnated water stand on the fields until it seeps down into the ground. Although no field has so far been abandoned because of salinization, there are spots of land along Reservoir Canyon that show the surface bleached white with alkaline salt. In any event, irrigation in Moenkopi agriculture is no more than a superficial addition to the traditional farming technique of the Hopi.

Simple or crude as this may seem, the farmers could not avoid the cumbersome question of water distribution among themselves. Innumerable troubles soon developed in this respect.

First, there existed differences in the time at which individual farmers were ready for irrigation. While a general framework of farming calendar might, at this time, still have been given by the solar movements observed in Oraibi and transmitted through informal means of communication to Moenkopi, this was certainly not minute enough to coordinate the economic life of Moenkopi, already diversified because of its involvement in the reservation community of Tuba City. Finally, Moenkopi had a wider range of choice of planting seasons owing to the shorter period of killing frost than in Hopiland proper.

Consequently, the order of individual irrigation did not always follow the most efficient route as might be imagined from the spatial distribution of farms and the course of the canal. Thus water was wasted by leakage into unprepared fields before it reached the field for which it was intended. Accusations of water theft were exchanged. Some were criticized for leaving the intake gates to their fields open while others were irrigating. The control of reservoir gates by individual irrigators was often neglected, leading to another cause of waste. Navajo and Hopi sheepherders were blamed for allegedly watering their sheep in the canal and soiling the water.

In the face of these novel difficulties, the village chief was almost impotent. Though his position was recognized by the local agency, he was unable to bring about any sanction against the saboteurs of cooperative labor or the pilferers of irrigation water. In turn, the chief was criticized for allowing such sloppy use of a gift from the government, which the villagers argued the Hopi should cling to in good faith lest the Navajo take it over. Thus toward the end of the 1920's, it was fairly obvious that a new and more powerful organization was called for.

I have already discussed the political aspect of an attempt at reorganization by the "Village Council." As far as the control and maintenance of the system were concerned, however, the "council" was as ineffectual as the traditional chief. Its effort to regularize the maintenance work by making attendance records of the labor contributors from the village was severely censured by the villagers as a blatant challenge to the people's spontaneity, one of the basic values of the Hopi. The donors of the funds to purchase a batch of tools, including shovels and picks, for the work on irrigation as well as road maintenance were limited to a small number of the residents of the upper segment, who were primarily dissidents to the traditional power. Thus, despite its avowed aim of unification of the village in community spirit, the "council" deteriorated into another faction against the traditional power group, concentrated around the chief in the lower segment of the village. Shortly after the failure of the "Village Council," the two segments, upper and lower, began sending out their own parties for the irrigation work.

The maintenance of the system by the work parties of the two groups has continued to the present time. Between the two, disputes over the distribution of water were not infrequent and there was even an attempt to bring the whole matter to a tribal court (Hopi Hearings, 1955:399).

In 1959, in order to improve the aggravated state of reservoir administration, the Keams Canyon and Tuba City agencies jointly issued a notice to install locks at the headgates of the reservoirs and to leave the keys in charge of the watermasters to be established respectively by the leaders of the two segments (see pp. 79–80). After a series of disputes, the locks were installed but the watermaster was set up only in the upper segment, the chief assuming the position in the lower segment.

Even this measure, designed to bring about responsible management of the reservoir system, was not successful. The people often bypassed the chief of the lower segment or governor and watermaster of Upper Moenkopi by circulating the keys, once borrowed, among the farmers. In order to borrow the keys, they crossed the line dividing the two groups (see p. 80) or, once the gates were opened, they were left open until all the neighboring farms were

Plate 6. Hopi reservoir shortly before irrigation begins in Moenkopi allotment fields.

irrigated. Farmers watched the time their immediate neighbors would finish their irrigation, thus coordinating the field preparation for irrigation within a small circle of operators on nearby farms. Though the water level is usually low, some chose the fall season to irrigate, thus avoiding personal entanglements. Disputes still flared up but they never precipitated into a serious issue for the village as a whole because the number of people irrigating from the reservoirs was reduced to only about a third of all farmers by this time.

(2) *Wash Irrigation.* At present, there are two types of Wash irrigation practiced by the farmers of Moenkopi. The first type depends on the diversion dam and a long canal, a part of which crosses the Wash through a flume to irrigate the Hopi fields in the *Ma'asau* area. The system was completed between 1915 and 1937 by the government. Since the canal courses through the Navajo farms first, irrigation of the *Ma'asau* fields has to wait for the Navajo to finish their irrigation (see Map 4). Thus cooperation is necessary between the Navajo and Hopi farmers. After the government ceased operation of the school farm in 1955, the need for this cooperation increased and the government remained in a supervisory position for the maintenance of the system. In 1960 the

Plate 7. Irrigation dam on Moenkopi Wash.

reinforcement of the canal with cement was carried out by cooperation of the Navajo and Hopi farmers under government leadership.

The following maintenance work schedule is observed at present and its main features appear essentially similar to those practiced previously. Labor contribution for canal cleaning is almost obligatory here, although no specific sanctions have been mentioned against truants. Occasionally, Navajo farmers in the same area are hired on a cash basis by those Hopi who are unable to join the cleaning party. At least a day's labor is expected to be contributed. No formalized arrangement as to setting the date for the work is present. However, since the cleaning work entails only that portion of the ditch that connects it to the main canal and since no Navajo is involved in this part of the canal, informal arrangements are usually made among the Hopi farmers without further difficulty. During this work the date for opening the gate by the flume is decided. The decision also depends on the Navajo farmers, who irrigate first and whose word the Hopi have to await before they start their own irrigation. If infrequently, the BIA announces the date for the Hopi irrigation through a notice at trading posts or the post office in Tuba City.

The irrigation is conducted in the spring, from late March to early April, when the Wash contains enough water. The farmers at

Plate 8. Irrigation canal and a culvert across Moenkopi Wash to the Hopi fields in Ma'asau.

the head and tail ends of the area assume responsibility for opening and closing the gates. Especially the one at the head, who opens the gate and irrigates his fields first, has to be ready to receive

Plate 9. Irrigated field in Ma'asau; note the intake gate.

from the last Navajo farmer. The subsequent order of irrigation in the *Ma'asau* area is also strict and one cannot obtain water if his fields are not ready by the time the water reaches there. The coordination of this work is done through mutual observations on the progress of the irrigation as well as daily, informal conversations in the village and fields.

Each plot is irrigated "brim full" or just enough to avoid overflow and only once. The water level in the Wash is not high enough for irrigation during the summer and fall. Depending on the number of plots in cultivation in a particular year, irrigation in the entire area of *Ma'asau* varies from one to two weeks. A field 10 acres in size takes about two days to draw water and irrigate after the water has reached the intake gate from the flume. While irrigating, the farmers vigilantly observe the fields night and day to prevent leakage as well as theft of water.

The second area that depends on the Wash water for irrigation lies to the northeast of the Moenkopi bridge. The farms in this area stand on an unassigned section of the land and are therefore illegal. No action, however, has been brought against the operators since the beginning of cultivation sometime after 1940.

Seven farmers in this area irrigate their fields with three gasoline pumps, each of which draws water for a distance of about 30 to 40 feet from the Wash through a flexible pipe, about half a foot in diameter. The seven farmers are divided into three pump-using groups on a kinship basis and each group chooses a time for irrigation at its own convenience. No coordination of the work is made among the three groups, however. Moreover, they often choose the fall season because the water seeps better into the soil by its frosting during the winter time. While this theory is only apparent, the farmers in this area are well aware of the complaints hurled against them by the other farmers downstream. This may be a more cogent reason to avoid the spring-time irrigation.

(3) *Spring Irrigation.* During the period of the Mormon settlement and shortly thereafter, irrigation from such springs as *Moenkopi, Ma:tsya, Ta:waki,* and *Tuviktsyala* was the only form practiced by the Moenkopi farmers. The technique of farming from these springs must have been similar to those described by Forde (1931:365–66) and others (Hack, 1942:36ff.). The fields by the present State Highway 264, near the upper segment site, still retain small plot demarcation and terracing, which are characteristic of the spring irrigation farms in Hopiland proper (see Map 2). At present, a few patches in the communal vegetable garden are still in use under this type of irrigation. The people often carry water in buckets from Moenkopi spring to irrigate some of these plots, while others obtain water from a tributary of Reservoir Canyon after it collects water from Moenkopi spring. The significance of these plots is presently nil and many are left unused.

More important of this type of irrigation are the fields in the *Shalako* area above the reservoirs along Reservoir Canyon. Five farmers have been operating on the land of about 40 to 50 acres since 1940. The farms are well irrigated by a series of rich springs that feed Reservoir Canyon.

To summarize the discussion of irrigation, it has been characterized by a disaggregative tendency throughout the history of Moenkopi. There is no coordination among the five distinct systems of irrigation presently used in Moenkopi. Though irrigation has been deemed indispensable for the success of farming in Moenkopi, its operation has been carried out without any community level organization. The Hopi farmers, in turn, exploited available alternatives of not only different sources of irrigation but also of non-irrigation farming. Thus one farmer expressed relief for the fact that he did not have to be dependent on one single system of irrigation.

Plate 10. Irrigation pump and a flexible pipe in Hu:yankikyö.

Dozier has argued that the absence of community-wide irrigation contributed to the persistence of the clan system among the Hopi (1960; cf. Kirchoff, 1955; Wittfogel and Goldfrank, 1943:27). The case of Moenkopi irrigation, then, partially corroborates his argument, since economic cooperation among bilaterally related households is preserved at the expense of community integration for the maintenance of a unified system of irrigation. Disaggregation of the source of irrigation, while vitiating community solidarity, allows the villagers to form the network of interactions based on close kinship relationships and further to take part individually in the outside economy.

Second, the Moenkopi irrigation technique has not been tightly incorporated into the whole complex of Moenkopi agriculture. It is highly reminiscent of traditional flood-water farming. Irrigation in general may be regarded as a technological achievement to partly free farming from the exigencies of nature by controlling the supply of water. Thus, even in Moenkopi there exists the theoretical possibility of expanding agricultural production into double cropping. No such attempt has ever been made, however. In fact, the village farmers are not as aware of increased and stabilized yields from irrigated fields as they are of the additional toil expended in irrigation farming. The total contribution of irrigation to agriculture in Moenkopi is summed up in stability of annual production and lessened chances for abandonment of land due to erosion processes in flood-water farming. In short, irrigation in Moenkopi has remained as a mere adjunct to the traditional flood-water farming technique.

NONIRRIGATION FARMING. As previously mentioned, dry farming has been practiced in the fields near *Pa:latuika* since the 1910's (see Map 4). During the last war, one household in the upper segment took up dry farming fields by Dinnebito Wash and has continued their cultivation until the present time. The fields at Red Lake and Coal Mine Canyon, now abandoned, appear to have been dry farming fields as well.

The farming technique in these categories of fields is basically similar to that adopted in the irrigated fields minus irrigation. The following description of the technical aspects of farming, therefore, applies to irrigation farming as well.

Farming now consists of plowing, planting, weeding, thinning, harvesting, and plowing in that order. The irrigation phase is inserted between plowing and planting and, optionally, between planting and weeding. Plowing after harvests is practiced only in dry farms. All but the plowing operation by tractors composed the traditional pattern of farming as it is still practiced in Hopiland proper. Moenkopi farming techniques thus reveal a highly conservative character in general.

(1) *Plowing.* It was the government at Tuba City that introduced *en masse* wagons, plows, and plow harnesses to the Indians as "issues" in return for their labor on the school farms and road constructions during the 1900's and 1910's (TCL). Similar issues were apparently being made in Hopiland proper (Watson, 1945:66). In Moenkopi as well as in Hopiland the use of horse plows was still extensive during the 1940's (Watson, 1945:66–67). In the latter part of the 1950's, however, horses and horse wagons were rapidly being replaced by automobiles (see p. 167) and with this, horse plows disappeared and tractor-drawn plows were introduced. The tractors were purchased in Flagstaff and soon became fashionable in the village. The number of tractor owners, however, remained small and even at present, does not exceed 20. Consequently, the machines were often circulated among related households in the village. Further, those without horse or tractor now hire two village tractor owners for plowing and pay wages to them. The two have also been employed by the Navajo farmers in the vicinity.

The tractors do not appear to have helped alleviate the shortage of farm labor. Due to the fragmentation of farm holdings, there now exist numerous plots into which tractors cannot be brought

Plate 11. Old Moenkopi Hopi ploughing a dry field after harvest.

for plowing. Further, scattering of the holdings resulted among some farmers in a restriction of use of their tractors in a certain number of their fields, but not in others to which they could not be moved effectively. Partly because of this limitation of tractors for farming purposes, one owner applies his to such other non-agricultural services as removing weeds and drifted sands from the house lots, a service for which he receives payment in cash.

It is not clear what contribution the plowing phase made to Moenkopi agriculture. Traditional cultivation as it is currently practiced in some parts of Hopiland proper did not require intensive plowing. Clearing fields of weeds with a pusher hoe and wooden rake in First Mesa (Beaglehole, 1937:37; Forde, 1931:389) was the only preparation made prior to planting, and the top soil itself was left undisturbed. Beaglehole states, "Native tools are now being superseded by American tools. The plough is of no great value, however, since ploughing renders the soil too light and causes over-quick evaporation" (1937:37). It is generally maintained, on the other hand, that the plowing process, including disking and harrowing, is an essential ingredient of dry farming, since it breaks up earthen clumps in the fields and enhances the capillary action of pulverized top soil (Webb, 1931:360ff.).

The contemporary Moenkopi farmers seem to hold Webb's view on plowing, which would explain the pre-irrigation plowing. At the same time, however, they seem to regard the elimination of weeds and remains of corn roots from previous years as another important aim of plowing. On the other hand, some farmers occasionally skip plowing in their irrigated fields and when they do plow, the operation is for the purpose of rebuilding a new pattern of plot demarcation by destroying all the pre-existing ridges.

Unlike irrigated fields, sand dune fields for dry farming receive plowing treatments before planting as well as after harvest. The exact function of plowing in this type of field is not quite clear, for sands in these fields are already fine enough to need no further pulverization. Yet it appears the esthetic preference of the Hopi farmers for tidy corn fields somehow calls for plowing of dry fields if only to rid them of wind-driven weeds.

(2) *From Planting to Harvest.* Apart from the irrigation and plowing processes, Moenkopi farming has remained unchanged from the traditional pattern. The following, therefore, notes only the features characteristic of Moenkopi farming today.

Though digging sticks or "planters" (*so:ya*), traditionally made of greasewood branches, are no longer in use, the sticks fashioned

Plate 12. Moenkopi man planting in a dry field near Moenkopi Wash; note the use of a digging stick.

out of steel pipes have been extensively employed in exactly the same manner as the former. Some also have been using thin hoes. The steel implements are obviously more effective in digging in the irrigated fields, whose soil is often harder than the sandy soil of dry farms. One informant mentioned an experiment with an automatic planting machine but it ended in an evident failure. Otherwise no serious efforts for labor-saving have been made in planting. Alternation of planting rows of corn is still practiced in both irrigated and dry farms.

After harvest, corn stalks are left in dry fields for fertilization of the soil as in the customary procedure. In the irrigated fields, however, they are either taken out of the fields to feed horses or simply burned. Some farmers collect corn husks for wrapping of tamales.

Use of fertilizers has not been very common. A few farmers

Plate 13. Young Moenkopi Hopi in a Ma'asau field.

bought insect sprays for their vegetable crops. In general, the attitude of the farmers to fertilization of the soil remains little changed and they still abhor a danger of contaminating the fields by the use of chemicals.

Plate 14. Dry field shortly after harvest.

PRODUCTIVITY OF IRRIGATED AND NONIRRIGATED FIELDS. The difficulties attendant to quantification of data have made it practically beyond my hope to make an accurate comparison of the productivity of the two types of fields. Yet it appears fairly certain that the labor input in a unit of irrigated fields is much greater than in the same unit of nonirrigated fields if only because of the irrigation itself. Further, given the same amount of capital outlay, a greater area can be brought under dry farming than irrigation. On the other hand, as previously indicated, the annual output in the irrigated fields is greatly stabilized due to independence of rainfall, and there is even a possibility of reaping double crops. Finally, the availability of land for the two types of farming may influence the relative rent and hence eventual cost of production. These factors, though isolable in theory, are so fractious in practical analysis that I give the following only as an indication of the village farmers' response to the two techniques of farming.

Irrigated fields in Moenkopi reflect higher relative productivity than the nonirrigated in the density of hills ($5' \times 5'$ to $3' \times 3'$ in the irrigated vs. $8' \times 8'$ in the nonirrigated). The farmers are aware of this difference. However, as mentioned earlier, they also assert that the irrigated fields demand greater care and labor than the nonirrigated. No specific preference for irrigated over nonirrigated fields has been expressed. I have already cited the instances of the Moenkopi farmers who left the village and their irrigated fields on marriage for other villages, where they have been engaged in dry farming. Though extremely scanty as evidence, these appear to indicate that the full potential of irrigation farming has not been exhausted in Moenkopi and corroborates once again the previously reached conclusion on the absence of integration between irrigation and the traditional pattern of farming.

To conclude, the absence of a lasting demand for subsistence

Plate 15. Man and young girl unloading the harvested corn from a dry field.

crops in the area and eventual participation in cash economy through wage work have left the technology of farming extremely conservative. Yet the farmers of Moenkopi are often proud of their farming activities and quote this heritage in comparison with the Navajo farmers in the same area. Though basic technological requirements are the same and the farmers of the two tribes are engaged in similar types of irrigation agriculture, the Hopi are wont to criticize Navajo farming techniques in terms of such relatively trivial points as the depth of planted corn seeds or the process of thinning the hills of corn. Apart from the economic significance, the present farming techniques are thus taken as a mark of tribal identity in this minority community on the Navajo Reservation.

Varieties of Cultivated Crops

Another striking index of the stability of subsistence agriculture in Moenkopi is the kinds of crops so far adopted by the village farmers. In the earlier period, the only crops in addition to the "Indian trinity" were cotton and wheat, which, however, remained marginal in the complex of Moenkopi agriculture.

The Navajo had long known of Moenkopi as "Where Cotton is Cultivated" (Van Valkenburgh, 1941:100). Mindelef (1891:33) and Christensen (1958:85) reported that cotton was typical of Moenkopi in the pre-allotment era. Indirect evidence of cotton in the early period is also found in a rock hollow called *Pavaukyaoki*, east of the village, which had been used for weaving (see p. 195). In 1911, however, it was already noted that "at present very little cotton [was] grown by the [Moenkopi] Hopis" (TCL, November 23, 1911), although Gregory found it still in cultivation in 1912 (1915:114).

The subsequent fate of cotton growing is unknown. At the present time no farmer appears to cultivate it. I could find only one farmer with a comparatively recent experience of raising cotton from 1948 to 1951 but never since.

Reference to wheat is still more scarce. Christensen noted it again for the pre-allotment period (1958:85). The Sun Chief mentions it for the 1900's (Simmons, 1963:108). Gregory found it in 1912 (1915:119). Though the cultivation of wheat is still remembered by many residents of Moenkopi, I could not obtain any indication of approximately when it disappeared. I suspect, however, that wheat dropped out of the Moenkopi crop complex much earlier than cotton, primarily owing to the availability of flour through the local trading posts since the early period.

After the withdrawal of the Mormons, the Tuba City Agency succeeded to the operation of the orchards and irrigated fields that the Mormons had developed in the area and conducted a fairly profitable enterprise based mainly on apples and hay (see p. 176–78). With encouragement from the Mormons and government, the Indian farmers planted a number of fruit trees in their fields. These included apples, pears, peaches, and apricots. Many trees still stand in the fields of Moenkopi and fruit is harvested in great quantity. As shall be discussed, however, they have not effectively been directed for sale but are mostly consumed domestically or used in ceremonial exchanges. In particular, there is no indication that fruit growing ever constituted a profitable enterprise as it did on the government school farms. Therefore, I regard fruit in Moenkopi as a variety of subsistence crop that continues to exist along with the other major crops.

The documents for the earlier periods indicate the early presence of the corn-bean-squash complex. John D. Lee noted the Hopi planting corn and melons in their summer settlement of Moenkopi during the 1870's (Cleland and Brooks, 1955). Stephen mentions "corn, beans, squashes, pumpkins and melons" in his letter of 1882 (HvJ, Def. Ex. G-245). A group of surveyors noted "corn, beans and melons" in 1906 (HvJ, Def. Ex. 243).

Corn occupies the most stable position in this complex of sub-

Plate 16. Moenkopi woman taking roasted corn out of a stone oven.

sistence crops at present. Its varieties are blue, white, yellow (*takeji qa'ö*, Forde, 1931:392; Voegelin and Voegelin, 1957:A8.10), and sweet corn (*tawakchi*, Forde, 1931:392–93). Occasionally, Walapai corn (*ko:nin qa'ö*, Voegelin and Voegelin, 1957:A8.10) is planted as well.

How the sweet corn (*Zea mays saccharata* Sturt.) (Whiting, 1950:69) was introduced to the Hopi is not known (Forde, 1931: 392–93). In Moenkopi at present it is the most popular corn, and households which lack labor to plant the other types of corn seldom neglect growing it. Apart from the suspected recency of its origin, the special position of sweet corn appears to be primarily because of the Hopi preference for roasted fresh sweet corn, a favorite item in the early summer menu.

The importance of white and blue corn is derived from its multiple uses not only in traditional foods but also as an object of ceremonial and kinship exchange. In addition, the blue corn is unobtainable in outside markets and it is widely believed that the yellow corn, though on sale in markets, is too hard to make corn meal. In many households white and blue corn often occupy the largest area of all the fields planted in corn.

Aside from these three varieties of corn, the others are optional and not infrequently omitted from cultivation. An informant who has been planting white corn for several years mentioned that its main purpose was for sale. However, such a status was not accorded to it by the others who planted it as well.

It is difficult to determine the next most prevalent crop in Moenkopi today. While two varieties of beans (Hopi lima and string beans) are raised in considerable quantity by some households, others do not cultivate either variety. On the other hand, musk- and watermelons are almost invariably planted on every family farm irrespective of the size of the patch.

Hack mentioned adaptability of beans to sand dune farms in comparison to melons (1942:33–34) and gave this as a reason for the prevalence of bean growing in Hotevilla, ". . . where over 60 percent of the cultivated land is watered by rainfall only, and thus is farmed by the method of sand dune agriculture" (1942:33). Some farmers in Moenkopi are aware of this, although no attempt has been made to concentrate beans on sand dune farms. Further, the difficulty of sand dune agriculture in Moenkopi makes the ecological separation of beans and melons difficult and has led to competition in which all present indications are that the melons appear to be driving the beans out.

This is first seen in the allocation of crops to respective fields. The corn plots are relatively stable and seldom are rotated with either beans or melons. On the other hand, the melons and recently sweet potatoes are more often switched around from one plot to another. In this process they tend to invade the bean plots. Thus the rule that " 'A melon field always keeps the same' " (Forde, 1931:391) does not apply in Moenkopi. Since no definite pattern of crop cycle is present in traditional Hopi agriculture (Beaglehole, 1937:36; Forde, 1931:391), crop rotation among the present Moenkopi farmers is largely a matter of individual adjustments based on considerations of such economic factors as available labor, domestic needs, amount of yield, and, marginally, salability.

Even in these terms, melons seem more advantageous than beans in contemporary Moenkopi. First, the processing of beans is slightly more cumbersome than melons, since the former require shelling, husking, and drying by women. Further, a tiny quantity of bean is almost meaningless for household consumption. Melons, on the other hand, can be appreciated as delicacies even if they are produced in small number. Finally, they can be sold more easily than beans. All relevant factors considered, melons are more advantageous than beans in the present economic context of Moenkopi. In melon patches, squashes, sweet potatoes, and pumpkins are often added as supplementary crops.

Plate 17. Communal vegetable garden in Lower Moenkopi; note the corn crop in the garden.

As with melons, a similar trend has been observed for vegetables, great varieties of which are now raised in the backyard gardens of Moenkopi homes. Occasionally, plots are prepared for vegetable crops in the corn fields outside the village. On the other hand, perhaps owing to the greater feasibility of home gardens and political antagonism in the village, many of the vegetable patches in the communal garden have been either abandoned or have lost their specialized use for vegetable growing. Some people have been planting corn in these plots. The vegetables now grown are chili, tomatoes, onions, carrots, cantaloupe, cabbages, and potatoes.

I could not decide which of these vegetables represent recent introductions from outside. Yet it seems the cultivation of vegetables in general has been increasing at the expense of wild vegetables, whose use had been limited in kinds as well as in quantity. The seeds of the vegetable plants, except for chili, are mostly purchased from outside and no attempt is made to preserve seed crops of the vegetables. The same applies to sweet corn seeds.[7]

---

[7] The purchase of vegetable as well as flower seeds seems common in other villages as well. A trading store in Second Mesa has had a display shelf of commercial seed bags for sale.

To conclude, the kinds of Moenkopi crops have been remarkably stable and dominated by the subsistence plants all through the periods under consideration. No commercial crops have been added. As the contact conditions of the dual economy changed, certain crops became comparatively more prevalent than others, while certain others disappeared. Yet the core feature of the crop complex (corn-melon-beans) has been retained so far.

Disposal of Farm Produce

Native exploitation of the environmental differences between the Tuba oasis and the Hopi highland did not reach a stage of community differentiation of agricultural production, and no institution for the exchange of field produce emerged between Moenkopi and other Hopi villages, including Oraibi. Most of the agricultural produce thus flowed through the channels of kinship and ceremonial relationships as shown by the Sun Chief's visits to his relatives in Moenkopi "in order to conserve our food supplies [in Oraibi]" (Simmons, 1963:93, 108).

In the early periods of the village, the farmers took their early crops to the *Niman* ceremony at Oraibi to display them in the plaza during the dance and to be distributed among the contributors' kin in the audience. This practice is still observed by a small number of farmers in the village, who take the crops to Hotevilla and Bacabi, the only two villages that still give the *Niman* on Third Mesa. After the disruption of the Oraibi ceremonial cycle, however, the majority of the Moenkopi farmers ceased to offer contributions at the *Niman* ceremony and chose, instead, to distribute their field products to their kinfolk in other villages on informal occasions, on the occasions of kachina dances, or such individual kinship ceremonies as birth and marriage.

The general pattern of kinship exchange of agricultural produce remains well preserved in the traditional framework. Three levels of exchange appear differentiable here in terms of frequency and kinds of goods exchanged. First, the exchange is reciprocal, most frequent, and close to sharing between sister households and between those of parent and child. Between brother and sister households, on the other hand, it is usually the former that contributes field produce without reciprocation from the latter. Outside this range of kin, exchanges are formal and assume a ritual character. This is especially true in the exchange relationships between the households of father's sister and brother's son; a brother's son is expected to take meat obtained through hunting or, as has been more frequently the case in recent years, purchased at outside stores, to his father's sister (*kiya'a*, Eggan, 1950:40–41; see p. 236). The latter reciprocates with cooked corn foods (e.g., *piki* or *pigami*). On the occasions of kinship ceremonies (first naming, Kachina initiation, or wedding ceremonies), a large number of clan relatives are involved in the exchange of various goods, including blue corn meal, *piki, tugu:viki, nokwivi,* or basket plaques and ceremonial bows and arrows. The Kachina ceremonies also provide contexts for exchange of corn, melons, and fruit among the kinsmen.

The amount of field produce expended for these exchanges is considerable. For example, about 50 pounds of blue corn meal is cited as "payment" for the gift of a basketry plaque by a paternal aunt on the occasion of a child's Kachina initiation ceremony (Eggan, 1950:51). The child usually obtains more than one plaque. In one case, a girl was given eight plaques, making the return of corn meal about 400 pounds. Taking 56 pounds for the weight of a bushel of shelled corn, the amount needed for the "payment" would be about seven bushels. Given 20 bushels as the average yield from an acre of irrigated land in Moenkopi and assuming that the size of a household holding is about 3.5 acres, two-thirds of which, about 2.4 acres, are planted in corn, we obtain 48 bushels as an annual yield of corn per household. Consequently, about one-seventh or 15 percent of the yield of corn is consumed for gift exchange. This type of large-scale exchange occurs only when a child is initiated to the Kachina society. However, the occasions for ceremonial exchanges of a smaller scale are far more numerous. Thus considered, the necessity to meet these obligations alone appears to be a sufficient cause for the continued cultivation of white and blue corn. The ceremonial need is thus a dominant motive for continuing farming at present. This illustrates again the fact that agriculture in Moenkopi carries an aspect of boundary maintenance today.

Some produce from the Moenkopi fields has been sold to the local traders and Navajo for cash since the early days of the village (TCL). No distinction was made in this practice between sale and nonsale crops. The traders even bought corn from the village farmers. It is not clear when they ceased to purchase agricultural products from the Moenkopi Hopi. During recent years the Hopi of Moenkopi and other villages have taken the place of the traders as buyers of the Moenkopi crops.

The sale of crops to other Hopi is much less frequent than to the Navajo. In sales to the Hopi, *piki,* made of blue corn, occupies a dominant position. However, as the village came to contain households without farms or with an insufficient labor force for farming, cash transactions involving crops increased within the village as well. The Hopi from other villages, especially from Polacca, are said to have been frequent customers of the Moenkopi farmers. I was not witness to this during the field work, however.

Barter as well as cash sale of field produce have been conducted with the Navajo and continue at present. The Navajo bring mutton and jewelry to the homes of their Hopi acquaintances in Moenkopi and barter them for corn, melons, and fruit. I could not determine the current rate of exchange and a few Hopi women who dealt with the Navajo denied the existence of any fixed rate. The relationships between the Navajo and Hopi in barter are often characterized by the Hopi as "friendship" and appear stable enough to last for several years. However, the trans-generational continuity shown between the Navajo and Zuni (Vogt, 1955) does not exist in these relationships, nor is there a tendency to exclude other Hopi or Navajo from these "friendships."

Another apparently ancient form of transaction with the Navajo which involves field produce is entirely unilateral. It occurs on the occasion of the Navajo *Yebechi* dances during the fall and winter. When a dance is ready, a group of masked *Yebechi* dancers visits Moenkopi and collects contributions of melons and sweet

Plate 18. Melons displayed in a Moenkopi house yard for a gift to Navajo *Yebechi* dancers.

corn from the homes in the village. No reciprocation, even in the form of such ritual goods as blessing or prayers for the welfare of the Hopi donors, is made by the Navajo in return for these gifts. The *Yebechi* have visited other Hopi villages as well, and the Hopi frequently present caricaturized *Yebechi* clowns in their kachina dances.

Most of the Moenkopi crops have at one time or another been sold for cash to the Navajo, who visit the village for that purpose. Melons appear to be the most popular item of purchase. The melons, in season, are displayed in the front yards of the Hopi homes and Navajo buyers visit one house after another, inquiring about prices and qualities of the melons, sometimes even haggling.

In barter as well as sale, it has been the Hopi women that have dealt with the Navajo visitors. All the harvested crops are controlled by women; one housewife once told me that "Corn, beans and everything belong to a man when they are in the fields but once they are harvested and brought into a house, they are women's" (cf. Titiev, 1944:181). Transactions are conducted either in Navajo or in English but never in Hopi. Cash payments are made on the spot.

The above exchanges by the peoples of the two tribes have often been interpreted as symbiosis of the Navajo pastoralists and Hopi agriculturalists. However, such an economic differentiation seems to be disappearing in the Moenkopi area for the following reasons. First, a process of mutual diffusion of the respective subsistence patterns has been going on through the interactions over a few centuries. Agriculture itself has become a well-established pattern among the Navajo in many areas (Brugge, 1964). This is especially true in the Moenkopi area, where a large number of Navajo families have been practicing a similar pattern of irrigation agriculture. As a result, the Navajo customers of Moenkopi are mostly from outlying camps where farming remains a minor activity. Navajo influence on Hopi economic life has been comparatively slight and yet it has left a distinct mark on the few Moenkopi sheepherders (see p. 168). Second, participation in cash economy through wage work has assumed an increasing importance in the two tribes. This has tended not only to replace barter with cash transactions but also to direct the Navajo to outside markets and away from Moenkopi.

Thus, there has existed a modicum of competition between the Hopi farmers and outside merchants, including traders and supermarkets on and off the reservation, for the Navajo consumer market. Soon after the harvest, some Hopi women have taken their melons and fruit in pickup trucks, driven by their husbands, to distant Navajo camps for sale. These trips, apparently an established practice since the last war, do not last more than a day and often terminate before all of the produce is sold.

The present sales activities in general are neither planned nor organized in terms of the available stock of farm products. Consequently, it is a common occurrence in the village that households find themselves in short supply toward the springtime, a lean season of the year. One housewife mentioned the lack of storage facilities as the reason for rush sale of melons and fruit. However, the fruit could be stored for winter consumption by drying or by making preserves, a practice known but no longer common in Moenkopi. Melons certainly pose a problem and yet it has been occasionally noted that they last well into winter. No preservation efforts are expended on vegetables except for chili, which seldom lasts over a year, however. Only the blue corn has been in surplus as it has been customary among the Hopi (Spicer, 1962:195).

Housewives do not appear particularly concerned with the stock of their agricultural supply. Foods are now easily available by purchase in the stores of Tuba City and Flagstaff. For the last 10 years, a vendor of agricultural products from Phoenix has been frequenting Moenkopi and other Hopi villages as far as Second Mesa in a bus loaded with eggs, vegetables, and many kinds of fruit. The service of this "Fruit Man," as the villagers call him, has been highly appreciated in Moenkopi, where he appears once a week almost all the year round. Thus, the Moenkopi Hopi have been buying all the crops they themselves produce except for blue corn. It is not infrequent that even sweet corn is included in this purchase and canned corn on the market appears to be their favorite. The purchase of subsistence crops, including canned corn, watermelons, squash, and chili pepper, was already noted in Hotevilla during the 1930's (Brainard, 1935:245–48).

I have mentioned that Moenkopi farmers do not distinguish between sale crops and those for domestic consumption. Of equal importance is the fact that the crops for sale are not the surplus as distinguished from those for home supply. Though two early agents in Tuba City referred to the sale crops as "surplus" (TCL), it is clear from the above description of their sales activities that the present households in Moenkopi sell their farm products irrespective of the adequacy of their own supplies. Absence of differentiation between sale and nonsale crops and resultant dependence on outside markets for subsistence materials they themselves produce have been observed among other groups of Indians who came to be involved in exchange economy through the products of their subsistence economy (see Mintz, 1959:21–22).

LIVESTOCK INDUSTRY

Reservation Control

The Indian Reorganization Act of 1934 provides a most convenient point of reference in the discussion of government policies regarding Indian grazing activities.

Prior to the act, governmental efforts were confined to improvement of the Indian stock by the introduction of breeding animals (TCL; KCL) and by construction of rainwater catches (TCL) and later windmills. The pre-IRA government, however, did not control the size of the herds or range for the Indian stock. The Indian range was generally regarded as coterminous with the reservation, and the government intervened in disputes over the range territory that occurred mainly between Indian and non-Indian herders.

The individual allotment of grazing land was similarly regarded as unfeasible. In 1903 a superintendent wrote:

I look upon the allotting of the grazing land as thoroughly impracticable and out of the question, for the reason that there is not enough grass on any quarter section; aside from the land scarcity for farming purposes, to support fifty head of sheep, and the scarcity of water will make allotment of grazing land impossible from the fact that the few only would have watering places and many would perish from the want of water (FDL, January 16, 1903; TCL).

Thus the government left the reservation land as an open range for the use of Indian livestock. Subsequent development of the livestock industry by the Indians, however, created the danger of depletion of the range resources and deterioration of the economic value of the stock animals through unplanned overstocking and overgrazing.

In order to rectify this, the Indian Reorganization Act initiated two basic programs: the establishment of land management districts and the institution of the permit system. This stock reduction program was carried out jointly on the Navajo and Hopi reservations.

Thus, in 1936 the original plan for 18 land management districts was laid out with "about 1,000,000 acres each" (Young, 1961:155).

In 1937 the plan was adopted and resident supervisors were appointed by the BIA to manage the districts (Adams, 1963:46). With the establishment of the districts, the movement of livestock over the district boundaries was prohibited. In 1937 also the Navajo Tribal Council, empowered by the federal government, placed the first grazing regulations in effect (Young, 1961:155).

The livestock count was executed on the two reservations in the same year and the carrying capacity of each district was determined. The capacity has been calculated in sheep units (SU). A head of cattle is given four sheep units and a horse five (see Brophy and Aberle, 1966:122). The excess stock was eliminated without compensation to bring down the stock to the capacity level. In 1940 the first grazing permits were issued on the basis of capacity and the 1937 count (Young, 1961:155).

After the last war, the government transferred some of the regulatory functions of reservation resources from the BIA to the Navajo tribe. Thus, in 1953 the Navajo Tribal Council, with the authorization of the Secretary of Interior of 1952, established grazing committees (Young, 1961:158; Adams, 1963:48; Shepardson, 1963:60), which replaced the district supervisors.

At the present time, a grazing committee is in charge of issuance of new permits and probation of inheritance as well as sublease of the older permits (Navajo Tribal Council, 1962:15, 17). The present regulations further specify such details as the location of corrals within a half mile radius from a windmill (Navajo Tribal Council, 1962:23). The maintenance of the windmills, once a responsibility of the BIA, is now charged to the Navajo tribe.

It is generally assumed by the BIA and Navajo tribe that a permit, composed of a number of sheep units, also includes a right over range sufficient to graze the permitted number of stock. Thus the "customary use area," established through continuous use of a range on the permit basis, is respected by not only the Indian herders but the government and tribe as well. However, in order to allow a flexible use of the available range within a district, the government or tribe has not attempted to plot the use areas or freeze their distribution. Thus a theoretical framework of open range system is still maintained within each district.

Through the stock reduction program, Moenkopi came to belong to District 3 with 1,773,397 surface acres, the largest of all the 18 districts on the Navajo Reservation. Its carrying capacity was set at 47,288 SU (Young, 1961:170), which stands at present. The Moenkopi herders were assigned 3,487 SU in 1942. In 1943, however, the units were increased to 3,497 and this has remained unchanged to the present time.

The inclusion of Moenkopi in District 3 meant not only alienation from the Hopi District 6 but also submission to the jurisdiction of a local Navajo grazing committee, from the participation in which the Hopi have been excluded (see p. 59). I shall discuss the consequences of these actions on the Moenkopi livestock industry in the following section.

Livestock Ownership and Usufruct Rights to Ranges

OWNERSHIP AND INHERITANCE OF LIVESTOCK. Since the introduction of sheep, horses, and cattle among the Hopi, they have been regarded as the property of individual males (Watson, 1945:68). The cattle, in particular, have been individually earmarked and branded since the early period in the area (TCL). The brands have been inherited with or without modification.

Individual ownership of livestock appears to have derived partly from the fact that a number of men in Moenkopi and perhaps elsewhere in Hopiland acquired their first herds through purchase in cash saved from their work in the government. The Moenkopi livestock industry thus had an intimate association with the money economy from the beginning. The exclusion of women from ownership, on the other hand, was mainly due to the herding practice which has been strictly a male activity. Thus a father may give a portion of his herd to his sons or nephews for the latter's service in herding (Page, 1940:45). The sons who have not rendered such service are often excluded from inheritance. A male in-law may own stock which his father-in-law has given him in return for the former's help.

There are cases, however, in which attribution of ownership between a married couple is not so explicit. Thus, if a man has only daughters, the husband of one of the latter usually runs his herd after his death, but the herd itself is regarded as belonging to the household as a whole. In one case, a man with only daughters gave his entire herd to a grandson, when he reached old age. The herd itself had been run by his son-in-law until the grandson came of age. His other daughters had gone to California after marriage and when one of them had to pay hospital bills for her husband, the old man told his son-in-law to sell two head of cattle and send the proceeds to her in California. This appears to indicate that though women may be excluded from direct ownership of the animals, they still retain a right to draw benefits from the sale of the livestock.

Watson noted women's ownership of livestock (mainly sheep) in Oraibi and New Oraibi but observed that the stock was tended by husbands or brothers (1945:68–69). Beaglehole mentions for Second Mesa that the inheritance of livestock (mainly sheep) is ". . . customarily . . . by his sisters, brothers, and clanspeople generally, the widow, sons and daughters inheriting none at all . . . today children as well as the close clan connections inherit from the father; that is, there is a tendency to allow members of the bilateral kin group to share in the disposal of the goods" (1937:11). No case of livestock inheritance by a man's sisters or brothers has been noted in Moenkopi. Nor do Page's cases of cattle inheritance at Oraibi during the 1930's show Beaglehole's customary type of inheritance.

The exclusion of Moenkopi women from livestock ownership stands in sharp contrast to the Navajo practice. Navajo women often run sheep flocks by themselves. Further, they butcher and skin the sheep. The Moenkopi women have been seldom seen doing this; when butchering is necessary, they either let the men do it or hire Navajo women in return for hides and the inside of the sheep.

The introduction of the permit system, however, has brought about some confusion in the rules of ownership of livestock. This is chiefly due to separation of the herding activity from the criterion of stock ownership, now to be accompanied by possession of permits. Thus two women have come to own permits since the system was adopted. One of them inherited her father's permits. Since she was working as a clerk at the Tuba City Agency, she was well versed in the bureaucratic procedure of probation. Thus she registered all the permits under her name. On the other hand, her brother had been running the cattle until he was incapacitated by an accident. Now the herd is tended by their father's mother's brother's son with the latter's herd. This arrangement was derived from the fact that their father and the present herder's father used to tend the cattle together. The second Moenkopi woman obtained the permits from her Navajo husband at his death. She has not yet owned a herd on these permits, however.

APPROPRIATION OF AND USUFRUCT RIGHTS TO RANGES. The customs relative to range rights have never been formulated explicitly among the Hopi. Page mentions, "The establishment of the original claims to range rights was a simple process of 'first come first served'. As long as the stock were not allowed to enter the cultivated areas they were free to graze near the villages" (1940:37). Though Watson reports the occurrence of grazing within the clan blocks (1945:68), it is not clear if the latter area was originally for farming. In Moenkopi, at least, the farming area has so far been well demarcated from the established ranges.

Because of the differences in herding practices between Moenkopi and Hopiland, it is difficult to speak of individual tenure of range land (Watson, 1945:69; Page, 1940:35) among the Moenkopi cattle herders. The latter have formed into several stable groups, each of which concentrated the herding activities around its own corral and range. Thus the ranges for cattle have been appropriated by groups instead of individual herders. Since all the available ranges were already appropriated during the 1930's, a newcomer usually joined one of the pre-existing herding groups on its range.

On the other hand, sheep ranges appear to have been appropriated on an individual basis. This again depended on the herding practice among the sheepherders, who usually remained close to the village.

Boundaries of the ranges have never been clear and a great deal of overlapping has occurred. Even today, it is not rare for the herds belonging to different herding groups to graze on the same range. In theory, however, the ranges already appropriated are respected by the herders, who seek permission from the original users before entering. Thus a Hopi herder from Hotevilla was met with threats of eviction from the Navajo herders when he and his brother moved their herd from the crowded range on Oraibi Wash to the range west of Dinnebito Wash in 1935. The Hopi cattlemen then offered services to the Navajo, e.g., procuring Hopi medicine, running errands as far as Winslow in a "jalopy truck," repairing and improving the roads of the range. It was only after offering these services that they were allowed to graze their herd on the Navajo range. Much the same procedure has been adopted among the Hopi herders as well.

The inheritance of range right per se does not exist among the Hopi herders of Moenkopi nor in Hopiland. The heirs usually make use of the area where the inherited herds have been grazing.

The content of the range right, finally, consists of the actual use of a certain range for herding purposes. No lending or borrowing of the ranges alone exists; one may have a flock without a range but never a range without a flock. A range is open to use by others when a herd or flock ceases to graze on it.

The permit system has not changed the basic characters of the range right except that one cannot claim a right to graze outside his own land management district.

Changing Volume of the Livestock Industry

Livestock operation by the Moenkopi Hopi was virtually nonexistent around the turn of the century. Only one man, a Navajo captive raised in Oraibi, built a sheep camp on a bluff south of Moenkopi Wash, about a mile east of the village. Otherwise, grazing activity was limited to Navajo sheepherders who had been increasing in the area and who often came into violent conflicts with the Mormon and gentile cattlemen over range distribution. In 1903 a superintendent mentioned that "the main reliance of these Navajoes for a living is their sheep" (FDL, January 16, 1903).

The number of Hopi sheepherders increased little during the first two decades since the establishment of the reservation in 1900 and probably did not exceed five. Even in 1937 the tally of Moenkopi stockowners showed only five sheepherders.

The range for these sheep was limited to the vicinity of the village, and the main watering spot was the Reservoir Canyon swamp area, where a sheep dip vat had been constructed (Gregory, 1916: map facing p. 144). A conflict was reported by Page (HvJ, Def. Ex. 230b) between the herders of the two tribes over the use of this area in 1937. However, apart from the upper reaches of the canyon, long in use as a Navajo range, the ultimate supervision by the government of the reservoirs contributed to securing Hopi access for watering purposes.

Saddle and draft horses must have already been prevalent in Moenkopi during the first decade of this century, since wagons issued by the government were extensively employed as an important means of transportation between Moenkopi and Oraibi, for freighting and farming. Horses do not seem to have been commercially raised, however. Burros were less common, perhaps because of the greater need for transportation in Moenkopi than elsewhere in Hopiland.

It appears fairly certain that cattle raising began much later than that of sheep. The first reference to cattle appears in 1909 (TCL), but they belonged to a Navajo. The existence of "a few cattle" on the Western Navajo Reservation as a whole is mentioned for 1910 (TCL), but tribal affiliations are not indicated. In 1911 "15,000 cattle" are reported for the entire reservation of the Western Navajo, along with "160 to 320 acres of grazing land each," allotted to the Hopi of Moenkopi (TCL). It is doubtful if these allotments were ever approved in Washington, since subsequent events do not give any indication of their official existence. In any case, it appears safe to assume that the Moenkopi Hopi came into the cattle business during the 1910's, shortly after the Navajo did the same in this area.

Three modes of entry into the business appear to have been common. First, the original herd was obtained from the local Navajo through trade of field produce or direct purchase in cash saved from government wages. Second, original herds obtained through purchase or inheritance in Oraibi were brought to Moenkopi. Page mentions in this connection that Oraibi had had very few cattle prior to 1902, when four Hopi "traded about $400 worth of goods and turquoise for cattle [in Jemez pueblo, New Mexico]" (1940: 45). At least one Hopi from Moenkopi brought a portion of this herd to Moenkopi during the 1910's. Finally, some sheepherders switched to the cattle business. Although this mode of entry into the cattle operation became popular only recently, one Hopi from Hotevilla had already made the change in 1927 and brought his cattle herd to the Moenkopi range during the 1930's.

All the cattle the Hopi came to own were beef cattle. No attempt has been made by the village stockmen to engage in dairy production. The raising of cattle was always been for commercial purposes. Consequently, with the rise in needs for cash, the number that came into the business increased and competition arose between the Navajo and Hopi herders over the available range land. Such conflicts between the two tribes are reported for 1914 (TCL) and for the 1920's (HvJ, Def. Ex. 230b).

These early conflicts were mainly due to the scarcity of stock water available to the herders. Before the government initiated construction of windmills around 1915, most of the stock water in the Moenkopi area was obtained from the tributary canyons of Moenkopi and Dinnebito washes or charcos (stock tanks to collect rainwater). The Navajo regarded the first source of stock water open to any herder's use, but some Hopi herders constructed camp houses and later even farms. These actions invited the violent resentment of the Navajo herders who feared the complete appropriation of water by the Hopi herders.

After the windmills became available, however, the limited water spots lost their former critical significance, and eventually most herders became dependent on the troughs constructed adjacent to the mills. Although disputes over the ranges thus decreased in frequency, the forage condition of the area was still so precarious that the herders were often forced to abandon one range and move elsewhere for better forage. This was another factor that contributed to the maintenance of flexible range rights among the Indian herders.

The state of range use by the Moenkopi herders shortly before the stock reduction shows little indication of overgrazing. In 1930, 1,300 head of sheep and 300 head of cattle grazed mainly to the south of the village, on Moenkopi Plateau and Coal Mine Mesa, which area was set aside for the Hopi herds through an agreement with a Tuba City superintendent (HvJ, Def. Ex. 196). In 1937, 1,000 sheep and goats, 300 cattle, and 40 horses were counted (2,400 SU), and 6,000 forage acres were regarded necessary to carry them. The subsequently proposed 65,000-acre area, deemed enough to provide the necessary forage acreage, however, consisted of the ranges that had already been in use by the Hopi herders from Moenkopi (HvJ, Def. Ex. 280b) and hence no serious problem of reduction was posed (HvJ, Def. Ex. 230b; see also Map 5).

In regard to conflicts between the Hopi and Navajo herders over range use, Page reports in 1937 that "There do not seem to be many outstanding complaints" (HvJ, Def. Ex. 230b). In fact, the 1937 count of Moenkopi stock was far less than the total amount allowed by permits subsequently issued on the basis of carrying capacity of the range. Hence, if most of the Moenkopi herders lost portions of their herds at the reduction, it was mainly because they could not round up their entire herds on short notice and thus were unable to have them registered *in toto*. However, from 1936 to 1942 overstocking was a fact in District 3, to which the Moenkopi range belonged (Young, 1961:171). Thus it was obvious that the increase of Navajo stock was the primary source of strain on the range capacity.

The significance of the stock reduction program to Moenkopi, then, lay more profoundly in the institutional innovations which came to affect the position of this Hopi community on the Navajo Reservation. First, the land management district system, which separated Moenkopi of District 3 from the Hopi Unit of District 6, was to prevent stock movement over the district boundaries. Some Hopi herders were frightened at the prospect of total alienation from Hopiland proper. In 1942 a Hopi superintendent reported: "Now it seems that some of the Moenkopi Hopis want to . . . move back to Old Oraibi bringing their livestock with them. One member from Moenkopi moved back to Oraibi with one hundred sheep before we were aware of the plan . . ." (HvJ, Def. Ex., III, 897).

Seeing a danger of ruination of the whole project, the Commissioner of Indian Affairs immediately wired back to refuse grazing permits to this Hopi herder (HvJ, Def. Ex., III, 898).

Second, freezing of the grazing permits within each district meant that the Hopi could no longer move their herds from Hopiland to Moenkopi even if they were to reside in the village by marriage. Since the livestock was owned and disposed of by men, grooms from Hopiland were forced to either abandon their herds to their kinsmen or to make other arrangements there. Livestock operation was thus closed to future newcomers to the village, and as land resources for farming were exhausted, Moenkopi reinforced further its image as a source of wage labor to the Hopi of Hopiland proper.

The Moenkopi herders were confronted with a unique problem of their own. While fencing appeared to secure their range from further Navajo encroachment, the herders had to comply with the regulations promulgated by the Navajo Tribal Council, in which they were not represented. Incentives for expansion of the stock operation, often spurred by competition with the Navajo herders, were now severely curbed by the limit set on the number of their permits. As the Navajo council came to assume greater functions in the management of grazing, the Hopi herders were deprived of opportunities for maneuvers which had been open to them when it was in the hands of local superintendents (see HvJ, Def. Ex. 196). Cut off from one of the major sources of increase in labor and capital for livestock business and subjugated under the control of an alien tribe, it did not take long for the period of decline of Moenkopi livestock operation to set in.

Tables 1–4 (see also Figures 3–5) show the subsequent changes in stock holdings and number of operators with permits since the stock reduction. They also indicate several trends in the Moenkopi livestock operation since that period. First, there is a general decline in holdings as well as number of operators for the entire period. The extent of the decline, however, depends on the kinds of stock animals. Thus, sheep and goats decreased more rapidly than cattle or horses. By 1950, while the cattle showed only a small decrease (134 SU less than in 1942), the sheep and goats represented only about half of the 1942 figure of 1,101 SU. If the 1940's were the period of decline in sheep, the 1950's were so for cattle; while the number of sheep has been maintained to the present at the level reached by the middle of the last decade, cattle holdings in 1958 were only slightly more than half what they had been in 1950, and they remained at the 1958 level until 1962 with slight fluctuation.

TABLE 1. Livestock Holdings of Moenkopi (1937–62)

Year	Sheep	Goats	Sheep and Goats	Cattle	Sheep Units	Permitted SU
1937	667	77	744	414	2,400	
1942	1,041	60	1,101	469	2,977	3,487
1943	1,080	70	1,150	518	3,222	3,497
1944	835	31	866	472	2,754	"
1945	601	11	612	420	2,292	"
1946	576	8	584	438	2,336	"
1947	517	12	529	414	2,185	"
1948	528	11	539	437	2,287	"
1949	507	13	520	411	2,164	"
1950	494	11	505	335	1,845	"
1951	468	7	475	323	1,767	"
1955	375	10	385	372	1,873	"
1956	290	9	299	365	1,759	"
1958	381	28	409	245	1,389	"
1959	336	15	351	286	1,495	"
1961	338	18	356	250	1,356	"
1962	376	16	392	274	1,488	"

Source: Land Operations Office records, BIA Western Navajo Subagency, Tuba City.

TABLE 2. Number of Livestock Operators (1937–62)

Year	Sheep and Goats	Sheep, Goats, and Cattle	Cattle
1937	3	2	33
1942	7	3	27
1943	6	3	26
1944	7	2	25
1945	7	3	25
1946	9	1	25
1947	8	1	21
1948	8	2	24
1949	8	0	25
1950	8	0	26
1951	8	0	23
1955	3	2	28
1956	4	2	30
1958	2	1	24
1959	1	0	26
1961	2	0	27
1962	2	0	28

Source: Land Operations Office records, BIA Western Navajo Subagency, Tuba City.

TABLE 3. Average Individual Holdings of Sheep, Goats, and Cattle (1937–62)

Year	Sheep and Goats	Head	Cattle (sheep units)
1937	148.8	11.8	47.2
1942	110.1	15.0	60.0
1943	127.8	17.9	71.6
1944	96.2	17.5	70.0
1945	61.2	15.0	60.0
1946	58.4	16.8	67.2
1947	58.8	18.8	75.2
1948	53.9	16.8	67.2
1949	65.0	16.4	65.6
1950	63.1	12.9	51.6
1951	59.4	14.0	56.0
1955	77.0	12.4	49.6
1956	49.8	11.4	45.6
1958	136.3	9.8	39.6
1959	351.0	11.0	44.0
1961	178.0	9.3	37.2
1962	196.0	9.8	39.2

Source: Land Operations Office records, BIA Western Navajo Subagency, Tuba City.

TABLE 4. Horse Holdings in Moenkopi (1937–62)

Year	Number of Horses	Number of Owners	Number of Owners of Horses Alone	Average Holdings	Permits for Horses
1937	126	42	13	3	
1942	103	43	14	2.4	168
1943	124	52	21	2.4	
1944	122	51	22	2.4	
1945	121	50	22	2.4	
1946	126	49	20	2.6	
1947	106	40	16	2.7	155
1948	128	46	18	2.8	
1949	143	50	21	2.9	
1950	93	36	7	2.6	
1951	105	39	10	2.7	
1955	103	37	12	2.8	
1956	88	34	9	2.6	
1958	37	28	8	1.7	
1959	46	28	4	1.6	141
1961	55	29	4	1.9	
1962	46	23	2	2.0	

Source: Land Operations Office records, BIA Western Navajo Subagency, Tuba City.

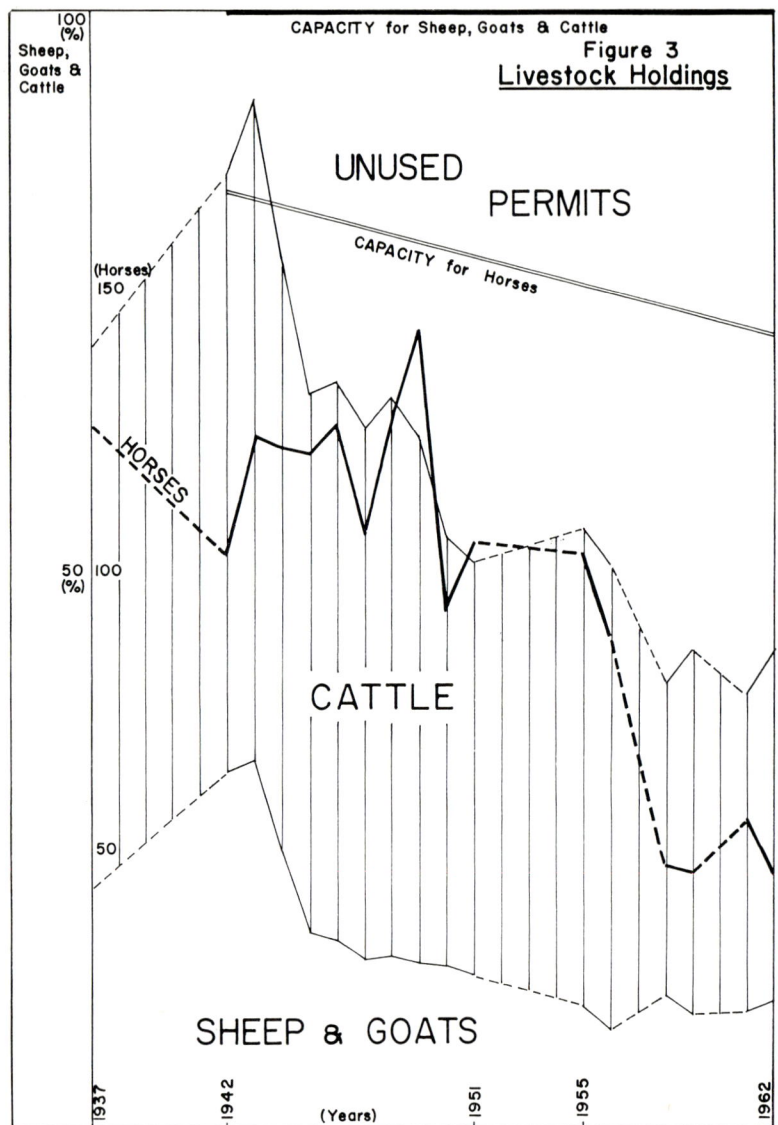

Figure 3. Livestock Holdings

The rapid decrease in sheep and goat holdings during the 1940's is not reflected in the number of operators; however, there is a sudden drop in sheepherders from eight in 1951 to three in 1955, and at the time of my field work in 1962–63, only two sheepherders were noted for the whole village. The number of cattle operators,

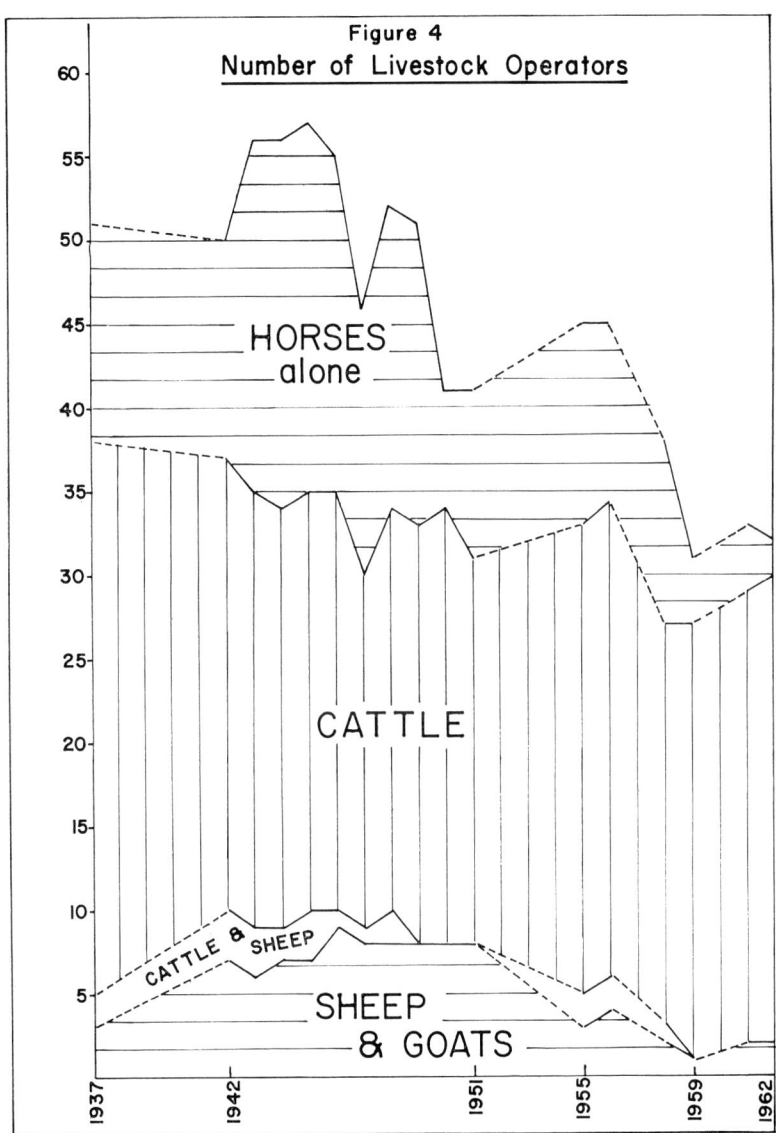

Figure 4
Number of Livestock Operators

on the other hand, showed a slight increase for the last two years (1961 and 1962).

The recent increase in the number of cattle operators is primarily because of the modern economic conditions in Moenkopi. First, while sheep need to be tended daily, cattle can graze wild during a

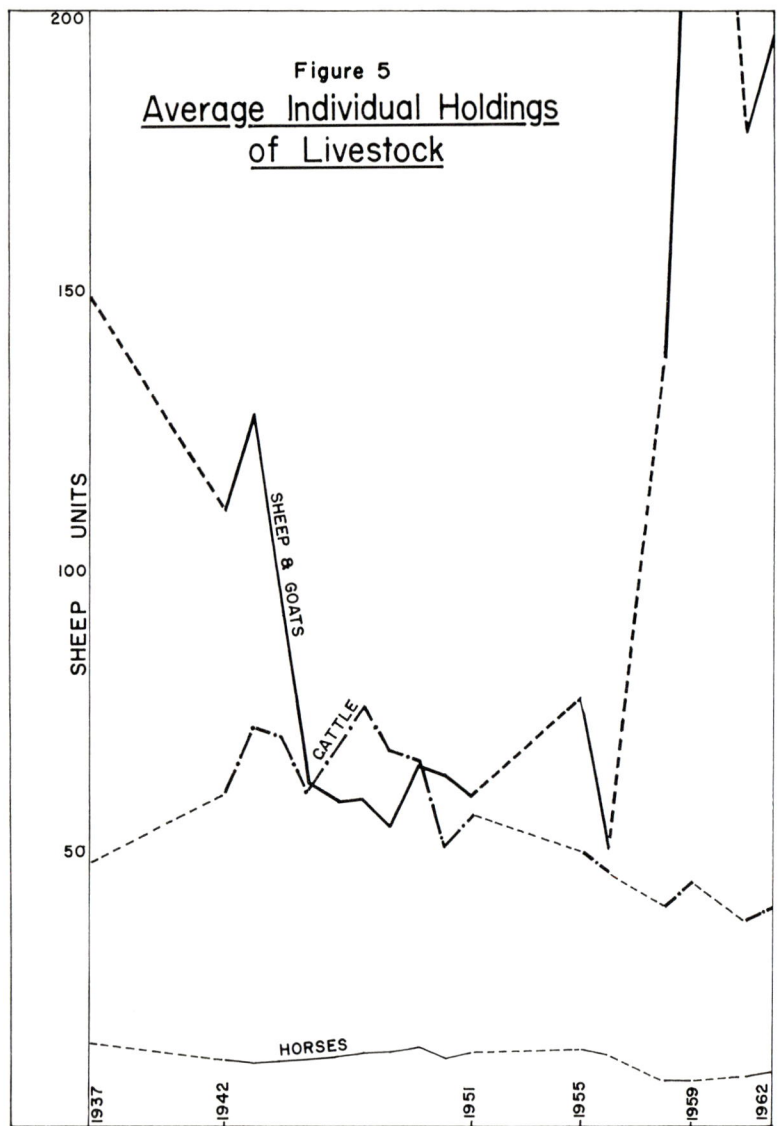

Figure 5
Average Individual Holdings of Livestock

good portion of the week (Kennard, 1965:27). Further, running cattle can be made easier through cooperation in herding groups, while sheep herding has not been operated on this basis in Moenkopi. Thus cattle-keeping does not deter men from working for wages on weekdays. Finally, as shall be discussed later, market demand for the two animals and their respective liquidity favor cattle under present economic conditions in Moenkopi. These factors induced many sheep operators to switch to cattle, while some young people lost no time in trading their inherited sheep for cattle.[8]

The government appears to be encouraging this trend, partly because of considerations of local Indian welfare and partly for conservation purposes. While sheep do not move very extensively, their utilization of the range grass can be more thorough than cattle and well-balanced utilization of the range cannot be expected as much from sheep as from cattle. Thus, while the total cattle holdings have been diminishing, the number of cattle operators has been growing, with a consequent reduction in individual holdings.

The simultaneous running of cattle and sheep has never been popular in Moenkopi. Although there were some who held both animals during the 1940's, they were the result of living in grazing camps. During the last decade, however, this practice as well as holdings of the two animals disappeared. Of the three that appear in the census for this type of holding, one belongs to Hotevilla, though grazing in District 3, while the other two adopted the Navajo pattern of herding and gave up living in Moenkopi.

Another notable trend in the last five years is the decrease in holdings of horses. This is clearly indicated in the number of those who own only horses. The latter dropped from 20 during the 1940's to 10 during the 1950's and to less than five in 1959. Their horses were saddle or wagon horses for transportation and their disappearance coincides with the influx of automobiles (see Kennard, 1965:27).

Combining all trends, there emerges an over-all decline in the livestock industry of Moenkopi, which had never reached the maximum number of permitted sheep units. Since 1958 about 2,000 SU or 57 per cent of 3,497 were left inoperative.[9] Undoubtedly, this decline is a result of Moenkopi's intensive participation in the wage economy. At the same time, one cannot deny the inhibiting effect of the cumbersome restrictions imposed on stock-holding by the government and the Navajo tribe. An old cattleman of Moenkopi

---

[8] Kennard has observed a similar trend in Second Mesa for 1961 and gives a similar explanation (1965:27).

[9] District 3 itself has remained well within the carrying capacity since 1943. Other districts which stayed within their respective limits for the same period of time are Districts 7, 11, 13, and 18 (Young, 1961:171).

mentioned that he had to butcher the sheep given him by his Navajo friends in return for plowing service, because the sheep did not belong to District 3. Such a case as this occurs not infrequently.

Discrepancy in actual stock and permit ownership, owing to the introduction of the permit system, has already been pointed out. The control by the Navajo tribe of the livestock operation also resulted in a great deal of reluctance on the part of the Moenkopi Hopi to follow faithfully the regulations in the transfer of permits either as inheritance or otherwise. Many do not take the trouble of changing titles to the permits after the deaths of original holders. Frequently, the relatives, mostly sons, run the stock under the deceased permittees' names. For the period of 20 years since 1942, only seven cases of legal transfer (mostly inheritance) have been recorded, and the rest, whenever noted, were either left inactive or kept by close kinsmen for their own use, without bringing the matter of formal transfer to the Navajo committee.

Herding Practices and "Outfits"

Herding practices in Moenkopi have shown a significant difference from the practices in Hopiland proper. In Moenkopi sheepherders have operated individually and cattle herders in groups. In Hopiland, especially on Third Mesa (Watson, 1945:74), the reverse has mainly been the case. Page mentions, "Cattle groups are not organized as are the sheep herding. This is due to the Hopi practice of not herding cattle" (1940:36). Beaglehole observed the same: "At the other two mesas [First and Third] . . . the usual practice is for cattle to graze wild, and for several men to pool their small flocks of sheep and goats" (1937:49).

Two factors appear to be involved in the absence of group herding of the flocks in Moenkopi. First, the number of sheepherders has always been small, 10 being the maximum maintained from 1942 to 1946. A few among them also tended cattle and their sheep were herded on the ranges close to the camp houses built near their cattle corrals. The rest of the sheepherders maintained ranges close to the village and used corrals either within or near the village. As among some sheepherders of other Hopi villages, their herding was a matter of daily commuting between the village and ranges.

Individual sheep herding in Moenkopi indicates Navajo influence. Among the latter, sheep flocks are tended by the flock-owning families (Kluckhohn and Leighton, 1948:59). The Navajo in the Dinnebito area once lodged a complaint against the Hopi sheep-

Plate 19. Sheep corral and a herding hut of an old Moenkopi man.

herders from Third Mesa because the latters' sheep invaded Navajo ranges, and they evaded the charges by transferring the blame among the members of the group (HvJ, Def. Ex., III, 663, 690). In Moenkopi, however, one sheepherder built his own herding camp with the help of some Navajo sheepherders and has been living there most of the time. He is fluent in Navajo, wears an "Indian hat" (Adams, 1963:80), and visits Moenkopi only on ceremonial occasions. He has even adapted the Navajo value of prestige based on the size of one's flock and boasts of his holdings to outsiders, when actually most of the villagers are turning away from sheep. Another man left the village around 1950 to live in the camp he built, married a Navajo woman, and has been tending his own as well as his wife's sheep. This man does not come to the village even on ceremonial occasions.

As previously mentioned, the cattlemen appeared in Moenkopi after the sheepherders appropriated the ranges near the village. In addition, the cattle operation required a larger area for range than the sheep. Thus they were compelled to seek the ranges farther out. In their search for ranges distant from the village, however, the Moenkopi cattlemen met the Navajo cattlemen who had already been using a large portion of the land. The Moenkopi cattlemen had to graze their stock on the Navajo Reservation in theory and

Plate 20. Sheep in the corral.

in the area already occupied by the Navajo in fact. Therefore, they could not rest in peace with the "practice of not herding cattle" (Page, 1940:36).

All the cattle operations so far recorded are in the form of group herding. The groups are formed most frequently by patrilineal relations (by brothers or by fathers and sons). The largest group, Outfit No. 1, was thus formed by eight partilineal relatives during the 1930's with a huge corral on Coal Mine Mesa. The group gradually absorbed the herds of other distant kinsmen as well as those of "friends." Smaller groups were organized on the same principle. Though much less frequently, male in-laws and such matrilineal kin as sisters' sons were also included in the groups.

The emphasis on patriliny in the cattle-herding groups of Moenkopi has been unique among the Hopi livestock operators. The group composition of sheepherders in Hopiland, for instance, does not reveal such patrilineal bias. Page mentions a sheep-herding group formed by an uncle and his nephews (sister's sons) or of friends.[10] I cannot determine if the patri- and matrilineal emphases are respectively associated with cattle and sheep-herding groups. However, the recent trend of switching from sheep to cattle in Moenkopi revealed a clustering, if for a short period of time, of

---

[10] Watson and Beaglehole do not specify relationships of group members.

matrilineal relatives, who once herded sheep independently, into a cattle-herding group (Outfit No. 5). The group was soon dissolved. The experience of this outfit, then, may indicate a peculiar difficulty of group formation by matrilineally related cattle herders.

The cattle-herding groups vary in size from three as minimum (Outfit No. 5) to 17 as maximum (Outfit No. 2). Outfit No. 2 is one of the oldest herding groups in Moenkopi (see Figure 6) and

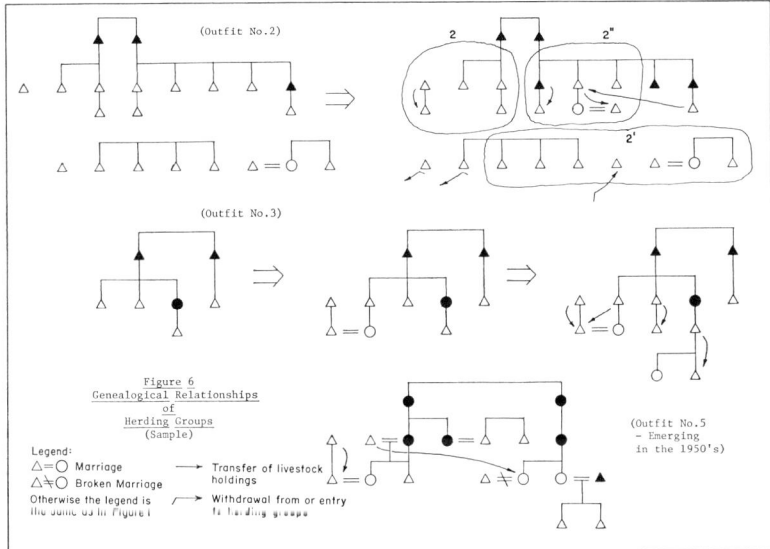

Figure 6
Genealogical Relationships
of
Herding Groups
(Sample)

Legend:
△=○ Marriage
△≠○ Broken Marriage
Otherwise the legend is
the same as in Figure 1

⟶ Transfer of livestock holdings
⤳ Withdrawal from or entry to herding groups

was begun by a man with BIA training in the mid-1920's. Their first corral was built on Coal Mine Mesa (see Map 6). As the group became larger, they increased the capacity of the corral, where the cattle sale began to be held for all Moenkopi as well as the Navajo stock in the area. However, as its size continued to grow, internal dissension broke out and in the late 1940's, it split into three groups, each of which built its own corral. This is the sole outfit that, starting around the same period with the other three, yet experienced such fission.

The other groups have been stable and while the corrals of two of them were later moved to other locations, the groups' organization remained fundamentally the same. Within each of the cattle-herding groups, however, there are occasional accretions and removals of members due to personality difference or difficulty in work arrangements, and it occasionally happens that a man goes from one corral to another, seeking the most favorable group he

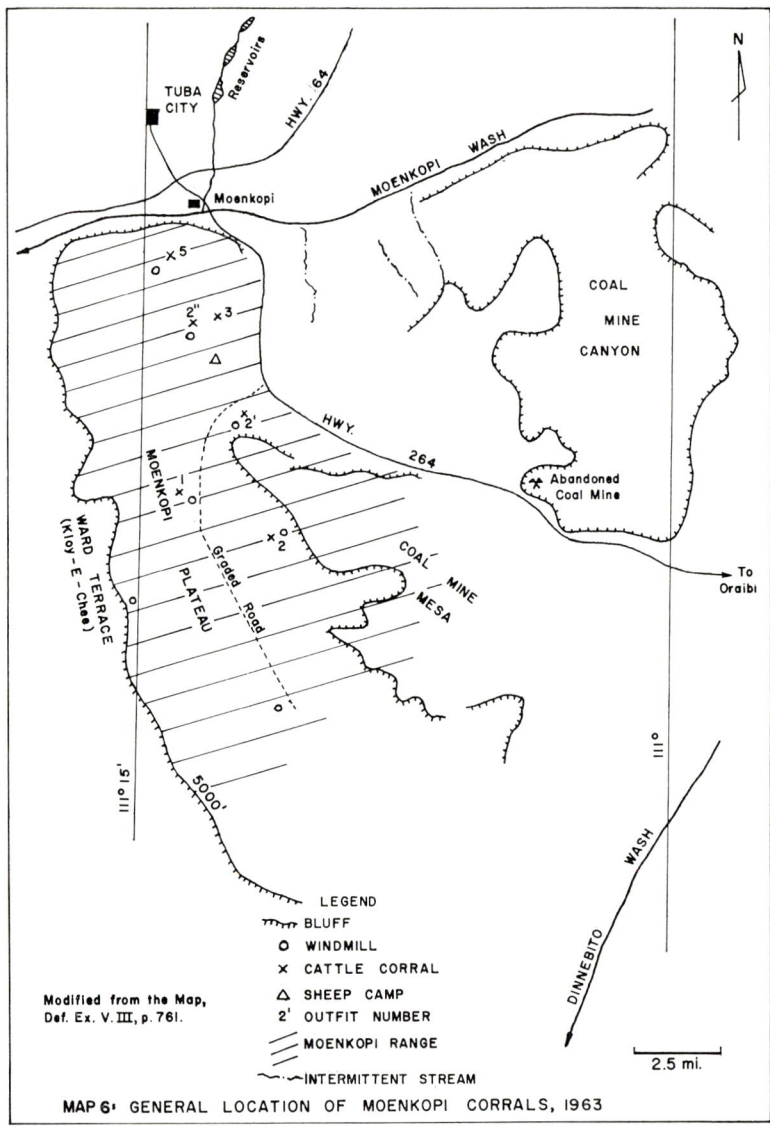

MAP 6: GENERAL LOCATION OF MOENKOPI CORRALS, 1963

can find. Those who have newly acquired cattle stock join one of the outfits already in existence. Thus, from the original four, there are now six outfits that properly belong to Moenkopi.

The locus of activity of each herding group has always been its corral, whose location was chosen with regard to the local water supply or windmills. At the present time, five outfits are distributed around three windmills on Moenkopi Plateau and Coal Mine Mesa. No outfit is now dependent on the natural water supply (see Map 6).

The group's task, now as formerly, consists of constructing and maintaining a corral, tending the joint herd, especially directing its seasonal movement to favorable pasturage within its range, and other chores (branding calves, rounding up for stock counts, conducting sales). These activities were once performed from the camps built by the corrals, where the cattlemen stayed almost all the year round, going back to the village only for reprovisioning. They even opened farms around the corrals. A few members of Outfit No. 5 built a solid rock house with a stove and kitchen. A number of men who stayed in the camps also ran sheep.

This camp herding, which developed before the stock reduction, disappeared as more labor was absorbed in wage work at Tuba City and elsewhere after the last war. In place of the camp living, it is now common for the group members to take turns inspecting the herd movement on weekends or during after-work hours. Otherwise it is left grazing wild. Thus, at present, labor shortage is a fact in livestock operation as well as other agricultural pursuits.

The competition with the Navajo herders over available range land had also existed on the Hopi Reservation. However, the Hopi herders there developed a somewhat different type of adjustment to this pressure. Page observed the following two methods of Hopi cattle grazing during his survey for the Soil Conservation Service in the latter half of the 1930's (1940:36). One is "to buy out Navajos living close [to] the village" for more range, while the other was to hire Navajo herders. The second method was especially common among the Hopi Tewa. On Second Mesa he found three cases of hiring Navajo herders for sheep herding alone, and two on Third Mesa for cattle herding (1940:46). Despite the long period of interaction with the local Navajo, the Moenkopi cattlemen adopted neither of these practices. One, who has had a Navajo herd his cattle since 1935, is originally from Hotevilla and has been a resident of Moenkopi since his marriage to a woman of the village. He is a brother of one of the two Third Mesa cattlemen Page observed.

The Navajo employee had already been herding the stock of other Navajo when the above three Hopi moved to the area by Dinnebito Wash. The Hopi decided to let this Navajo take care of their herds on his range in about 1935. This arrangement differs from the First Mesa practice in which the Navajo herd the Hopi stock on the Hopi ranges (Page, 1940:39, 42). The Hopi and Navajo herders also made the agreement whereby "what we [Hopi] would be able to carry to him [Navajo herder], we would: firewood in winter, corn, melons or flour and other groceries once in a while." When they sold cattle for, say, $600, $10 to $50 in cash or $20 worth of groceries were given to him. Beyond these, no explicit terms of the contract were made. The relationship has continued even after the stock reduction, and at the present time the cattle of these Hopi herders are taken care of by the original Navajo herder as well as by his son-in-law. This arrangement recently acquired an added significance as the Moenkopi men were progressively taken to wage work and deprived of the time for herding. In spite of the advantages, however, this is the only case of such an arrangement between the herders of the two tribes.

Sale of Livestock

Since the introduction of the livestock industry, stock sale has provided a major source of cash income in Moenkopi. Although sheep often contributed to domestic consumption as one source of meat (Kennard, 1965:25), cattle have seldom been slaughtered for sheer subsistence needs. Their importance lay in the cash income derived from them. While the local trading posts have been the major buyers of lambs, wool, and hides from the sheepherders, cattle raisers often sought their market outside the reservation.

During the 1910's and 1920's, when the Hopi cattle operation had just begun, buyers came from outside through permission of the local BIA. However, in the late 1930's some Hopi were driving their cattle to outside markets by themselves, and a California paper once reported three Hopi youths from Hotevilla arriving at a town in California after a long drive in the summer of 1935. While such a feat has never been performed by the Moenkopi cattlemen, hauling cattle to Phoenix through contracts with a Flagstaff trucker was a common practice during the late 1940's. Outside cattle buyers also entered the reservation from Phoenix or Cortez and Denver, Colorado, and sales were conducted in designated corrals. Since the stock reduction, the BIA made a special effort to improve the marketing of Indian livestock on the reservation. Finally, about five years ago, a white buyer settled in Tuba City in order to concentrate on cattle buying, and thus, many Hopi cattlemen who ceased to haul since around 1955 have been dependent on him as the only constant buyer in the area.

Engagement in cattle sales obviously familiarized the herders with price changes, and many quoted experiences with price differentials in different areas. When they hauled cattle, price quotations from a slaughter house in Phoenix were consulted in a newspaper.

At present, a lamb is said to be sold to a local trader for $10 to $15.[11] The price for wool and hide has not been obtained.

In contrast to sheep, one informant gave the price of a spring calf at $10 to $20 in 1919 and mentioned that he used to sell 60 to 70 calves in one year. Even if this was a pre-reduction year, the number sold appears exaggerated. At the present time, the same informant said that six calves a year from his herd of 15 head was the best yield he could obtain. His average is two calves a year. The price of a spring calf now ranges from $70 to $85, while yearling steers can be sold for slightly more than $100 a head.

Many cattlemen in Moenkopi mentioned the difficulty in recent years of keeping calves long enough to sell at optimum price. Two indicated as a reason theft by Navajo, while another suspected the same by his own people. Others accused the open range system of fostering such unscrupulous behavior. Generally, however, shortage in labor due to intensive wage work appears to be the main cause for lack of constant management of the livestock operation and, consequently, for the low calf yield.

The potential profits possible in cattle raising are thus offset by the low level of calf production from small herds. On the other hand, the low prices offered to sheepherders are complemented by the increase in size of an average flock (250), in addition to the traditional use of sheep in ceremonial and kinship exchange. Thus considered, it is not the cash income alone but the labor expenditure for herding, opportunities for wage work, and availability of a relatively wide and seasonally less variable market to meet the demand for cash in emergency that are also taken into consideration in the recent preference for cattle.

WAGE WORK

Since the beginning of the BIA administration in Tuba City, Moenkopi was intricately tied to this agency town through employment in government enterprise. Two conditions contributed to creating this relationship. First, Moenkopi's proximity to Tuba City involved the village as a segment of the new reservation community. Second, the agency conducted a large scale of economic enterprises which the Mormon settlers originally developed in this oasis environment. The government was thus early established in the minds

---

[11] One herder mentioned $4 to $5 per lamb in bad years.

of the villagers as the major dispenser of cash. Gregory noted such an atmosphere in 1912: "They [the Hopi of Moenkopi] ask nothing of the government except protection from the Navajo raiders and an occasional opportunity for remunerative employment" (1915: 119).

Opportunities for Wage Work

Although the churches and trading posts employed a small number of Indians on an irregular basis, it was the Tuba City Agency which provided incomparable opportunities for wage work to the Indians of the area. The agency operation of business enterprises, initiated for its own maintenance, soon developed into a large-scale operation of school farm, orchard, and coal mine.

The size of the farming operation by the agency was already impressive during the 1910's. Although the acreage of fields in actual cultivation annually varied, it had a capacity of about 80 acres of orchard and vegetable garden in Tuba City and about 250 acres of alfalfa and corn fields on the alluvial plain of Moenkopi Wash about three miles from Tuba City (FDL; TCL). The orchards were irrigated by a series of three small reservoirs in Tuba City, and the farms on the plain by the water from the Wash. The crops in these fields included fruit (grapes, apples, peaches, apricots, plums, and pears), vegetables (potatoes, turnips, carrots, cabbage, onions, beans, peas, and beets), and several varieties of corn, wheat, and alfalfa (TCL). The agency also maintained a hog farm, from which bacon was produced, but since the Navajo children showed a strong dislike of it, it was eventually sold to other agencies (TCL). Though not for outside sale, milk cows and calves were also fed within the farm (TCL). The fruit was sold either fresh, or dry, canned, or as preserves (TCL). Tuba apples became the most famous product of the area (Gregory, 1915:118). Thirty varieties of apples were planted and numerous prizes were captured in the Arizona State Fair in 1912 and 1914 (TCL). Unable to dispose of the surplus apples, the agency acquired a cider mill in 1912, and vinegar and apple cider were produced and sold (TCL).

The market for the bulk of the school farm produce included not only the day schools in Hopiland but such other spots as Leupp, Kayenta, Fort Defiance, Lee's Ferry, and the off-reservation town of Flagstaff (KCL; TCL). Gallup and even Phoenix were contacted for the sale of apples in 1914 (TCL).

During the winter, when the hay fields were vacant, the land was leased out to white stockmen for wintering their horses (TCL).

Plate 21.   Coal mine once in use by the Tuba City Agency.

Another government enterprise, coal mining, was developed about 15 miles southeast of Tuba City (TCL). Since 1904 the agency employed a white miner from Flagstaff and obtained coal initially for use at the agency itself but later for sale to local traders and missionaries (TCL).

Finally, the jurisdictional area of the agency, from Lee's Ferry to the Little Colorado, was utilized as a trail for sheep herds between Utah and Arizona, and the agency charged tolls of the sheep drovers who made use of it (TCL).

Through these enterprises the Tuba City Agency was able to raise profits which were accumulated at the "Treasury" in Washington as the "Indian Moneys, Proceeds of Labor, Western Navajo Reservation" (TCL). Thus the agency received little financial support from the nation but, economically, it was a self-supporting business establishment with a fair amount of success. The uniqueness of the Tuba City Agency in these respects had a direct impact on the number of wage work opportunities made available to the Moenkopi Hopi. In fact, the common types of employment in any reservation town of the Southwest during this period (interpreters, judges, policemen, cooks, laundry workers, janitors, housekeepers, freighters, carpenters, stone masons) were insignificant when compared to the volume of jobs offered through the agency business operations. Freighting alone included not only the delivery of agency supplies and mail from Flagstaff but also that of school farm products to all the day schools in Hopiland and Flagstaff and of coal from the mine to Tuba City.

Temporary employment was provided for the maintenance of school farms, irrigation ditches, and dams, cutting and baling hay, and harvesting, canning, and preserving of fruit.

The avenue of Hopi participation in the wage economy of the reservation town through freighting was very simple. The agency issued wagons in return for the Indians' labor on irrigation dams and ditches (TCL). The hay for the wagon horses was also obtained through work on the school farm (TCL). Once they acquired wagons, the Hopi immediately went into the freighting business not only for the government but also for local trading posts (TCL). Some managed to accumulate money capital to later buy sheep from the Navajo. The popularity of freighting was such that an agent reported that almost every family in the village had a wagon (TCL). In order to constantly provide these Indians with wage work opportunities, the agency applied the funds of "Indian Moneys" to pay for irregular Indian labor on the farms and in the coal mine (TCL). Dependence on wage work was especially prominent among the young Indians, for whom the agency requested release of the above funds on the ground that they "have no personal property and depend entirely on what they earn from day to day for a living" (TCL).

It appears that the Moenkopi Hopi were accorded a more favorable chance for wage work by the Tuba City Agency than the Navajo in the area. In a report in 1907 an agent mentioned that the Hopi ". . . supply a large part of the fuel for this school; they get more than their share of the Government freighting; they have more calls for their labor, at fair wages than they care to supply

... they are doing better each year; of late they had ceased to grumble, something unusual in a Hopi" (TCL, October, 1907). When a day school was built within the village in 1905, the agency took additional care to give wage work to the parents of the school children so that they could properly feed and clothe them (TCL).

Government employment during this period was restricted to irregular jobs. However, as the young men returned from off-reservation boarding schools, they were encouraged to occupy agency positions with the explicit aim of protecting them from reverting to the primitive ways of the Indians. Thus, in 1912 a Moenkopi Hopi held regular employment at the Tuba City Agency (TCL).

Another feature of the wage work in this early era was the number of women employees, mostly returnees from the off-reservation schools. They were hired as laundry women (TCL) and later as regular housekeepers at the Moenkopi Day School (TCL). Thus sexual discrimination was absent in wage work from the very beginning.

The comparative abundance of employment opportunities in the vicinity of the village and isolation from the railroad towns along the Little Colorado helped to ameliorate the need for off-reservation wage work. In Hopiland proper some school children in Keams Canyon worked in beet fields in Gallup, New Mexico, or Rocky Ford, Colorado, during the short summer vacations as early as 1909 (KCL). In 1913 some families from Oraibi left for Grand Canyon to work at the Harvey House there (KCL). For the people of Moenkopi, however, such an opportunity came only in 1914, when boys from the Tuba boarding school spent a summer in the beet fields at Rocky Ford and girls in "good white homes in Flagstaff as maids and housekeepers" (TCL). These jobs were arranged by the agents in charge. In the case of sending school girls to Flagstaff, the agent took the initiative and contacted the Ladies Aid Society of the Presbyterian Church at Flagstaff to locate hiring homes (TCL). The boys' work gangs sent to Rocky Ford followed the same procedure already in practice on the Hopi Reservation (TCL). The care taken by the government in sending Indians under supervision to off-reservation establishments often amounted to fearful concern. Though a Santa Fe agent contacted the Tuba City Agency for Indian wage laborers as early as 1905, the agent in charge declined the offer on the basis of isolation as well as inexperience of the Indians (TCL). When an offer was made to hire Indian students at Albuquerque in 1913, the agent declined it for the same reason (TCL).

Thus, the extent of wage work economy in the Tuba City–Moenkopi area during the 1910's was strongly conditioned by the presence of government enterprises, which placed the Hopi of our village in a far superior position in comparison to other villages of Hopiland. Inevitably, Tuba City induced many Hopi from Hopiland to either migrate or temporarily move to earn needed cash. Such a pattern of interaction is well illustrated by the Sun Chief's frequent visits from Oraibi, his native village, to Moenkopi, where he worked for the agency or for the missionary and others (Simmons, 1963:144, 145, 155, 180, 191, 203). One of the two reasons he wished to return to Moenkopi during this period was "to earn money" (Simmons, 1963:141). Even after he settled down in Oraibi after marriage, he visited Moenkopi frequently "for a few days and earn[ed] some money" (Simmons, 1963:269).

The government extended its paternalistic protection to the Indian employees on their path to civilization and was particularly concerned to keep them employed. The entire framework of the wage economy was thus tightly closed within the reservation community, and the government was the sole provider of Indian needs through wage payment.

This pattern of wage economy continued for the following decades without much change. Though the shortage in operating funds and reluctance of the central office to expand the agency enterprises in Tuba City (TCL) resulted in contraction of acreage under cultivation on the school farm and orchard, and though the successive agents made proposals to release portions of the land to the local Indian farmers (TCL) and to lease to a former Mormon settler (TCL), the school farm enterprise was maintained in its major form for a long time. Thus the wage economy during the 1920's was still dependent on the paternalistic "superintendent system" (Spicer, 1962:361). Only cotton picking in southern Arizona was now added as a new opportunity for off-reservation wage work. However, the cotton industry in Arizona, though it attracted a large number of Indian laborers, quickly collapsed with the nation-wide depression toward the end of the decade. Besides, its significance was largely limited to the people of Hopiland proper. Not many from Moenkopi availed themselves of this opportunity.

While the school farm operation did not show a remarkable expansion, wage labor was now absorbed in the construction of new agency plants, including a hospital, and expansion and maintenance of the older plants in Tuba City. Though not confirmed in the available documents, it appears as well that the Irrigation

Department engaged some Hopi labor in an irrigation improvement project during this period. The project itself was applied at that time to the Navajo Reservation extensively.

With the IRA, the Collier administration of the Indian Bureau set out on a program of reservation development among the Navajo and Hopi Indians. In order to execute the stock reduction program for the entire Navajo and Hopi reservations, a number of Hopi from Moenkopi were employed on the economic survey crews or as range riders. Construction of extensive road systems and soil and water development programs also provided new avenues of wage work through the Tuba City Agency. U.S. Highway 89, connecting Salt Lake City and Flagstaff across the Colorado River through the Navajo Bridge, was paved during this period and Tuba City was now connected to Flagstaff by a magneto phone system, "the longest in America" at the time (Adams, 1963:45).

However, World War II and subsequent curtailment of governmental funds resulted in contraction of agency activities within the Navajo and Hopi reservations (Adams, 1963:47). As a result, wage work opportunities through the agency decreased. On the other hand, the county's war efforts induced many Indians to leave their reservations through draft and enlistment in the military service. A considerable number of young Hopi served in the military during World War II. At the same time, other villagers left Moenkopi for work on newly created military installations, mainly in Flagstaff, to meet the nation-wide shortage in unskilled labor (Adams, 1963:50). Off-reservation wage work was thus secured for the Indians as a definite alternative during the last war. The trend of out-migration from the village to off-reservation towns appears to have been established through the extensive experience gained during this period.

In general, the period from the stock reduction to the end of World War II may be taken as an unstable and yet preparatory one for reorientation of the reservation economy. Although the livestock business increased during this period, subsistence economy was still characteristic and the major link with the outside market was provided through trading posts. More important, off-reservation towns were regarded as places of wage work only for those who could afford to leave the village, though their number was gradually growing.

During this period the government was conducting several research projects for the reorientation of the Indian economy, which later resulted in a multitude of legislation. The first such attempt was relocation of Indians on more fertile land on the Colorado River Indian Reservation (Spicer, 1962:207; Fontana, 1963). Two families from Moenkopi moved out to Poston, Arizona, through this project to take up farm allotments there. The relocatees have never returned to the village. More important to Moenkopi is the Navajo-Hopi Long Range Rehabilitation Program of 1950 (Young, 1955:iii; Kelly, 1953:77–81), with appropriations for such projects as school construction, hospital and health facilities, irrigation, soil and water conservation, road construction, housing, and others (Kelly, 1953:77; Young, 1955:v). The program allocated about $90 million for the period of 1951 to 1962 (Young, 1961:5). It was chiefly the Long Range Program that seriously transformed the economic structure of the Navajo and Hopi reservations and, concomitantly, that of Moenkopi.

For such a development program, Tuba City appeared equipped with a battery of natural resources. Its geographical location made it a stop-over point between northern Arizona and the Four Corners area. It was surrounded by nationally famous tourist spots, including the fact that it was in genuine Indian country. It also had untapped sources of underground water. "A sleepy Mormon village" (Colton and Baxter, 1932:64) of the 1930's was thus suddenly changing into a bustling tourism center during the last decade.

The decade between 1951 and 1960 marks a period of unprecedented growth in wage work in the Tuba City and Moenkopi area. The construction of paved Routes 1 and 3, connecting Tuba City respectively to Shiprock and to Window Rock through the Hopi District, was completed by 1961. Using State Highway 89, Flagstaff came within a two-hour drive, a trip that once took the Mormons about three days (see Map 7). Since the two routes converge at Tuba City, the latter became a final link between Flagstaff and the reservations. A sole post office, whose first postmaster was significantly a trading post manager (see Adams, 1963:276), has been in operation in Tuba City since the early 1950's. In 1954 dial telephone service was set up at Tuba City. Many Hopi were employed in the construction of roads and the placing of telephone poles. In 1955 an air strip was completed in Tuba City (Young, 1955:37) and has since been in use for mail service and emergency patient transport. With it, an air control tower was built between Tuba City and Moenkopi.

New school and hospital buildings were built during this decade. Public school plants (for all grades divided into elementary and junior and senior high) were completed and placed in operation in Tuba

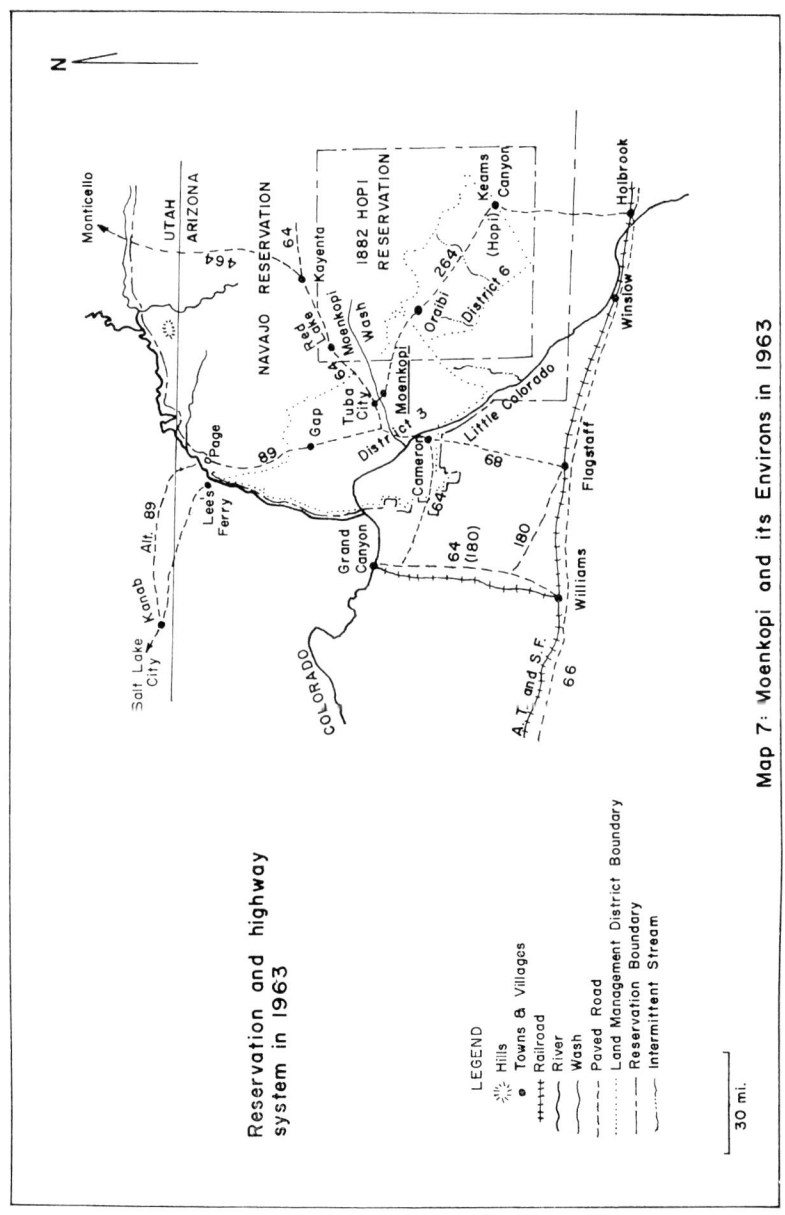

Map 7: Moenkopi and its Environs in 1963
Reservation and highway system in 1963

City in 1956 (Young, 1957). A new hospital with 75 beds was completed in the fall of 1954 and is operated by the Public Health Service (Young, 1955:22ff.). The old hospital with 28 beds (Young, 1952) was then transformed into nurses' quarters. With new schools and hospital, a series of housing constructions was carried out, one of them along a dirt street named after the radio program, "Allen's Alley." These structures were to accommodate the expanded personnel in the BIA and other services.

The Tuba City BIA, which was consolidated into the Navajo Agency in 1935 (Young, 1961:597), was re-established as the Western Navajo Subagency in 1955 (Young, 1961:602) and has been operating the offices of land management, plant management, roads, education and welfare, and others, in which many Indians are now employed.

The BIA buildings also increased. In 1963 a boarding school for the Navajo children completed the expansion of its original plant, along with new quarters for the school personnel.

Though the subagency was charged with the task of development in its own jurisdictional area of the Navajo Reservation, it also took the lead in the development of Tuba City itself and has built three water towers so far. In cooperation with the Navajo tribe, a system of sewer lagoons for Tuba City was constructed to the north of Moenkopi during this decade. A city dump was prepared to the northwest of the village of Moenkopi.

As a result of these changes in Tuba City, the agency decided to halt the management of the school farms, the operation of which had been putting a heavy strain on the agency budget (Payton, personal communication). In 1944 the school orchard in Tuba City was abandoned. The school farm in Moenkopi continued to be cultivated until 1955, primarily for hay production. However, in that year the entire 270-acre tract was assigned to 13 Navajo and one Hopi farmers under tribal control. Ten years after the war, therefore, the economic link of Tuba City with the outside world was entirely reversed and the agency came to depend more heavily on budgetary allocation from the federal government. Thus, while the employment level of the Indian labor force was raised to an unprecedented degree, the wages flowed directly from the national budget and the small areal self-sufficiency was completely eliminated.

The Navajo tribe was also an important contributor to the local economy. In 1960 a Tuba City Community Center was opened to promote community activities of local Navajo chapters, including Tuba City and Coal Mine Mesa. Its recreational activities attracted many from Moenkopi. The tribal police and court expanded their capacity during the second half of the decade. The tribe also operates a huge warehouse and a park by Reservoir Canyon. The Hopi are excluded from employment in these tribal enterprises.

With the improvement in communication and the boost in Indian income, private business enterprises appeared successively in Tuba City. No longer was the Tuba oasis marginal to outside retail business (Voget, 1961–62:245). A supermarket was located at the junction of Routes 1 (present State Highway 64) and 3 (present State Highway 264) in 1956. This belonged to the Kerley interest but was sold to a trader of Indian artifacts in Sedona, who later added a gas station. The Tuba as well as Kerley trading posts now run gas stations. Another gas station started around the same time as a branch enterprise of a Gallup auto dealer, also specializing in repair work on government and tribal vehicles. The sole restaurant in Tuba City was opened by a young Navajo in the early 1950's and remains the only Indian-owned business at this writing. A laundromat, another gas station with a garage, and a Desert Freeze ice cream shop were opened during 1963–64. A motel and trailer court have been operated by the Tuba Trading Post since the early 1950's, and the Kerley Trading Post opened its motel in 1964, to replace an old trailer court. A uranium mill, operated by an outside concern, was built about 10 miles east of Tuba City in 1958 and with it, electricity was drawn to Moenkopi and Tuba City.[12] These developments have precipitated a tribal plan for a shopping center at the junction of the two routes, which has already been publicized.

Expansion in wage work opportunities was not limited to the Tuba City area alone. The government also set out to build larger school plants at other sites on the reservations and has employed the Indians for operation of school buses, as cooks and janitors, night watchmen, etc. The Indian employees are provided with their own living quarters, whose maintenance called for the further employment of Indian labor.

The off-reservation wage market has also been growing for the Indians. In 1956, when construction of the Glen Canyon dam began (Young, 1961:269), a large group of Hopi was recruited from Moenkopi and lived in Page for the project. Cameron, Flagstaff, Belmont, Sedona, Williams, and occasionally even Phoenix were

---

[12] BIA generating plant had been supplying electricity to the government quarters until then. The plant is still in operation on a limited basis.

reconnoitered by the job hunters from Moenkopi. Many Hopi laborers rushed to the cheap housing area in Flagstaff to stay for the duration of their jobs, and a few taverns attracted these Indian laborers in town. Others sought their relatives in Flagstaff and elsewhere to stay as temporary boarders while working. Finally, a number of Moenkopi Hopi managed to create stable homes in rented houses and apartments in these towns through semi-permanent wage work.

The government has been encouraging this trend of off-reservation employment through the Relocation Service Program since 1952. The program includes employment in Los Angeles, San Francisco, Denver, and Chicago (Young, 1961:233ff.). No Hopi from Moenkopi, however, has left the village in this program yet.

Pattern of Wage Work

Until after World War II, wage work activity was a matter of choice to the Hopi of Moenkopi. Though the need for cash was clearly recognized, their engagement in wage labor was irregular and temporary. Aside from occasional jobs at the agency, all the villagers concentrated most of their time and energy on life within the village. The traditional pattern of life, farming and ceremony, dictated their employment for wages, and the Sun Chief could and did quit a job in order to participate in the Powamu ceremony at Oraibi (Simmons, 1963:191). The nature of the majority of jobs (freighting and labor at the school farm and orchard at harvest times) was of short duration, and little conflict was felt between the traditional occupations within the village and wage work in Tuba City. In short, wage labor for the people of Moenkopi during this period did not occupy a critical role in their daily existence, and a few villagers, it seems, lived without any experience in government employment (see p. 50).

A significant change seems to have occurred, however, soon after some of the returnees from the off-reservation schools assumed regular employment at the agency. Though only a select few in number, they were given quarters in the agency buildings, shared life with the non-Indian agency personnel, and drew regular monthly checks from the government. These permanent Indian employees at the agency were thus exposed to a regimented wage work pattern. Moreover, since the agency staff was very small in size during this early period, it was inevitable that the Indian employees be strongly incorporated into the tiny community of the agency personnel. Thus they tended to identify their interests with the government and to regard the government as the source of their security and prestige vis-à-vis their fellow villagers. This appears to be one of the origins of the factional cleavage based on government wage work.

During the last war, when off-reservation employment rapidly became common, many young men left the village to work in the off-reservation towns. The war expanded the labor market of the Indians beyond the reservation. The earlier pattern of seasonal work gangs, organized by the Tuba City Agency, was thus replaced by a more voluntary form of wage work which required the Indian laborers to stay in town for a prolonged period of time. Partly helped by the vocational training they received in the off-reservation boarding schools and partly motivated by the lure of town living and pressure of the conservative constraints on reservation life, the Hopi now took their families to the towns and established households there. Corresponding to the contraction of opportunities for wage work on the reservation during the war and subsequent decades, labor migration to off-reservation towns increased and established itself as a pattern of wage work in Moenkopi for the years to come.

Through off-reservation employment, the Indians came to form fairly stable relationships with their white employers, who tended to assume patronizing attitudes toward Indian employees. This appeared to apply particularly to small businessmen, whose interactions with the Indian individuals often extended beyond the realm of job performance. The Indians, on the other hand, attempted to maintain these personalized relationships by inviting them to their homes on the reservation for native ceremonies or making frequent gifts of Indian curios to their white "patrons." Many Hopi who settled in off-reservation towns maintained such ties individually and thus protected themselves from total alienation in these towns. This pattern of life in the towns appears to account partly for the absence of voluntary associations among the Indian residents themselves.

Since 1950 the job opportunities on the reservation have again expanded mainly through the Navajo-Hopi Long Range Project, and there has been a slight reversal of the flow of the Moenkopi labor force from the towns back to the village. At the same time, the Navajo laborers, some of whom formed a small settlement south of Tuba City during the 1940's, increased in number, and a labor reserve of the Navajo was established as a constant feature of Tuba City. This settlement is now designated as South Tuba by the Navajo Police of Tuba City, though it does not contain any coherent aspect of a community (Levy, 1962b).

Hopi laborers, at any rate, could now look to both the reservation and off-reservation towns as their wage work market, and this expanded horizon, along with the increased dependence on wage earnings as the source of cash, brought about a change in the people's attitude toward employment by the government. Previously, the upper group actives of Moenkopi could effectively threaten the lower group people by saying that those against the government could not hold jobs in the BIA, but the threat lost its power with the influx of wage work opportunities. In 1955, moreover, the Assistant Indian Commissioner made it clear in his meeting with the villagers of Moenkopi that irrespective of political orientation, government jobs were open to every Indian (Hopi Hearings, 1955). On the other hand, those "traditionals" who made a point of not being dependent on government checks tempered their position and ceased to insist on the same for other Hopi (see p. 62).

By eliminating the ideological barrier within Moenkopi regarding government employment, the Hopi of the other villages now came to look upon it as an area freed from "traditional" restrictions, where one could exploit a chance to live like a *Pahana* or white man. Even an old respected leader of "traditional" Hotevilla told his people to go out to live in Moenkopi if they were not satisfied with the Hopi way of life in his village. Various kinds of modern household equipment, often disapproved of in other villages, were thus openly approved in Moenkopi. Finally, the improvement in employment opportunities in Tuba City attracted numerous Hopi to Moenkopi, which presented itself to Hopiland proper as a colony of wage laborers.

During the last decade, many non-Moenkopi Hopi have come to temporarily reside in the village for jobs in Tuba City. They are mostly men, though a few families are also included. They live in the vacant rooms of their relatives or rent the houses of people who moved out for work elsewhere. To accommodate them it is now common in Moenkopi to use store rooms and *piki* houses. These people seldom establish permanent residence and never build their own houses.

Four features of the contemporary wage work pattern among the people of Moenkopi appear to characterize the degree of participation in the labor market of the northern Arizona region and, further, of the nation.

First, the vocational training the Indians received in the past is now given opportunities for meaningful application. In the past the off-reservation boarding school education emphasized vocational aspects. However, the acquired skills were often lost upon the return of the students to the reservation, where few contexts for the application of such skills were provided. In recent years the governmental projects on the reservation have increasingly demanded semi-skilled laborers, and previous training became an important asset for the Indians to be employed by the government. As shall be mentioned later (see pp. 202ff.), the Indian laborers can further use their knowledge obtained in the government schools for spending their wage incomes. These circumstances activated the latent labor force on the reservation, whose quality had been further improved through experience in off-reservation employment and military service during the last war.

With the trend toward pubilc school instruction on the reservation, the vocational aspect of curricula appears to be de-emphasized. This has been a concern of some Moenkopi residents, who tend to see the value of education only in vocational training. Even among the present youngsters, however, strong preference of wage work appears to prevail. In a test conducted in two classes of eighth graders of the Tuba City Junior High School, consisting of 53 Navajo, Hopi, and white students, the following occupations were mentioned as preferable summer employment: auto mechanic, lumber mill worker, pharmacy assistant, supermarket attendant, and farm hand for boys, and baby-sitting, cabin maid, and housekeeper for girls. Only three out of 20 boys gave farming as their choice while nine chose auto mechanic.

Second, the channels of information through which local jobs in the Tuba City area are sought out often consist of groups of related households. Thus there is a slight tendency for a group of relatives to dominate a certain sphere of jobs. For instance, one of the secretaries in the hospital has her father's brother's wife, a San Juan woman, working also as a secretary there. Her brother's wife, a Navajo, is a nurse in the same hospital. In addition, her sister and her male and female cousins all worked in the hospital previously. This nepotistic tendency, however, is constantly offset by the abundance of jobs themselves and the great amount of turnover through lay-offs. In particular, the jobs are not appropriated as "use-right" by any group of related households (Adams, 1963:101).

Job hunting in the on- and off-reservation towns is frequently initiated along this line of interaction. In the case of off-reservation employment, the white "patrons" of relatives living in off-reservation towns are often resorted to. However, the use of the State Employment Agency office at Tuba City has been on the increase, mainly owing to the participation of Indians in the trade unions of the region. I have seen, finally, one case of a job application made through the local paper in Flagstaff, a procedure only rarely relied on.

Third, the growing specialization of skills (Kennard, 1965:28) among many wage laborers of Moenkopi (see Table 5) has been accompanied by their integration into the trade unions, which include electricians, plumbers, bricklayers, carpenters, and unskilled laborers. Through the trades acquired at off-reservation schools, young Hopi join the unions and obtain certificates from them. A recently married boy was once hired as an irregular laborer on a construction project of the Tuba City Public School. He was hired by a white foreman of the crew. However, after three days' work, the foreman gave way to criticisms raised by none other than three Moenkopi laborers who belonged to the union, and the boy was fired. He later made two attempts to pass the test given by the office of the local at Flagstaff but without success. At present, union members are employed in the main on construction jobs executed outside the framework of governmental and tribal employment. Thus the barrier is still maintained by the government in protection of Indian labor on the reservation.

Unionization of Indian labor has posed a serious question elsewhere on the Navajo Reservation. However, since the unionization of some of the Moenkopi laborers has become an established fact, this question has not been a serious one in the Tuba City–Moenkopi area so far. On the other hand, because the governmental agencies still remain the major sources of employment, the process of unionization is considerably slowed down. The abovementioned boy, for instance, eventually assumed a BIA position as a janitor and thus circumvented the union problem.

Emancipation of Moenkopi laborers as free proletarians is not complete in two further regards. First, the BIA contracts with outside firms for work on the reservation give priority to the Indians by the "force account method" (*Navajo Times*, May 30, 1962; see Brophy and Aberle, 1966:70). While this places the Moenkopi laborers in a favored position, they are categorically eliminated from the jobs provided by the Navajo tribe, which primarily employs Navajo labor. The Navajo laborers appear, though implicitly, to be given priority over the Hopi in the case of outside contracts on the reservation as well. A Hopi electrician, applying for a job in Shonto, was rejected allegedly because the State Employment Agency gave the Navajo preference for work on the Navajo Reservation.

TABLE 5. Wage Earning Occupations of the Hopi of Moenkopi and Tuba City, 1962–63

Male[a] Occupations	Government	Private
Electrician	2	1
Carpenter	3	1
Bricklayer-mason	1	1
Plumber	3	
Painter	2	
Heavy equipment operator	2	
Truck driver	2	
School bus driver	4	
Auto mechanic		3
Gas station attendant		6
Boiler man	7	
Cook	6	1
Butcher		1
Road survey assistant	4	
Store clerk		3
Grade school teacher	1	
Secretary	2	
Lab technician	1	
Janitor and night watchman	10	
Irregular laborer (construction)	6	14
Unknown	3	
Total	59	31

Female[b] Occupations	Government	Private
House maid		2
Saleswoman		1
Waitress		2
Laundromat attendant		1
Baby sitter		7
Cook	2	
School matron	4	
Post office clerk	1	
Grade school teacher	1	
Secretary	1	
Nurse	3	
Hospital helper	1	
Unknown	2	
Total	15	13

[a] Independent store operators and medicine men are not included.
[b] Peddlers, medicine women, and independent store operators are not included.

Perhaps because of the fear of discrimination, the Hopi workers enjoy the reputation of being consistent, hard-working laborers. Some white BIA employees expressed an opinion that the Hopi are steadier in work than the Navajo, who rush to town with their checks to get drunk and do not report to work the next day.

Punctuality is often attributed to the Hopi and a few white workers appear to find their shop confidants more often among the Hopi. In spite of the rise of South Tuba, such a relationship still seems to characterize the Hopi and white workers in Tuba City.

The last feature of wage work in Moenkopi is the people's reaction to unemployment. In the past, loss of a job did not prompt the people to look for another elsewhere. Their labor was easily turned to the traditional sphere of productive activities in the village. The barrier of laws in the reservation system at the time, communication in the form of language and spatial mobility, education, skill, and finally, small need for cash due to the restricted consumer market, all contributed to maintaining their labor market in the limited area of the Tuba City Agency. These conditions are now either ameliorated or have disappeared.

The source of unemployment mainly exists in irregularity in the volume of employment provided by the government. Lay-offs are now frequent and do not assume seasonal regularity, though in the case of construction laborers slack seasons often fall in winter. Even among the latter, however, job hunting in remote areas reached by automobile is not infrequent. Many Moenkopi laborers now do not wait to resume work in Tuba City but seek out other employment on and off the reservation. Unemployment compensation is widely applied for and appreciated. The previously mentioned boy had to bear snide domestic gossip exchanged among his in-laws on his unemployment, which was not compensated. Drunkenness is bad not so much because it is against the Hopi value of temperament as because it jeopardizes a job.

The village provides a refuge for the unemployed, who engage in farm work. The impact of the wage economy left the traditional economy short of labor. Thus the unemployed usually direct their labor to the latter sphere. This is another feature of the structure of Moenkopi's participation in the money economy, which is compartmentalized from the subsistence economy by reservation control of the land capital.

Income from Wage Work

It is difficult to trace the changes in wage earnings by the people of Moenkopi through the period under consideration. Fluctuations in the real value of the dollar over time, in its purchasing power, and in its value in comparison with other forms of income make it very difficult to treat the wage income as a universally comparable measure. The correlation of dates and earning rates is also highly limited, especially for the earlier period. The following information is given only with the aim of providing some indication as to possible changes in the amount of wage income of the villagers.

The first type of data comes from the very early period between 1902 and 1915. The wage rate during this period is as follows:

$1.00/day (labor in the school farm and orchard; labor in coal mining)
1.25/day (freighting) ($1.00 freighting for a trader)
2.00/day (labor in coal mine with a team)
4.00/day (coal mining itself)
2.00 to 2.50/day (carpenter and stone mason)
1.50 to 3.00/week (house maid in Flagstaff; the latter wage is for a trained house maid)

For the fiscal year of 1910, the following distribution of annual wage income is reported (TCL, August 31, 1910, and October 31, 1910).

Agency personnel (non-Indian)		Indian regular employees	
Superintendent	$1,800	Farmer and laborer	$351
Physician	1,200	Laborer	398
Teacher	720	Forest guard	33
Industrial teacher	720	Policeman	241
Matron	600	Judge	84
Cook	600	Laundress	220.50
Seamstress	540		
Laundress	340		

As the data indicate, there appears to have existed parity between the wage of non-Indian employees and the Indian employees of the government. This is also shown by the fact that a white housekeeper at the newly built Moenkopi Day School was paid wages of $30 per month, which rate continued when a Hopi girl from Moenkopi took over the job. Another example is coal mining. At the beginning of the operation, the Indians were afraid to risk their lives in mining and the agency employed a white miner from Flagstaff for $4.00/day. The same wage rate was maintained when two Indians were employed for the operation later.

I could not determine if Indian labor was in reality cheap by off-reservation standards. Within the reservation, at least, the rates have been set by the federal government for the regular employees in accordance with national civil service law and, when an Indian is to be employed, his wages are set according to his job on the same standard as non-Indians. This parity might not have existed for irregular jobs, in which most of the Indians were engaged, and some gap may have existed between on- and off-reservation employment of the same nature. Even if this had been the case, the difference does not appear to have been exploited by off-reservation business nor did the Indians provide their labor for the cheaper on-reservation rate in the off-reservation market. The Navajo as well as the Hopi have never projected themselves as cheap labor to the outside world.

In regard to present employment in the governmental agencies, Brugge writes, "Federal wage scales are set by civil service law and are not adjusted to wages for comparable work in private industry, so that PHS and BIA wages would not be the same as union scales" (1965, personal communication). However, there appears to exist a conscious effort by the government to maintain the wage rate of Indian labor at the national standard. In BIA employment, therefore, hourly wages range from the national minimum of $1.25 per hour for irregular labor to $3.75 per hour for heavy equipment operation, along with additional pay for overtime. Thus annual individual wage incomes vary from $2,500 to $5,000, and in some cases, go beyond $8,000.

Despite these apparent efforts by the government, its operation at present is not large enough to realize full employment of the labor force on the reservation. Mainly as a result of this, another characteristic of wage incomes of the Moenkopi Hopi is that their cash income often includes four or sometimes more sources, each for a short period of time. One man in Moenkopi drew his wages for the year of 1961–62 from a local supermarket, the Land Operations BIA, the Forest Fire Fighting Service, and the Moenkopi Day School (Keams Canyon Agency). Sources of wage incomes of a number of the Moenkopi Hopi are thus characterized by considerable instability.

Since the local BIA sets the wage rate, private business also keeps pace by setting minimum wages, seniority rule, and incentive payment. In the local labor market, therefore, the Indian workers are protected from possible competition by the monopsonic control of the government which brings them up to the national standard.

CRAFT INDUSTRY

Despite its favorable location for the sale of native craft goods, Moenkopi never became a significant center of craft industry. In the early period local trading posts as well as village stores dealt with a small amount of craft goods (TCL). However, as more lucrative wage work drew villagers away from traditional economic engagements, craftsmen too left their industry unattended. The possibility of marketing craft work was never exploited and native arts declined.

This is most clearly seen in weaving. Along with cotton cultivation, previously mentioned, weaving appears to have been an ancient art that was once popular in Moenkopi. A huge rock hollow (*Pavaukyaoki*), east of the lower village, had long been used for weaving and is still claimed by the Water Coyote clan of Moenkopi (see Map 4). A large loom was spanned in the holes drilled in the rock walls. In 1911 a superintendent reported that "a few of the Hopi men at Moenkopi have taken up the weaving of blankets very similar in workmanship and design to the Navajo product" (TCL). However, the popularity of weaving largely disappeared with native cotton by the end of the 1920's, and in 1938 it was already a dying art. It was noted in that year that, apart from those with knowledge of the craft and others able to knit ceremonial stockings, there were only three regular practitioners of native weaving in Moenkopi (MacLeish, 1940:292) and "no more than half a dozen who produce articles for the purposes of trading or selling" (MacLeish, 1940:291). In 1962 I could identify only one old weaver in the lower segment, who produced native cotton dresses on order.

Rather a low level of native craft industry had already been observed in other arts in 1938. MacLeish states, "There appears to be little doubt that this particular village [Moenkopi] stands below the level of the others in respect to weaving and other native arts" (1940:291).

Women's crafts, pottery and basket weaving, are now also rare. One woman in the lower village did produce salable pottery for some time but has ceased to do so for the last three years. Another woman learned the craft from Elizabeth White of New Oraibi, who developed new techniques of pottery baking and endeavored to popularize it among the Hopi women. Despite repeated attempts, however, the woman has not been successful in commercial production.

Women's basket making was noted in 1915 (TCL). Recently several women of the village learned basket weaving but none to my knowledge produces for sale. One old woman in the upper segment, known for her basketry, came from Bacabi originally and is the only successful basket maker. Though silversmiths were mentioned in a report of 1911 (TCL), there is no male silversmith in

Moenkopi at present. One woman in the lower segment acquired the art during her residence among the Zuni with her Zuni husband; she maintains a tiny shop in her house and has been engaged in the craft for the past fifteen years.

The most widespread craft at present is the making of kachina dolls and water color paintings, neither of which requires elaborate skill or training. Though a few in the village are acknowledged as excellent kachina doll carvers by many villagers themselves, a majority of the male adults appear to produce one or two dolls in a year. The time for kachina doll carving is no longer concentrated on the Bean dance period; instead, the availability of time, presence of orders, and urgent need for cash appear to dictate actual production. In order to meet sudden needs for cash, it is not infrequent also to sell dolls that have already been distributed to girls in the households. On the other hand, men occasionally buy from their fellow Hopi to fulfill their obligations to give dolls to their nieces at the Bean dance. Water color paintings are as frequently made and sold as kachina dolls.

To an innocent outsider, the prices of these craft goods seem inordinately high. A doll, 10 inches high, usually costs from $10 to $15, depending on the manner of its carving and decoration. The time for its production may range from 10 to 15 hours and hence its price is not necessarily unreasonable when compared with the current minimum hourly wage. In fact, it is a low-priced commodity. Impressions of expensiveness of craft goods are thus not on the supply side but rather on their demand, which is erratic and easily saturated in the limited market of Tuba City. This inelasticity of demand, due to the narrow local market and wide alternatives of wage work, restricts production of craft goods by the people of Moenkopi to leisure hours when they are free from regular wage work. Also because of wage work availability, no attempt has been made to organize the craft industry and to create arts and crafts centers, which have been common in the relatively isolated villages of Second and Third Mesas.

On the other hand, the market of Tuba City, consisting of government employees, craft goods traders, and passing tourists, has been left open to those from other villages who travel out there to sell their products. Often they stop in Moenkopi to have their relatives contact possible buyers in Tuba City. Moenkopi children are often commissioned to sell their goods in town and are often seen visiting from house to house in the darkness of the Tuba City streets. Outside customers, in turn, come down to the village in search of craft products and are frequently disappointed to find none available in any of the homes they contact. Lack of institutionalized markets between the producers and customers of native crafts, then, reflects, in addition to the lower level of production itself, the extent of its decline in the face of an encroaching cash economy based on wage labor.

COMMERCE

Inter-Tribal Trade

It has been mentioned that barter exchanges of Hopi agricultural products for Navajo mutton have long been an established pattern of economic transaction between the two tribes. Craft goods were also included in the exchanges and Hopi beads were frequently bartered for Navajo horses. These interactions still continue between the Hopi of Moenkopi and local Navajo, who visit the village almost all the year round.

Unlike the unorganized pattern of Hopi and Navajo barter, the Walapai visited the Hopi villages in parties at specific times of the year and their visits in the past are well remembered by the older villagers even now.[13] A party of men, women, and children visited Moenkopi on horseback toward spring and summer each year, carrying buckskins and fig cakes; they stayed in temporarily built shelters or in some of the Hopi houses in Moenkopi for about a week. Each night they sang and gave dances around a camp fire, and young Hopi joined and learned their songs. Their annual visits were made along the old Havasupai trail and Moenkopi was the terminal point of their trading expeditions. Their trade included the Navajo of the Tuba City area as well (Hill, 1948:375). This type of trade continued during the 1920's but by the middle of the 1930's, the Walapai ceased to appear in Hopiland and Moenkopi. With the end of Walapai trading parties, organized inter-tribal trade entirely ceased to exist.

Barter with other Indian groups in Moenkopi is strictly limited to the Navajo at present. In place of colorful trading parties, what we observe in Moenkopi today is an occasional visit of a lone pickup truck of Santo Domingo apple-sellers timidly stopping in the plaza, or sporadic job hunters of the Sioux or Eskimos. This

---

[13] Although I could not obtain similar information about the Havasupai, I suspect they also maintained fairly regular trading relationships with Moenkopi (cf. Spier, 1928:376).

somewhat dreary picture of contemporary Moenkopi trading activities was, however, brightened by a brief period of native store operations in the village.

Village Stores

In comparison to the Navajo, the Hopi appear more enterprising in business activities. In Hopiland proper, Tom Pavatewa, a Tewa, opened a store as early as 1894 (Page, 1940:41). This may rank as the first Indian store on the Hopi and Western Navajo reservations. In New Oraibi, Sam Pawki was running a store by 1908, when there were already two other posts operated by non-Indians there (KCL). In Moenkopi one store was being operated along with one trading post in Tuba City in 1906 (TCL). In 1910 there were three stores in operation in the village (TCL). Since the three white-operated trading posts were scattered in Tuba City, Red Lake, and Blue Canyon (TCL), one may surmise that the Hopi stores absorbed a considerable volume of business in the direct vicinity of Tuba City and Moenkopi alone. The number of stores appears to have continued increasing, and in 1914 another store was opened by a young Hopi, who, it was reported, "is doing quite a business . . . [while others] do a rather desultory trading business" (TCL, March 9, 1914).

These four stores during the 1910's were, in a superintendent's description, "small concerns and do best little business" (TCL, August 31, 1910). In addition to general merchandise, they handled Hopi baskets and plaques (TCL), presumably for the modicum of tourist trade developed through the agency employees. Their main clients were local Navajo but the pattern of transaction at this time is unclear.

How long these stores lasted in the subsequent decades was not determined. In 1930, however, another Hopi store was established outside the village and developed a vigorous business activity to the fear of the superintendent, who complained that the Hopi stores tended to spread their operations into the Navajo territory (HvJ, Def. Ex. 195a).

Active store operation by the Hopi of Moenkopi ceased to exist in the post-war period, when outside business made aggressive entry to the Tuba City area through contracts with the Navajo tribe and when, at the same time, employment opportunity improved through the renewed government projects for reservation development. Between 1940 and 1960, one store with a gas station, a restaurant which once employed a white cook, and an automobile repair shop appeared and disappeared. At present, the village contains only two stores, one auto repair shop, and a shoe repair shop, each of which is increasingly under pressure from the growing involvement of the area in the general American economy.

One store in the lower segment is owned by an old man who formerly ran a bus service between Tuba City and Flagstaff. One day in 1950 the bus was destroyed when it accidently plunged into an arroyo near the village. He then turned the garage into a store (see Map 3). The inventory of this store is limited to canned meat, bottled soft drinks, Crackerjacks, and other small commodities. The net value of the stock probably never exceeds $100. Its operation is highly irregular, usually closed on weekdays but to be opened only on request. Its business is thus limited mainly to weekends and kachina dance occasions.

The other store is located in the upper segment (see Map 3). Its operator, who works in the plant management section at the Tuba City Agency, rents the store building from a villager, who himself ran a store there. Both are active members of the Upper Moenkopi Council. The store is open after 6 P.M. on weekdays and all day Saturday and Sunday. The time schedule is obviously reciprocal to the store hours in Tuba City. Because it is the only store open in the evenings, Tuba City residents, in addition to regular Navajo clients, occasionally patronize it. Villagers are more *quivi* (particular), and political antagonists of the manager family make a point of avoiding it. The store's inventory is far superior to that of the lower segment store and includes fresh meat. To a limited extent, it also functions as a communication link, but its effect is restricted only to the council families and hardly resembles trading posts which provide focal points of Navajo life on the reservation.

There is an auto mechanic in the upper segment who has been operating fairly successfully for the last 10 years (see Map 3). He also belongs to the Upper Moenkopi Council and was once a secretary of the council. His chief clients are again Navajo, whose language he speaks. His business practice is not very clear, but he does advance credit. On the other hand, his work schedule is quite flexible and months may pass by before a car is finally repaired. He is favored, however, by much less acute competition because until quite recently, there was only one repair shop in Tuba City which was operated by a white mechanic.

The shoe shop, next to the Upper Moenkopi store (see Map 3), is run by an old Upper Moenkopi Council member who seldom stays in the shop. He learned the trade at Tuba City Agency but his customers are very few in number nowadays.

Peddlers and Food Sales

As the need for cash and dependence on market products from outside increased, the villagers sought various means to satisfy these demands. Some village women are engaged in the peddling of surplus fruit, Hopi bread, tamales, and *piki* in Tuba City and, occasionally, in distant Navajo camps. During the 1940's two women in the village were engaged in selling hamburgers at local rodeo meets of the Navajo and during the Squaw dances. Though not confirmed, the issue of peddling permits by the Navajo tribe was said to have discouraged this activity. At present, Tuba City is the only major market for the few food peddlers of Moenkopi.

It appears also that during the 1930's, with the initiative and cooperation of a Moenkopi Day School principal, an attempt was made to promote native craft industry and sale of farm products to the outside residents. It came to be known as the Moenkopi Fair and, in 1939, its twelfth event was held on the day school grounds (Hopi Hearings, 1955:293ff.). Though the fair ceased to be given after the last war, individually organized food sales took its place and continue up to the present within the village. These are co-operative sales activities organized by a few women of Moenkopi. In the upper segment, the council has taken an active interest in organizing sales and men have helped women by conducting the business themselves; in violation of the traditional division of labor, they even cook hamburgers and prepare chili dishes for sale. On the other hand, no men among the households antagonistic to the council have been seen with their wives in giving actual sales. The food sales were originally planned for the outside non-Hopi residents, mainly of Tuba City, but at present the majority of the customers consist of the villagers and sales participants themselves. In the past, the food sales were organized intensively during the Christmas season to attract outside customers. Such a time preference disappeared recently and small-scale sales came to be given in increasing frequency irrespective of season. Thus, instead of increasing the cash income of the participant households, the food sales became a mechanism to recirculate a small amount of surplus cash among the villagers themselves.

SUBSIDIARY INCOME

In order to meet sudden needs for cash, the people of Moenkopi resorted to various financial sources both in and outside the village. A few medicine men who are still active in the treatment of Navajo patients appear to have been one of the important loan agencies within the village. As the fees for treatment have been more often taken in cash in recent times, their cash earning ability became a formidable asset to the people of Moenkopi. One of the two village medicine men, the father of the present Lower Moenkopi chief, deals with two or three cases a day all the year round excepting winter; one treatment seldom costs less than $5 and $10 or $20 payments in cash are not unusual. When cash is not available, he accepts Indian jewelry. His clients include the Navajo from areas as distant as New Mexico, Utah, and Colorado. The other medicine man maintains his "clinic" in a farm shed in his fields but otherwise operates on the same basis. There is one medicine woman in Moenkopi; her clients are said also to be Navajo.

Both of the medicine men are reputed for their large bank savings, and the people of the lower segment often look to them for emergency funds, ranging from $10 to $50 at a time.

Outside the village, however, trading posts appear to have functioned as loan agencies in the past (Adams, 1963:220), although the nature of this relationship between the posts in Tuba City and people of Moenkopi in the earlier period was not clarified. At the present time, trading posts appear to be rapidly losing their loan function to off-reservation finance companies, from which the majority of the village households appear to obtain credit through the inevitable purchase of automobiles in Flagstaff and other off-reservation towns. Because of the lack of acceptable securities, the Indians were unable to obtain credit from the off-reservation loan agencies until about the middle of the last decade (Kelly, 1953:79; cf. Voget, 1961–62:245; Brophy and Aberle, 1966:110–11). However, with the increase of automobile ownership by the Indians on the reservation and consequent breakdown of territorial control by the trading posts of their markets (Adams, 1963; Young, 1961: 246–47), banks and loan agencies began extending loans to Indians regularly employed or with livestock (Young, 1961:246–47). They also keep themselves well informed of the repayment records and credit standing of their Indian clients in the major towns along Highway 66, with the result that few delinquent accounts appear to exist, at least among the Moenkopi Hopi. Easy credit and installment purchase of household equipment also bind many residents to the off-reservation commercial houses.

Within the reservation itself, a voluntary credit union was formed among the Indian and non-Indian residents of Tuba City, and a few families of Moenkopi have been long-standing members. Although an earlier agent at Tuba City once declined the offer of loans to the Indians on the basis of their ignorance (TCL), a few loan channels through the government have also been popular since the Indian Reorganization Act, and three modern-style cinder block houses were built during the last decade with money borrowed from this source. The Hopi revolving funds, created through cooperation of the government and Indians, have shown an excellent record so far (see Brophy and Aberle, 1966:109).

With the increase in available sources for family financing, the importance of local trading posts inevitably decreased. Credit at the posts is now maintained only for groceries, which the villagers acquire at the posts only when ready cash is not available. At present, the most constant credit carriers at the posts are limited to the Indian post employees and Navajo Indians.

Cash income through government welfare funds on the Navajo Reservation did not begin until 1945, although both New Mexico and Arizona initiated a general public assistance program in 1936 (Young, 1961:29). In 1949, however, the state welfare program was extended to the Navajo and Hopi Indians through an agreement between the federal and state governments (Kelly, 1953:123; Young, 1961:294, 296–97; Adams, 1963:48). At present, the Keams Canyon Agency extends placement services to the Hopi of Moenkopi, whose state welfare funds are administered by the Coconino County Department of Public Welfare at Flagstaff. Of the five welfare programs now applied to the Hopi and Navajo reservations, Moenkopi has several cases of Old Age Assistance and Aid to Families with Dependent Children but none in the Aid to the Blind or Aid to the Totally Disabled categories.

Finally, since the late 1940's a few older men and women have been drawing retirement checks, derived from their employment at the Tuba City Agency in the past.

SPENDING PATTERN

All the wages from government employment have been paid in checks. It is not clear how the wages from other types of employment, e.g., trading posts and missions, were paid in the earlier period. At present, the payment of salaries in checks is the usual practice of most of the governmental and private employing agencies.

The Sun Chief tells of his savings from wage work, deposited at the agency in Tuba City (Simmons, 1963:203). This seems to have been a common practice of many Indian laborers from Moenkopi. They went back to the agency to draw their savings out as the occasion demanded. Local trading posts appear to be the only institution in the area that cashed the Indians' checks during this period. Since the checks were issued to individual laborers, the cash they obtained at the trading posts was usually kept and disposed of by these individuals, and no attempt was made to pool the wage earnings within a household under the control of any single member. Since the nature of available jobs at the agency mainly demanded men's participation, the households became dependent on male wage earnings, most frequently husbands.

Individual control of wage earnings seems to have continued in its essential form well into the 1930's. Brainard observed the following in Hotevilla during her field work of 1932:

Money income in the form of wages or salaries being a newer form of property and its division not provided for in the mores, has remained in the control of the husbands. This lack of a set pattern for the allocation of finances was expressed by one woman in her surprise at the question, 'Who does the buying for the family?' and her reply, 'Why, whichever has the money.' Two families were known in which the wives were given a certain share monthly of the husband's income, for the needs of the home, the remainder having been invested. While the pressure of community criticism would have served to prevent a man's appropriating for his own use all of his wages (to the extent of failure to provide for his family), the correspondingly changed status of the husband, as a source of money income, has become increasingly apparent (1935:305–6).

On the other hand, cash funds earned by a husband were primarily applied to the needs of his own household, and while no contribution of cash to the parental household of either spouse was ever made, purchased goods were often given to them in gift exchanges (Brainard, 1935:253). This pattern still prevails in Moenkopi today.

The exclusively individual and hence male control of cash income is no longer observable in Moenkopi. Only one woman in the lower segment mentioned to me that a man of the house usually keeps the purse string and when a woman does so, she is ridiculed for "wearing long pants." Even in Hotevilla, several women I interviewed were unanimous about their control of cash income. At least in Moenkopi, this change from male to female control over cash corresponds to the increased solidarity of the nuclear family household (see pp. 249–51).

In the early stage of marriage, the spouses appear to test out each other about the control of incomes and a period of uncertainty usually ensues. When the couple is living in the house of the parents of one or are without children, they tend to keep their cash income separately, doling out whatever it is deemed necessary to contribute. When a household of their own is established and a woman settles down with the sole responsibility of homemaking, she finally achieves control over the family finances. Wives also appear to prevail over husbands in control of cash even when both are employed. This arrangement, however, is not without occasional conflicts.

All the government pay checks are now mailed to the Tuba City Post Office (see Adams, 1963:275). With the endorsement of their husbands at home, women then cash them, mainly at the supermarkets in Tuba City or in Flagstaff. In the case of construction workers or employees in private enterprises, the checks are directly handed out to the men, who give them intact to their wives. Often men's lack of control over their cash earnings leads to domestic discord, for, weary of unremitting daily labor, they become reluctant to surrender checks immediately after their issuance and flee to town where they "get boozed up," eventually spending the night in the town jail.

Apart from the well-established couples, no sharing of cash income is practiced even among the household members. Thus an old man of a family never lets anyone else cash his retirement checks and he spends them at his own discretion. A young unmarried daughter of another family saves her earnings, making only monthly contributions to grocery purchases in the family.

The control of wage income by a married couple and by unmarried individuals is also reflected in the fact that those in off-reservation towns usually do not contribute by sending cash to their relatives in the village. Although they may bring gifts in kind and give out small allowances to the children on the occasion of their visits to the village, sending of cash, regularly or irregularly, has not been a custom in Moenkopi.

A single major difference that characterizes today's spending pattern in Moenkopi is intensive dependence on the off-reservation towns for purchases (see Table 6). In the earlier days, local trad-

TABLE 6. Expenditure and Frequency of Checks Issued by One Upper Moenkopi Household between November, 1955, and July, 1958

Item	Flagstaff	Tuba City	Others[a]
Supermarket A	$ 570.15 (31)[b]		
" B	58.00 (3)		
Household appliances and clothing			
" A	494.78 (18)		
" B	211.00 (16)		
" C	64.00 (8)		
Electric appliances A	15.17 (4)		
" B	5.00 (1)		
Auto appliances A	375.00 (20)		
" B	76.00 (5)		
Auto and household appliances	75.25 (10)		
Clothing A	112.35 (11)		
" B (?)	60.70 (6)		
Bank A	475.90 (18)[c]		
" B	198.00 (7)		
Family finance A	959.73 (28)		
" B	138.00 (7)		
Car loan	589.79 (18)		
Butane	151.83 (10)		
Oil, kerosene, etc. A	74.00 (10)		
" B	9.50 (3)		
Electricity	16.65 (2)		
Camera and stationery	(1)		
Liquor	(1)		
Supermarket C		$ 173.50 (20)	
Trading post A		790.82 (26)	
" B		1,006.36 (25)	
Car insurance			$10.00 (1)
Magazine subscription			26.55 (4)
Specialized dress shop			60.20 (7)
Record shop			21.65 (1)
Trading post C			13.50 (2)
Personal (Hopi)			(1)[d]
Personal (non-Hopi)			(23)
Total	$4,730.80 (238)	$1,970.68 (79)	

[a] This column also includes one check issued to a garage in Moenkopi, another for the service of hauling coal by a Moenkopi Hopi, and 29 other unspecified checks issued to the fellow villagers of Moenkopi.
[b] Numbers in parentheses indicate the number of checks issued.
[c] Some entries under "Bank" are not included.
[d] This check was issued to a Hopi from Hotevilla for his service of hauling rocks.

ing posts and village stores absorbed the greatest volume of commercial transactions in virtual exclusion of the off-reservation stores, which supplied the trading posts on the reservations on a credit basis. The amount of business conducted at the trading posts, however, showed a drastic decline since the war and, along with the village stores, the trading posts came to occupy a secondary position for the people of Moenkopi.

The significance of the two trading posts in Tuba City is thus limited mainly to the Navajo clients in the isolated areas of the reservation. To the Hopi of Moenkopi, their importance lies in the ease of obtaining credit; when the villagers run short of cash in a particular month, they revert to the trading posts to acquire goods on credit. Only the employees of the Tuba City Trading Company, which hires the Hopi, appear to spend the majority of their income at this store, mainly on account of the credit.

The supermarket at Tuba City occupies an intermediate position between the trading posts and off-reservation stores. The market does not extend credit, in part because the volume of business is too large to be handled on a credit basis, in part because a considerable proportion of the transactions are with passing tourists, non-Indian residents in Tuba City, and Indians from diverse parts of the reservation. In short, the great fluidity of the consumer market makes it impossible to establish the stable territorial control which many trading posts exert in defense of their business (Adams, 1963:169–70). On the other hand, the Tuba supermarket cashes salary checks for the Indian employees in Tuba City. Its store inventory is the largest in the area and can meet most daily needs.

For the villagers, purchases at this supermarket consist mainly of groceries. Though the store has a considerable stock of clothing, yardgoods, and shoes, buyers of these items are mostly Navajo. The Hopi rely on off-reservation stores for purchases of this type.

On weekends the majority of the villagers rush "to town," i.e., Flagstaff, for shopping, which is a day-long affair, much tinged with a recreational atmosphere, and invariably includes eating at Mexican or Chinese restaurants. It is not unusual for a family to spend $30 or $40 on one outing.

It seems difficult to account for this increased preference for shopping in Flagstaff rather than in the local stores. Of course, there are still a number of household appliances that are unobtainable except in Flagstaff, and their purchases there include a week's supply of groceries as well. The villagers explain that prices are higher in the local stores. Though this "price for isolation" (Adams, 1963:140) does exist in Tuba City and Moenkopi, it is a moot question if the weekly shopping at a town 80 miles distant offsets the difference and presents a more economical proposition. In fact, the frequency of visits to Flagstaff varies extensively from household to household, and one young woman, fairly sophisticated in domestic finance, mentioned that she restricts her trip "to town" to once a month because the cost of the trip is self-defeating. Thus it appears that the only way to make it economically feasible is to make a large purchase in one visit, a procedure that requires considerable planning. Unfortunately, data available on the question of planned spending is still insufficient for a detailed discussion.

Finally, purchase through national mail order houses is now a widespread practice in Moenkopi. Sears' catalogues are a common asset of the majority of the village households; some also have Montgomery Ward and Spiegel catalogues, from which dresses especially are frequently ordered.

Little data were available on the commodities purchased for cash during the earlier period. The Sun Chief mentions the purchase of groceries in a trading post during the 1910's (Simmons, 1963:203). In the early days of the Tuba City Trading Company, it was "the white man's groceries" (Simmons, 1963:203) and dry goods (mostly work pants, shirts, and uncut cloth) that occupied the largest volume of sale.

At the present time, groceries and automobile purchase and upkeep appear to share the position of greatest expenditure in a majority of the households. Next comes the purchase of household appliances (refrigerators, washing machines, gas ranges, vacuum cleaners, radios, phonographs, bathroom equipment, house building materials). These "consumer durables," including automobiles, are frequently acquired on the installment plan from off-reservation dealers, thus binding many Hopi households to the off-reservation economy. Utility payments include butane gas and, in the case of homes in the upper segment and a section of the lower one, electricity. The cost of the two kinds of utilities does not amount to more than $10 a month. For the rest of the homes, kerosene for lighting purposes occupies a part of the utility payment. Firewood and coal for heating and cooking are also obtained by purchase from a few fellow villagers or Navajo haulers. There is a trend now toward increased dependence on purchased firewood because of the restriction imposed by the Navajo tribe upon individual utilization of reservation resources (see p. 101).

One household has installed a telephone, while a few households both in the upper and lower segments subscribe to Flagstaff and Phoenix newspapers.

Differences in family finance occur in response to those of the above expenditures that can be cut back and to any other additional expenditures which may be involved. Thus the households which make extensive use of field produce appear able to accumulate savings from their cash earnings. On the other hand, completely nonfarm households, though still few in number, are forced to depend heavily on market-bought groceries. While they acquire a portion of their subsistence crop needs from the farming households of their relations, this contribution to total food consumption is secondary.

Even among the farming households, domestic consumption of the crops varies and, in many cases, the white and blue corn crop tends to be accumulated as surplus. A significant difference in grocery expenditure thus arises, depending on the extent of white and blue corn consumption.

Diverse preferences in diet are another factor causing differences in family spending. In the consumption of meat, the villagers are unanimous in preferring beef to pork, chicken, and mutton. Many families, however, consciously strive to eat mutton more frequently because it is less expensive. On the other hand, beef is bought and consumed for a short spell right after pay days. Reliance on market meat supply and prevalence of refrigerators, powered either by electricity or gas, has virtually eliminated dry meat processing in Moenkopi.

The present pattern of family income spending in Moenkopi shows a remarkable difference from that of an isolated community such as Shonto on the Navajo Reservation. Having indicated a serious discrepancy between subsistence spending and "luxury consumption," Adams mentions that ". . . rapidly expanding sources of income [in Shonto of 1952] have not been matched by any comparable development of a consumer's market for material goods" (1963:141). The Navajo of the Shonto community thus direct their "surplus income" (Adams, 1963:141) to "what White people would term luxuries, both material and nonmaterial: luxury dress, luxury ornamentation, luxury foods, and ritual activity" (Adams, 1963:140). Except for a few regular government and tribal employees, the Navajo do not save (Adams, 1963:141). Material possessions, consisting of "'hard goods,' 'soft goods,' and livestock" are still the basis of prestige and psychological security, and their conception of economic life is "a seasonal one" (Adams, 1963:140).

More recently, Kennard observed this phenomenon of "luxury

consumption" in the Second Mesa village (1965). There the traditional wedding ceremonies are conducted with an escalated volume of wedding garments, foodstuff, and other gifts of modern housekeeping items (1965:28). Ceremonial activities are increased in frequency and duration (from one day to two days for each dance), with an apparent change in the emphasis of these ceremonies from religious (placatory and procreative) to secular and recreational aspects (1965:29). Kennard mentions further that "It almost seems as if the 'waste not' values of a culture that survived precariously despite recurrent famines . . . have been supplanted by those of the affluent society" (1965:29).

Luxury spending is not absent in contemporary Moenkopi, especially in the lower segment. A number of houses now own more than one transistor radio each. An unwed mother, who maintains a household in Lower Moenkopi with her sister and father, purchased a stereo-phonograph with savings from her welfare payments. A young married couple owns a TV set, which has been stacked away in their home in Lower Moenkopi for several years. Another young man had bought a TV set and an electric hair drier for his wife, who had been living in Kayenta for employment reasons. Television reception is possible in Kayenta. Recently, however, the two decided to move to Tuba City, where the man managed to obtain government housing. The wife quit her job in Kayenta and upon their move to Tuba City, the TV set was put away, for reception in Tuba City is very difficult. A few households in the upper segment now have more than one car each, of which usually one is disabled or nearly so. The prevalence of tape recorders in Moenkopi is almost disgusting to a fieldworker. A battery-run short wave radio is kept in the house of the chief of Lower Moenkopi; he also has two tape recorders and two transistor radios. One may also argue that a 1963 Oldsmobile sedan is a luxury item for the chief. Numerous abandoned automobiles alongside the reservation roads indicate the haphazard manner of maintenance. Finally, as Adams pointed out (1963:139), the exemption from payment of taxes, rent, water, public school tuition, medical treatment, and others uniformly alleviate the burden of basic expenditure for the Moenkopi residents. As a result of this, spending efforts of the villagers are often directed to the purchase of those items which are disconnected from the traditional pattern of life and carry, in the background of an ancient pueblo, a note of luxuriousness.

In spite of these similarities, there are significant deviations from the Shonto or Second Mesa communities in the manner of spending by the people of Moenkopi. First, spending in ceremonial activities has been overtly or covertly discouraged and the sponsors of kachina dances are becoming scarce. The Basket dance, in which a quantity of contributed goods is distributed to the audience, has not been seen in the village for more than a decade. Strictly village kachina dances are now limited to two, one by each segment. Moreover, the decrease in ceremonials in Moenkopi is explicitly associated with the need of cash for daily household management. One woman in the upper segment mentioned that she simply could not afford to give a Basket dance.

Second, the notion of "frugality" or "thrift" is now meaningfully related to the cash economy in which Moenkopi is involved. Thus, while many households have been in debt to one or two loan agencies, some households have succeeded in saving. The extent of household saving is difficult to determine and ranges from a meager $25, forgotten to be withdrawn, to $50,000 by the medicine man of the lower segment. Apparently some of the saved cash is hoarded, and a rumor runs that one old woman keeps savings from her relief payments in an empty coffee can (see Kennard, 1965:26). Since the cash income varies little between the two segments of Moenkopi, I suspect the lack of public utilities in the lower segment may help its residents to save more. The surplus cash is rarely redirected to interest-generating purposes. No one to my knowledge owns investment stocks.

Expressed motives for saving are also varied and yet all include an element of future expectation in the form of house improvement, purchase of automobiles or tractors, and education of children beyond public schools. Many villagers now take education of children quite seriously. At the time of my field work, only one girl of school age was kept out of school by the wish of her parents. Though basic expenditure is incurred by the federal government, the villagers are also aware of economic responsibility of education in clothing children and providing opportunities to further their educational careers in off-reservation schools. With the possibility of attaining higher economic goals, inculcated through previous educational experiences, they appear to deviate from reinforcing the traditional values through luxury consumption but attempt frugal spending and produce savings in order to realize the objectives that were once unattainable. No doubt, with the involvement in the off-reservation consumer market, the level of aspiration for improvement of economic status has risen in an unprecedented degree since the 1950's, and the availability of such basic utilities as electricity, running water, and a sewage system has made domestic investment in households significant. A shiny steel sink, once an isolated piece of furniture, no longer presents a disconcerting sight in a vacant dining kitchen when it is now organically connected to a refrigerator and a gas range in the same room.

The increase in household investment has another important consequence. Since the efficient use of consumer durable goods requires further spending, e.g., electricity, gasoline, propane gas, and, in the case of the homes belonging to the Upper Moenkopi Council water system, water, a new demand for cash is generated and further binds the villagers to the cash economy. The economic reason on which some villagers in the lower segment base their refusal to accept electricity is thus not ill-founded because it is not a simple matter of "paying the light bill." Public utilities in general have this aspect of mutually reinforcing expansion of spending contexts.

Finally, the possibility of urban conveniences in a society of fellow tribesmen, in addition to enlarged wage work opportunities, induced a few migrant families from off-reservation towns to return to the village. Two of them built new, sturdy, cinder block homes across Highway 264, contrasting with the older homes in the village but contributing to the increase of community wealth in Moenkopi. Since there is a competitive element in the attitude of the villagers toward adoption of alien cultural items in Moenkopi (see p. 95), the existence of these homes appears further to encourage them to vigorous participation in the cash economy.

In contrast to spending on consumer durables, investment in productive capital goods has been limited to tractors and corn grinding machines. This is chiefly due to the governmental control of land and livestock as previously discussed. Given the organizational framework of farming and grazing economics at present, the possible returns from investment in these sectors of the economy cannot equal the return of enjoyment obtained from comfortable homes equipped with modern household goods. The present cash spending pattern of Moenkopi, then, is largely a consequence of the economic structure of the reservation.

The increase in "social wealth"[14] has thus provided an im-

---

[14] "Social wealth" includes not only such material wealth as roads, running water, sewer systems, electricity, and other public utilities, but also such intangible wealth as schooling and job experience and skills.

portant context in which the increase in cash income can be directed to the improvement of the living standard. Prior to the installment of the community sewer system in the upper segment, it was common to observe cinder block houses juxtaposed with shabby outhouses. Now these latter are gone.

Perhaps in Moenkopi today there exist more households in debt to loan agencies than those with savings. It may also be argued from this that the spending spree of the Moenkopi households is a "demonstration effect" (Bauer and Yamey, 1957:138; Firth and Yamey, 1964:382), resulting from intensive contact with the off-reservation consumer market.

It cannot be argued, however, that the present spending pattern in Moenkopi is deleterious to the economic development of the community. Kennard's Second Mesa villages appear to provide an instructive contrast in this regard, for these villages are without the basic utilities that Moenkopi is now equipped with. Hence the increased cash is often squandered on traditional ceremonies in Second Mesa. The same may apply to the "luxury spending" of Shonto. The latter in 1952 was linked to the off-reservation labor market through employment on the Santa Fe Railway, but its consumer market was isolated and limited under the control of a local trading post (Adams, 1963:141, 145). The Second Mesa villages of 1961 had access to the outside market through improved road systems (Kennard, 1965:27), but were without significant community wealth. Our village shows *de facto* isolation from the off-reservation labor market by major reliance on the BIA and other governmental employment. It is, however, irrevocably involved in the off-reservation consumer market. Finally, it possesses indispensable utilities for home investment, which demands further involvement in cash economy. In the consumption sector, then, Moenkopi appears far more integrated into the national economy than the other communities in comparison.

ECONOMIC INTEGRATION AND INTERACTION OF SUBSISTENCE AND MONEY ECONOMIES

Throughout the history of Moenkopi, two sets of factors conditioned economic change. The first set consists of the factors common to a majority of the communities of the Navajo and Hopi reservations. To begin with this set, the Moenkopi area has been marginal in regard to the national economy (see Spicer, 1962). Isolation from the developing American economy resulted from the generally inhospitable desert environment, the absence of attractive mineral resources amenable to small-scale extraction, the difficulty of access to major towns that eventually developed in the environs, and a labor force couched in an alien cultural background. It would have required a great amount of investment for any industry in this area to be economically successful in the national competitive market. The plantation could have been one such alternative, had the land possessed potential for specialized agricultural or mineral production and had continuing demand for possible products existed (see Geertz, 1963). Neither of these conditions obtained in Moenkopi. Native commercial or livestock operations also held out small promise. Consequently, except for the initial effort by the Mormons to develop the area in a strategy of commercial and subsistence agriculture, no serious attempt occurred to make the land pay. The marginality of this land thus protected the area from the encroachment of private industries and perpetuated a subsistence economy in Moenkopi.

Second, the government controlled land capital through the reservation system. Irrespective of the concrete measures taken by the government for protection of the Indian land, it was obvious that not only did the exclusion of outside capital eliminate the possibility of integration of the areal economy into the national structure, but also no incentive was created for operational expansion by the indigenous population in response to the extent and strength of a local market. The locus of initiatives for economic integration thus shifted to the government. At the same time, the Indians, legally unable to sell the land by themselves, had only their labor to exchange for cash.

The final factor of the first set is contact with the national consumer market. Since the imposition of the reservation system, the government has allowed the intrusion of consumer products from the national economy to the Indian communities. In fact, it even fostered and encouraged such a tendency as a means of civilizing the Indians. If the consumer market of the Indians was in any way isolated from that of the nation, it was primarily because of the restricted Indian cash income, difficulty of communication, lack of mobility, structure of the mercantile market, paucity of spending contexts, and because of the conscious control by the government over the trading business on the reservation. In any event, the Indians have been in contact with the consumption sector of the national economy either through licensed trading posts on the reservation or retail stores outside it. It was this contact that prompted the Indians to divert their labor from subsistence activity to money-procuring occupations. In view of the strategy of economic development and integration, then, the Indian consumer market loomed as an important variable. On the marginal and government-controlled reservation, the consumption life of the indigenous population became a prime mover of economic change (see Murphy and Steward, 1956), and the government emerged as an agent that manipulated it on the basis of cash income, communication, and spending context.

To summarize, the reservation system imposed on the marginal area excluded land capital and alternatives of commercial production as means of economic integration of the community and thus provided the basis for a persistence of subsistence economy. There remained, however, Indian labor, cash income derived from its sale, and consumption of that income as variables manipulated by the government. The condition of the Moenkopi "dual" economy was, then, set in allocation of labor between the two economies and contexts for consumption of the output therefrom.

While this condition might be universally present on the reservation, Moenkopi was endowed with a second set of factors which uniquely facilitated economic change in the community. The first factor in this second set is its proximity to the "reservation community" (Spicer, 1962:353–54) of Tuba City. If "differentiation of White contacts" is one of the factors for varying degrees of culture change in the Indian communities of the Southwest (Adams, 1963:93, 146), Moenkopi, of all the villages of Hopiland, came under the strongest acculturative influence that emanated from Tuba City. Since the majority of governmental projects were initiated from this reservation community, Moenkopi became their first recipient. This applies most clearly to its participation in wage work. Because of the availability of wage work in Tuba City, on-reservation employment was often more important to Moenkopi than off-reservation employment; hence, it was difficult to maintain the spatial dichotomy between the traditional productive activities in the village and nontraditional ones outside it (see McFeat, 1962). The village was the base for both types of economy.

The second factor is the colonial role of Moenkopi to Old Oraibi and other villages of Third Mesa. Its secular and exploitative orientation, as represented in the absence of clan houses and important ceremonies and in the capacity to transfer the "sacred" sphere of life to its mother village of Oraibi, helped adjust the community to the dictates of changing economic conditions. The structural position of Moenkopi vis-à-vis Third Mesa villages created in Moenkopi an accommodative "stance" to the outside economy.

The final characteristic of Moenkopi is its minority role on the Navajo Reservation. In addition to its colonial role, its location on the reservation of an enemy tribe placed the villagers in a competitive position with the Navajo and tended not only to tinge their economic behavior with aggressiveness but also to encourage cooperation with the government, which they regarded as their protector from the Navajo. This made them comparatively more receptive to economic opportunities present in the area.

To summarize, economic integration of Moenkopi depended not only on the condition of the "dual" economy, manipulated by the government through the reservation system, but also on these three unique structural features of the village.

With these preliminaries, we shall now summarize the characteristics of interaction of the two economies and degrees of integration of the Moenkopi economy with that of the nation. The data previously presented enable us to discern three periods of the village economy in terms of distinct modes of governmental resource control, economic initiatives taken by the government, respective volumes of the three major productive activities in the village and their mutual relationships, and, finally, contact with the national labor and consumer market (see Figure 7 and Table 7).

The first period of the "dual" economy (1903–35) was dominated by the subsistence sector, and only surplus labor from farming was directed to wage earning. Wage work was limited to government enterprise in the reservation community of Tuba City and the jobs were irregular and temporary. Though the school farm and orchard were oriented toward production for an outside market, the profit incentives in this operation were weak, and no attempt was made by the government to exploit the Indian wage earners through company stores. It was thus far from a plantation, but rather one of its main objectives was to give the Indians a chance to earn cash.

The consumer market, supported by Indian wages, was firmly controlled by local trading posts and village stores, and seldom if ever did the villagers make direct purchases in off-reservation stores. Isolation of the consumer market partly resulted from the limited amount of cash available to the Indians. The isolation of the market also created a small demand for subsistence crops which the local traders bought from the Moenkopi farmers, thus reinforcing the need for farming.

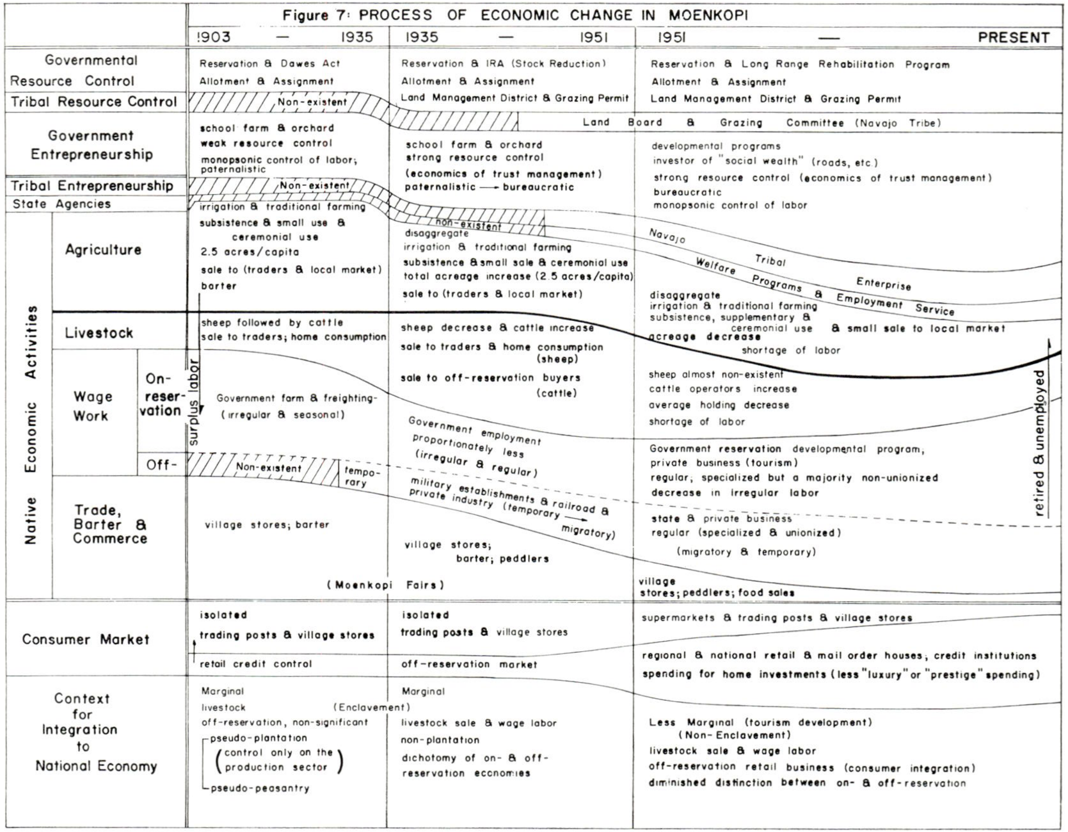

216 MODERN TRANSFORMATIONS OF MOENKOPI PUEBLO

Figure 7: PROCESS OF ECONOMIC CHANGE IN MOENKOPI

		1903	1935	1935	1951	1951	PRESENT
Governmental Resource Control		Reservation & Dawes Act		Reservation & IRA (Stock Reduction)		Reservation & Long Range Rehabilitation Program	
		Allotment & Assignment		Allotment & Assignment		Allotment & Assignment	
Tribal Resource Control		Non-existent		Land Management District & Grazing Permit		Land Management District & Grazing Permit	
Government Entrepreneurship		school farm & orchard weak resource control monopsonic control of labor; paternalistic		school farm & orchard strong resource control (economics of trust management) paternalistic → bureaucratic		Land Board & Grazing Committee (Navajo Tribe) developmental programs investor of "social wealth" (roads, etc.) strong resource control (economics of trust management) bureaucratic monopsonic control of labor	
Tribal Entrepreneurship		Non-existent		Non-existent		Navajo Tribal Enterprise	
State Agencies		irrigation & traditional farming		disaggregate irrigation & traditional farming subsistence & small sale & ceremonial use total acreage increase (2.5 acres/capita) sale to (traders & local market)		Welfare Programs & Employment Service disaggregate irrigation & traditional farming subsistence, ceremonial use, supplementary & small sale to local market	
	Agriculture	subsistence & small use & ceremonial use 2.5 acres/capita sale to (traders & local market) barter				acreage decrease	
Native Economic Activities	Livestock	sheep followed by cattle sale to traders; home consumption		sheep decrease & cattle increase sale to off-reservation buyers (cattle)		shortage of labor sheep almost non-existent cattle operators increase average holding decrease shortage of labor	
	Wage Work — On-reservation / Off-	Government farm & freighting (irregular & seasonal) surplus labor		Government employment proportionately less military establishments & railroad & private industry (temporary & migratory)		Government reservation developmental program, private business (tourism) regular, specialized but a majority non-unionized decrease in irregular labor state & private business regular (specialized & unionized) (migratory & temporary)	
		Non-existent	temporary				
	Trade, Barter & Commerce	village stores; barter		village stores; barter; peddlers (Moenkopi Fairs)		village stores; peddlers; food sales	
Consumer Market		isolated trading posts & village stores retail credit control		isolated trading posts & village stores off-reservation market		supermarkets & trading posts & village stores	
Context for Integration to National Economy		Marginal (Enclavement) livestock off-reservation, non-significant [pseudo-plantation control only on the production sector pseudo-peasantry]		Marginal livestock sale & wage labor non-plantation dichotomy of on- & off-reservation economies		regional & national retail & mail order houses, credit institutions spending for home investments (less "luxury" or "prestige" spending) Less Marginal (tourism development) (Non-Enclavement) livestock sale & wage labor off-reservation retail business (consumer integration) diminished distinction between on- & off-reservation	retired & unemployed

TABLE 7. Income Distribution of the Hopi and Navajo Indians

Year	Agriculture		Livestock
Hopi		(per cent)	
1936	44	(56)[a]	12
1942	22	(57)[a]	35
1949			
1952		(25)[a]	
1955			
Navajo			
1940	14	(56)[a]	44
1949			
1952		(46)[a]	
1955		(11.1)[a]	
1955 (Shonto)	1.3	(17.6)[a]	16.3
1960		(9.5)[a]	
1961–62 (Rainbow Bridge)	2	(50.2)[a]	48.2

Year	Wage	Welfare	Arts and Crafts	Other	Per Capita Income	Source
Hopi		(per cent)			(dollars)	
1936	40				150	1
1942	43				70	2
1949					67	3
1952		(75)[b]			216	4
1955					212	3
Navajo						
1940	30		9	3	82	5
1949					105	3
1952		(53.9)[b]			337	4
1955	74.6	7.2	5.6	1.5	450	6
1955 (Shonto)	66.5	8.2	4.3		290	6
1960	71	14.7	1.2	3.6	521	5
1961–62 (Rainbow Bridge)	36.4	13.4			398	7

[a] Numbers in parentheses represent the total percentage of agriculture and livestock.
[b] Numbers in parentheses represent the percentage of remainder of income sources.

Sources: 1. Human Dependency Survey, 1939.
    2. Long Range Project, 1944; Thompson and Joseph, 1944:25.
    3. Kelly, 1957:73.[1]
    4. Kelly, 1953.
    5. Young, 1961:213, 228–29.
    6. Adams, 1963:146, 148.
    7. Shepardson and Hammond, 1964:1037.[2]

[1] The size of a Hopi household is assumed to be six while that of a Navajo household is five.
[2] BIA and USPHS services are not included.

The livestock industry began to rise during this period and the products were brought to the national market through the intermediary of trading posts and itinerant off-reservation buyers. However, the industry was highly segregated from its national counterpart because of reservation control of Indian ranges.

To sum up, Moenkopi economy in the first period was mainly closed within the limits of the reservation. The role of the government was dominated by an entrepreneurial aspect. The off-reservation economy was in contact with Moenkopi only through such "intercultural role" players as the government and traders. Otherwise, it was bereft of significance to the villagers.

A similar condition of the "dual" economy lasted into the second period (1935–51). Though farm acreage expanded considerably, the per capita volume indicates that the expansion was due to an increase in the village population.

During this period, however, two sources of cash income, livestock and on-reservation wage work, underwent serious changes. First, through the stock reduction program the government set out on a policy of more stringent "economics of trust management" (Kelly, 1957:76). The incentive for livestock operation, through which feeble contact was maintained with the outside economy, was now dampened by the new conservation measures on grazing resources. Consequently, the industry, which was germinally oriented to specialized economic production and hence incorporation into the national market through product distribution, degenerated into an activity only supplementary to wage work.

Second, as a result of World War II, there was a reduction in the volume of government wage work on the reservation, while at the same time the flow of the Indian labor to the off-reservation labor market increased. Temporary off-reservation employment was then followed by a trend for migrants who found stable employment to settle down in off-reservation towns. The dichotomy of the "stay-at-homes" and migrants (Dozier *et al.*, 1957:159ff.) thus emerged during this period. The loss of a portion of the village labor force through migration, however, did not affect the character of "dual" economy because their contribution to the village economy in either labor or income was nil. Due to individual control of cash income, the migrants, once settled in off-reservation towns, seldom sent any of their income back to the village.

The consumer market was as isolated as in the previous period. Though the villagers visited the off-reservation towns on occasion, the frequency of their visits remained low and was seldom for the purpose of shopping. The dominance of subsistence economy continued.

The final period (1951–62) represents a partial breakdown of the "enclavement" (Spicer, 1962) that characterized the two previous periods and saw irreversible displacement of the subsistence economy.

During this period per capita acreage of farm land decreased to one acre, too small for survival of a single individual. Intensive participation in the wage economy resulted in a labor shortage in the subsistence sector. The flow of labor was reversed and it was the surplus labor from wage work that was applied to farming. Apart from the unemployed, the chief labor force in farming consisted of those incapable of wage work, i.e., the retired old men. A growing demand for cash brought a quantity of farm products to sale. This resulted in a shortage of food crops which was remedied by purchase. Decrease in continuous demand for subsistence crops due to greater accessibility to market products left the entire complex of farming technology extremely conservative. This, in addition to a shortage of farm labor, left farm holdings in a state of fragmentation, and many plots remained unoperated. Though the capital basis of farming was protected in the framework of the reservation system, a point of no return was reached and cash economy became irreversibly dominant over subsistence farming in this brief period of ten years.

Persistence of subsistence agriculture at present assumes small economic significance. Upon the basis of legal compartmentalization of the land capital for the traditional economy, it continues, apart from supplementing the wage income, to provide ceremonial foodstuff unobtainable in the outside market. It is thus an activity to maintain tribal identity in opposition to the Navajo farmers in the area (see Table 8).

TABLE 8. Occupational Differentiation of Households in Moenkopi, 1962–63

	Upper Moenkopi	Lower Moenkopi	Total
Farming–livestock operation– wage work	7	10	17
Farming–livestock operation	3	4	7
Farming–wage work	26	22	48
Farming	3	2	5
Wage work	12	7	19
Unemployed	5	6	11
Total	56	51	107

Bureaucratic restrictions on the livestock operation left this industry in as much an isolated position as subsistence farming, although greater liquidity of livestock came to be more appreciated and induced more individuals to enter the cattle business.

The degree of integration of present-day Moenkopi economy into the national economy is most cogently indicated in the volume and quality of wage workers. First, improvement in the quality of the village labor force through military experience, off-reservation employment, and training in off-reservation schools and local BIA offices has tended to weaken the dichotomy between on- and off-reservation employment as economic alternatives. Unionization of skilled and unskilled laborers has brought them into the national labor market. While these represent the integrative aspect of the Moenkopi work force, a few protective measures adopted on the reservation and the psychological security provided in the life of the village tend to restrict the movement of the Moenkopi work force on the reservation. Off-reservation employment still poses a hurdle in social and psychological terms, though the improvement in communication mitigated the threat of alienation from the village. Thus, as soon as the employment opportunities were improved in Tuba City and other newly established reservation communities, a modicum of labor force flowed back to the village from the off-reservation towns.

The reservation consumer market of the villagers merged with that of the off-reservation market during this period. Territorial control by the trading posts through the credit system (Adams, 1963) broke down and the village stores, few in number, continued only nominal existence. The villagers became dependent on a supermarket on the reservation or on retail stores and loan institutions outside. This interaction is maintained by the increase in household investment, which has created a sustained demand for cash and for purchase of goods in off-reservation towns.

Both phenomena are chiefly the result of the development project by the government, which increased the "social wealth" of the Indian country and provided the context for household investment. As communication improved and Indian wage income increased, private business has been induced into the reservation community to absorb the burgeoning consumer demand through contracts with the government and the Navajo tribe. The opportunities for a better life are now assured within the village itself and this again has encouraged some migrants to return to the village. The distinction of life patterns on and off the reservation have decreased in this respect as well.

In sum, Moenkopi today displays a trend away from "enclavement." This consists in the growth of man-power capable of participation in the national wage labor market and the growth of household capital, demanding further spending in the national consumer market. In the process of this integration, the government played the role of entrepreneur and monopsonic buyer of Indian wage labor and that of "social investor" on the reservation.

Spicer has argued that the enclavement of Indian reservations in the Southwest is a consequence of isolation from the national economy due to marginality of their land, labor, and resources (1962:585). The absence of a labor intensive, capital extensive plantation economy in this part of the United States further contributed to its isolation by eliminating the possibility of creating a part-society peasantry (Wolf, 1957). However, as the national economy developed, its demand for labor reached even the Indian reservations. This appears to be the stage of Shonto or Second Mesa, as compared previously. In these communities the consumer market is either isolated or not entrenched enough to induce further involvement in the national economy. Contexts for spending are limited to "luxury" goods. It is clear, then, that the role of the government as entrepreneur and "social investor" is indispensable in providing a way out from such isolation of marginal Indian reservations.

Although the above describes necessary conditions of the process of economic change, they cannot be sufficient ones. It can be argued, for instance, that despite the governmental efforts for integration, the population might remain impassive to the new opportunities unless under political coercion. The trap might not work because, for socio-political reasons, the people might refuse to take advantage of "civilization." Such a situation has been present in Hopi society as shown in the "conservative" faction of the tribe.

In the case of Moenkopi, however, the particular setting of the community disposed the population to respond to and to take advantage of these opportunities. Its geographical proximity to Tuba City exposed Moenkopi to a maximal number of contacts with the white world in this part of the reservation. The colonial role of Moenkopi made the population receptive to economic advantages and never brought the economic aspect of the "traditional" *vs.* "progressive" cleavage into serious dispute. The cleavage between upper and lower segments of the village allowed the households individually to take part in the wider economy, while retaining a tie with the communities in Hopiland (see pp. 95ff.). The competition with the Navajo favorably oriented the Hopi to the governmental projects. To conclude, in addition to the government as entrepreneur and "social investor," it was the unique setting of Moenkopi that contributed to achieving the above-described mode of integration into the national economy.

8

Process of Kinship Transformation

A DEMOGRAPHIC PREAMBLE

Table 9 provides population estimates for Moenkopi for the years between 1903 and 1962. Some comments are in order on these figures. The larger estimate of approximately 200 for the 1903 population of Moenkopi was made by the superintendent about four months before he moved to Tuba City from Blue Canyon. Two years later he made the same estimate. Gregory's 1903 figure of 100 was based on his knowledge of increasing migration to Moenkopi during the years after 1910. Since the later figures by the two succeeding agents give fewer than 200 as the village population and are based on an intimate knowledge of Moenkopi, Gregory's 1903 estimate seems to be the more reasonable of the two. The settlement pattern given by Mindelef in 1897 also fits more comfortably an estimate of 20 households than one of 40. For the 1914 figure, I take as the most accurate estimate the mean between 210 and 225, since the population of Moenkopi is here considered as the number of people in more or less permanent residence in the village.

In the succeeding estimates only three figures need be commented on. The 1943 estimate of 550 by the Long Range Project seems exaggerated. This estimate was made during the war years when the village population could not have been higher than in later years. There is, moreover, no indication of increased migration to Moenkopi from other parts of Hopiland during this period. Stubbs's census, based on the BIA figure of 1948, included out-Moenkopi Hopi, who are indicated as such in the census. I have

TABLE 9. Population Trend

Year	Moenkopi	Third Mesa[a]	Hopi
1903	200		
	100[b]		
1904	200		1,878[l]
1905	150		
1907	150		
1908	162[c]		
1910	182		2,009[l]
1911	183[d]		
1912			2,272[l]
1914	250		
	210–225[e,f]		
1923			2,336[l]
1930			2,752[l]
			2,600[l]
			2,848[l]
1932	388[g]	1,377[g,i]	3,647[g,i]
1936		1,479[k]	3,028[k]
1937	409		3,248[l]
1943	550[h]	1,968[h]	4,100[h]
1948	486[g]	1,609[i]	3,468[i]
	640[i]		
1950	400[j]	1,396[j]	3,028[j]
1962	592		4,000[m]

[a] The figures for Third Mesa include the Moenkopi population.
[b] Gregory, 1915:117.
[c] TCL, April 4.
[d] Male, 83, and female, 100.
[e] " . . . in permanent homes in Moenkopi" (a letter to Gregory).
[f] Gregory, 1915:119, "in homes."
[g] Colton and Baxter, 1932:47.
[h] Report on the Navajo-Hopi Long Range Project.
[i] Stubbs, 1950:xv.
[j] A letter of the Keams Canyon BIA to Stubbs.
[k] Page, 1940:14, plus the Moenkopi population of 1937.
[l] A report to the Land Claims Commission.
[m] U.S. Department of Interior, 1962; an approximate count.

studied this census and, by eliminating the outside residents, I have obtained the lower figure of 486, which is here adopted. The 1950 figure of 400, given in a letter to Stubbs from the BIA, appears to be an underestimate as do the figures for Third Mesa and Hopiland. This census was taken in April, when a number of Hopi and Navajo (Young, 1961:320) out-migrate for wage work, returning to the village shortly before the planting season in May and June. Since the period of absence from the village is only temporary, amounting to merely two or three months, these individuals should have been included and the resident population as defined above should have been considerably larger than the figure given. Since wage work migration in Moenkopi frequently includes entire families, a comparison of census figures from different years, without attention to the months during which the censuses were taken, may display a much larger fluctuation in resident population than actually has occurred. For example, if 20 families migrate in this manner, a quarter of the village population could easily be left out of the census.

In general, the censuses tend to underestimate the resident population. A comparison of the 1962 census with my field data revealed that about 20 families were missing from the tallies. Among those left out were families that do not go along with the Upper Moenkopi Council. Since the census was taken by a Upper Moenkopi Council member, there is an indication that political bias is also a factor to be taken into account in evaluating the census data. I have profited from the official census because my own data were biased toward the families that do not belong to the Upper Moenkopi Council.

Incorporation of the above comments on the choice of adequate estimates does not produce an easily comprehensible growth curve. The most reasonable approximation would, in fact, be a straight line, if one neglects rapid growth due to migration in the early period from 1903 to 1915. It is even possible to devise a simple mnemonic formula for this line by taking the annual increment of 10 persons. This means that the growth rate of the village population is constantly decreasing!

The slow growth of the Hopi population since the establishment of the reservation has already been noted in the past, and the Hopi themselves often contrast it with the rapid increase of the Navajo and attribute it to the Navajo practice of polygyny and Hopi practice of the native religion. The latter is quoted most often by the Upper Moenkopi Council members, apparently to imply that the improvement of Hopi life is impossible without total abandonment of the religious practices save the kachina cult. They maintain that the practices "sacrifice" the young people and hence prohibit population growth.

If by "sacrifice" is meant high death rate among the young, this has not been the case for the last 20 years at least. On the contrary, the availability of medical services in Hopiland, especially after the last war, cannot be less and may be greater than among other tribes, e.g., the Navajo. The Hopi, in addition, usually have less difficulty in availing themselves of the government medical service than the Navajo, a large number of whom are still located in inaccessible places. Colton's comparison of the growth rate between the dispersed Navajo and nucleated Hopi (1936:342–43) does not seem to apply for the period after the war, and yet this is the period when the resident population in Moenkopi does not show as high a growth rate as in the period between 1937 and 1948.

On the other hand, the low rate of increase is understandable if we resort to the difference between the "tribal" and "service" population as defined in the Navajo censuses (Young, 1961:312). The former refers to the Navajo, including those with the quarter degree of Navajo blood, *irrespective of residence,* while the latter refers only to those Navajo residing on the reservation and accessible to government services. In the case of the Navajo, the ratio between the two categories of population amounted to at most 10 per cent in 1950 (7,000 off-reservation Navajo and 70,000 "tribal" Navajo; Young, 1961:320). Even by assuming the higher (4 per cent) growth rate for the off-reservation Navajo between 1950 and 1960 and much lower (2 per cent) for the "service" population for the same period, the ratio does not amount to more than 15 per cent in 1960. On the other hand, the Hopi Agency gives an estimate of 1,200 residing outside the Hopi Reservation in 1962 and 4,000 Hopi on it, and the ratio becomes about 24 per cent (U.S. Department of Interior, 1962:6). It is apparent from this that the off-reservation residents occupy a more important position in the population growth among the Hopi than among the Navajo.

These considerations seem applicable with greater cogency to Moenkopi. The analysis of the Moenkopi population profile according to age group shows no major difference from the swiftly increasing Navajo. For 1948 and 1962 more than half of the village population is in the age group under 20, while in 1937, 48.7 per cent is in this group (see Tables 10 and 11). The age group between 25 and 45 occupies from 20 per cent to 25 per cent both in Moenkopi and among the Navajo. A slight difference exists in the case of the groups adjoining this age group. The 20–25 group shows a larger percentage among the Navajo than in Moenkopi, while the two older groups, 45–60 and 60 and over, are larger in Moenkopi than among the Navajo. As a result, the average age of the Moenkopi population is slightly greater than that of the Navajo: 23 to 26 in Moenkopi for the three periods, and 17 to

TABLE 10. Age Distribution of Moenkopi Population

Age	1937 Male	1937 Female	1948 Male	1948 Female	1962 Male	1962 Female
0– 5	30	26	42	50	55	75
–10	29	24	32	32	45	42
–15	26	23	39	38	41	35
–20	21	20	27	22	21	23
–25	15	19	24	16	16	22
–30	21	17	13	11	20	17
–35	9	21	14	16	11	15
–40	10	9	15	11	18	13
–45	9	8	9	18	16	9
–50	11	8	9	8	6	11
–55	7	2	9	7	9	9
–60	6	6	4	3	7	13
–65	9	4	7	6	9	6
66–	12	7	12	6	20	13
Total	215	194	256	244	294	303
Average age	25.5		22.9		23.4	
Village population	409		500		597	

TABLE 11. Comparative Data of the Moenkopi and Navajo Populations

	Moenkopi		
Age Group	1937	1948	1962
Under 5 years	13.7	18.4	21.8
6 to 15 years	25.0	28.2	27.3
16 to 20 years	10.0	9.8	7.4
21 to 25 years	8.3	8.0	6.4
26 to 45 years	25.4	21.4	20.0
46 to 60 years	6.8	6.6	5.8
61 years and over	10.7	7.6	11.3
Under 20 years	48.7	56.4	56.5

	Navajo[a]		
Age Group	1930	1950	1961
Under 5 years	16.86	17.01	16.04
5 to 14 years	28.61	29.28	29.99
15 to 19 years	10.93	10.93	10.60
20 to 24 years	9.94	8.83	9.52
25 to 44 years	21.57	20.27	21.45
45 to 59 years	7.16	7.98	7.77
60 years and over	4.94	5.70	4.61
Under 20 years	56.40	57.22	56.64

[a] "Tribal" population; Young, 1961:326.

18 among the Navajo in 1960. Both, however, are far below the U.S. national average of 29.5 (Young, 1961:325).

Similarity in the age structure of the two groups may indicate that the growth pattern of the Moenkopi population is in accord with the rapidly growing Navajo. In this light, the factors suppressing the similar rate of growth in Moenkopi seem fairly obvious. As we noted above, the Moenkopi population tends to be slightly older than the Navajo "tribal" population. This appears to indicate that the out-migration in Moenkopi is a more significant factor in regulating the population of the village. Moreover, since there is no particular age group that shows marked deficiency in percentage, one may expect that the migration occurs by whole families rather than by individuals.

It is difficult to estimate the extent of family migration from Moenkopi. For one thing, the village not only produces out-migrating families but also receives many individuals from other villages through marriage. Recently, in-migration to Moenkopi by family has drastically decreased, but the number of people marrying into Moenkopi, both male and female, has not shown appreciable decrease; from 20 to 30 people have been coming in the 10-year period between 1937 and 1948 and between 1948 and 1962. In regard to the out-Moenkopi residents, my computation shows that in 1948, 36 couples lived outside while 89 lived in Moenkopi, and in 1962, 52 couples lived outside Moenkopi against 109 in the village. Since the identification of Moenkopi families living outside is much dependent on the knowledge of the residents, these figures are underestimates. I suspect that more than 30 per cent of the Moenkopi population is actually staying outside the village at present.

It is a fairly certain assumption that this ratio is on the increase. The residential area of Moenkopi has reached a saturation point; the houses built recently, small in number, are mostly outside the traditionally defined area of the village. At the same time, it was frequently noticed that young couples were compelled to rent houses that have been vacant. In the upper segment, the use of *piki* houses or storerooms for residence was not infrequent. Though economic conditions in the Tuba City area have improved considerably in the last five years, many people from Hopiland proper are unable to find a place to stay for work in Tuba City and some are even forced to commute more than 40 miles. While this is the case with the Hopi from other villages, the original Moenkopi residents often leave the village for such reservation towns as

Kayenta, Shonto, Kaibito, and Leupp or others off the reservation. Thus, beneath the seeming stability of the demographic curve, there exists a highly volatile movement of people in Moenkopi.

Increasing population with high mobility and limited residential resources has been creating innumerable kinds of pressures on the traditional social structure of Moenkopi. It has challenged the organization of the little pueblo in a number of respects, some of which have already been discussed. In this chapter we shall confine our attention to the transformations of kinship and household organization as they have been affected by the changing demographic and economic conditions.

CLAN

The traditional organization of Hopi kinship is based on the extensive application of a matrilineal principle. Generally, this principle operates on three levels of segmentation: a maximal segment of clan, an intermediate level of lineage, and a minimal segment of a woman and her unmarried daughters. The Hopi clans are further grouped into several phratries. However, this grouping is not based on matrilineal descent. The minimal segment of a woman and her unmarried daughters usually occupies a single room or a separate house and forms a part of a lineage household composed of several such units under the headship of a dominant female, who is usually mother or older sister to the other women. The women of such a household make up the core of a matrilineage.

We shall first consider maximal matrilineal grouping of "clans" among the Hopi. The membership of a particular clan is categorically transmitted through one's mother. Members of a given clan do not claim descent, putative or otherwise, from a common ancestor or ancestress, however. Formal genealogical relationships are absent between segments of a clan as such. Each of the Hopi clans carries one or more "names" that have reference to "some object, personage or aspect of nature" (Eggan, 1950:80).

The clan is not a corporate group as defined by Radcliffe-Brown (1950:41). There are no occasions when a considerable portion of adult members, either male or female or both, take part in a common activity. It lacks any role of group representative, and, more particularly, a clan does not have a "clan head." "Clan lands" refer to land belonging to the members of clans resident in a specific village or on a mesa. Though the same clans are often represented in different villages and on different mesas, land holdings do not cross village or mesa boundaries. Land holding is localized and clans are dispersed.

The last characteristic of a Hopi clan may indicate that an economic basis of clan solidarity is represented only by the local portion of a clan found in a village and that it is this "subclan," to use Gough's terminology (1961a:477), that fits Radcliffe-Brown's definition more comfortably. The village segment of a clan is often, if not invariably, represented by a man, who assumes a priestly position for the ceremony belonging to that clan segment. Its members gather for the performance of their life-cycle rituals. Each "subclan" maintains a "clan house" or occasionally a "shrine," where the paraphernalia of the clan's ceremony are kept. An elderly woman (*soho*) usually resides in this house (Connelly, 1956:12).

The relationship between "subclans" in the traditional scheme of Hopi society is not very clear. Because of clan differentiation into village segments, a member of a certain clan from one village cannot and does not acquire rights in a piece of land belonging to the same clan in another village, nor can he perform in the ceremony of that clan there except by reinitiation. On the other hand, kin terms are extended to clan members irrespective of their village affiliations, and clan ties that override villages are often acknowledged in gift giving at kachina ceremonies or in the exchange of presents at kinship ceremonies, particularly weddings.

However, this distinction between a clan and its village segments is considerably obscured by the fact that each mesa contains more than one village; interactions are significantly more frequent among the villages on the same mesa than between villages on different mesas. The villages on the same mesa retain explicit genetic relationships, which are often expressed in the difference in organization of ceremonies given in respective villages as well as by mutual participation in them. One such relationship is that of "mother" and "colony" villages. As Eggan mentioned (1964:178), intermarriage between the mother and colony villages is more frequent than between villages of different mesas. The people of Shichomovi and Shipaulovi go to Walpi and Shongopavi respectively for the Kachina initiation and other rituals. The Wuwuchim and Snake ceremonies are not given in Shichomovi but only in Walpi on First Mesa, while Shipaulovi joins Shongopavi for the Wuwuchim ceremony. The same situation, though to a different degree, prevailed between Oraibi and Moenkopi prior to the 1906 split of Oraibi. Since then, however, growth of other settlements on Third Mesa and disruption of religious practices in Oraibi disturbed the modal differentiation of ceremonial status among the villages on the mesa.

The above characteristics of the villages on a given mesa may make it appear more appropriate to limit the term "subclan" only to that segment of a clan confined to the mesa. However, such is not the case in Shipaulovi where land is fairly definitely separated from the Shongopavi farming territory (Forde, 1931:367). On the other hand, the clan segments of Shichomovi are so closely merged to those of Walpi not only in land (Forde, 1931:366) but also in rituals (Steward, 1931) that the former do not present sufficient traits to justify the corporate "subclan" status.

To conclude, the corporateness of Hopi clans is highly variable and depends on the particular historical circumstances of village communities on each mesa. Despite minor variations, however, the first level of segmentation of the clans has been the three mesas. On each mesa, the degree of further segmentation is dependent on the status of respective communities as "mother," "guard," and "daughter" villages. On this level, further, the boundary of each clan segment is not drawn in a uniform manner and, in the case of Oraibi and Moenkopi, is entirely absent. This flexibility in boundary formation at the mesa level of clan organization contributed to the maintenance of mutual ties between communities in the process of adaptation to the meager natural environment in the past.

Phratry as a Stabilizing Factor

The fluidity in the boundaries of clan segments of different orders, however, indicates an important characteristic of Hopi clanship. Unlike some African segmentary lineage societies, all the Hopi clans carry in their traditions accounts of merging and phratral association with each other. While segmentation occurs within a clan, such processes have not been recorded for the emergence of new clans. In fact, what characterized demographic processes that altered the constellation of clans in villages or mesas was mostly extinction or assimilation, and when a new clan was noted among the Hopi, it emerged not through the process of segmentation but through introduction from outside, as in the case of numerous Navajo clans in the Hopi clan system. More typically, the native interpretation of clans in a phratry is invariably made in terms of such episodes as association through a period of migration from the Underworld and participation in common experiences during that period (Eggan, 1950:78–79), but never as a result of segmentation. In this respect, the Hopi phratries are also different from those of the Western Apache, among whom phratral ties are based on common descent (Kaut, 1957:40). One indeed obtains an impression that no clan has ever been born since the time of origins in the Underworld. New clans were introduced into Hopi society mainly through adoption or marriage with female members of alien tribes.

On the other hand, the clans, once emerged, are "immortal" (Eggan, 1950:110; 1964:179). Two mechanisms are provided to insure this. In order to revive a dying clan in a village, a clanswoman may be "reseeded" from another village (Eggan, 1964:179). If members of a clan die out in a village, the clan name, associated ritual, and land that belong to it will be taken up by its linked clan of that village (Forde, 1931:372–75; Eggan, 1950:64–78; 1964:179). These practices result, on the one hand, in a seeming proliferation of names claimed by respective clans and on the other, a complicated pattern of phratry groupings often beyond the bounds of a village, thus obscuring clear-cut localization of segments.

The absence of genealogical links beyond the level of clans and association of clans into phratries based on mythical experiences reflects the process of clan formation among the Pueblo Indians, as reconstructed by Steward (1937). He argued that the Pueblo clans were formed essentially through the process of accretion and amalgamation of formerly localized and independent units into large villages for the purpose of defense, and not by segmentation of unilineal kin groups into units of a lower order through population growth in a certain locality (1937:96–99). To paraphrase this argument in the present discussion, phratral associations of clans among the Hopi should be interpreted as a phenomenon independent of the intra-clan segmentation process.

Moenkopi Clans

A survey of clans represented in Moenkopi over time is made difficult partly by phratral associations. Often identification of clans differs from one informant to another; multiple clan identities may be given by an informant to a certain individual, whom another informant assigns to a single clan. Even for one's own clan, one may prefer to mention membership in a more prestigious clan while suppressing another. Apart from such biases, some, especially the young, are sometimes ignorant of the names of clans linked into respective phratries (Eggan, 1950:135–36).

Table 12 needs some comment. Eggan (1950:65, 72–73) and Titiev (1944:87) mention that the Tobacco clan has long been extinct in Oraibi. In Moenkopi, however, its members are clearly separated from the Rabbit clan, although they merge and cooperate in kinship rituals and father's sisters of the one are regarded

TABLE 12. Moenkopi Clans

Clan	Allottee or His Spouse	1906[a]	Migration after 1906[b]	1937	1948	1962
Rabbit	+[c]	+	+	+	+	+
Tobacco				+	+	+
Parrot		+		+	+	
Kachina			+			
Bluebird					+	+
Snake				+	+	+
Lizard		+				
Sand			+	+	+	+
Sun		+	+		+	+
Sun's Forehead				+	+	+
Reed	+	+		+	+	+
Greasewood		+	+	+	+	+
Coyote		+	+	+	+	+
Water Coyote	+	+	+	+	+	+
Ma'asau	+	+	+	+	+	+
Badger			+	+	+	+
Pi:kyas	+	+	+	+	+	+
Patki			+	+		
Crane			+			

[a] Titiev, 1944:88.
[b] Titiev, 1944:94. Only women's clans are listed. Titiev gives another list of clans in Moenkopi elsewhere (1944:92), which includes the Kachina clan. However, the list's reference to time is lacking (1944:89, footnote 168) and hence left out of consideration.
[c] + indicates presence.

The Oraibi clans not included in the above table are: Bear, Spider, Eagle, Bow, Kokop, Le (Lehu or Millet), Cedar, Gray Badger, Navajo Badger, Butterfly, Sivap, Chicken Hawk, and Squash. The 13 clans were present in Oraibi in 1906 (Titiev, 1944:87) as well as during the 1930's (Eggan, 1950:vii, 65–66).

as such by the members of the other clan.[1] Titiev shows three women of the Kachina clan moving to Moenkopi after 1906 (1944:94), but my survey did not register this clan. Although one woman, claiming to be both Kachina and Rabbit, settled in Moen-

---

[1] B. Wright of the Museum of Northern Arizona mentions that at least one man of the Tobacco clan was present in Oraibi before 1906 and that the Tobacco clan was ousted from Oraibi after the split of the village.

kopi after 1937, an attempt to separate the two was unsuccessful. The members of the Rabbit clan also claim membership in the Kachina clan. Similarly, the Snake clan of Moenkopi, despite Eggan's note on its near extinction on Third Mesa (1950:69), turned out to be a powerful clan group, and the distinction between the Lizard and Snake clans was meaningless, for the members of the latter all claimed also to be Lizard. Considering the fact that "in Stephen's time [late nineteenth century] the Snake clan was reduced to one family" (Eggan, 1950:69), it may be suspected that the Snake clan members were formerly Lizard clan people who claimed to be Snake. Neither Eggan nor Titiev gives the Sun's Forehead. My informants were, however, emphatic on the point that the "genuine" Sun clan was absent until after 1937, when a woman of that clan moved to Moenkopi from New Oraibi through marriage, and that the "Sun" clan members, many of whom came from Oraibi, were actually the Sun's Forehead people. They also provided me with a tale explaining the origin of the Sun's Forehead in Oraibi. Because of this, I have separated the two in the table. I suspect also that the Sun clan mentioned by Titiev (1944:88, 94) was identical to my Sun's Forehead clan, for there was no evidence of the clan in Moenkopi prior to 1937. Finally, my survey failed to turn up the Crane clan, which Titiev mentions as moving to Moenkopi after 1906. My informants did not recall the former existence of any Crane woman in the village.

The table clearly indicates that the majority of the Moenkopi clans (10 out of 14) were already established in the village by 1906. Fluctuation in clan composition from that time to the present has remained comparatively small. Since then, the Parrot clan disappeared when the last female member died after 1948. The Patki clan, which migrated to Moenkopi after 1906, was eliminated when the remaining clanswomen moved back to Old and New Oraibi out of frustration in land disputes with the Pi:kyas and the government. On the other hand, the village gained five new clans from Third and Second Mesas, including the Bluebird clan of Mishongnovi.

The experience of the Patki clan indicates another characteristic of the clans in Moenkopi. Because the village originated as Oraibi's farming colony, the Moenkopi clans were not "planted" there in a manner to insure continuity of the respective clans. No clan has built its clan house in the village, but all the clans, including Pi:kyas, maintain such structures in the parent village of Oraibi. As a result, no attempt was made to revive an extinct clan in Moenkopi. On the other hand, there is an indication that the village was regarded as a repository of "seeds" for other villages, and an abortive attempt was once planned to transfer a Coyote woman to Mishongnovi to rejuvenate that clan there.

Further, the ceremonies in which clans played broadly differentiated functions were mostly given in Oraibi. Consequently, solidarity of the clan as a ritual-holding group did not develop in Moenkopi. In fact, the Moenkopi clans derived their ceremonial significance from their association with Oraibi.

Finally, land in the Moenkopi area was in individual tenure from the early period, and an alien clan member was not barred from opening a field on an unclaimed portion of the village territory. In addition, irrigation as a major form of farming required village-wide cooperation. Thus, agriculture by fellow clan members was no longer an effective means of labor cooperation unless the bond of locality was first upheld for the maintenance of irrigation works (Dozier, 1960). These factors tended further to reduce clan solidarity and, in its stead, to introduce new clans by bringing women in from other villages. Thus, not only did the Moenkopi clans tend to be unstable but, as the economic prospect remained favorable or even improved, heterogeneity of clan composition also tended to increase.

Although the majority of in-marrying women belonged to one or another of the clans already extant in Moenkopi, they were often genealogically unrelated to clanmates of the village clans. This also resulted in an increase of lineage segments within respective clans (see below).

Present Significance of Clans in Moenkopi

Though the Moenkopi clans are now deprived of religious and economic bases for solidarity, they remain extremely important in two spheres of village life. In the first place, clanship in Moenkopi is an important mechanism in the regulation of marriage.

Two exogamic rules are most frequently cited by the villagers. One is based on the unilineal groupings of clans and phratries, the other on cognatic distance of blood relationship. Exogamy based on clans and phratries consists of exclusion of one's own clan and phratry and one's father's clan and phratry. Within this rule, the force of application as well as native theories vary appreciably between one's own clan and phratry exogamy and paternal clan and phratry exogamy. The first is based on the consideration that once you marry a clan or phratry mate, your kinsmen will be confused as to which side (bride's or bridegroom's) to take in the subsequent exchanges of goods and services. This explanation well summarizes the social background of marriage, since the distinction between bride's and groom's groups in terms of clan and phratry plays an important role in the wedding ceremony (Eggan, 1950:54–55) and is preserved for the children, whose life-cycle ceremonies are organized between their own and paternal clans (Eggan, 1950:46–47, 60).

One may also expect a similar confusion as a result of marriage to *kiya'a* (father's sister) for, to her husband's clanspeople, she now occupies a new position, *mö:wi* or female relative-in-law, which conflicts with her role of *kiya'a* in some of the prestations. As *mö:wi*, she is entitled to respect from her husband's people but as *kiya'a*, she stands in a joking relationship with them (Eggan, 1950:39–40). The *kiya'a* is also entitled to meat from *miyi* or grandchild, who is now her husband, but the *mö:wi* is expected to share it with her husband's people. In the wedding ceremony, a mud fight cannot be well organized now that the attackers, i.e., *kiya'a*, are the attacked by stealing their own grandchild for marriage (Eggan, 1950:40).

In addition to these complications in marriage to paternal clans, the villagers add that if you marry *kiya'a*, a lizard (*monongye*) will follow you and the people will immediately know (Titiev, 1938:105). What happens to them is not explained.

It is also questionable if these prohibited marriages, based on clanship, are in the category of incest. They are not regarded as heinous or criminal nor is there any fear of physical injury or harm. In fact, marriage in all these forms does occur. However, the frequency of marriage in the paternal clan is far greater than intra-clan or -phratry marriages.

The second type of marriage prohibition assumes more closely the character of incest and is based on genealogical distance (Eggan, 1950:57). There does not exist any clear-cut limit beyond which marriage is allowed. Some explain the prohibition of marrying one's actual father's sister's or mother's brother's daughter on this ground. According to them, marriage with such kin has deleterious effects on children, an explanation possibly of recent origin.

It has been impossible to determine the paternal clan affiliation of all the married couples found in the census, many of whom are long deceased. The following data are, therefore, presented with a hope for future elaboration.

In regard to the intra-clan or -phratry marriage, the 1937 data show not a single case among the 59 resident couples whose clan affiliations are known. In 1948 there were two intra-phratral marriages among the 76 couples (2.6 per cent). The partners to these marriages were all from Moenkopi. The two marriages still existed in 1962. No intra-clan marriage was found in 1948. In 1962 there was one marriage within the Pi:kyas clan; the husband in this case came from Shongopavi. With three marriages, the percentage is up to 3.1 per cent of 96 cases. Another intra-clan marriage existed in the same clan and the husband in this case came from Shipaulovi; the couple lived in Tuba City, however.

Only one measure was obtained on marriage to paternal clans and phratries. In 1962 there were 11 such marriages (four to the clans) out of 96 married couples, i.e., 11.5 per cent. Since there were 32 undetermined cases, the percentage probably represents the minimum.[2] This figure turns out to be slightly higher than Titiev's 10 per cent for 1932 at Old Oraibi (Titiev, 1938:110; 1944:36; Eggan, 1950:345) and may or may not point to a small change in the observance of marriage regulations.

There are other indications of the relaxation of marriage rules. First, the villagers are now well aware of marriage with *kiya'a*, and, while they gossip about such cases, no sanctions are imposed. Second, the prohibition based on genealogical distance shows clearly a trend to obscure the distinction between own and paternal relations.

Finally, the organization of kinship exchange has always involved an element of choice within a wide range of appropriate relatives. In a wedding ceremony, not all the *kiya'a* of a village or a mesa gather to wash the hair of a bride or groom. Innumerable factors determine the actual attendance of the available *kiya'a*. In present-day Moenkopi, where factional disputes are rife, it often happens that one neglects certain *kiya'a* in preference to others on political grounds and withdraws from patterned interactions with the former for ceremonial exchanges. Further, since any collection of *kiya'a* is usually segmented into several lineages, a choice of acceptable ones is easily made from among them. The present chief of the lower segment married one of his *kiya'a*, who did not belong to his father's lineage. She was incorporated in his lineage not as a *kiya'a* but as a *mö:wi* or female in-law. The latter has a maternal half-sister by a political antagonist of the

---

[2] More than 80 per cent of the undetermined cases involve husbands from outside Moenkopi.

chief and though the sister is also his *kiya'a,* the chief has almost no interaction with her nor has he made any gift to her so far. Most of his "significant" *kiya'a* in the village are found among the women of his father's lineage.

Modifications and reductions in the life-cycle ceremonies show the contemporary functioning of clanship in Moenkopi. Since most births now take place in the Tuba City hospital, birth rituals are not performed in full sequence. The hair washing, naming, and dedication of new-born babies to the sun by *kiya'a* are the rituals most frequently observed. Further, without waiting for the prescribed 20-day period before the washing, many relatives celebrate the birth when the mothers are still in the hospital. No new mothers abstain from salt for the prescribed period. Naming of a new-born baby, customarily restricted to its *kiya'am* (Titiev, 1938:106; Eggan, 1950:48), is now occasionally done by a wider group of kinswomen. Thus, in the naming of a baby born of a Hopi father and a Navajo mother, not only his clanswomen, including his own mother, but also his father's sister and mother took part. It was the baby's father's father's mother who dedicated him to the sun and not his father's *kiya'a.* The baby's father's father's sister then mentioned that she was now his *kiya'a* because she washed his hair and named him, but she was also his *so'o* or grandmother because of his relationship to her.

Because of the unmanageable complexity of the rite under modern conditions and its prolonged time involvement, many households curtail the phases described in the wedding ritual (Eggan, 1950:54–55). Often the whole ceremony is reduced to the hair-washing phase, and the other phases are replaced by a mere feast with the attendance of the couple's relatives. Weaving of a wedding garment is only rarely done in Moenkopi, though it is still common in other villages. Often the ceremony is completed after a baby is born and hence the hair washing of the couple and their baby is simultaneously performed.

Occasionally, omission of a prescribed ritual becomes a means to circumvent the difficulty of neat differentiation of the kin. In a feast for an intra-clan marriage, invitations were issued irrespective of exact kinship relationships to the couple, and at the feast itself much comment was exchanged among the participants as to whose side they were to take. However, since it was an American-style reception, no serious problem arose.

Apart from the expense for preparation of the ceremony, the villagers are loath to suspend their routine wage work and household chores to carry through the sequence of the Hopi wedding ceremony (see p. 210). At the same time, more and more marriages are contracted in off-reservation schools or a short while after graduation, and marriage licenses are drawn from off-reservation town offices.

Use of the village graveyard and public graveyard in Tuba City is compartmentalized; the former is restricted to the deaths that occur within the village and the latter to those outside it. Since most deaths now take place in the hospital, use of the public graveyard has been increasing. The relatives who take part in funerals at present are not differentiated by lineality. While custom prescribes that adult women of the deceased's father's side should retouch the corpse, I have seen a dead woman's daughter-in-law, who had experience as a practical nurse, treating the corpse and dressing it in *kanelkosa* (woman's traditional black cotton dress), which was bought from an old weaver in the village.

In conclusion, though the clans in Moenkopi still appear to function as an effective exogamic unit, the degree of relaxation in the rule of clan exogamy has been slowly increasing. Disorganizing pressure on Moenkopi clanship has long been at work, mainly in the form of changes in the economy, and, while the clans still provide a basic organizational framework for individual kinship rituals and attendant exchanges, their actual performance has been greatly modified, often in negligence of clan affiliations. Many young people of Moenkopi today are ignorant of the clan affiliation of their fellow villagers. Only a few young villagers can present correct information in regard to phratral association. Increasing ethnic heterogeneity of the community has also contributed to diminishing the significance of clanship.

The clans also play an important role in the present political parlance of Moenkopi. In the traditional system ceremonial roles were allocated to numerous clans in a village (Titiev, 1944:59–60). Several of these roles also assumed a political character, and as a result, the village presented itself as a "theocratic state" (Colton, 1934). To illustrate, the village chief of Oraibi was at the same time chief of the Soyal ceremony. The Kokop (Fire) clan controlled the Momchit or society of death, from which the warriors (*kalé:-taqa*) were recruited. Hence the clan claimed the role of protector of Oraibi. The Pi:kyas clan head is a lieutenant of the chief and controls the *Aholi* kachina during the Soyal ceremony. The Crier chief (*Chakmongwi*) was selected from the Greasewood clan in Oraibi (Titiev, 1944:60), whence some claimed the clan was the chief's adviser.

With the Oraibi split in 1906 and the subsequent lapse of ceremonies, many positions were left vacant and no succession occurred even in such a conservative village as Hotevilla. Only the chiefly status is now weakly recognized in Oraibi, Hotevilla, and Moenkopi. In spite of the utter disorganization of the politico-religious system, however, many of the present "traditionals" often justify their participation in village and tribal politics on the grounds of past association of the clans with political positions. Further, loss of the ceremonies that supported the offices and the absence of unified codices of tradition forced some to attempt to rationalize their clans' roles by means of the emergence myth from the Underworld or, more flagrantly, from the sheer absence of such roles in the tradition. Thus, the Reed clan affirms its guard role by the myth in which a reed was used for a road of ascent from the Underworld. The Water Coyote clan of Moenkopi is assigned the position of protector to the Pi:kyas clan because of its lack of ceremonial roles. On the other hand, some accusatory remarks and rumors, hurled by the "traditionals" against their opponents, often refer to the latters' clan affiliations. Thus, the Greasewood clan is said to be a troublemaker in Moenkopi, while the Rabbit clan members are malicious gossipers. The women of the Sun's Forehead clan are reputed to have fair skin, and this clan, which had no ceremonial function, was said to have been admitted to the village on the condition that it submit its women to the pleasures of the village males. They were thus the home wreckers of Moenkopi. A cursory checking of the clan affiliation of the inhabitants makes it immediately clear that not all the members of these clans fit their characterizations and that a considerable number of them are active in traditional politics. Clan membership is not the only determinant of political activities, which involves the far more complicated processes of village and household membership, affinal relation, occupation, sex, and age. Finally, because only the males take part in overt political activities, continuity of these activities along clan lines is almost never achieved, and one's cause, once justified on the ground of his clan affiliation, is often lost in the next generation with no one to follow him. These observations suggest that clanship in village politics provides the participants with acceptable "political idioms" which are meaningful in understanding the conflicts in the acculturation process.

LINEAGE

In the discussion of lineage and clan among the Hopi, it has been customary to follow Goldenweiser's definition that a lineage is a unilineal kin group in which actually traceable genealogical relationships unite the members, while such a genealogy is absent in a clan (1937:361; Radcliffe-Brown, 1950:39–40). As Titiev noted (1944:48), this definition is not without serious difficulty because genealogical knowledge of an individual fluctuates owing to numerous factors, including kinship, sex, age, and above all, memory capacity.

Despite its operational difficulty, this definition of a lineage played an important role in the discussion of the clan-lineage relationship among the Hopi (Lowie, 1929; Titiev, 1944:44–46; Eggan, 1950:76–77). Briefly, it was Parsons, in particular, who held that a Hopi clan is a large maternal extended family and that no purpose could be served by trying to differentiate segments within it. By introducing Goldenweiser's definition, however, it was possible to identify segments within a clan. Thus, Lowie and others following him enumerated, within the context of a village, actual numbers of segments in respective clans that were isolated by the absence of genealogical links in the knowledge of selected informants. The point appeared to be made, therefore, when White counted 39 segments in the 21 Oraibi clans (Titiev, 1944: 48–49; Eggan, 1950:77). The more, in fact, the better!

The discovery of lineages, however, was accompanied by more significant findings on their structure. Lowie first confirmed that such a group was often a unit of succession to ceremonial offices belonging to clans (Lowie, 1929:330; Titiev, 1944:46). Later Forde found that lineage groups were the clan segments that actually control clan land (1931:373).

Formation of Lineage Segments in Moenkopi

Though the lineage was thus successfully isolated from the clan, the process of its formation has not been clearly stated in the literature. Only Titiev has made an explicit attempt to reconstruct it (1944:46–48). In essence, he regards it as a part of the developmental cycle of a domestic group and, as such, internally regulated.

An examination of Moenkopi lineages, however, reveals a feature somewhat aberrant from the postulated internal segmentation and fission. The accompanying table compares number of lineages in respective clans for the four Hopi communities. Moenkopi lineages were "formally" constructed from the 10 genealogies obtained in the field and additional data from the informants mainly regarding deceased members' relationships (Table 13). The table shows that the number of segments in respective clans of Moenkopi is greater than in other villages. This is not entirely owing to the imperfection of the data because the generation depth of many Moenkopi lineages is as great as in other villages and sometimes greater. A number of segments in Mishongnovi and Shipaulovi do not go beyond three generations. The number of segments in Moenkopi varies more widely than in the other villages; for example, Moen-

TABLE 13. Lineage Segmentation of Clans

Clan	Mishongnovi[a]	Shipaulovi[a]	Old Oraibi[b]	Moenkopi[c]
Bear	2	2	3	
Carrying Strap	1			
Spider		2		
Parrot	1		1	
Parrot or (Kachina-Crow)			1	
Kachina (Crow)	1		1	
Snake				4
Lizard (Snake)	2		3	
Sand			1	
Sun			2	
Sun's Forehead		5		6
Eagle	1		1	
Reed			2	3
Greasewood			2	2
Bow			1	
Coyote			3	4
Water Coyote			2	4
Ma'asau (Hovahkop-Kwan-Kokop)	1		1	3
Badger	2		4	4
Butterfly	2		1	
Rabbit (Tobacco)			4	3
Pi:kyas	3		1	1
Cloud	1			
Patki			2	
Squash (Hawk-Crane-Pumpkin)	1		1	
(Chicken Hawk)	1			

[a] Lowie, 1929.
[b] Titiev, 1944:49.
[c] Members of unlisted clans are composed of a single household and hence omitted from the table. The organization of phratries followed Titiev, 1944:49.

kopi varies from a one-lineage clan to a six-lineage clan, while Mishongnovi includes one- to three-lineage clans. Finally, there are many detached females in Moenkopi who married into the village, are not yet old enough to form lineages, and are not related to other lineages in the village.

The three characteristics of Moenkopi lineages are derived from its colonial character which caused it to absorb unrelated segments from Old Oraibi and other villages and from its recent establishment as a community. The question remains, however, as to why the segments in each clan at such old communities as Mishongnovi and Old Oraibi are so few in number, whereas many Moenkopi clans contain more numerous segments. If the segmentation and fission of Hopi clans resulted from household expansion, should they not contain more lineage segments than they actually do? Or is fission as a consequence of immigration an essential part of the process as happened in Moenkopi? Was there some amalgamatory process which kept the proliferation of segments in check? Or, finally, did the restricted economy eliminate the excess segments? These and other questions are unanswerable at the present stage of my research. It is evident, however, that no segmentation or fission of the type Titiev described has occurred in Moenkopi so far (see below).

Economic Basis of Lineage Grouping

All of the segments in Moenkopi started through migration from Third Mesa and later from other areas as a search for better economic prospects. Because the time of the migration coincided with the breakdown of the clan land system and the occupation of "outland" in the Moenkopi area and because individual farm land tenure soon came to be sanctioned by the government, appropriation of land by a small number of clans did not result. Instead, individual lineages of numerous clans soon became established in the village.

In the subsequent development of Moenkopi, no fission occurred in the migrant lineages, including even the single lineage of the Pi:kyas clan and one of the Water Coyote lineages, which are the oldest settled ones in the community. In the case of these two lineages, a special situation contributed to their comparative solidarity. As indicated before, they occupy the largest portion of the choice irrigated land still in cultivation in Moenkopi. The Pi:kyas clan held an important position in the politico-religious regime of Moenkopi and Old Oraibi. The Water Coyote clan has been allied to the Pi:kyas through affinal ties since the allotment period. These factors obviously stabilized their lineage structure.

Generally, however, conditions in Moenkopi were not conducive to the development of large lineages. When the land surplus disappeared by the end of the 1930's, the possibility of wage work emerged as a bright prospect. A cash economy made rapid inroads to Moenkopi after World War II. Inefficient and poor farm productivity ceased to be an important threat to survival.

A cash economy based on wage work income tended to discourage cooperation among kin. Cash-earning activity became the primary concern of the individual family, and unit of consumption became limited to a small household. Traditional contexts for economic cooperation succumbed to the increasing need for money. To aggravate this, ceremonial activities, which reaffirmed ties of kinship, gradually became a matter of community recreation. Religious positions disappeared with the lapse of the respective ceremonies in Oraibi.

The foundation that supported lineage solidarity—land and ceremony—thus collapsed under the pressure of new economic opportunities and the intervention of the government. On the other hand, a trickle of women attracted by the comparative abundance of job opportunities kept coming into Moenkopi through patrilocal residence, while the young residents of the village sought further chances in off-reservation towns and left the community. The lineages in Moenkopi thus became further fragmented. The newly established households, then, sought diverse relationships within the community for interaction, and a neat lineal differentiation in the structure of their kinship relationships was mostly abandoned.

Lineage Differentiation

In Moenkopi there is no evidence that a "clan house" has ever been built. Consequently, the Moenkopi lineages have not been segmented in the manner Connelly described for Shongopavi (1956). Of the "prime," "reserve," and "marginal" lineages, however, indications exist that all the Moenkopi lineages except, perhaps, for those of the chiefly Pi:kyas and associated Water Coyote, belong to Connelly's "marginal" category. It has already been pointed out that the community itself was created for the households which had less land at Old Oraibi. Permanent maintenance of dwelling structures has never been regarded as imperative in

Moenkopi. The *ki:kya* where Nashileowi, the first chief of Moenkopi, once resided and where kachina masks and other ceremonial paraphernalia for the kachina rituals were stored (see Map 3), was allowed to fall into ruin after her death. She died childless and, because no woman of her lineage moved into the house, the ceremonial goods were removed to *Iskiva*, which belongs to the Water Coyote clan of the village (see Map 3). The Pi:kyas clan of Moenkopi maintains its "clan house" and shrine in Old Oraibi. All other clan segments in Moenkopi also have their "clan houses" in Old Oraibi, which are preserved and maintained by their relatives who live there or in Hotevilla.

The chieftainship of Moenkopi, now recognized mainly by the lower group, was not confined to any particular segment of the Pi:kyas lineage, but in the last succession the last chief's mother's sister's daughter's son assumed the position, although there were men in the former chief's direct segment, e.g., his sister's daughter's son (see pp. 70–71). Succession to other religious positions that were once held by members of this lineage became obscured and the positions were left vacant. At present, the lineage contains only a handful of Powamu members, many of whom have never had a chance to conduct kachina ceremonies.

That continuity of residence in houses in Moenkopi was not an aim in itself is shown by the abandonment of a number of houses in the lower segment site as the population moved up to the upper segment. Clans like Greasewood and Coyote either sold their houses or left them in ruin, and Moenkopi at present reveals an unbalanced distribution of clans between the upper and lower segment sites (see Table 14).

The absence of lineage differentiation in Moenkopi is primarily because the community was not built for ceremonial purposes. It was originally a place for the excess population from Oraibi, and it has remained primarily an area of economic exploitation. Temporary residence is still characteristic of many of the present inhabitants of the village. None of the clans or their lineage segments were committed to stay in the village to uphold Hopihood. The village was formed of a loose union of "marginal" segments of Oraibi, and its component kin groups changed at the mercy of economic fluctuations from the larger society. One result of this change, which eventually dominated the social structure of Moenkopi, was the emergence of a nuclear family household as the most viable economic unit.

TABLE 14. Clan Distribution in Upper and Lower Moenkopi, 1962

Clan	Upper Moenkopi		Lower Moenkopi		Total	
	Male	Female	Male	Female	Male	Female
Rabbit	6	11	12	21	18	32
Tobacco	7	3	2		9	3
Parrot	1		2		3	
Bear	1		3		4	
Bluebird	2	2			2	2
Snake	3	3	12	10	15	13
Sand	2	1	3		5	1
Sun			2	2	2	2
Sun's Forehead	20	24	20	19	40	43
Reed	12	16	34	33	46	49
Greasewood	17	15		2	17	17
Coyote	30	30	6	7	36	37
Water Coyote	7	9	18	18	25	27
Ma'asau	9	10	7	18	16	28
Badger	11	11	5	5	16	16
Pi:kyas	9	11	9	8	18	19
No clan[a]	2		5	6	7	6
Non-Hopi	3	1	2	3	5	4
Unknown	4	6			4	6
Total	146	153	143	152	288	305

[a] Children through marriage with alien tribes without clan system, e.g., Walapai.

NUCLEAR FAMILY HOUSEHOLD

Household Group

Identification of a household group has been a problem among several authorities on the Hopi. Titiev (1944) and Eggan (1950) put more emphasis on the lineage, while Beaglehole (1935) and Brainard (1935) saw in a biological family the basic form of a Hopi household. The former defined the form of a household as a matrilineally extended family of three generations (Titiev, 1944:7, 46; Eggan, 1950:29) whose primary function was socialization or "primary orientation" (Eggan, 1950:30). In regard to coresidence of the group, Titiev stated that the group lives "under the same roof" (1944:46), while Eggan differed from him and said that it "normally occupies a set of adjoining rooms which it uses in common" (1950:29–30). Eggan specifically warned against its confusion with a census household (1950:337). His use of the term, however, was not entirely consistent as shown in the following statement: "If his [a child's] mother's sisters should live in separate *households*, their homes are equally his" (1950:30–31; my italics). Both Titiev and Eggan noted the occasional equivalence of a household group *minus* in-married males and a lineage (Titiev, 1944:46; Eggan, 1950:30), and Titiev, in particular, considered the group to be a stage in the development of a lineage and clan (1944:46).

On the other hand, Brainard followed the BIA census definition of 1930, in which a household consists of: ". . . those persons who were sharing a common dwelling unit and the activities and responsibilities [connected] with its maintenance" (1935:158). In her survey of Shipaulovi and Mishongnovi, Beaglehole followed Kroeber's definition of a household as a group sharing one and the same hearth (Kroeber, 1917:123) and found that the biological family of father, mother, and children was the modal household group (Beaglehole, 1935:43). Brainard, who came to the same conclusion as Beaglehole (1935:195), noted her disagreement with Eggan's description and suspected that the latter might represent a condition in the past (1935:195). Although her definition recognizes an economic aspect of the household, a trait peculiarly absent in Titiev and Eggan, she mostly ignores the consequence of interactions above the level of individual house groups.

These differences regarding the identification of a household group are not unique to the Hopi. Writers on the subject of social organization also hold divergent views on the definition of a household. Murdock, for instance, generally omits discussion of the household and uses the term only for the purpose of description (1965:23, 29). To him, a family, whether nuclear or composite, is coterminous with a household (1965:1, 23). In a recent article to distinguish the two groups conceptually, Solien defines a family "as a group of people bound together by that complex set of relationships known as kinship ties, between at least two of whom there exists a conjugal relationship." On the other hand, a household "implies common residence, economic cooperation, and socialization of children" (Solien, 1960:106). Finally, Goody avoids the use of the blanket term "household" and attempts to differentiate kinds of "domestic groups" in different situations or functional contexts (1958:56). According to this view, the functions implied in a household by Solien may be performed separately by different units, and Goody specifically concerns himself with the domestic groups that emerge in the process of food production and consumption (1958:56). In particular, Goody considers that coresidence is not a necessary criterion of a domestic group because the unit of food production and that of food consumption or preparation do not always coincide with each other (1958:56, 82–83).

In the following analysis of the Moenkopi households, then, I shall define a household group as a unit which cooperates in food production either through farming or through wage work and shares the right over distribution of the fruits of this productive activity. This rather awkward definition is a result of the following considerations. First, it takes care of the fact that a simple biological family, housed in a single room of a pueblo, has long been known among the Hopi as well as other Pueblo Indians as the unit of food consumption (Kroeber, 1917; Lowie, 1929). Surveys by Beaglehole (1935), Brainard (1935), and others, including a portion of one industrial survey conducted by the BIA in the 1920's, all confirmed the existence of this unit among the Hopi. Second, it identifies a lineage grouping, discovered by Lowie (1929) and Forde (1931), as a household type in the pre-wage work period. This unit represented an intermediate level of integration between the clan grouping and room-dwelling unit. Though not coresidential, it controlled the use and inheritance of the land it demarcated from clan land. At the same time, men who married women of the lineage cooperated in farming, and their produce was distributed among the component units which consumed it. In terms of food production and distribution, then, a lineage was the household unit. The general trend in Hopi household structure indicates a change from *lineage households* to *nuclear family households* or room-dwelling units. This definition serves to differentiate these types of households and to trace such a change in Moenkopi.

The Moenkopi Household in the Past

In default of adequate information, it is almost impossible to reconstruct the household composition for the early period of Moenkopi. What follows is extremely speculative and should be taken critically.

During the early period of seasonal residence, the Moenkopi population maintained only temporary homes in the buildings that Mindelef observed in the last century. Ties with Oraibi were kept alive through participation in rituals for a short while after the government entry into the area. It was through their respective clans that each house group was closely knit into the religious complex of Oraibi. During its stay in Moenkopi, the house group was only an economic organization, and a considerable portion of its farm produce was taken to Oraibi (see Simmons, 1963:93, 108) and distributed among its sister households. Unmarried young men of the lineage often visited the Moenkopi house to help in the farm work (see p. 123).

The new fields opened by individuals in Moenkopi were occasionally transferred to male members of their matrilineages who had migrated to Moenkopi from Oraibi or to the husbands of female members residing in the village. The migrants constructed their own houses in Moenkopi, often helped by their local matrilineal male relatives or their women's husbands. Men who married in Oraibi took their wives to Moenkopi and sought land belonging to their wives' lineages there. If the women's lineages had no land, they asked permission of the village chief to open fields. Unmarried men coming to Moenkopi also asked permission if they could not obtain land from their lineages. A Coyote clansman and his friends reclaimed a number of fields in the early 1910's. While he worked on his fields, he lived in the household of his sister's daughter, whose husband worked a portion of his fields. The produce from his field was distributed in his lineage household both in Moenkopi and Oraibi. After his marriage to a woman from Bacabi, however, he eventually moved away and left his Moenkopi fields to his sister's daughter and her husband (see p. 112). This type of land disposal was apparently common until about 1920, when surplus land was still available. The lineage household was the prevalent norm at that time.

Emergence of the Nuclear Family Household

The disorganization of Third Mesa ceremonial life through the village split in 1906 weakened the tie of Moenkopi with the mother village. At the same time, economic activity in the village required new kinds of efforts and caused the reorganization of social groups. Absence of clan lands in Moenkopi was a potent factor. Customary Hopi law had no particular provision regarding new fields opened by men, who, as a result, had to choose whether these should go to their own or their wives' lineages. Actual choices appear to have depended greatly on the marital status of each man. If a man moved with his wife to Moenkopi, the fields he opened there usually passed into the possession of his wife's people. If he was unmarried, they went to his own lineage. As the surplus land was taken up and as government regulation of the movement of the population became more stringent, however, migration for the sole purpose of reclamation dropped to nil. Land then came to pass most frequently from a man to his own children (see pp. 111ff.).

The development of lineage land ownership was further inhibited when, in the course of land transmission, the sons continued to work on the father's fields even after marriage (see p. 113). Continuity of land inheritance through women of the lineage was then broken, and both men and women came to claim the rights over the same land. The matrilineal principle of land inheritance gave way to a bilateral one.

The governmental efforts to encourage individual land ownership furthered this process and the land a man acquired from his father and continued to work now belonged to him and his family. With the establishment of the local Land Board in the Navajo tribe shortly after the last war and probation of inheritance of allotment fields, the concept of individual land "ownership," irrespective of sex, became further entrenched, and the people adapted the allocation of farm labor to these changes through concentration on their own fields.

Certain transitional steps to the new pattern were observed. Cooperative farming between sibling households may still occur in planting and harvesting, when a feast is given, but the major burden even of these operations is borne by individual families (see p. 123). With the introduction of farm machinery, house groups began to share their use, but machinery is most commonly shared by brother households and not sister households. These machines are never bought out of pooled funds, which do not exist in any form except among married couples (see pp. 203–4). Perhaps because agriculture has been a man's occupation, newly introduced tools reinforced the man's position in the household.

Another important factor in the breakdown of lineage solidarity in Moenkopi is participation in cash economy through wage work. I have already discussed the individual pattern of wage work and consequent disposal of cash income. Unlike farming, the capital basis of wage work economy was provided by the government and other alien agencies. The Hopi had no control over it. Since the government retained the ultimate right over natural resources, involvement of the Hopi in the national market economy was made only through wage work and spending in the national consumer market.

As men were progressively involved in this economy, their position as providers of the household was increasingly reinforced in the total economic complex. Moreover, by engaging in wage work, men became free from the controls of their own and their wives' lineages, which could not offer wage work. In the disposal of wage income, lineage groups could not intervene (see pp. 202ff.). Just as the room-dwelling unit traditionally controlled the consumption of field produce, it came to exercise exclusive control of the wage income from the labor of a husband. The wage work of the Hopi of Moenkopi based on a nuclear family unit contrasts with that of the Navajo or Papago, who migrated in extended family groups for off-reservation wage work and collectively spent wages earned by the entire extended family (Spicer, 1962:490). Wage work, in addition to reinforcing the economic solidarity of a nuclear family household, also segregated the family from other similar units of a lineage.

Though the Hopi were isolated from the "unitary market system" of the nation (Gough, 1961b:640) in regard to natural resources on the reservation, their participation in the system through wage work and the consumer market so reinforced the economic position of a husband as to result in the adoption of the nuclear family household as the basic unit of the economy.

Reinforcement of the economic status of the husband also modified his position as a father, for he became economically indispensable for the maintenance of the household. On the other hand, his role to his sister's children as "mother's brother" lost its previous significance. This was especially so when the school assumed a greater socializing function. The mother's brother is no longer a disciplinary figure in Moenkopi. Discipline is enforced either by the mother or the father.

Present Size of Moenkopi Households

The variation in household size in Moenkopi at the time of the field work (1962–63) is given in Table 15.

The one-person households in the table require comment. One in the upper segment is an old divorcée who alternates her residence seasonally between her own house in the village and that of one of her daughters in Grants, New Mexico. Although she has a married daughter in the village, she rarely visits her and never eats in her house. However, her grandchildren in the village often visit at her place and spend much of the play period there. On the other hand, her daughter seldom sets foot in her mother's place and, apart from infrequent exchanges of food (corn and meat), there is no significant amount of interaction between them. Since she frequents the Mennonite Church in the village, her

TABLE 15. Distribution in the Size of Present Moenkopi Households

Number of People	Number of Households	
	Lower Moenkopi	Upper Moenkopi
1	2	3
2	2	5
3	3	9
4	11	6
5	6	7
6	5	7
7	5	5
8	4	7
9	7	1
10	3	2
11	1	1
12	1	2
13	1	1
Total	51	56

affairs are mostly taken care of by the missionary family. The daughter has been caring for her father, who, though now married to a Navajo and living in the latter's house in Tuba City, frequently visits her house and helps in farming and other household chores. A childless widow in the upper segment, a Cherokee woman, lives isolated from her deceased husband's relations but supports herself through work in the Mormon church and occasional baby-sitting.

A comparison of the size of households in Moenkopi with that from other villages at different periods (see Table 16) has not produced a clear-cut picture. A divergence in average household size and distribution appears to be derived partly from the different definitions of a household and partly from incompleteness of respective surveys. It is likely that the government censuses missed a certain number of households and that families which would not be considered as households using the definition presented above were counted as independent households. In the 1962 government census, the portion for Moenkopi omitted more than 30 per cent of the constituent households and had to be supplemented from my own data. At the same time, children are often omitted from the count, thus reducing the household size.

As for the second possibility, Brainard herself reconstructed the tables of "households" for respective villages in which some of the households were found to consist of more than one census family (1935:160), and there were numerous cases in her tables

TABLE 16. Household Size Comparison of Selected Hopi Villages

	N	1	2	3	4	5	6	7	8	9	10+	Mean
Moenkopi (1962)	107	4.7	6.1	11.3	15.9	12.2	11.3	9.3	10.3	7.5	11.3	5.83
Hotevilla[a] (1950)	99	9.1	12.0	20.2	13.1	11.1	15.2	10.1	7.0	1.1	1.1	4.39
Bacabi[a] (1950)	39	12.8	25.6	15.4	17.9	7.7	5.1	7.7	5.1	—	2.6	3.00
Third Mesa[b] (1930)	241	12.5	17.0	14.1	14.5	13.3	18.7	7.5	3.7	2.1	1.7	4.10
Shipaulovi[c] (1934)	16	—	6.3	6.3	6.3	18.7	12.5	18.7	18.7	6.3	6.3	6.25
Mishongnovi[c] (1934)	35	—	5.7	8.6	11.4	11.4	—	11.4	25.8	11.4	14.3	6.83
Hopi[b] (1930)	593	12.6	16.0	14.8	15.2	13.9	11.5	8.1	5.1	2.0	1.4	4.20

[a] BIA Census, 1950 (Keams Canyon Agency).
[b] Brainard, 1935:214–15.
[c] Beaglehole, 1935:42.

of households which contained three census families. Taking this into account, the average household size in the four Third Mesa villages was recalculated:

	Hotevilla	Bacabi	New Oraibi	Oraibi
Number of households	77	31	53	33
Number of census families	93	34	56	38
Mean family size	4.5	3.8	4.7	3.2
Mean household size	5.5	4.2	5.0	3.7

Average size of a household on Third Mesa..........4.8

Since Brainard's house count was made in 1935 (1935:203), five years after the census taking, the population should be assumed to have grown during this time. Such is indicated by her own statement: "The house members were charted as they were given in the (census) records, *which did not account for all of the rooms*" (1935:160; my italics). At the same time, the number of slots given in the tables for notes on the "significant relationships" of the household members is 122 in the case of Hotevilla, and if each of these slots is to be taken for a "census family," the number is significantly larger than 93. These ambiguities in Brainard's analyses were not accounted for in her dissertation. It has been my experience also that the "census family," despite its emphasis on coresidence, tended to ignore it and, instead, was often identified by the family names. Consequently, a house that contained married-in husbands and their "families of procreation" was divided into respective "census families" under the family names of these men and made it seem that they were localized in several houses. In this respect, it should be noted that the government censuses are primarily concerned with head counts or individual tallies and generally do not give house affiliation.

From these considerations, it may be concluded that the size of a present Moenkopi household has not appreciably changed from that computed by Beaglehole and Brainard for the 1930's on Second and Third Mesas. Unfortunately, Brainard dismissed the difference between household size and the size of a census family as insignificant (1935:203), and she did not discuss the difference between Beaglehole's data and her own. I deem it fairly safe, therefore, to discard Brainard's figure of 4.2 as the average size of a Hopi household or even as the size of the census family. Contrary to Brainard (1935:214), the adjusted figure (about 6) shows that the size of a Hopi household is significantly larger than the national average of 1930 (3.8). Our figure also shows a slight increase from that for the period prior to 1900 (Beaglehole, 1935:42; Kroeber, 1917:123). The latter varies from 3.6 in Walpi to 5.4 in Mishongnovi with an average of 4.7. Whether this increase is owing to the reduction of a lineage household, composed of multiple house groups, into a nuclear family household in a single house with a compensatory increase in the size of each group in a house, or is simply owing to population increase cannot be determined from the available data. Indications, however, point to the latter possibility.

Forms of Moenkopi Households at Present

For a further analysis of the nature of Moenkopi households, three types of household groups are distinguished: *bilateral, matrilineal,* and *patrilineal.* The use of lineal terms here is only for the sake of description and does not imply the existence of any particular descent rules. Murdock has objected to the use of such terms as patri- or matrilineal extended family on the ground that they connote the existence of respective descent rules (1965:34). However, his alternative proposal based on marital residence is not without difficulties when applied to the modern household in Moenkopi. First, marriage residence is so variable as to make the classification on that basis of small significance. Second, there are occasions when men move to their children's homes in their old age or when women return with their children to the village after divorce to live in the homes of their brothers. These cases defy Murdock's type of classification. The main concern in the present analysis is in identifying the frequency of chains of matrilineal relatives in the households and not in residence per se. Lineality for the sake of description, finally, has not been abandoned in recent studies of household organizations (see Hammel, 1961).

The lineality of a household is determined by the following criteria. First, the *size criterion:* That lineality that covers or accounts for the maximum number of a household's members in a single group is the lineality of that household. If this does not resolve the classification, the *continuity criterion* is applied: If a household contains a chain of a man (woman) and his daughter-in-law (her son-in-law) or, in her (his) absence, his son's (her daughter's) children, the lineality of that household is patrilineal (matrilineal). If this does not resolve the classification either, that household is bilateral. Because of the particular interest in the bilateral household, it is further divided into:

1.1 One-person household.
1.2 Sibling household (siblings alone).
2.1 Two-person household (husband and wife).
2.1.1 Modified two-person household (couple and a sibling or siblings of either spouse).
2.2 Nuclear family household.
3 Bilaterally extended family household (more than two-generation span; see below).

The frequency of these types of households in Moenkopi is given in Table 17.

TABLE 17. Types of Households in Moenkopi

	I[a]						II[b]	III[c]	Total
	1.1	1.2	2.1	2.1.1	2.2	3			
Upper Moenkopi	3		4	1	30	1	12	4	55
Lower Moenkopi	2	1	2		27	2	11	6	51
Total	5	1	6	1	57	3	23	10	106
Percentage	4.7	0.9	5.7	0.9	53.7	2.8	21.8	9.4	

[a] Bilateral household.
[b] Matrilineal household.
[c] Patrilineal household.
Unknown case—1.

A formal application of the criteria runs into difficulty in one case. This consists of a man, his daughter, and her children. A matrilineal group can be formed of the daughter and her children and accounts for the maximal number of the household members. However, if she has only one child, regardless of its sex, the group should be bilateral because the size of the maximum matrilineal group is the same as that of the maximum patrilineal group, i.e., two, and yet there is no chain as described in the second criterion. Thus the types defined here contain some ambiguity in borderline cases. Nevertheless, the entire definition is retained primarily because it not only is inclusive of the descriptive definition given earlier of the types of families but also makes it possible to deal with variations from the ideal types given in current descriptive definitions.

PREDOMINANCE OF NUCLEAR FAMILY HOUSEHOLD. A glance at the above table clearly indicates the dominance of the nuclear family household, which, when combined with two-person households (I.2.1), includes nearly 60 per cent of Moenkopi households. This frequency deviates drastically from some of the past studies of household types in Hopi society. Thus Beaglehole's study in Second Mesa in 1934 revealed only three such cases out of 16 households (18.8 per cent) at Shipaulovi and 10 of 35 (28.6 per cent) at Mishongnovi (1935). In her survey of the households in Hotevilla, Brainard counted 16 households out of 77, each consisting "of more than one family" (1935:197). Taking the rest for the nuclear family households, their percentage is 55. However, as she notes, one "family" is in the form of "a man, and his wife, and either or both parents and children" (1935:197) and hence slightly larger than the nuclear family herein defined. The figure, then, must be taken as representing the possible maximum and could well be smaller in reality.

The prevalence of the nuclear family household type is the result of a recently increasing preference for neolocality and the feasibility of early "fission" of a young household as a result of participation in the modern economic conditions and the breakdown of the traditional agricultural society.

EXTENSION IN HOUSEHOLD GROUP. In order to examine the factors leading up to this situation as well as to explore the structural relevance of a nuclear family in the developmental cycle of a present-day Moenkopi household group, we shall now analyze the nature of the extended household and its position in the kinship system of Moenkopi.

(1) *Frequency of Extension.* By *extension* is meant here an accretion of relatives other than those in an already extant or reasonably constructed nuclear family within a household. A *reasonably constructed* nuclear family is one constructed by a maximally possible number of household members. Thus a household of a woman, her children, and brother is extended by the last member. A *lineally extended* household has a more than two-generation span and consists of any combination of the following kin: a man (woman), his wife (her husband), his (her) child (children), its spouse (that of one of the children), the latter's child (children), its spouse (that of one of the children), the latter's child (children), its spouse (that of one of the children), and so on. As a marginal case, a household of parents and their son (daughter) and his (her) spouse is here defined as lineally extended.

A *laterally extended* household includes members who cannot in any manner be described by the categories mentioned in the lineal extension and yet who belong to the same generation as at least one member of the component nuclear family, extant or reasonably constructed. *Lineal-lateral extension* is 1) for a lineally *and* laterally extended household and 2) for a household with members who are not counted in either extension. With these typological definitions on extension, we find:

Lineal extension	24	75.0%
Lateral extension	3	9.4
Lineal-lateral extension	5	15.6
Total	32	100.0

As this shows, cases of lineal extension far exceed lateral. The "avoidance" of lateral extension is also shown in the fact that there is not a single case of two or more married couples in a single generation in any of the extended households in Moenkopi. Such cases seem to have been comparatively rare even in the past. Beaglehole lists only one with two sisters and their husbands out of 13 extended households in Mishongnovi (1935:43). Sixteen extended households of Hotevilla included four, each of which contained more than one couple in the same generation in 1910 (Brainard, 1935:198–200). Brainard, however, mentions that "No maternal group included more than one married daughter" (1935: 198).

The frequency of households each containing more than one married couple is also small in the village at present. Only 11.3 per cent (12) of all households consist of two-couple households. No household contains three or more couples. The relative frequency for Second Mesa is 18.8 per cent (3) in Shipaulovi and 11.4 per cent (4) in Mishongnovi as of 1934 (Beaglehole, 1935). In Brainard's Hotevilla sample, 14 per cent (11) out of 77 households were made up of two or more couples in 1930 and only two of these contained three couples each.

The frequencies for the types of lineal extension in the three villages are:

	Moenkopi (1962)		Shipaulovi (1934)		Mishongnovi (1934)	
Matrilineal	17	58.6%	9	69%	20	80%
Patrilineal	9	31.0	2	15.5	0	0
Bilateral	3	10.3	2	15.5	5	20

While the table does not differentiate our village from the others, an examination of the households with two couples in Moenkopi reveals that half of them are patrilineal and the rest matrilineal.

In fact, matrilineal extension of the Moenkopi households contains features deviant from what is commonly accepted in the notion of extension.

(2) *Continuous and Discontinuous Extension.* A domestic group develops in the manner of a cycle in which the group reproduces itself while giving rise to various categories of kin in different stages (see Goody, 1958). In the course of development Moenkopi households extend beyond the simple nuclear family groups and then contract and finally disappear. Many of the extended households in Moenkopi probably are a result of this internal growth and represent intermediate stages in the developmental cycle. I shall call the extension due to a continuous process of household development *continuous extension*. On the other hand, there are, especially among the present-day households of Moenkopi, extensions resulting from accretions of household members who had once left their natal households and, in some cases, married outside and even raised children there, but who later returned to their natal households because of divorce, death of a spouse, economic difficulties, and other reasons. Since this type of extension involves a period of discontinuity in the cycle, I shall call it *discontinuous extension*.

This classification does not purport to be universally applicable and, in particular, for the societies where the extended household is the norm, it is a trite one. That such classification can be made meaningful in the present analysis shows in itself a particular aspect of the Moenkopi social structure. On this basis, the extensions are divided as follows:

	Continuous		Discontinuous		Total
Matrilineal	5	29.4%	12	70.6%	17
Patrilineal	5	55.5	4	44.5	9
Bilateral	2	66.7	1	33.3	3
Total	12	41.4	17	58.6	29

Thus, discontinuous extension far exceeds continuous. In order to see the implications of this distribution, let us first examine the genesis of continuous extension.

Continuous Extension. In the traditional pattern of household development, a nuclear family expands first by marriage of one of the daughters in the family. A newly married couple usually resides in the wife's household (matrilocal) and raises one or two children there. Beaglehole mentions that "The tendency today is for the married daughter to remove to a separate household as soon as her family is enlarged by two or three children" (1935:44). In the meantime, another daughter may bring her husband to the house, thus expanding the group. Before this happens or shortly after the second couple is formed, the first couple may leave to establish its own household. Sons leave for other households on marriage. The original household may thus be continued and maintained by at least one daughter and her husband even after her parents die. In this scheme a house building is seldom abandoned.

However, only five Moenkopi households exhibit this stage of extension in the traditional scheme of cycle. One in Lower Moenkopi consists of a mother and daughter, their husbands, and the daughter's children. All the daughter's siblings, both male and female, have either married out and established their own households in and outside the village or have been working off the reservation. The daughter's husband is also from Lower Moenkopi and is intermittently employed as an unskilled construction laborer. Her father is a long established sheepherder and stays in his camp, seldom returning to the village (see p. 169). Thus the young couple assumes the major burden of household upkeep as well as caring for the aged mother. The house itself is quite large by village standards and has often been used as a stage for kachina dancing in the past. The young husband also tends the farms belonging to this household as well as his own obtained from his father.

The second example, in Upper Moenkopi, is a family of 12, consisting of the parents, their children, a husband of one of their daughters, and the children of another daughter. The last had once been married to an Eskimo and both resided in this household until they divorced and the husband left. After this, the second daughter married a boy from Second Mesa and both started living there. Within a period of about six months, during which time the couple lived in this household, their marriage ceremony was completed. The young husband as well as his father-in-law were employed in Tuba City. A similar household composition, representing a slightly more advanced stage of development, is found in one household in Lower Moenkopi, where the young couple have children now.

A further stage in the traditional cycle is a household in the lower village, consisting of an old man, his divorced daughter, and her children.

Continuous matrilineal extension may also occur without involving marriage. Thus one household in the lower village contains two sisters, each with children born of irregular unions; they have never married and have remained in their present household most of their lives. Their father works on the farm, while they receive government welfare and are occasionally employed in Tuba City.

Seven cases of continuous extension deviate from the norm of "matrilocality." The junior couples in all but three of these cases consist of Moenkopi men and their wives from outside the village (New Oraibi, Hotevilla, one Navajo from the Tuba City area, and one New Mexico Pueblo girl). The last marriage was a union of a man from the village and a Pueblo girl who had been working as a practical nurse in the Tuba City hospital. The two men with Hopi wives from other villages began their marriages in the homes of their own parents and one at least raised his family there. One moved to his father's house soon after the marriage feast was given in the girl's house in Hotevilla. Both men have older sisters, all of whom established their households elsewhere in and outside the village. The couple from Moenkopi is now residing with the boy's parents. The girl is the third oldest (17 years old) of 13 children while the boy is 21. His only sibling is an older brother living next door with his family. The economic condition of the couple has not allowed them to live in a separate house, let alone with the girl's parents; the boy has been working in a Tuba City service station. The other four men are also employed in Tuba City. As shall be shown later, patrilocal residence has been extremely common in Moenkopi and these cases must have been frequently repeated in the recent past. The fact that the actual number of such cases is rather small appears entirely due to the recently much curtailed period in the extended stage of the cycle and to the displaced position of an extended family in the modern household structure of Moenkopi.

Discontinuous Extension. The majority of extended households in the village are of this type. The circumstances for this are as follows.

a) Divorce and Separation. Women with their children, i.e., a matrifocal family in form, or men alone often join their natal households after divorce or separation. The five women who have returned to the village lived in Tuba City, Red Lake, Cameron, Grand Canyon, and Flagstaff respectively and raised their families there. After divorce or separation, they all came back to the homes of their parents, sister, or brother, where they had once lived before marriage.

Four men returned to their natal households or to the home of a sister. These men left their children with their previous wives. As a result, a man's return seldom results in extension and when it does, as in these cases, the extension is either lateral or lineal-lateral.

b) Employment and Unemployment. This is another frequent cause of temporary extension at present. In four cases men brought their wives and children to their parental households in the village. Three of the four wives are from Walapai, Kochiti, and Zia respectively and one is a Hopi from Hotevilla. The man with the Hotevilla wife and another with an alien wife are employed in Tuba City, while a third commutes to Kaibito. The man with the Walapai wife had been working in Phoenix, where he originally married and raised a family. However, when he lost his job after an auto accident, he returned with his family to his parents' household in Moenkopi.

Three Moenkopi women brought their families to their parents' homes from outside the reservation. Two have Pima husbands, and one is married to a Hopi from New Oraibi. The latter had been residing in Flagstaff, where her husband worked as an electrician. When construction of a Navajo boarding school began in Tuba City in 1960, the husband acquired a job there and moved to his in-laws' home. In 1962 his family began constructing a home on one of the farms of his father-in-law and was in the process of moving out of the in-laws' house.

A fourth woman returned to her brother's home in the upper segment with her Zuni husband and children. The brother had been living alone in a house that belonged to his long deceased mother. He works on the farms belonging to him as well as one belonging to his brother and eats at the latter's home. He has not married. Thus a discontinuous lateral extension resulted from the return of his sister's family. Soon the Zuni husband found a job at Kaibito, where he stays during the workdays.

c) Management of Parental Household. A woman married to a man from Mishongnovi came back to the village with her family from Flagstaff in order to manage the household of her parents. The woman's father had been working in Kayenta, where he had been assigned government housing. Consequently, he took his wife there and left his children in the care of his daughter. Her Mishongnovi husband, in turn, works on the farms of his wife's parents and occasionally does wage work in Tuba City.

A somewhat reverse arrangement was made in another household. A daughter lived in Phoenix, married a man from Hotevilla, and raised a family. While in Phoenix, she sent her daughter to her mother's home in the village to be taken care of there so she might also work in the city.

d) *Care of the Aging Parents.* A daughter and her husband returned from Phoenix in order to help her sick mother and attend to the household chores. Her husband had been working as an accountant in a grocery store in Phoenix but when the news of her mother's ailment arrived, they decided to leave for the village. Her sick mother had been virtually alone in her house. Since the return of the daughter's family, her mother's sister has also come into the household from Tuba City because of divorce. The daughter has one older sister, living in Leupp, and three older brothers, all married, but only one of them lives in the village.

One case of lineal extension of the discontinuous type involves a man moving to his daughter's household. The daughter established her household in the upper village on marriage to a man from Hotevilla. Her father, in the meantime, had been living with his two sons in a house in the lower segment after separation from his wife. Before 1935 the latter moved up to the upper village, where her new husband built a two-story house. As his two remaining sons married, his children discussed the welfare of their aging father. It was decided that his sole daughter would accept him in return for his services on the farms belonging to her household. With his move, he also brought a field opened by him down in the *Ma'asau* area. The original house in the lower village was eventually sold and the proceeds went to the daughter.

e) *Care of Orphaned Children.* A couple in the lower segment "took in" the children of their daughter after her death outside the village. The daughter's husband apparently abandoned the children and his whereabouts are unknown.

f) *Borderline Case.* There is one case difficult to classify. A girl from the lower segment married a man from Shongopavi. The couple then moved to the house where her mother's brother had been living. Her parents were living in the same village but in another house. Both structures are claimed by her mother, who inherited them from her mother. The mother's brother, when living alone, ate in his sister's house and helped to work on her farms. During this period, he was thus a part of his sister's household. Though the man is now eating in his house of residence with his sister's daughter's family, he continues to work on his sister's farms. The girl's husband is not a well-settled man; he does not help on the farms and has frequently changed jobs. He is away from the village much of the time.

Since the beginning of an autonomous household was made with the move of the young couple, it may be argued that the present set-up, including the couple and their children and the girl's mother's brother, is a result of continuous development. The girl has not lived outside the village before or after marriage. It is finally difficult to determine to what extent the present household is independent from the mother household. However, because the course of its development deviates from the traditional continuous pattern in its move out of the parental household on marriage, it is included in the discontinuous category of extension.

The majority of these extensions are temporary. In one case, the nuclear family of a Moenkopi youth left for Phoenix after about three years' stay in his parents' household. Their departure was occasioned by employment obtained by the youth through the aid of the local BIA. In another, a divorcée left for Flagstaff, where she stayed at her brother's home while looking for a job there. She left her children in her parents' home. During their stay in the village, however, those who return become easily reincorporated in the life of the recipient households and perform the duties expected of the household members. Activities mainly revolve around the traditional type of undertaking, such as farming, sheep herding, and in the case of women, household chores. Since these activities are often neglected because of a shortage of labor, the returnees appear to find little problem in readjusting themselves to village life.

As the above examples show, discontinuous extension is, in the main, a result of involvement in the outside wage work economy and most often represents a temporary retreat from striving to make good on and off the reservation. Most of the returnees do not regard their stay in the village as permanent but are looking for another opportunity to get out of the village or establish their own households within it. Their return is thus not conditioned by any felt need to continue the original household.

The composition of a Moenkopi household is thus flexible and unstable at present. In order to adjust to the difficulties in contemporary family life, a household emits its segments to on- and off-reservation communities outside Moenkopi. At the same time, it absorbs previous members who meet any difficulty outside. The instability of Hopi household composition may not in itself be a novel phenomenon, for divorces and separations have been common in the traditional Hopi society (Titiev, 1944:39; Eggan, 1950:56).

Yet today the circumstances of return often derive from the irrevocable commitment of the village to the economic conditions of the larger society.

Finally, the direction of return, apart from cases of divorce and separation, is not unequivocal. Four families were pulled to their husbands' side, and three to the wives'. In cases of divorce and separation, the children appear to be invariably taken by their mothers, although in two cases, it was otherwise. The solidarity between a mother and her children, however, has not remained unchallenged.

Modern Developmental Cycle and the Moenkopi Household

The predominance of nuclear family households corresponds to the increasing preference among the young people to establish their own households and become, even if partially, independent from the parental ones. This preference for neolocality has long been recognized by writers on the Hopi. Beaglehole mentions the desperate attempt of a man to move out of his in-laws' house, which was frustrated by his mother-in-law who followed him to his new residence (1935:44). According to her, this man was eager to build his own home but "For economic reasons, he is [was] unable to do this" (1935:44). In Moenkopi, economic conditions in and outside the village have improved considerably and as a result, young couples do not hesitate to set up independent households at the earliest possible opportunity.

In the order of "budding off" from the parental household, there appears to be a slight tendency for the older children to marry out first, leaving the younger ones at home. Contrary to Titiev's statement (1944:47), there is no trend for the eldest daughter to take over the parents' house. No explicit rule was stated by the villagers as to which of the siblings should stay to take care of the aging parents and eventually inherit the house. While a daughter was most often cited as the one who should do so, the villagers were vague about her position in the sibling group.

It appears, then, that the extended household is no longer stable, nor does it represent a built-in segment in the developmental history of all the households. The early "budding off" of a child's household also implies that the process described by Titiev (1944: 46–47) of segmentation of a lineage group does not hold in Moenkopi today. The split does not occur at a later stage when a daughter (Titiev's #3) raises her children within her mother's household, but at marriage, when she leaves her parental home to create her own household. Two factors underlie the accelerated fission.

First, the older house structures have long ceased to be objects of inheritance. In the beginning no sanction was provided against the abandonment of Moenkopi houses. Then, when the Tuba City Agency decided to allocate house sites in the present upper segment in 1914, the young people immediately took the opportunity to move out of the crowded pueblo in the lower segment. New houses were rapidly built and the older ones in the lower segment were either abandoned or sold to new migrant families or rented out. Finally, when the upper segment site began to be filled up, the opportunity was already present for the families of the third generation to establish homes either in off-reservation towns or in government housing units. In this process of expansion, the inheritance of older houses often became superfluous; now better homes could be obtained with a small effort, so that by the time a house became an object of inheritance, most of the children had already established themselves in their own homes. Thus the inheritance of houses remained and still remains undefined. In native theory, new houses in the village are built for wives and hence belong to them. Thus, at divorce men usually leave the houses. However, the inheritance precipitated by the death of an original couple is not a formalized procedure, but involves mutual arrangements among the possible heirs. Often the houses remain vacant to be used by families on occasional visits from off-reservation towns. In one case the inheritance became a legal dispute not because the house was needed by any party but because one of the possible heirs tried to secure her title over it, thus inviting the claims of others. The result was an equal division among the children, while its use alone was left to the initial claimant. What appears to happen most frequently and is regarded by the villagers as an acceptable procedure is that a young couple, usually a daughter and her husband, come back to the household to attend to the needs of the aging parents and they inherit the house. In so doing, however, the child's family does not abandon its abode elsewhere; hence, after the death of the parents, houses often remain without residents.

It may be expected, however, that inheritance of house structures shall become a major question in the near future, since recent houses include such improved features as toilet and kitchen facilities and they are generally much larger than the old "rooms" in the lower segment. The parents who raised families in the older houses and who continued living there for awhile sometimes move up to the improved houses of their sons and daughters in the upper segment and use their own houses only for sleeping or renting.

The decline of agriculture and bilateral division of land also undermined the continuity of a household group. Through the onrush of wage economy, farm land ceased to be a powerful cohesive factor for the young members of the household; land was no longer a mark of economic independence but was distributed to the descendant households where farm labor was available. Thus it did not accrue to the parental authority, by which the landholding parents could have appropriated the labor contribution of the children. The land thus distributed did not entail any subsequent relationship between donor and recipient households nor was there any other specific prestation between them. On the part of the parents, no attempt was made to retain a major portion of the land in order to secure the future welfare of the descendants who would carry on the maintenance of the household. The land ceased to be a factor in the continuity of a household group. A corollary to this is the fact that among the villagers, the older men, whose descendants established their own households, never retire from ordinary farm labor. They are not only not in a position of any authority vis-à-vis their descendants, but the sole avenue through which their existence is taken care of is their own labor contribution to the descendants' households. Thus an old man of 80 was finally taken into the household of his daughter on condition that he take care of the farms of his son-in-law, his wife's mother's brother, and his own. On rare occasions, an old man is able to secure his later economic support by giving out his land or livestock to the children and, in turn, receiving their care. This may also happen between him and his distant junior kin. The trend is incipient and yet it appears the nature of the change is that economic goods may eventually become a means to insure the position of the parents and thus to induce the continuity of a household.

To conclude, the phase of extension in the developmental cycle of a Moenkopi household is, at least at present, no longer a part of the process. While the nuclear family household has assumed a far greater significance as a form of domestic group in Moenkopi, it is not a trans-generational corporate group but rather an organization resulting from adjustment to the swiftly changing economic conditions surrounding Moenkopi. The high frequency of discontinuous extension among the extended households in the village

268 MODERN TRANSFORMATIONS OF MOENKOPI PUEBLO

today indicates a mode of accommodation in this process of change from the corporate lineage household in the traditional farming society to the nuclear family household in the wage economy.

Matrifocal Family in Moenkopi

There are four households (3.7 per cent) which fit the formal aspect of Solien's definition of matrifocal family (Kunstadter, 1963:56). Each of these consists of a mother and her children. There is one that comprises a father and his children (patrifocal). The frequency of the Moenkopi matrifocal family is much smaller than the 9 per cent among the Mescalero Apache (Boyer, 1964:596). Of the four mothers, one is a widow of 70 and has a son of 49 who farms their land as well as works for wages in Tuba City. The second is also a widow, age 56, with children ranging from 17 to nine. Her household, however, has long been supported by that of her married daughter who lives in the village, and when the latter moved to Kaibito, she joined her with all her children. The third mother is a widow of 34 and has eight children. She has long been a recipient of welfare funds. It was rumored that a young man of the village was regularly visiting her and about a year after the census was taken, the young man moved into her house. The mother of the last household, a divorcée who had a Pima husband, works in the Tuba Boarding School as a matron and is also partially supported by her 24-year-old daughter in the household, who is occasionally employed in Tuba City. While wage earnings provide their economic base, she also has an older daughter living in her *piki* house and obtains a supply of field produce from her son-in-law, who works on land inherited from his father. Thus, aside from the last mentioned, which itself fits only uncomfortably Solien's definition, there is no household in Moenkopi that has confined "the effective and enduring relationships within . . . those existing between consanguineal kin" (Kunstadter, 1963:56) of the household.

There is a comparatively rich opportunity for a woman to be the breadwinner of the household at least before she reaches senility, and since there are now those kinds of jobs which demand prolonged separation of husbands from homes (construction work, road building, and forest fire fighting), it may be expected that the matrifocal family may develop more frequently. However, women who work as matrons and cooks in remote boarding schools on the reservation may also be separated from the household for extended periods. These separations due to job conditions are usually regarded as temporary, and most men and women who are away from their own homes in the village appear to take particular pains to get back on their weekly days off. When the women are away during the workdays, their children, often already married in the village, take care of the fathers' households. Men as well as women who are thus temporarily absent from the households are regarded as still belonging to them and except in the case of widowhood or divorce, the families remain intact.

Finally, in their move out of the village for wage work, the family members, especially husbands, prefer to move as a family unit. The existence of farms and relatives, irrespective of laterality, to be taken care of in the village, the availability of family residence in the job areas, and the difference in occupation between the spouses often prevent such a movement, but, as soon as these problems are solved in some way, they tend to vacate houses in the village in order that their direct families may form their own households. Occasional difficulties in conjugal and familial relations often derive from the frustrations caused by men's prolonged alienation from family life and women's fear, in turn, of alienation from their relatives and from the intimacy of village life.

While the man's position has increasingly been incorporated in his own household as provider through extensive participation in the wage economy, divorce and widowhood are dealt with by discontinuous extension, which vitiates the emergence of the matrifocal family. Apart from one-person households, therefore, no household in Moenkopi is without some men to perform the role of provider.

To conclude, the household structure of today's Moenkopi can be described as *bilaterally oriented*. Apart from the solidarity of mother and children, revealed at divorce, no salient matrilineal feature is present in the household group.

MARRIAGE

In the preceding sections on the household, it was suggested that residence and the stability of contemporary marriages were factors contributing to the prevalence of the nuclear family household. The present section on marriage deals with these factors in some detail.

Residence

RANGE OF MATE SELECTION. During the 1910's, men with their wives migrated from Third Mesa villages to establish homes in

Moenkopi. In 1914 Gregory stated that "each marriage of a Moenkopi resident with a man or woman from the Tusayan villages usually results in the founding of a new home on the Tuba Oasis" (1915:119). About 20 years later, Titiev observed, "In former times the custom of matrilocal residence was probably universally observed with the possible exception of inter-mesa marriages where a wife went to live in her husband's village. More recently, all brides of Moenkopi men have gone there to live" (1944:16). The examination of the local origins of married couples found in the 1937 census reveals that 27 per cent of the couples originated outside Moenkopi (see Table 18). At the same time, however, the frequency of brides settling with Moenkopi men in the village was only about an eighth of the entire marriages and far smaller than that of bridegrooms coming from outside. Despite serious changes in other types of marriage, the ratio between in-marrying brides and bridegrooms remained the same for subsequent periods (see Tables 18 and 19).

On the other hand, the immigration of couples originating outside the village has been swiftly decreasing since 1937 (see Table 20) and, conversely, the young people appear increasingly to choose their mates from within the village. This indicates that since the end of the last war, the village has become more and more closed to the Hopi from outside Moenkopi. In fact, for the two post-war censuses, I was able to find only four couples that migrated to Moenkopi.

The village remains open, however, for those who marry the children of Moenkopi, and the proportion of men and women moving to the village through marriage shows but a small change for the three periods. Of these marriages between Moenkopi and other villages of Hopiland, the majority of the spouses are recruited from Third Mesa (see Table 21), confirming Eggan's statement: "Intermarriage between mesas has played a relatively minor role in Hopi socio-cultural integration. . . . Within each mesa there is more intermarriage, particularly with the colony villages" (1964:178).

There is a slight indication that since the last war, marriages to the Hopi of Second Mesa have been increasing. Two women from Shongopavi and Mishongnovi have been established in the village since 1948.

Inter-tribal marriages also show a significant increase since the war (see Table 18). In this type of marriage, there is no appreciable difference between sexes. While the ratio among all couples

TABLE 18. Local Origins of Married Couples in Moenkopi

Husband-Wife	1937		1948				1962			
			Increment		All		Increment		All	
Intra-village	18	(28.6%)	17	(32.7%)	29	(32.6%)	20	(37.0%)	42	(38.6%)
Moenkopi-other village	8	(12.7)	9	(17.3)	13	(14.6)	8	(14.8)	16	(14.7)
Other village-Moenkopi	19	(30.2)	13	(25.0)	26	(29.2)	16	(29.6)	30	(27.5)
Immigration	17	(27.0)	2	(3.8)	10	(11.2)	2	(3.7)	9	(8.3)
Inter- (Moenkopi-alien)			6	(11.5)	6	(6.7)	5	(9.2)	6	(5.5)
tribal (alien-Moenkopi)	1	(1.6)	5	(9.6)	5	(5.6)	3	(5.6)	6	(5.5)
Total inter-tribal	1	(1.6)	11	(21.2)	11	(12.4)	8	(14.8)	12	(11.0)
Total	63		52		89		54		109	

TABLE 19. Local Origins of Married Couples Resident outside Moenkopi

Husband-Wife	1937		1948			1962	
			Increment	All		Increment	All
Intra-village	3	(60.0%)	8	(27.6%)	9	(28.1%)	2	(15.4%)	9	(19.2%)
Moenkopi–other village[a]			4	(13.8)	5	(15.6)			7	(14.8)
Other village–Moenkopi			4	(13.8)	4	(12.5)	3	(23.0)	7	(14.8)
Once immigrated couples	2	(40.0)	1	(3.4)	2	(6.3)			2	(4.3)
Inter- (Moenkopi-alien)			2	(6.9)	2	(6.3)	5	(38.5)	10	(21.3)
tribal (alien-Moenkopi)			9	(31.0)	9	(28.1)	2	(15.4)	9	(19.2)
Total inter-tribal			11	(38.0)	11	(34.4)	7	(53.9)	19	(40.5)
Unknown			1	(3.4)	1	(3.2)	1	(7.7)	3	(6.4)
Total	5		29		32		13		47	

[a] A few in this slot are in other villages of Hopiland by matrilocal marriage.

Note: The cases represented here were identified through censuses, genealogies, and individual interviews. The actual number of cases may well exceed the figures herein presented.

TABLE 20. Immigration of Married Couples

Husband-Wife	1937	1948 Increment	1948 All	1962 Increment	1962 All
Old Oraibi–Old Oraibi	7		2		
Old Oraibi–New Oraibi	1		1		
Old Oraibi–Bacabi	2	1	3		3
New Oraibi–New Oraibi	1				
New Oraibi–Mishongnovi		1	1		1
Hotevilla–New Oraibi	1		1		1
Hotevilla–Hotevilla	3		1		1
Bacabi–New Oraibi	1		1		1
Shongopavi–Hotevilla				1	1
Shongopavi–Shongopavi				1	1
Old Oraibi–unknown	1				
Total	17	2	10	2	9

resident in the village remains small, it is the most prevalent form of marriage outside the village. In 1948, 34 per cent of the couples whose spouses were from Moenkopi or who once established homes in the village and then moved out were married inter-tribally, and in 1962 about 41 per cent were so (see Table 19). It appears from this that inter-tribal marriages tend to be more frequent among those from Moenkopi who live outside and intend to stay there. Many such couples who came back to the village and made homes eventually left after several years' residence. Since this is the only type of marriage in which the resident couples are less frequent than those outside, it may be concluded that the village is still a difficult place to live for those from other tribes.

The range of mate choice has thus clearly expanded during the last 30 years. While it is mainly confined within the Indian groups (see Table 22), inter-tribal contacts have been increasing through common experience in boarding schools, BIA and off-reservation employment, and, less frequently, tribal politics and pan-Indian movements. Marriages soon after graduation from the boarding schools appear especially frequent nowadays, and the young couples usually take jobs outside the areas of their origin.

NEOLOCAL RESIDENCE. In traditional Hopi society, matrilocal residence was a "normative" mechanism which buttressed the matrilineal theory of land and house ownership and secured the continuity of lineage and clan. Theoretically, the position of a husband under this set-up was reduced to that of a mere inseminator and

TABLE 21. Local Origins of In-Marrying Spouses

			Third Mesa				
			Old Oraibi	New Oraibi	Hotevilla	Bacabi	Subtotal
MALE		1937	14 (73.7%)	1 (5.3%)	1 (5.3%)	2 (10.5%)	18 (94.7%)
	1948	Increase	1 (7.7)	1 (7.7)	7 (53.9)	1 (7.7)	10 (77.0)
		All	9 (34.6)	2 (7.7)	8 (30.8)	3 (11.5)	22 (84.5)
	1962	Increase	6 (37.5)	3 (18.8)	2 (12.5)		11 (68.7)
		All	10 (33.3)	4 (13.3)	5 (16.7)	3 (10.0)	22 (73.4)
FEMALE		1937	5 (62.5)	1 (12.5)	1 (12.5)	1 (12.5)	8 (100.0)
	1948	Increase	2 (22.2)	2 (22.2)	1 (11.1)	2 (22.2)	7 (77.7)
		All	4 (30.8)	3 (23.1)	1 (7.7)	3 (23.1)	11 (84.5)
	1962	Increase		3 (37.5)	3 (37.5)	1 (12.5)	7 (87.5)
		All	3 (18.7)	5 (31.2)	4 (25.0)	2 (12.5)	14 (87.5)

a small addition to the lineage labor force. As Titiev states, "a woman's material welfare depend[ed] very little on her husband" (1944:43).

In Moenkopi, however, men played an important role in the household in the colony, where no such guarantee of a large kin group existed. They appropriated land and provided their households with its produce. Through the equal or bilateral division of land, a parental household was dissolved into several descendant households, each exhibiting a certain amount of economic autonomy. This autonomy increased further as the Hopi were more intensively involved in the cash economy based on wage labor.

These changes in economic conditions immediately surrounding the village encouraged early fission from parental households and resulted in neolocal residence among the young. Young couples now seldom remain in the parental household of either spouse until children are born.

PROCESS OF KINSHIP TRANSFORMATION 275

				Second Mesa				
			Shon-gopavi	Mishong-novi	Shipau-lovi	Subtotal	Tuba City	Total
M A L E	1937			1 (5.3%)		1 (5.3%)		19
	1948	Increase	2 (15.4%)	1 (7.7)		3 (23.1)		13
		All	2 (7.7)	2 (7.7)		4 (15.4)		26
	1962	Increase	4 (25.4)		1 (6.3%)	5 (31.2)		16
		All	6 (20.0)	1 (3.3)	1 (3.3)	8 (26.7)		30
F E M A L E	1937					1 (11.1)	1 (11.1%)	8
	1948	Increase	1 (11.1)			1 (7.7)	1 (7.7)	9
		All	1 (7.7)			1 (12.5)		13
	1962	Increase		1 (12.5)		2 (12.5)		8
		All	1 (6.2)	1 (6.2)				16 12.2

TABLE 22. Alien Spouses Resident in Moenkopi

1937		1948		1962	
Husband	Wife	Husband	Wife	Husband	Wife
White		2 Navajo		2 *Pima*[a]	
		2 Zuni		2 Zuni	
		Laguna		Laguna	
				Zuni	
			2 Navajo		Navajo
			San Juan		*Choctaw*
			Santa Clara		*Walapai*
			2 Cherokee		*Zia*
					Kochiti
					N. Mex.
					Pueblo
Total					
1		5	6	6	6

[a] Cases in italics are new additions.

Within the village many new houses have been constructed to accommodate new couples since 1914, and with financial help from the government, larger and sturdier houses have appeared in the upper segment. During the 1950's, however, there were few house sites still available, and the newlyweds began using *piki* houses and storerooms as their homes and renting houses left vacant by the people living in off-reservation towns. If neither alternative was available, a temporary hut was constructed to house a young couple. In one case, a temporary partition was built to accommodate a couple in an already crowded home in the lower segment.

As a consequence of neolocality, the relationship of wife and husband has been undergoing change. Though the paternal position is now secured in the economic structure of a household, it is still the wife who usually makes management decisions and the husband who executes them. Occasionally, however, a woman continues to depend on the members of her parental household, especially her parents, in matters of child rearing. This leads to decreasing interaction between the father and his children, and some men are dissatisfied with this situation. On the other hand, some men are frustrated because they seem to think of their fatherly role as being too burdensome. While the framework of a nuclear family household is already firm in the economic structure of the village, the process of internal adjustment is still going on.

The new residence practice has also caused an acute strain in the relationship between a man and his in-laws. Now that he has his own home to attend to, he often withdraws from service to his in-laws. Traditionally, a male in-law or *mö:nang* was a young man of strength, as his epithet, *pekanghoya* or "warrior twin," indicates (see Simmons, 1963:274). He was expected to cooperate with his father-in-law in farming, grazing, and hunting, and in return he acquired sexual access to his wife and daily food and lodging from the in-laws. However, through participation in a wage economy, he has ceased to depend on the in-laws' land to provide for his wife and children. He provides a house for his family and is fed by his wife with the food they buy with his salary. With the majority of the adult villagers involved in daily wage work, farming tends to be a secondary occupation and a shortage of farm labor results. People now find it difficult to recruit their sons-in-law's labor for farming. A boy whose wife started working in Kayenta chose to stay in his own parents' home in the village and seldom returned to the home of his parents-in-law, thus avoiding the performance of all services, including farming. His in-laws complained bitterly about his behavior, saying that while after the marriage ceremony the groom "belongs to them," he does not like helping with their farming. Neolocal marriage also has resulted in the dislocation of women from their own lineage. Quoting from Forde's case studies (1931: 382), Titiev noted a divorcée's difficulty in obtaining labor services from her clan relatives and rightly attributed it to her moving "into [a] separate house" (1944:43).

INSTABILITY OF RESIDENCE. Mainly because of modern economic conditions and improved transportation facilities, married couples, both young and old, now have high residential mobility. Even in the old days, the colonists of Moenkopi divided their residence between the village and Old Oraibi. In recent times, as they acquired automobiles and the road systems improved, the range of their movement became far greater than the area once covered on foot or horse.

For about half of the couples living in Moenkopi, homes in Third Mesa or Second Mesa villages are still maintained by the parents of either spouse who live there. Moenkopi's colonial dependence on Hopiland proper prompted the people to divide their residence between the village of one of the spouses in Hopiland for ceremonial occasions and Moenkopi for economic activities. Many of these couples still maintain this pattern of dual residence.

Far more important, however, is residence outside Moenkopi for employment reasons. Such residence includes off-reservation towns and, recently, those developed on the reservation itself. Many who live in government quarters consider this residence to be only temporary. Their homes in the village continue to be utilized for occasional returns on vacations or, more frequently, on ceremonial occasions and during the farming season. In an early stage of dual residence a couple may live apart, one residing near the place of employment and the other in the village. Men commonly live outside the village while engaged in construction work and their wives maintain households in Moenkopi. The ties of these men with the village are very stable and their return visits are weekly. In extreme cases a couple may retain three homes: one in the husband's job area, one in Moenkopi where he was raised and built a house after marriage, and the last one in his wife's village in Hopiland.

A wide spectrum of subtle differences is observed in the manner in which emigrant couples and families retain ties with the mother community of Moenkopi. There are couples who migrated to a town shortly after being married in the village, who raised families in the town, and whose children are already building their households there. Some young men migrated to town and married and "settled down" there. Many families now residing outside have some tangible evidence of ties with Moenkopi in the form of house buildings, once lived in or inherited without ever having been lived in, or similarly acquired farms. Generally, those presently living in government quarters have stronger ties with the village since their present residence is inevitably temporary. However, even couples who have married outside and formed stable households and who, as a result, have little stake in Moenkopi, still maintain various degrees of relationship with the village through the relatives of either spouse. A woman from the lower segment who married a Hotevilla man in an off-reservation town shortly after the war finally reached Connecticut where her husband died. Eventually she remarried a white there and raised more children while working in a fountain pen factory. After more than 10 years' absence from her village, she recently returned with her children for a visit during the summer. Such incidents are not rare. A man from New Oraibi who had long lived in Tuba City as a government employee and who had not had any relationship with Moenkopi, save the fact that his brother lived there through marriage, recently moved in and built a house. One wonders if, in fact, a migrant ever reaches the stage where he finally disassociates himself and his family from Moenkopi and is "assimilated" in the population of larger American urban concentrations. In any event, it is clear that most migrants continue to think of Moenkopi as their place of origin and to identify with it, however tenuous their tie with it may be. In this respect the community has been transformed from a colony of Old Oraibi into a village which is now the center of migration itself.

Divorce

Titiev (1944:39–43) and Eggan (1950:56) first pointed out the "brittleness" of marriage and the high frequency of divorce among the Hopi. On the basis of marital records of the inhabitants of Old Oraibi during the period 1900–1905, Titiev calculated that about 34 per cent of the inhabitants experienced divorce in their lifetimes (1944:39). Both argued that the high instability of Hopi marriage shown in the ratio was primarily due to the complementarily operating matrilineal lineage and household organization (Titiev, 1944:43; Eggan, 1950:56). What happens, then, to the stability of marriage when such groups cease to function as in the case of Moenkopi?

DIVORCE RATE. The computation of divorce frequency is not a simple task, mainly because exhaustive records on each individual are almost impossible to obtain. There are also definitional difficulties involved in the notion of divorce. As Titiev pointed out (1944:40–41), what was once thought of as divorce or remarriage by some informants may turn out to be a prolonged separation or extramarital cohabitation, respectively. While divorce does not include any formalized procedure even at present, unless it raises a question such as division of property and children or acceptance of public assistance (Brophy and Aberle, 1966:56–57), the remarriage is regarded by many as simply a shift of residence on a man's part. Further, in actual computation there is a problem of defining a population on which to base the calculation. Thus, even Titiev's statistics may be questioned if they are not free of informants' bias in reconstructing the village population of about 30 years ago. Unfortunately, he did not state explicitly what kinds of inhabitants were included in the statistics and it is only after the consultation of his table (1944:345) that one realizes his computation of those individuals who have had marital experience. Even then, however, it may be questioned if the divorces reported for a certain individual occurred during the period of 1900–1905 or after, when certainly more new couples were formed and old couples died out. Similarly, some of the divorces may have occurred before the period under consideration. While his data are impressively exhaustive in regard to individual records, the statistics based on them are generally not amenable to an unequivocal interpretation.

In the present analysis an attempt was made to compile the kinds of statistics that would enable some comparison with Titiev's. Individuals who are currently married, or have been married, were chosen from the corrected census of 1962. Thus they include the divorced, separated, and widowed. But while Titiev's data apparently included divorces which occurred after the 1900–1905 period, the present data includes only those divorces which took place prior to 1962. Second, Titiev omitted the young "whose marriages were of such recent date as to preclude the possibility of divorce" (1944:40). The present data includes such marriages. Consequently, the percentage of the divorced and separated obtained from Moenkopi might rise further if the data were placed on a similar comparative basis, i.e., 30 years prior to 1962.

	Single Marriage	Divorced	Widowed	Separated	Total
Male	87	20	7	2	116
Female	86	27	7	0	120
Total	173	47	14	2	236

Rate of divorce Male.................(20 + 2)/116 or 19.0 per cent.
    Female..............27/120 or 22.5 per cent.
    Total...............(47 + 2)/236 or 20.8 per cent.

Note: 1) The widowed consist of those without an experience of divorce.
  2) Non-Hopi residents are excluded.

The above ratio is thus much smaller than Titiev's 34 per cent. Unfortunately, again, we have no means of checking how much of the difference is real and how much is simply due to the difference in comparative basis. As for Titiev's figure itself, Eggan suspects that the high rate might have been caused by the realignment of affinal relationships during the turmoil in Oraibi at that period and hence represents a situation not exactly normal (1964: 183). All factors considered, however, it still appears that the present figure for Moenkopi divorce is *appreciably* lower than Titiev's and may represent an actual drop in the divorce frequency. This impression is somewhat reinforced by the low frequency of divorce within the village for the two time periods. Between 1937 and 1948, 9.5 per cent or six of the 63 marriages found in 1937 ended in divorce, and between 1948 and 1962, 9 per cent or eight of the 89 marriages found in 1948 ended similarly. When we take only the couples newly listed in the 1948 census, we find only 8 per cent or five out of 58 ending in divorce in 1962. Finally, 21 marriages or 33.2 per cent of those found in 1937 still exist in the 1962 census.

Divorce, in fact, seems more difficult now. The often reported picture of a Hopi woman placing her husband's belongings outside the door as a sign of divorce is no longer observable in Moenkopi. In its turn, it is not infrequent for a wife to go after her husband who has run away on a drinking spree in town. A man who did not return home on his days off but chose to stay in Window Rock with his Navajo girl friend was soon found out by his wife and daughter, who drove more than a hundred miles to bring him home. Another man, long dissatisfied with his wife, pleaded in drunken tears to his sister that he be allowed to stay and visit another woman in the village but the sister resolutely told him to stick to his present wife and family. He had to obey. The stability of marriage in contemporary Moenkopi, if it does not connote harmony and euphoria in marital relationships, appears to be in conformity with the changing familial organization. Before going into this, we shall examine what types of divorce are current among the people.

FACTORS OF DIVORCE. Two factors need to be considered in evaluating divorce rates among the Moenkopi Hopi: residence location and tribal affiliation. While numerical information has not been obtained, the marriages in towns on and off the reservation appear especially brittle when compared to marriages within the village. For the period of 1937–48, one out of five marriages resident outside the village dissolved in divorce, while in the next period of 1948–62, five out of 36 or 13.9 per cent. In addition to general unfamiliarity and isolation in the urban settings away from the village, women often find it difficult to spend their days without much interaction in a strange neighborhood. While men are easily absorbed in their work and recreational milieu through specialized jobs and regimented into routinized labor schedules, women are mostly unorganized and left isolated at their homes. Thus it appears that while the problems of Indian males in town arise mainly due to tension from rigid regimentation of their lives, women suffer from alienation and lack of interaction. At the same time, the Indian families in off-reservation towns do not possess any formal organization of their own and kinship interaction is at a minimum.

In addition, Indian families in town seldom own homes and even among those who have lived away from the village long enough to raise grandchildren, rented apartment living is common. Except within the narrow confines of a rented house, then, women's activities in town are usually extremely restricted, and while the husbands are away at work, they occasionally shop and do the laundry and idle away the rest of their time in front of the TV. Blinds are always down and their homes usually present a dreary outlook to the passer-by. Occasionally women may succeed in obtaining part-time employment as store clerks, laundry workers, school cooks or maids, baby-sitters, and cleaning women for private homes and motels. In comparison to men, however, their lack of skills and difficulty with English appear to drive them into a far less advantageous position, especially when other minority groups are making an aggressive inroad on job markets in town. Generally women appear to prefer employment on the reservation where the competition is restricted and interactions with fellow Indians are much more frequent.

Successful and long resident Indians usually have close white "friends" in town, who often turn out to be their employers. The absence of lateral links among the Indian families and their orientation to the isolated, vertical "patron" relationship with individuals of the superordinate group place women in a still more difficult position. It has been frequently observed that in order to alleviate this, they often call their relatives in from the village and let them stay in their homes. At the same time, women go back to the village even on days when the husbands are at work and return to pick up the latter in town. This emotional pull of the village on women and the economic one of the town on men appears to make stable marriages more difficult and leads to frequent divorce.

When divorce occurs, it is usually the women who return to the village with their children, thus producing discontinuous extension in the parental households. The divorcée from town does not seem to find it difficult to readjust to village life; she can not only rely on the help of her near relatives but often contributes to the recipient households in the traditional sphere of economy, where labor is usually in short supply.

Mixed marriages appear to be as unstable as marriages outside the village. Such marriages within the village pose a greater difficulty to the alien spouses who move to the village. It has been mentioned to me by way of a joke that Navajo men cannot stand the overpowering manners of Hopi women, while Navajo girls prefer generally docile and domestically oriented Hopi men. Divorces occur in both combinations, however. Cultural differences are real not only in the case of Navajo-Hopi marriages but in others as well. An Eskimo boy, who finally ended up in Moenkopi, married a girl but had to run because, it was said, he couldn't take lamb and missed salmon too much. Such differences are also reflected in the native attitudes toward other tribes. A Walapai girl, although she persevered, had to suffer from abusive comments of the village wives that she was "out of a chicken coop in Peach Spring." A Pima girl could not take such unfriendly comments about her tribal origin and ran away. The Pueblos, on the other hand, are well received and one Zuni husband is the delight of the village for he is able to make interesting kachina dolls. The language barrier is another difficulty. Finally, the different degrees of acculturation become another cause of frustration in Moenkopi. A fervent pan-Indianist, who is a Cherokee herself, once commented that she never ceased to wonder at the difference between the Navajo and Hopi in Tuba City and her own tribe, one of the "Five Civilized Tribes" of Oklahoma. The difference hits hard the young Indians of alien tribes who married the Hopi in the "enlightened" atmosphere of boarding schools and were then brought into *piki* houses in Moenkopi.

Perhaps it is because of the last factor that mixed marriages appear to be more successful in off-reservation towns. Here again, the men have the advantage. Many men return to the village with foreign wives but for employment reasons are anxious to return to the towns as soon as possible.

A number of divorces also occur among the resident couples in the village. Titiev gives for "the most common grounds for separation . . . stinginess, laziness, violence of temper, and above all, adultery" (1944:40). Among the young couples in Moenkopi at present, emotional incompatibility generally carries less weight than economic factors in household maintenance. Husbands working outside the village and leaving homes entirely in the hands of wives, or their prolonged unemployment while their wives are earning wages, both appear to endanger conjugal stability. When a young husband is still resident in his wife's parental household, his unemployment emerges as a sign of economic incapacity and becomes an object of snide remarks not only among the members of his marital household but in the community in general. When he is employed and living in his wife's parental household, he is further burdened with demands that he help with the farm work. When the wives are from other villages, they are often confronted with the problem of isolation from their own kinfolk and cooperation with her husband's people.

A stage of stability is reached when the couple establishes its own household either in a rented or newly constructed house. The problem at this point of household development revolves around the economic as well as the psychological investment that each spouse is willing to make. Squabbles regarding the use of income, its allocation, and the question of giving financial help to the parental households of the spouses appear to threaten the marriage. A husband, disgusted with the fact that his income is squandered by his wife on her people, may run to town and drink up his paycheck, or he may withdraw to his parents' home. Unresolved frustrations accumulated in the daily work in Tuba City may result in the abandonment of one's family.

Divorces occur even if the couples have children to rear. Of six divorces that happened in the village between 1937 and 1948, four couples had unmarried children before divorce. The others had no children. Between 1948 and 1962, three couples with children divorced. When a divorce occurs, the children are most often kept by the women, though in two cases the men have kept the children. The latter were married to women from other villages of Hopiland. One of them was once regarded as the wealthiest man in the village; he built a house of comfortable size as well as a restaurant. A portion of the house was then remodeled into a store. He bought farms from a Navajo allotment holder. He married and divorced a Hopi from Bacabi and two Navajo women and has kept all the children from these unions. Even if men provide houses for their wives, it is usually they who leave the wives and children there and go back to their mothers' or sisters' homes. Thus matrifocal families do occur at divorce. However, their frequency as well as stability are not great enough to make them a prevalent family type.

While the presence of small children does not totally insure a marriage, it does have a cohesive effect to a certain degree, as indicated by cases of divorce that occur in the later stage of household development.

Six cases of divorce between 1937 and 1962 occurred after the children were grown and married. In one of these cases, divorce was not followed by remarriage but each spouse lived in the household of one of the children; a woman lived with her son's family in her own house, while her ex-husband was taken care of by his daughter's family in her house which was built by her husband. The latter arrangement was made so that the old man could contribute to the household through working on the thus far neglected farms. Another old divorcée was similarly invited into her daughter's household. One old man returned to his sister's daughter's household while his former wife lived alone in the house. She and another woman, whose husband married a Navajo in the later stage of life, have been supported by their children's households in various ways while living alone. Another divorcée called an old man from Hotevilla into her house that was built by her former husband, but the cohabitation was of short duration, and she had to be partly supported by her daughter's household. In only one case, an apparently stable marriage ensued between two older people, each of whom had their children all married. Finally, an old sheepherder turned cattleman married a Navajo woman and left the village.

So far as the life history of these people is concerned, they reveal firm roots in the village among the children they successfully raised, in the fields they long cultivated, and in the livestock they tended. In spite of this extensive participation in village life, however, their later stage in life was accorded with anything but the secure atmosphere of retirement in the families they themselves created. Perhaps because of this insecurity derived from disorganization of the lineage system, the old couples attempt to insure their later life by reorganizing their respective relationships in regard to the households of their descendants or through a new marriage. Since a small portion of such economic resources as farms and livestock usually remains in the hands of an old husband, he redirects them from his original household to his own interests. Because of the lack of continuity in the household group, he can reinvest them either in one of the households of his children or he can establish a new household through remarriage. A wife, on the other hand, retains the house structure, into which she admits the family of one of her children or a new husband. But the later stage of marriage may not involve such economic difficulty that it ends in divorce or separation, and it is well to notice that cases of married couples in old age are just as frequent as broken marriages in the village.

Kinship and the Stability of Marriage

The brittleness of Hopi marriage has been associated by Titiev with the pervasive matrilineal household organization (1944:43). His argument is that when a matrilineal organization assumes economic as well as child-rearing responsibilities, a marriage with a particular male counts little and since, apart from the procreative aspect of marriage, each individual has secure protection from his or her own lineage, marriage does not create a lasting relationship between the spouses. Eggan's view is essentially in accord with Titiev's and he significantly adds that the "tempo [of divorce] has probably increased in recent times" (1950:56).

We have already shown that the divorce rate at Moenkopi since 1937 is relatively low and indicated the higher rate of divorce among the couples residing in off-reservation towns than among those within the village. A matrilineage as a land- and ceremony-controlling group no longer exists in Moenkopi and there is no clan house which the members of a lineage endeavor to maintain. Instead, a household emerges as a bilaterally supported economic unit for the rearing of descendants. Neolocality in the early stage of marriage enables a young household to achieve independence from a parental one before its offspring are assimilated into the latter. In the traditional set-up, a husband's economic contribution to his marital household did not go beyond his labor, but in Moenkopi he often brings the land inherited from his parents. His wages, moreover, are obtained without any help from his wife's people. Further, he often provides a new house for his family. His salary is now indispensable in the cash economy of the village and, as discussed previously, cannot be replaced through borrowings from the relatives. In short, the economic contribution of a husband to a new household is far more substantial now than during the previous period of matrilineage. Thus desperate efforts are often made by women in the village to bring misguided husbands back home; and husbands can ill afford to lose the investment already made in the home buildings and modern equipment by divorce. Besides, when his children are grown and start working on his farm, it is difficult for a man to take the land away from them at divorce. Because of individual land tenure, neolocal marriage, and wage-earning ability, a man's commitment to marriage is far greater than in the traditional system. A woman's loss of economic position through the breakdown of clan land and house ownership puts her in a dependent position on her husband. Her wage-earning ability, in addition, is more restricted than a man's in general. In such a set-up, divorce becomes a precarious proposition to make. Thus divorce occurs in a fairly early stage of marriage when the stake in it still remains small or in a much later stage when one can rely on already established descendant households. It is not so much the mere existence of small children as the amount of commitment already made and of stake established that makes the couple cohere to each other. In short, marriage is now considerably more stable than it once was, and correspondingly, the matrifocal family becomes only an unstable, passing phenomenon. In the past, what prevented the emergence of matrifocal family was the capacity of intact matrilineages to absorb such segments. Today, however, it is derived from the increasing incorporation of a husband into a household, which is due to the change in the economic structure of the community.

What is currently common as an accommodation of broken families due to divorce is the discontinuous extension of a household group. This results most often from the divorces of couples outside the village. It should be noted that in this type of divorce, it is mostly women and their children who withdraw to the village while men stay in town, often in the homes they had been living in. The return of divorced women and their children presents a definite problem in household economy on the part of the recipient households. However, the returnees as well as the recipients usually readjust to each other in the same household by directing the increment labor to a neglected sphere of the household economy. A unique characteristic of the present household in Moenkopi appears to lie in this capacity to reintegrate additional members into the household economy without much strain.

Despite apparently more frequent divorces outside the village, an increasing number of young people venture into town to try their lot. There seems little doubt, then, that discontinuous extension represents a type of familial adjustment in the face of the community's frantic efforts to take part in its expanding economic horizon.

9

Contemporary Moenkopi

RESERVATION STATUS

At present the BIA administration of Moenkopi is broadly divided between the Tuba City Subagency of the Navajo Reservation and the Keams Canyon Agency of the Hopi Reservation. The former has ultimate charge of land resources that the villagers make use of, while the latter assumes the remainder of federal responsibilities, including off-reservation schooling, welfare allocation, and community projects. Both agencies offer employment opportunities to the people of Moenkopi.

The location of Moenkopi on the Navajo Reservation is less significant with respect to other governmental services. Thus the villagers are entitled to free medical services of the PHS at both Tuba City and Keams Canyon.

The Navajo Tribal Council directly controls the use of land for farming and grazing by the people of Moenkopi through a local Land Board and grazing committees. The actions of these two organizations are sanctioned by the Navajo Court in Tuba City. Since the Hopi Tribal Council possesses neither authority nor power in this matter, the minority status of Moenkopi is most acutely felt in this area. Mainly motivated by this disfranchisement regarding land matters, it has been rumored that the Hopi Council is preparing a legal suit against the Navajo Council in order to secure title over the area formerly claimed by the Hopi.

AGENCY COMMUNITY

The approximate size of the contemporary population of Tuba City is 1,500, consisting of about 800 Navajo, about half of whom live in South Tuba, an emergent community of wage-working families (Levy, 1962a:787); about 100 Hopi; and the remainder whites.

The proliferation of governmental agencies and the absence of unified coordination of these agencies and of community affairs characterize present-day Tuba City.

Aside from daily wage labor, the institutions in which the Hopi of Moenkopi participate in Tuba City include the BIA for land matters, PHS for medical care, public schools for education, Navajo Tribal Council for grazing permits (grazing committee), land assignment (Land Board), recreation and sports events at the community center, Navajo Tribal Court and police for legal problems, state employment agency for employment, and private business establishments for purchase of daily supplies. Participation in these institutions mostly occurs on an individual basis. No "corporate" relationship between Tuba City and Moenkopi exists except for relations between the Upper Moenkopi Council and local organizations of the Navajo Tribal Council to handle occasional crisis situations, and between the two Moenkopi basketball teams (Moenkopi Elks and Moenkopi Knights) and the teams of the Navajo and local whites, organized in terms of the respective institutions in which they are employed. Aspects of the life of Moenkopi Hopi are now conducted in Tuba City to such an extent as to include births at the PHS hospital and burials at the community graveyard.

Tuba City is also important as a locality for political activities of those Navajo and Hopi Indians who are not content with the present councils of the respective tribes. As previously indicated, the relationships of the Indians of the two tribes have become increasingly bureaucratized since the establishment of the tribal councils. Accordingly, Keams Canyon and Window Rock are identified as the centers of activities of the Hopi and Navajo tribal councils. Those Indians whose political ideas are not represented in the councils seek Hotevilla and Tuba City as the places for their activities. Hotevilla was chosen because it is a "traditional" Hopi village with a number of active Hopi politicians. On the other hand, the choice of Tuba City appears to have resulted because the Navajo local organizations of Tuba City do not strongly identify with distant Window Rock and the Hopi of Moenkopi are not strongly drawn to their own tribal council at Keams Canyon. Thus, while the two councils were wrestling over the disposal of the 1882 Executive Order Reservation with the help of their respective BIA agencies, a sentiment of friendly cooperation between the "conservatives" of the two tribes was expressed in a cartoon in the *Navajo Times* of October 3, 1963, depicting Navajo men, residing on the 1882 Reservation, proposing to Hopi girls of "traditional" Hopi villages of Second Mesa, with the caption indicating this as the most reasonable way to resolve the conflict. The Hopi "traditionals" and the Navajo living within the Executive Order Reservation as well as others dissatisfied with the present Navajo Council met in Hotevilla to discuss the problem in 1963. On May 21, 1964, the *Navajo Times* reported a calumet smoking ceremony held by a few Hopi "traditionals" from Moenkopi and Hotevilla and local Navajo in the Tuba City Community Center "for recall of Bill H.R. 9529."[1] The proposed bill was concerned with the division of the surface rights between the two tribes on the 1882 Reservation. In the second meeting at Hotevilla in 1964, the Hopi "traditional" politicians were hailed by the Hopi and Navajo present for their success in burying this bill.

On a more informal level of interaction, Tuba City provides the locale for a sort of double standard of Hopi conservatism. The "traditionals" denounce, for example, the white man's hospital and refuse to visit the one in Keams Canyon. Yet they do not hesitate to frequent the hospital in Tuba City. The Hotevilla "traditionals" may resent having to present a dance on behalf of the white establishments and yet it was a Hotevilla dance group that took part in the opening of a new white gasoline station in Tuba City in 1964. It may be feared, then, that the rumored suit over the territory of the Tuba City area, if actually filed, may only discourage the existing atmosphere of informal accommodation between the two tribes.

OFF-RESERVATION TOWN

Flagstaff is important to Moenkopi at present for three principal reasons. Food provisions and household equipment are purchased

---

[1] J. E. Levy mentions in a personal communication that the majority of the Navajo participants are regarded as "traditionals" by the Navajo.

there for cash; it offers opportunities for employment; last and somewhat less important, it has recreational facilities. Though Moenkopi is in Coconino County and Flagstaff is its seat, no direct transactions between the two occur on such administrative matters as applications for welfare, which are mediated by the Keams Canyon Agency. The people of Moenkopi who earn their wages in Tuba City spend the greater portion of their income in Flagstaff.

The present relationship between Moenkopi and Flagstaff is thus bereft of the mediation which was once the role of traders and trading posts at Tuba City. The people of Moenkopi are now directly involved in the consumer market of the northern Arizona region, which centers in Flagstaff.

COMMUNITY STRUCTURE

Moenkopi, with a population of 600, has extensively surrendered its community functions to Tuba City and Hopiland. New babies are born in the PHS hospital in Tuba City, where they usually go through the naming ceremonies. Children are initiated to either Kachina or Powamu societies in one of the villages of Third Mesa. Toward the end of the 1950's, the Keams Canyon Agency planned to scrap the Moenkopi Day School in order to integrate the education of Moenkopi children into the public schools in Tuba City. The plan was not executed because of strong opposition by both the upper and lower segments. As a result, the children spend

Plate 22. Hopi students at Moenkopi Day School.

Plate 23. Moenkopi Hopi graves at the Tuba City community graveyard.

four or five years of primary education in the village but receive the remainder in Tuba City until they graduate from a senior high school there. The majority of adult activities, including wage work, recreation, and native ceremonies, take place outside the village as well. An increasing number of the villagers die in the Tuba City PHS hospital and are buried in Tuba City. It is no longer far fetched to say that the crucial events in the life cycle of the Moenkopi Hopi frequently occur outside the village.

Ceremonial activities in contemporary Moenkopi are at low ebb. Only two kachina dances are given in respective segments in a single year. At least one of them is organized by the residents of either segment, while another is usually from Old Oraibi in the case of Lower Moenkopi or from New Oraibi and Bacabi in the case of Upper Moenkopi. Many residents take part more often in the dances given in other villages of Third Mesa than in their own.

In Lower Moenkopi the Kachina initiation of children has been performed in Old Oraibi for a number of years. Upper Moenkopi, on the other hand, has had its initiation in their former kivas in Lower Moenkopi; yet when it was given in 1963, only two boys were initiated. In the same year, many children from Upper Moenkopi were brought to New Oraibi for initiation. While Kachina and Powamu societies are now the only remaining ones to which initiation is still permitted in Moenkopi, there are already about 10 youngsters, ranging from 15 to 25 years of age, who have not been initiated into either of these societies. They shall never be initiated. On the other hand, some children, who know less Hopi than English, having been brought up outside, are taken to Hopiland and initiated to the Kachina society. The children of alien mothers who do not have clan organizations in the tribes of their origin, such as Walapai, are also initiated. The Kachina initiation thus appears to be regarded as a mark of tribal identity rather than the first step to the more esoteric societies of Hopi religion.

Other ceremonies such as Wuwuchim and a phase of Soyal long ceased to be practiced in Moenkopi. Social dances are still occasionally held by the two segments and yet their occurrences are fewer than in the past according to some informants. *Ngoitewa* or playful exchanges of gifts between fathers' sisters and brothers' sons, which occur soon after the snake dance, are still vigorously and gaily performed in Shongopavi but no longer observable in Moenkopi. While the ceremonial dependence of Moenkopi on other villages of Hopiland has thus been on the increase, life in Moenkopi itself is inescapably becoming dull and drab.

The Mennonite and Mormon churches and the day school in the village continue their existence mainly for the performance of the "charter" functions of religious services and formal instruction.[2] Participation in activities such as sports events, movie showings, rummage sales, and shower room service by these establishments is limited to a small number of residents in the village, while the majority of participants are recruited from the surrounding Navajo camps in the case of the Mormon church.

With such a "bedroom or dormitory town" feature in present-day Moenkopi, the prevalent attitude of the people is characterized by deep apathy to the common problems of their community. The involvement of Moenkopi in outside institutions is now so extensive that an old Hopi resident once expressed uncertainty as to whether he could still regard himself as a Hopi.

Social control in Moenkopi today is based on appropriation of the domestic water and sewer systems by the Upper Moenkopi Council in Upper Moenkopi and on the "ownership" of the residential site, as recognized through the inheritance probation, by

---

[2] "The term 'charter' may conveniently be used to designate the basic operational sanction or raison d'etre of an institution" (Adams, 1963:215), whereas the "ancillary" functions refer to those performed in addition to the "charter" functions, either "wittingly or unwittingly" (Adams, 1963:220–21).

Plate 24. Mormon church in Upper Moenkopi.

the Lower Moenkopi chief in Lower Moenkopi. The Upper Moenkopi Council further depends on the Hopi Tribal Police to curb certain deviant actions in the upper segment. Other minor offenses are under the jurisdiction of the Navajo Tribal Police stationed in Tuba City. Thus an emphasis is now laid on external control by groups outside the village itself. In regard to the social control of Lower Moenkopi, it must be observed in passing that the residential site there is a part of the chiefly allotment and that despite the original intent of allotments to create private ownership of land, they are now ironically the basis of holding the community of Lower Moenkopi together.

The two segments derive their support in political action from the Hopi Tribal Council and its affiliated villages and from the anti-council villages. While the authority of Oraibi over Moenkopi is now much less effective in deciding issues, tribal factionalism provides the two segments with informal leverage in conducting the political affairs of Moenkopi. They are, therefore, colonial extensions of the two factions of the tribe.

The existence of Upper and Lower Moenkopi as two separate units of decision-making and social control, when conjoined with extensive involvement in outside institutions on an individual basis, appear to allow a wide variety of individual interactions between the resident relatives of the two segments. This is partly

Plate 25. Soap suds in a Moenkopi irrigation canal because of the seepage of detergent used by Tuba City residents. Moenkopi is susceptible to the evils of urban America.

facilitated by the differential degree of adoption of alien goods among the households of the two villages. To illustrate, a young man of Lower Moenkopi has purchased a pair of electric clippers. Although his house is not equipped with electricity, he cuts hair at his father's brother's house in Upper Moenkopi in return for taking a bath there. Such reciprocal interactions along lines of direct kinship also take place between the relatives in the village and Tuba City, the former providing farm products in exchange for the opportunity to take baths at the homes of the latter.

BASIS OF VILLAGE ECONOMY

The current farm land condition of Moenkopi appears to represent only an unstable and intermediate stage, affected by the legal inhibition of smooth land transfer on the basis of individual land ownership and inefficient employment of land. There is no trend toward concentration of farm land resources in a few hands and the development of a landed class in Moenkopi today. In this respect, the reservation system emerges as a shackle. On the other hand, if outside commercial or industrial interests are allowed to compete for the land, the meager money capital of the villagers may lead to their total alienation from their own land through a process of appropriation by powerful outside capital. The reservation system is a protection in this respect.

In order to improve the utilization of available farm land, some village farmers are interested in forming an agricultural cooperative, but the political and economic climate in and outside Moenkopi does not favor such a proposal.

There are trends in the village that indicate a slight shift in the land tenure pattern toward individual "ownership." One of them, administrative action of inheritance probation of allotment lands, has already been mentioned. Improvements on the residential sites, either communal or individual, also have brought about a change in the ownership concept toward individual "property." It may be noted that these trends toward "individual ownership" represent a movement contrary to what is currently being practiced in many Indian tribes. The incorporation of tribal economic enterprise based on tribal land holdings has been a trend among these tribes (Shepardson, 1963; Woodbury and Woodbury, 1964; Getty, 1961–62:181–86). Concrete organizational particulars aside, corporate tribal enterprise is a direct development of the Collier theory of tribal land control. On the same premise, the Hopi Tribal Council recently leased some land strips on the reservation for mining purposes against strong opposition from the "traditional" faction. The direction in which the pattern of land tenure is developing in Moenkopi is thus in conflict with trends toward tribalization.

This conflict is also present in Tuba City. There numerous businesses operate through the leasing of sites from the Navajo Tribal Council. Though the Hopi of Moenkopi patronize them quite intensively, all the profits from the lease are thus culled by the Navajo tribe. Because the land the Hopi use is either assigned by the Navajo tribe or allotted by the government, the development of tourism in Tuba City proceeds without any economic advantage accruing to the Hopi except for the employment it offers. Under these circumstances, we may not disregard simply as an impossible dream the proposition once advanced to me by the chief of the lower segment to build a tourist stop on a spot within his allotment which he had already chosen from his shrewd observation of the number of travellers pausing there to appreciate the surroundings. The rumored legal suit by the Hopi Council, previously mentioned, should take this aspect of the problem into account as well.

Wage work in Tuba City occupies the most important position in Moenkopi economy today. The village is a labor reservoir primarily for Tuba City and, to a lesser extent, for other reservation communities and off-reservation towns. This corresponds to the role of Moenkopi as a wage work colony to other villages of Hopiland, especially Third Mesa. It is still fairly common for the Hopi from outside Moenkopi to reside temporarily in the homes of their relatives in the village during their employment in Tuba City. Village youths marrying girls from other villages tend not to move to their wives' villages. Men already employed in Tuba City seldom relinquish jobs to reside matrilocally after marriage.

A majority of the Moenkopi wage laborers are employed by the governmental agencies in Tuba City and remain unorganized. However, a considerable number of construction laborers from Moenkopi, including electricians, carpenters, bricklayers, plumbers, and unskilled laborers, now belong to the respective trade union locals.

Agriculture and livestock operations are practiced as subsidiary activities of the employed and as the primary occupations of the unemployed youths and retired old men. Apart from the small contribution it makes to contemporary subsistence in Moenkopi, the villagers are engaged in farming primarily to procure the ceremonial foodstuff of white and blue corn. Due to the absorption of the village labor force into wage work, farm labor is now in short supply. In order to cover this shortage, there is a trend to integrate two major productive activities within a household by maximally utilizing the available household labor force even at the expense of the traditional division of labor.

Business operations in the village are subjugated to Tuba City, which stifles entrepreneurial incentive among the villagers. While tourism has been growing as a potential field for business enterprise in the area, no communal effort has been made so far to take advantage of it. This intensifies the labor reservoir character of Moenkopi.

Little money is spent within the village at the present time.

This situation is rather unique in modern Hopi villages for in Hopiland proper the majority of the villages have their own community stores and a considerable number of cash transactions are still conducted within the communities. This constitutes an economic aspect of contemporary "surburban" Moenkopi.

Extensive participation in the wage work economy through limited specialization of skill and in the regional consumer market and, finally, bureaucratic restriction on the movement of capital goods (land and livestock) has inhibited the development of socioeconomic class stratification within the village. The wide range of wage income differences among households in the village is not stable enough to create economic classes primarily because the employment condition is not constant and because the accumulation of wealth does not insure continuity over succeeding generations. While it is possible to accumulate wealth within a single generation and to invest it in nonproductive home improvements, its transfer is fraught with the danger of dispersal or hoarding (see pp. 265ff.). The situation has been aggravated by a volatile housing condition. Because of the marginal agricultural production, investment in productive capital has remained minimal.

Aside from these objective conditions that hinder the formation of economic classes, the Hopi deny their existence among themselves. The question, "Who is the richest man in the village?" was received with varied degrees of hostility and did not produce consistent response. Though it is still a code of etiquette that wealth shall not be displayed nor poverty exposed, the current differences in income and spending patterns often show up in the size of house structures, internal decorations, dresses, and the possession of automobiles. Such differences, which may lead to invidious comparisons, are effectively shielded by compartmentalizing the Hopi and white man's way of life. Thus when a woman of a relatively poor household was asked by her child why their family was not decorating for Christmas, she said, "We are Hopi and Christmas is for the white people."

In appearance, therefore, the wage economy superimposed itself on an undifferentiated Hopi community so that it has not produced within the community structural cleavage which would have precipitated divergent economic interests into sub-groups. By a curious process of institutional manipulation of the reservation system, Moenkopi emerges today as a crossbreed of the traditional Hopi economy and wage economy. Under the thin veneer of a proletarian complex, agriculture is still persistently pursued whenever opportunities are available. Wage workers in Moenkopi are not genuine proletarians who find their only means of defense in organized unionism, but each of them is a singularly individualistic entrepreneur who allocates his as well as other household members' labor into available spheres of economic activity.

The present standard of living, measured in terms of cash income and material possessions, is unprecedently higher than in the past or even in comparison with other villages of Hopiland today. To illustrate their comparative affluence, a woman in charge of voluntary charity programs for the village homes volunteered to give me three pairs of trousers, which she discarded as unfit for distribution.[3] I have already mentioned the aspect of luxury consumption in Moenkopi (see pp. 209–10). This by no means indicates that all the Moenkopi households achieve the middle-class standard of American society. Rather, the nature of poverty that exists in Moenkopi today is unstable and represents a passing stage in the perennial process of acculturation. Specifically, the villagers do not regard the materially poor as being deprived. The impression of poverty emerges only when comparisons are made with the white homes of Tuba City or other communities in off-reservation towns.

HOUSEHOLD ORGANIZATION

The prevalent form of the household group in Moenkopi today is the nuclear family. The basic orientation of the village economy, i.e., wage work, tends to reinforce the solidarity of the nuclear family as a household unit through the sharing of cash income by married couples. Governmental control of land and livestock based on individual use, on the other hand, inhibits the growth of any larger kinship group to assume productive significance.

Dependence on wage earnings as the basis of household economy accelerates the fission of young households from parental ones through neolocal residence. The period of extension in a parental household group after marriage of one of the children is extremely curtailed and often absent. On the other hand, the composition of household groups existing in the village is very unstable because of frequent migration of household members to distant reservation communities or off-reservation towns for wage work employment or because of their return to sibling or, more

---

[3] I wore the trousers during my field work as town dress.

likely, to parental households (see pp. 261ff.). Thus while maintaining a nuclear basis, the household itself remains fairly flexible in its group composition.

Though farming and grazing still provide opportunities for cooperation, it occurs between bilaterally related households. Cooperation of related households in present-day Moenkopi takes on the character of neighborhood helpfulness elsewhere in small communities. If mutual helpfulness is the case with related households, however, competition characterizes the relationship between unrelated neighbors. The unit of production and consumption is the nuclear family household, while the unit of cooperation in productive activities is the *ad hoc* group of bilaterally related households in the village. Economic ties of Moenkopi households with those in Oraibi through matrilineal kinship are not present today.

10

Summary and Conclusion

Preceding chapters have discussed the processes of change with special reference to political, economic, and kinship institutions. I shall now present a developmental scheme of successive periods, each of which shows a stage of adjustment to the factors of modernization. The construction of these periods is based on the external factors and mediating agencies of these factors and on the social characteristics of Moenkopi which emerged as a result.

DEVELOPMENTAL SEQUENCE

Mormon Settlement Period (1875–1903)

CONTEXTS, FACTORS, AND MEDIATING AGENCIES. The Morman colonization of the area marks the period prior to the more intensive process of modernization of Moenkopi. Although the federal government was gradually succeeding in making the Southwest amenable to the settlement of the whites by pacifying the warring Indian groups, its efforts had not yet reached the Hopi region during this period. Stabilization of the area for lasting settlement of the Indian as well as white colonists was left to the Mormons.

With the establishment of their community in Tuba City, the Mormons began missionization and agricultural development. The former was aimed at the Indians who dwelled in the general area of northwestern Arizona (Navajo, Paiute, and Hopi). The second was concentrated in the immediate vicinity of the Tuba-Moenkopi area, where the water supply was enough to make irrigation feasible. The agricultural improvement of the area included construction of a series of dams, reservoirs, and extensive canals. Mormon agriculture was primarily for subsistence, but some of the Mormon settlers kept livestock and maintained a close contact with the non-Mormon stock market in northern Arizona. Otherwise their commercial activities, based on a small number of farm products and Indian trade goods (Navajo wool and sheep hides), occupied a more important position as a link with the larger economy that had been developing along the Santa Fe Railway in the south and Salt Lake City in the north.

Unlike the federal government, whose main objective during this period was to maintain peace between different Indian groups and between Indians and white settlers, the Mormons in Tuba City and Moenkopi were confronted with the additional problem of their own survival in the arid environment. As a result, their interests were liable to conflict with those of the Indians over the limited resources in the area. These conflicts became manifest with the Navajo over the livestock range and with the Hopi over the farm land. To aggravate this, national resentment against the Mormons and continuing development of the regional economy drove the Mormon settlers into a still more difficult position, which eventually led to their withdrawal after the government compensated them for their improvements on the land.

EFFECTS ON MOENKOPI. The Mormon colonization of the area eliminated the Navajo menace to the tiny Hopi settlement of Moenkopi and allowed a comparatively stable occupation of the locality for more than a seasonal residence. All the Hopi settlers of Moenkopi were from Oraibi, and they consisted of those deprived of agricultural resources in their mother village. In Moenkopi most of them irrigated small tracts of farm land from the nearby springs. All the Hopi residents of Moenkopi frequently returned to Oraibi for religious practices; only social dances were given in the settlement.

A characteristic of the relationships between the Hopi and Mormon settlers during this period is complete lack of institutionalized modes of interaction. Although the Mormons occasionally recruited labor from the Hopi as well as from other Indians, they performed most labor themselves. They were thus extremely self-sufficient and exclusive. Lack of orderly interactive mechanisms between the two groups frequently resulted in violent encounters, especially during the last decade of the nineteenth century, when the competition for farm land became more stiff. The Hopi farming in the Moenkopi area, therefore, continued in the traditional pattern of small-scale spring irrigation, and the Hopi adopted few crops from the Mormons. Nor did the Hopi profit from the elaborate irrigation works of the Mormons. As a result of competition for farm land, the Hopi were reduced to the position of sharecroppers for the Mormons on land they had formerly cultivated for their own subsistence.

Although there were informal, daily contacts between Mormons and Hopi, these interactions did not lead the Hopi to adopt any significant traits of the white man's culture. Mormon missionization among the Hopi was entirely a failure, and, since the settlers did not attempt to educate the Indians into the ways of the white man through schools or other means, the Hopi remained relatively insulated from the impact of factors of socio-cultural change. What was accomplished during this period was to prepare the Hopi for a more intensive and structured course of change through the Indian reservation system.

Western Navajo Reservation Period (1903–35)

CONTEXTS, FACTORS, AND MEDIATING AGENCIES. This is the first period when the federal government attempted consciously to bring about changes to Moenkopi in the framework of a newly established reservation, separating Moenkopi from the reservation of the Hopi. The general intent of the government during this period was to assimilate the Indians into the larger American society through individual land allotment and off-reservation boarding school education. The governmental agency at Tuba City encouraged agriculture among the Hopi of Moenkopi on the basis of allotment and assignment of land and through the issue of agricultural tools and wagons. The agency also took over the operation of farms, orchards, and the irrigation complex developed by the Mormons and marketed a portion of the farm products to other locations on and off the reservation. Unlike the Mormons, the agency conducted these operations not for the sake of areal development per se but for the economic welfare of the Indians in their charge, whom the agency enterprises provided irregular wage work. It also organized the work gangs of the Hopi youths in the Tuba City boarding school for summer wage labor in Flagstaff and elsewhere off the reservation.

The government also set out on an extensive and often rigid program of education of the local Indians through a day school in Moenkopi, a boarding school in Tuba City, and off-reservation boarding schools. In the last of these educational institutions, the

Hopi youths came into intense contact with the Indians of other tribes.

To promote agriculture, American cooking, and general hygiene in Moenkopi, the agency helped to organize the Moenkopi fairs, baby competition, and cleaning days.

The agency personnel during this period generally maintained a strong paternalistic attitude toward the Indians and regarded them not only as the "wards" of the government but also as children in the care of an individual agency employee. A few Indians were admitted to this administrative establishment as judges or policemen, and they assumed attitudes toward their fellow Indians similar to those of the whites.

Several Protestant missions took the place of the Mormons during this period, and, together with two trading posts, introduced additional factors of change. The trading posts sold market commodities to the Indians, who purchased them with the cash earned in wage work. Missions offered an ordinary set of religious programs (Sunday services and schools, Bible reading classes, and Christmas programs) as well as more secularly oriented activities such as sewing classes. These private institutions also provided the Indians with a small number of wage work opportunities.

Off-the-reservation contacts increased. The Indians frequently visited Flagstaff on their freighting trips to haul governmental supplies and mail. These visits increased the familiarity of the Indians with various aspects of town life, but the Indians' lack of purchasing power and small demand for the merchandise available in the towns gave these visits little significance other than to provide preconditioning for future relationships with Flagstaff. On the other hand, the area was visited by a few off-reservation buyers of Indian cattle, sheep drovers, and ranchers.

After the middle of this period, automobiles became common among the whites on and off the reservation, but they did not become available to the Indians until the next period.

During this period the area was more isolated from the surrounding off-reservation communities than during the Mormon period, primarily because governmental operations in the area were directly supported by the federal government and did not require intensive economic transactions with the off-reservation communities.

EFFECTS ON THE EXCLAVE FROM ORAIBI. Moenkopi during this period can still be characterized as an exclave from Oraibi.

Although kachina dances were performed in Moenkopi, the villagers returned to Oraibi for such major ceremonies as Wuwuchim, Soyal, and Powamu. Kinship interactions were frequent and involved the exchange of farm products, labor, and mutual visits. Many Third Mesa residents came to Moenkopi in order to earn cash wages at the Tuba City Agency. Considerable immigration of the people of Third Mesa occurred during this period, resulting in the expansion of the total farm acreage. The population of Moenkopi, however, remained essentially members of "marginal lineages" of Oraibi.

The people of Moenkopi were only peripherally involved in a cash economy through wage work and purchase of market goods in Tuba City. The Hopi established a number of stores in Moenkopi, replacing a great deal of aboriginal barter and exchange. During the middle of this period, the Hopi placed livestock operation on a commercial basis. These trends, in addition to the main reliance on irrigation farming for subsistence purposes, represent a process of adjustment to the local conditions which set Moenkopi apart from other villages of Hopiland.

The characteristic nature of local Moenkopi economy, the minority status of the colony on the reservation of an alien and formerly enemy tribe, and consequent competition with the latter generally contributed to the solidarity of the whole village of Moenkopi. The young men of the village, however, were not satisfied with the subordinate status of Moenkopi to Oraibi and demanded greater autonomy in the management of village affairs. This led to creation of the village council, which, for a short period of time, acted as an indigenous agency mainly to deal with the federal government represented at Tuba City. Although the council failed, the attempt exposed the conflicts between the older and younger generations, between the traditional subsistence economy and the new cash economy, and between religious and secular affairs.

Transitional Period (1935–51)

This period can be divided into sub-periods, each of which involved events of major national significance and introduced new factors to the reservation. The changes initiated by these particular factors, however, did not evolve fully because they were soon altered. Each sub-period was unstable in this respect, and yet, throughout the two, the trend of Moenkopi from an exclave of Oraibi toward a more independent "community" appears to have continued.

Sub-period I (1935–41): The Indian New Deal

(1) *Contexts, Factors, and Mediating Agencies.* This period began during the Great Depression in the nation. In order to restore the living conditions on the Indian reservations, the federal government altered the previous policy of forced assimilation through individual land allotment and off-reservation boarding school education. It abolished further land allotment, attempted to restore the Indian land basis, placed new emphasis on day school education, and generally encouraged native cultural activities. This was implemented by the Indian Reorganization Act.

The basic purpose of the new governmental measures was to improve the economic conditions of the Indians through recovery of the productive potential of the reservation land in order to build economic self-sufficiency based on the traditional subsistence pattern; little thought was given to the possibility of integrating the Indian economy into the money economy of the nation. In this sense, it was a reversal of the previous policy.

On the Navajo and Hopi reservations the measures included the stock reduction program to improve the carrying capacity of the reservation ranges, an increase in the number of wells to water the stock, and the introduction of a better marketing procedure. In the agricultural sector the irrigation systems were improved and expanded. In order to meet a rising demand for cash, the federal government through the Hopi Agency established a revolving credit fund for the Hopi. The government also set out to develop the road systems on the reservations and expanded the agency building for better management of the reservation resources and the individual welfare of the Indians (hospitals, schools, and other agency offices). The number of mediating agencies within the federal agency at Tuba City increased as well. These projects provided a greater number of employment opportunities to the local Indians and especially to the Hopi of Moenkopi. The government also encouraged participation of Indians in the administrative branch of the agency for execution of its policies.

Educational innovations were minimal in Moenkopi since the Hopi already possessed day schools. The administrative affiliation of the Moenkopi Day School was changed from the Tuba City Agency to the Keams Canyon Agency.

One of the most important of the new governmental measures was the creation of tribal self-government not only for the promotion of Indian self-determination but also as a mediating agency between the federal agencies and native societies. Thus were the Hopi Tribal Council, Tribal Court, and Police organized.

The expansion of governmental activities on the reservation overshadowed those of private agencies; the influence of the missionaries in the village as well as elsewhere in Hopiland decreased considerably. Only the trading posts continued their activities among the Indians without much modification.

While a majority of the governmental endeavors were directed to the development of reservation life, a number of individual Indians migrated to off-reservation towns for wage work and settled there. The majority worked as household servants and maids in white homes in Flagstaff, but a few found more skilled jobs. Apart from this voluntary migration, however, there was no immediate link between on- and off-reservation societies.

(2) *Effects on Moenkopi*. Initiation of the tribal government as a major mediating agency among the Hopi intensified the factional disputes in Moenkopi and resulted in deterioration of ceremonial and agricultural cooperation. The first attempt by the government to use the tribal councils to implement the stock reduction program ended in failure among the Hopi and met with strong resistance among the Navajo. Otherwise the impact of the two tribal councils on Moenkopi was negligible during this period, partly because there were few issues and partly because of the intensification of tribal factionalism. The general trend in Moenkopi for independence from Oraibi continued. Ceremonies were now performed separately by the two factional segments in the village, and, owing to a decline in religious activities in Oraibi, an increasing number of them, including initiation to the Kachina society and a portion of the Soyal ceremony, were held at Moenkopi.

Farming continued to be the basis of subsistence and the farming area was enlarged. Expansion of agriculture was accompanied, however, by fragmentation of the irrigation systems, which weakened the control of the chief which had been based on a unified irrigation system. The volume of wage work continued to increase and correspondingly the number of village stores. The local consumer market, however, remained isolated from the off-reservation market. During this period, livestock sales to the external market formed an important link with the national economy. In addition to the emerging mode of individual disposal of farm land, it contributed to weakening the solidarity of matrilineages by creating wealth (land and livestock) which was transmitted from a father to his children. The new grazing regulations imposed by the Indian Reorganization Act severed Moenkopi from Hopiland and Third Mesa, thus further contributing to the trend toward isolation and independence.

Migration of individuals to off-reservation towns began during this period without the intervention of the agency. The number of migrants was small and the barriers between the village and off-reservation towns was so great that transformation of Moenkopi continued with little influence from institutions external to the reservation.

Sub-period II (1941–51): Impact of National Emergency

(1) *Contexts and Factors of Change.* The policies of the Indian New Deal for improving reservation conditions were abruptly altered during and after World War II, when opportunities for off-reservation employment and military service afforded important alternatives to the Indians. In World War I the Indians of some reservations had enlisted in the armed forces, but it was only during World War II that there was extensive participation by all Indians.

The state of national emergency was important in profoundly affecting reservation life in general. First, it reduced funds for the continuation of the governmental projects initiated by the Indian Reorganization Act. Second, the nation-wide shortage in the irregular labor force resulted in a greater demand for Indian labor to fill the gap created in off-reservation governmental and private industries (military installations, fire fighting in national forests, and railroad and lumber companies). For recruitment of off-reservation labor, the state sent out its own employment agents, following the initial stage when trading posts recruited Indian laborers.

The war also heightened the interest of the Indians in off-reservation affairs, and they sought knowledge on the progress of the war and other national affairs through the radios and newspapers that became available in small numbers during this period.

Wartime conditions generally discouraged the activities of the governmental and private agencies on the reservation. The volume of employment in these agencies decreased and missionary activities further deteriorated, although trading posts and village stores continued their existence without much change.

(2) *Characteristics of Moenkopi.* The main economic effect of the war on Moenkopi was to establish off-reservation wage em-

ployment as an alternative to reservation jobs, and nuclear families migrated to outside towns. In addition, many young men entered military service. Outside employment prepared the Indians for more intensive wage work on the reservation in the following period and further increased its economic importance.

Attempts to reorganize the reservation economy in the traditional subsistence pattern were retarded owing to the reduction of federal funds and to increasing dependence on cash income through wage labor off the the reservation. Migration of so many persons from the village caused reduction in farm acreage. Otherwise the village economy remained isolated and changed little from the preceding period.

Migration of families from Oraibi to Moenkopi ceased during this period. Ceremonial activities on Third Mesa deteriorated greatly, but the initiation ceremony to the Kachina society continued to be given by each of the two segments of Moenkopi, which became further separated on the basis of spatially distinct residential sites. In terms of economy and ceremonial activities, Moenkopi was now nearly an independent community.

Western Navajo Subagency Period (1951–present)

CONTEXTS, FACTORS, AND MEDIATING AGENCIES. This period is characterized by the increasing involvement of Moenkopi with agencies of federal, state, and private institutions; the reservation became of value more for its land and mineral resources than for its agricultural production, and Moenkopi gained greater access to opportunities outside the reservation. Today Moenkopi is exposed to more features of the larger society, and there is a corresponding increase in the number of agencies that mediate these features.

Functions of the federal government have been divided between several agencies where they were formerly centralized in the Bureau of Indian Affairs, and many new functions were delegated to the tribal governments. The state extended many agencies to cover Indian affairs, and private business and missions played a more important role on and off the reservation.

There was a proliferation and separation of federal agencies, which performed their numerous functions without central coordination, although they were all located in Tuba City. They became bureaucratic rather than paternalistic. To promote its Long Range Rehabilitation Program, the BIA Agency at Tuba City controlled land operations, road construction and maintenance, plant management, education, and welfare placement. Through the agency in Keams Canyon, it controlled education, credit service, and welfare placement.

The goals of these federal agencies included increase in school enrollment, better housing, road development, range improvement, electrification, development of water and sewer systems, and tourism. The last acquired importance owing to the proximity of the reservation to roads leading to the Grand Canyon and other scenic spots of national fame. Health matters were turned over to the Public Health Service, and postal affairs to the U.S. Post Office.

Federal and state agencies continued employment service for off-reservation work in military installations, forest fire fighting, private construction work on the reservation, and recruitment into the armed services; they also undertook programs of relocation to urban centers.

Innumerable features of the larger society were introduced to the reservation by private agencies. Missions sponsored sports events, motion pictures, rummage sales, and children's programs as well as religious services. Tuba City had a supermarket, a resident cattle buyer, service stations, and two trading posts, and the people now had access not only to newspapers and radios but also to telephones and began to depend extensively on automobiles instead of horses and wagons. Moenkopi acquired an automobile mechanic, a store, and a Mormon church in addition to the already existing Mennonite church.

Many of the new federal programs were carried out with the aid of the tribal councils or left entirely to them. The Navajo Tribal Council controlled the resources of the reservation through its Land Board and grazing committees and enforced the law through its police and courts, and it provided a community center for recreational activities. Moenkopi, although on the Navajo Reservation, was represented through the Upper Moenkopi Village Council on the Hopi Tribal Council and its day school was under the Hopi Agency. Under the auspices of the Hopi Tribal Council, the upper segment of Moenkopi developed a local water supply, a sewage system, and paved roads.

The intensive development of resources of the reservation and the exploitation of tourism not only increased the total wealth but made a much greater number of wage jobs available. There was also created a greater demand for electrical appliances, automobiles, telephones, and the other amenities of Western culture, which now became available locally. Even food had to be purchased owing to the decrease of local subsistence farming.

Modernization of the people of Moenkopi was also furthered by their new roles with respect to state institutions and private business and associations off the reservation. The state provided welfare programs, highways, and education in the higher grades. The people could find employment with private companies as well as on state projects, and they were able to obtain loans from credit companies to purchase such consumer durables as automobiles, vacuum cleaners, and gas heating and cooking facilities. Automobiles increased their territorial mobility, while the services of state employment agencies as well as the presence of friends and relatives in the white towns facilitated out-migration from the reservation. In their new situations, many were so far detached from their native villages that they joined local labor unions, an important step toward proletarianization.

CONTEMPORARY MOENKOPI. The shift of the reservation economy from a subsistence, nonmoney economy to a wage-based money economy appears to have been largely accomplished during this period. As the opportunities for wage work on the reservation have greatly increased through the federal Long Range Program, a major portion of the village labor force has been absorbed into wage earning activities. Under this program, Indian wage labor is devoted to the creation of such "social wealth" as improved road systems, on-reservation boarding schools, and domestic water and sewer systems in addition to the generally improved level of education. Moenkopi has profited by its proximity to Tuba City, which it joined in the use of electricity. The availability and use of public utilities has created a further demand for cash.

The contexts for cash spending have also multiplied by the entry of various private businesses to Tuba City, where they leased operational sites from the Navajo Tribal Council. With the increase in cash earnings, availability of credit from off-reservation loan companies, and greater accessibility of off-reservation markets through extensive adoption of automobiles, the Hopi of Moenkopi have become tightly bound to the consumer market of the northern Arizona region and hence to that of the nation.

The integration of Moenkopi into the national economy is not limited to the consumption sector alone. Many Moenkopi construction workers now belong to national trade unions. The factors that caused the shift from a subsistence economy to a money economy have transformed the community from a farming colony of Oraibi to a labor reservoir and a community that is suburban Tuba City.

Despite a long history of interactions between the Hopi of Moenkopi and the Navajo in its environs, Moenkopi has maintained its ethnic distinctiveness from the surrounding Navajo culture. Frequency of intermarriage between the two groups of the Indians has remained comparatively small and their cooperation in economic pursuits is small. The common involvement in the conditions of modernization in the greater Tuba region has tended to eliminate contexts for symbiotic relationships and to emphasize the competitive aspects of their interactions. The existence of the Hopi Tribal Council and "traditional" villages of Hopiland proper have helped Moenkopi to continue its cultural isolation from the Navajo. As a result Moenkopi today reveals no major influence from the Navajo either in its social structure or culture.

Participation in the national cash economy through wage work appears to have brought a culmination in the trend toward strengthening the nuclear family household, which is now solidified as an economic unit at the expense of lineage households. This has further severed economic ties between the households of Moenkopi and those of Oraibi. At the same time, the group composition of each household remains extremely flexible owing to volatile economic conditions. Finally, the solidarity of the nuclear family household has induced a shift in domestic authority from the mother's brother to the father and/or mother.

Proliferation of the agencies that mediate new functions from the larger society to the village has meant extensive surrender of the community functions of the village to these agencies. The people of Moenkopi also have come to take part more frequently in the ceremonies given in other villages of Hopiland than in their own.

The split of Moenkopi into two decision-making units has aggravated this process of its suburbanization with respect to Tuba City. While the Upper Moenkopi Village Council now acts as the sole mediating political agency within the village, a major portion of interactions with the agencies of change are maintained by individual residents without any intermediate coordination among themselves. In fact, the factional situation in Moenkopi allows such individual participation in the agencies of change without jeopardizing the political boundary of the village.

GENERAL TRENDS

Throughout the four periods, the following processes have been operative with differing degrees of intensity and velocity. They consist of partial integration of Moenkopi economy into national economy, emergence of the nuclear family household, and suburbanization of the village community.

Integration into National Economy

1) The marginality of the land around Moenkopi and the virtual exclusion of land capital from the national market resulted in continuous decline in traditional occupations and especially in subsistence farming as the village economy became increasingly dependent on cash wages. Traditional occupations now persist only for ceremonial purposes and hence for the maintenance of tribal identity.

2) Agriculture in Moenkopi has never been commercialized, nor have the lands been appropriated as plantations or haciendas, which would have transformed the people into a peasantry type of society.

3) Participation in the national economy took the form of wage work, largely on government projects, and consumption of the wage earnings largely through purchase of private market products. The commitment to the cash economy has become irreversible as opportunities for earning cash and desire for more kinds of consumer goods increased.

4) The change in the village economy is assuming the character of "proletarianization." This process is kept in check, however, by the reservation control of farm land, on which a majority of the Moenkopi residents pursue subsistence farming. It is far more evident among the Hopi who live off the reservation.

5) Throughout the process of economic change, the government was most effective as the monopsonic control of the Indian work force and "social investor" on the Navajo and Hopi reservations.

Emergence of the Nuclear Family Household as the Corporate Unit

1) Through individual right of disposal of the farm land, through intensive involvement in the cash economy by wage work, whose capital basis evaded the control of larger kin groups, and through disruption of the ceremonial life in the mother village of Oraibi, solidarity of matrilineage groupings as an effective household broke down.

2) Dependence on cash income mainly from the wage earnings of a husband reinforced his position in the nuclear family household. The traditional pattern of individual control of wage income

eliminated interference of a lineage in the disposal of cash. It shortened the developmental cycle of a household group, increasing the stability of marital bonds and shifting domestic authority from the mother's brother to the father and/or mother.

3) The relatively greater strength of the nuclear family household at the expense of the lineage household has not resulted in atomistic isolation of households resident in the village. Differential degrees of adoption of alien cultural goods in the households, especially between those in the upper and lower segments of the village, call for reciprocal cooperation in bilaterally related households. The traditional modes of cooperative labor within the village have been superseded by *ad hoc* cooperation within a small range of related households.

4) Increase in alternatives of productive activities both on and off the reservation, instability of employment conditions, heightened need for wage income, and general improvement in communication facilities have resulted in an increase in mobility of family groups of Moenkopi and has led to high flexibility in household composition (discontinuous extension).

Suburbanization of Village Community

1) Instability of employment conditions, relative paucity of skilled laborers, lack of investment of productive capital by the villagers owing to scarce funds, and governmental control of land capital inhibited the emergence of socio-economic classes within the village.

2) Moenkopi has been assuming a greater significance as a wage labor reservoir for Tuba City than as a farming colony of Oraibi.

3) Control of community affairs has been dislocated from traditional, internal agencies to federal and tribal agencies external to the village. The village has surrendered its control of secular community functions to the establishments in Tuba City and Flagstaff, while it has placed the control of religious activities again in the villages of Third Mesa. This has resulted in mounting indifference of the residents to community affairs and deterioration of community cooperation.

4) Linkages of the community with outside agencies have increased and their nature has become more bureaucratic. Accommodation to the new roles created by these linkages has been accomplished through a new political unit, the tribal council and its branches, rather than by wholly replacing the traditional political structure.

5) The emergence and persistence of the two decision-making units, each with an amorphous membership, has partly articulated the linkages of individuals to the outside through these segments. Surrender of community functions to outside agencies and institutions, however, has led to increasingly direct participation of individual households in the larger society, and it has resulted in an absence within the community of voluntary associations for mediation of the factors of change, except for the Upper Moenkopi Village Council.

The above trends appear considerably widespread in small communities throughout the world. They coincide with three of the four processes identified by Leighton and Smith for seven communities from India, Japan, Southeast Asia, and North and South America (1955:81–82). The suburbanization process alone has been a serious problem to many small towns of the United States (Vidich and Bensman, 1960; Lyford, 1964). Increase in the number of direct linkages of the small nuclear family household to state and national institutions and a resultant increase in the corporateness of the household, when subsistence economy is replaced by cash economy, have been frequently cited as a major trend of social change in the modern era not only among the American Indians (see Spoehr, 1947) but among other groups of the world as well (see Gough, 1961b; Moore, 1963:98, 102–3).

These processes represent in essence the global trend of industrialization and modernization (Steward, 1967), many factors of which have been mediated to Moenkopi through the Indian reservation system. In the course of this transformation, the unique conditions of Moenkopi endowed the community with a greater potential than any other Hopi village for the introduction of and active response to the factors of modernization. The location of the area in an oasis environment provided Moenkopi with potentially exploitable resources, while the dual affiliation of the village in the reservation system and its proximity to Tuba City exposed Moenkopi to a greater number of factors and their mediating agencies than if it had had an unambiguous affiliation to a single agency. The secular orientation of Moenkopi in the traditional social system and its minority status in the reservation framework of its former enemy, the Navajo, disposed the people to manipulate these factors to their advantage whenever an opportunity was present. It is under these conditions, then, that Moenkopi today emerges as the most profoundly transformed of all the Hopi villages.

Bibliography

Aberle, David F.
    1951   "The Psychological Analysis of a Hopi Life History," *Comparative Psychology Monographs*, vol. 21, no. 1, serial no. 107. Berkeley, Calif.

Adams, William Y.
    1963   *Shonto: A Study of the Role of the Trader in a Modern Navajo Community*. Bureau of American Ethnology, Bulletin 188. Washington, D.C.

Andre, Walter W.
    1964   Personal communication (March 18). Pierre, S.D.

Auerbach, H. S.
    1943   "Escalante's Journal (November, 1776)," *Utah Historical Quarterly*, 11:27–113.

Bauer, Peter T., and Basil S. Yamey
    1957   *The Economics of Under-developed Countries*. University of Chicago Press.

Beaglehole, Earnest
    1937   "Notes on Hopi Economic Life," *Yale University Publications in Anthropology*, No. 15. New Haven, Conn.

Beaglehole, Pearl
    1935   "Census Data from Two Hopi Villages," *American Anthropologist*, 37:41–54.

Blout, S. E.
    1911   *Moqui & Navajo Allotments* (map). Western Navajo School, Tuba City, Ariz.

Boissevain, Jeremy
    1964   "Factions, Parties, and Politics in a Maltese Village," *American Anthropologist*, 66:1255–87.

Bolton, Herbert E.
    1950   *Pageant in the Wilderness—The Story of the Escalante Expedition to the Interior Basin, 1776*. Utah State Historical Society, Salt Lake City.

Boyer, Ruth M.
   1964   "The Matrifocal Family among the Mescalero: Additional Data," *American Anthropologist,* 66:593–602.
Brainard, Margaret
   1935   "The Hopi Family." Unpublished doctoral dissertation, University of Chicago.
Brandt, R. B.
   1954   *Hopi Ethics.* University of Chicago Press.
Brophy, William A., and Sophie D. Aberle
   1966   *The Indian: America's Unfinished Business.* University of Oklahoma Press, Norman.
Brown, Estelle A.
   1952   *Stubborn Fool.* Caxton Printers, Caldwell, Idaho.
Brugge, David
   1964   "Navajo Land Usage: A Study in Progressive Diversification." In Clark S. Knowlton (ed.), *Indian and Spanish American Adjustments to Arid and Semiarid Environments,* Contribution No. 7 of the Committee on Desert and Arid Zone Research. Texas Technological College, Lubbock.
   1965   Personal communication (December 17). Window Rock, Ariz.
Carlson, Vada
   1964   *No Turning Back.* University of New Mexico Press, Albuquerque.
Christensen, Christian L.
   1958   *Diary of Christian Lingo Christensen* (mimeo). Brigham Young University Library, Provo, Utah.
Cleland, Robert G., and Juanita Brooks (eds.)
   1955   *A Mormon Chronicle: The Diaries of John D. Lee, 1848–1876.* Huntington Library, San Marino, Calif.
Colton, Harold S.
   1934   "A Brief Survey of Hopi Common Law," *Museum Notes of the Museum of Northern Arizona,* 7:21–24. Flagstaff.
   1936   "The Rise and Fall of the Prehistoric Population of Northern Arizona," *Science,* 84:337–43.
Colton, Harold S., and F. C. Baxter
   1932   *Days in the Painted Desert and San Francisco Mountains.* Northern Arizona Society of Science and Arts, Bulletin No. 2. Flagstaff.
Connelly, John C.
   1956   "Clan-lineage Relations in a Pueblo Village Phratry." Unpublished M.A. thesis, University of Chicago.
Contzen, Phillip
   1905   *Township No. 32 North, Range No. 10 East, Gila and Salt River, Meridian Arizona* (map). Surveyor General's Office, Phoenix, Ariz.
Coues, Elliott
   1900   *On the Trail of a Spanish Pioneer: Garces Diary, 1775–1776* (2 vols.). Harper, New York.

Crane, Leo
   1925   *Indians of the Enchanted Desert.* Little, Brown and Co., Boston.

Cushing, Frank H., J. Walter Fewkes, and Elsie C. Parsons
   1922   "Contributions to Hopi History," *American Anthropologist,* 24:253–98.

Dozier, Edward P.
   1954   "The Hopi-Tewa of Arizona," *University of California Publications in American Archaeology and Ethnology,* 44:259–376.
   1960   "The Pueblos of the Southwestern United States," *Journal of Royal Anthropological Institute,* 90:146–60.
   1966a   "Factionalism at Santa Clara Pueblo," *Ethnology,* 5:172–85.
   1966b   *Hano: A Tewa Indian Community in Arizona.* Holt, Rinehart and Winston, New York.

Dozier, Edward P., George E. Simpson, and J. Milton Yinger
   1957   "The Integration of Americans of Indian Descent." In G. E. Simpson and J. M. Yinger (eds.), "American Indians and American Life," *Annals of the American Academy of Political and Social Science,* vol. 311. Philadelphia.

Dunning, R. William
   1962   "Some Aspects of Governmental Indian Policy and Administration," *Anthropologica,* 4:209–32.

Earle, Edwin, and Edward A. Kennard
   1938   *Hopi Kachinas.* J. J. Augustin Publishers, New York.

Eggan, Dorothy
   1943   "The General Problem of Hopi Adjustment," *American Anthropologist,* 45:357–73.

Eggan, Fred
   1950   *Social Organization of the Western Pueblos.* University of Chicago Press.
   1964   "Alliance and Descent in Western Pueblo Society." In R. A. Manners (ed.), *Process and Pattern in Culture.* Aldine Publishing Co., Chicago.

FDL
   Various years   Fort Defiance Letterbooks.

Firth, Raymond
   1939   *Primitive Polynesian Economy.* Routledge, London.

Firth, Raymond, and Basil S. Yamey (eds.)
   1964   *Capital, Savings and Credit in Peasant Societies.* Aldine Publishing Co., Chicago.

Fitchen, Janet M.
   1961   "Peasantry as a Social Type," *Proceedings of the 1961 Annual Spring Meetings of the American Ethnological Society.* Seattle, Wash.

Fontana, Bernard L.
   1963   "The Hopi-Navajo Colony on the Lower Colorado River: A Problem in Ethnohistorical Interpretation," *Ethnohistory,* 10:162–82.

Forde, Daryll
 1931 "Hopi Agriculture and Land Ownership," *Journal of Royal Anthropological Institute,* 61:357–411.
Fox, J. R.
 1961 "Veterans and Factions in Pueblo Society," *Man,* 61:173–76.
Friedl, Earnestine
 1963 "Studies in Peasant Life." In B. J. Siegel (ed.), *Biennial Review of Anthropology 1963.* Stanford University Press, Stanford, Calif.
Geertz, Clifford
 1963 *Agricultural Involution.* University of California Press, Berkeley.
Getty, Harry T.
 1961–62 "San Carlos Cattle Industry." In F. W. Voget (ed.), "American Indians and Their Economic Development," *Human Organization,* 20:181–86.
Gibbons, Helen
 1963 "Chief Tuba of the Saints," *Improvement Era,* November.
Gluckman, Max
 1956 *Custom and Conflict in Africa.* Free Press, Glencoe, Ill.
Golden, John
 1951 "Political Factioning among Three North American Indian Tribes: The Hopi; Klamath-Modoc; and Fox." Unpublished M.A. thesis, University of Chicago.
Goldenweiser, Alexander A.
 1937 *Anthropology.* F. S. Crofts, New York.
Goody, Jack
 1958 "The Fission of Domestic Groups among the Lodagaba." In J. Goody (ed.), "The Developmental Cycle in Domestic Groups," *Cambridge Papers in Social Anthropology,* No. 1. Cambridge, England.
Gough, Kathleen
 1961a "Descent-Group Variation among Settled Cultivators." In D. M. Schneider and K. Gough (eds.), *Matrilineal Kinship.* University of California Press, Berkeley.
 1961b "The Modern Disintegration of Matrilineal Descent Groups." In D. M. Schneider and K. Gough (eds.), *Matrilineal Kinship.* University of California Press, Berkeley.
Gouldner, Alvin W.
 1959 "Reciprocity and Autonomy in Functional Theory." In L. Grass (ed.), *Symposium on Sociological Theory.* Evanston, Ill.
Gregory, Herbert E.
 1915 "The Oasis of Tuba, Arizona," *Annals of the Association of American Geographers,* 5:110–19. Chicago.
 1916 *The Navajo Country: A Geographic and Hydrographic Reconaissance of Parts of Arizona, New Mexico and Utah.* U.S. Geological Survey, Water-Supply Paper 380. Washington, D.C.

Haas, Theodore H.
1957 "The Legal Aspects of Indian Affairs from 1887 to 1957." In G. E. Simpson and J. M. Yinger (eds.), "American Indians and American Life," *Annals of the American Academy of Political and Social Science,* vol. 311. Philadelphia.

Hack, John T.
1942 "The Changing Physical Environment of the Hopi Indians of Arizona," *Papers of the Peabody Museum of American Archaeology and Ethnology,* vol. 25, no. 1. Cambridge, Mass.

Hammel, E. B.
1961 "The Family Cycle in a Coastal Peruvian Slum and Village," *American Anthropologist,* 63:989–1005.

Hammon, George P., and Agapito Rey
1953 *Don Juan de Oñate: Colonizer of New Mexico, 1595–1628.* University of New Mexico Press, Albuquerque.

Hill, W. W.
1948 "Navajo Trading and Trading Ritual: A Study of Cultural Dynamics," *Southwestern Journal of Anthropology,* 4:371–96.

Hopi Hearings
1955 Hopi Hearings, conducted by a team appointed by Commissioner of Indian Affairs, BIA Phoenix Area Office. Phoenix, Ariz.

Human Dependency Survey
1939 Statistical Summary, Human Dependency Survey, Navajo and Hopi Reservations (mimeo). Washington, D.C.

Humphrey, Robert R.
1955 *Forage Production on Arizona Ranges, IV: Coconino, Navajo, Apache Counties (A Study in Range Condition).* University of Arizona Experiment Station, Bulletin 266. Tucson.

HvJ
Healing v. Jones, Civ. 579 Pct., Defendant's Exhibits, II (nos. 2–557; 1930–38); III (nos. 497–556; 1939–58).

Indian Voices
1965 Special section. September. Chicago.

Ives, Joseph C.
1861 *Report upon the Colorado River of the West, explored in 1857 and 1858 by Lieutenant Joseph C. Ives.* U.S. Engineering Department, Washington, D.C.

Jones, Volney H.
1950 "The Establishment of the Hopi Reservation," *Plateau,* 23:17–25.

Johnson, Burke J.
1964 "The Muddle of Moenkopi Wash," *Arizona Days and Ways* (Sunday supplement to *Arizona Republic,* September 27). Phoenix.

Kaut, Charles R.
1957 "The Western Apache Clan System: Its Origins and De-

velopment," *University of New Mexico Publications in Anthropology*, No. 9. Albuquerque.

KCL
Various
years Keams Canyon Letterbooks.

Kelly, Isabel T.
1934 "Southern Paiute Bands," *American Anthropologist*, 36: 548–60.

Kelly, William H.
1953 *Indians of the Southwest: A Survey of Indian Tribes and Indian Administration in Arizona.* University of Arizona Press, Tucson.
1954 "Applied Anthropology in the Southwest," *American Anthropologist*, 56:709–19.
1957 "The Economic Basis of Indian Life." In G. E. Simpson and J. M. Yinger (eds.), "American Indians and American Life," *Annals of the American Academy of Political and Social Science*, vol. 311. Philadelphia.

Kennard, Edward A.
1965 "Post-War Economic Changes among the Hopi," *Proceedings of the 1965 Annual Spring Meetings of the American Ethnological Society.* Seattle, Wash.

Kirchoff, Paul
1955 "The Principles of Clanship in Human Society," *Davidson Journal of Anthropology*, 1:1–10.

Kluckhohn, Clyde, and Dorothy Leighton
1948 *The Navajo.* Harvard University Press, Cambridge, Mass.

Kroeber, Alfred L.
1917 "Zuni Kin and Clans," *Anthropological Papers of the American Museum of Natural History*, 18:39–205. New York.

Kunstadter, Peter
1963 "A Survey of the Consanguine of Matrifocal Family," *American Anthropologist*, 65:56–66.

La Farge, Oliver
1957 "Termination of Federal Supervision: Disintegration and the American Indians." In G. E. Simpson and J. M. Yinger (eds.), "American Indians and American Life," *Annals of the American Academy of Political and Social Science*, vol. 311. Philadelphia.

Lasswell, Harold D.
1931 "Faction." In *Encyclopaedia of Social Sciences.* Macmillan Co., New York.

Leighton, Alexander H., and Robert J. Smith
1955 "A Comparative Study of Social and Cultural Change," *Proceedings of the American Philosophical Society*, 99:79–88. Philadelphia.

Levy, Jerrold E.
1962a "Community Organization of the Western Navajo," *American Anthropologist*, 64:781–801.
1962b "South Tuba: A Western Navajo Wage Work Community." Paper presented before the annual meeting of the American

Anthropological Association, Chicago. MS, Ethnology Papers, Window Rock Field Office, USPHS.
 1964 Personal communication (June 8). Window Rock, Ariz.
Long Range Program
 1944 Long Range Program for the Hopi Tribe, Arizona (mimeo). Keams Canyon, Ariz.
Lowie, Robert H.
 1929 "Hopi Kinship," *Anthropological Papers of the American Museum of Natural History*, 30:361–88. New York.
Lyford, Joseph P.
 1964 *The Talk in Vandalia: The Life of an American Town*. Harper, New York.
MacLeish, Kenneth
 1940 "Notes on Hopi Belt-Weaving of Moenkopi," *American Anthropologist*, 42:291–310.
McFeat, Tom F. S.
 1962 "The Malecite Family Industries: A Case Study," *Anthropologica*, 4:291–310.
Mindelef, Victor
 1891 *A Study of Pueblo Architecture: Tusayan and Cibola*. U.S. Bureau of American Ethnology, Eighth Annual Report. Washington, D.C.
Mintz, Sidney W.
 1959 "Internal Market Systems as Mechanism of Social Articulation," *Proceedings of the 1959 Annual Spring Meetings of the American Ethnological Society*. Seattle, Wash.
Moore, Wilbert E.
 1963 *Social Change*. Prentice-Hall, Englewood Cliffs, N.J.
Murdock, George P.
 1965 *Social Structure*. Macmillan, New York.
Murphy, Robert F., and Julian H. Steward
 1956 "Tappers and Trappers: Parallel Process in Acculturation," *Economic Development and Cultural Change*, 4:335–55.
Navajo Times
 1962 May 30, vol. 3, no. 19. Window Rock, Ariz.
 1963 October 3, vol. 4, no. 37. Window Rock, Ariz.
 1964 May 21, vol. 5, no. 21. Window Rock, Ariz.
 1965 July 22, vol. 6, no. 29. Window Rock, Ariz.
Navajo Tribal Council
 1954 *Duties and Responsibilities of the Land Board for Major Irrigation Project* (pamphlet). Window Rock, Ariz.
 1962 *Navajo Reservation Grazing Handbook*. Window Rock, Ariz.
Page, Gordon B.
 1940 *Hopi Agricultural Notes* (mimeo). Soil Conservation Service, Navajo Area.
 1954 "Hopi Land Patterns." In *Hopi Agriculture and Food*, Reprint Series, No. 5. Museum of Northern Arizona, Flagstaff.
Page, G. B., and O. Lavantu
 1937 *Tuba City Agricultural Holdings* (map). Department of Agriculture, Soil Conservation Service, Navajo District.

Parsons, Elsie C.
- 1925 "A Pueblo Indian Journal," *Memoirs of the American Anthropological Association*, No. 32. Menasha, Wis.
- 1931 "Review of R. H. Lowie's 'Notes on Hopi Clans' and 'Hopi Kinship,'" *American Anthropologist*, 33:232–36.
- 1933 "Hopi and Zuni Ceremonialism," *Memoirs of the American Anthropological Association*, No. 39. Menasha, Wis.
- 1936 "Early Relations between Hopi and Keres," *American Anthropologist*, 38:554–60.
- 1939 *Pueblo Indian Religion*. University of Chicago Press.

Payton, Lee
- 1965 Personal communication (July 28). Shiprock, N.M.

Provinse, John, et al.
- 1954 "The American Indian in Transition," *American Anthropologist*, 56:387–94.

Radcliffe-Brown, Alfred R.
- 1950 Introduction. In A. R. Radcliffe-Brown and D. Forde (eds.), *African Systems of Kinship and Marriage*. Oxford University Press.

Rubin, Vera
- 1961 "The Anthropology of Development." In B. J. Siegel (ed.), *Biennial Review of Anthropology 1961*. Stanford University Press, Stanford, Calif.

Shepardson, Mary
- 1963 "Navajo Ways in Government: A Study in Political Process," *Memoirs of the American Anthropological Association*, No. 96. Menasha, Wis.

Shepardson, Mary, and Blodwen Hammond
- 1964 "Change and Persistence in an Isolated Navajo Community," *American Anthropologist*, 66:1029–50.

Siegel, Bernard J., and Alan R. Beals
- 1960 "Pervasive Factionalism," *American Anthropologist*, 62:394–417.

Simmons, Leo W. (ed.)
- 1963 *Sun Chief: The Autobiography of a Hopi Indian*. Yale University Press, New Haven, Conn.

Solien, Nancy L.
- 1960 "Household and Family in the Caribbean," *Social and Economic Studies*, 9:101–6.

Spicer, Edward H.
- 1954 Letter to editors, *American Anthropologist*, 56:890.
- 1962 *Cycles of Conquest: The Impact of Spain, Mexico and the United States on the Indians of the Southwest, 1533–1960*. University of Arizona Press, Tucson.

Spicer, Edward H. (ed.)
- 1952 *Human Problems in Technological Change*. Russell Sage Foundation, New York.
- 1962 *Perspectives in American Indian Culture Change*. University of Chicago Press.

Spier, Leslie
 1928 "Havasupai Ethnography," *Anthropological Papers of the American Museum of Natural History,* 29:83–392. New York.

Spoehr, Alexander
 1947 "Changing Kinship Systems," *Anthropological Papers, Field Museum of Natural History,* 33:155–235. Chicago.

Stephen, Alexander M.
 1936 "Hopi Journal" (ed. E. C. Parsons), *Columbia University Contributions to Anthropology,* No. 33. New York.

Stern, Theodore
 1961–62 "Klamath Livelihood, Tribe, and Reservation." In F. W. Voget (ed.), "American Indians and Their Economic Development," *Human Organization,* 20:172–80.

Steward, Julian H.
 1931 "Notes on Hopi Ceremonies in Their Initiatory Form in 1927–1928," *American Anthropologist,* 33:56–79.
 1937 "Ecological Aspects of Southwestern Society," *Anthropos,* 32:87–104.
 1951 "Levels of Sociocultural Integration," *Southwestern Journal of Anthropology,* 7:374–90.

Steward, Julian H. (ed.)
 1967 *Contemporary Change in Traditional Societies* (3 vols.). University of Illinois Press, Urbana.

Strong, William D.
 1927 "An Analysis of Southwestern Society," *American Anthropologist,* 29:1–61.

Stubbs, Stanley A.
 1950 *Bird's-Eye View of the Pueblos.* University of Oklahoma Press, Norman.

TCL
 Various years Tuba City Letterbooks.

Ter Haar, B.
 1950 *Beginselen en Stelsel van het Adatrecht.* Groningen, Djakarta.

Titiev, Mischa
 1938 "The Problem of Cross-Cousin Marriage among the Hopi," *American Anthropologist,* 40:105–11.
 1944 "Old Oraibi," *Papers of the Peabody Museum of American Archaeology and Ethnology,* 22:1–277. Cambridge, Mass.

Thompson, Laura
 1950 *Culture in Crisis.* Harper, New York.

Thompson, Laura, and Alice Joseph
 1944 *The Hopi Way.* University of Chicago Press.

U.S. Department of Interior
 1962 *Hopi Indian Agency* (mimeo). Keams Canyon, Ariz.

U.S. District Court for the District of Arizona
 1962 Opinion of the Court, *Healing* vs. *Jones* (No. Civ. 579, Prescott). San Francisco.

U.S. Geological Survey
   1957   *Marble Canyon* (map). Denver, Colo.
U.S. Weather Bureau
   1960   *Climatological Survey.* Washington, D.C.
Van Valkenburgh, Richard
   1941   *Dine Bikeyah* (mimeo). Window Rock, Ariz.
Vidich, Arthur, and Joseph Bensman
   1960   *Small Town in Mass Society.* Doubleday, Garden City, N.Y.
Voegelin, Carl F.
   1959   "An Expanding Language, Hopi," *Plateau,* 32:33–39.
Voegelin, Carl F., and Florence M. Voegelin
   1957   "Hopi Domains," *Memoirs of the International Journal of American Linguistics, Indiana University Publications in Anthropology and Linguistics.* Baltimore.
Voget, Fred W.
   1961–62 Commentary. In F. W. Voget (ed.), "American Indians and Their Economic Development," *Human Organization,* 20: 243–48.
Vogt, Evon
   1951   "Navajo Veterans," *Papers of the Peabody Museum of American Archaeology and Ethnology,* vol. 41, no. 1. Cambridge, Mass.
   1955   "A Study of the Southwestern Fiesta System as Exemplified by the Laguna Fiesta," *American Anthropologist,* 57: 820–39.
Watson, James B.
   1945   "The Historical Development of Hopi Economy and Its Relations to Other Aspects of Culture." Unpublished M.A. thesis, University of Chicago.
Webb, Walter Prescott
   1931   *The Great Plains.* Ginn and Co., Boston.
Whiting, Alfred F.
   1950   "Ethnobotany of the Hopi," *Museum of Northern Arizona Bulletin,* No. 15. Flagstaff.
Wittfogel, Karl A., and Esther S. Goldfrank
   1943   "Some Aspects of Pueblo Mythology and Society," *Journal of American Folklore,* 56:17–30.
Wolf, Eric R.
   1955   "Types of Latin American Peasantry: A Preliminary Discussion," *American Anthropologist,* 57:452–71.
   1957   "Closed Corporate Peasant Communities in Mesoamerica and Central Java," *Southwestern Journal of Anthropology,* 13:1–18.
   1959   *Sons of the Shaking Earth.* University of Chicago Press.
   1966   *Peasants.* Prentice-Hall, Englewood Cliffs, N.J.
Woodbury, B. Richard, and Natalie F. S. Woodbury
   1964   "The Changing Patterns of Papago Land Use," *Proceedings of the XXXVth International Congress of Americanists, Mexico, 1962.* Mexico City.

Wright, Barton
    1964   Personal communication (May 20). Flagstaff, Ariz.

Young, Robert W. (ed.)
    1952   *The Navajo Yearbook, Report No. 1.* Navajo Agency, Window Rock, Ariz.
    1955   *The Navajo Yearbook of Planning in Action, Report No. 5.* Navajo Agency, Window Rock, Ariz.
    1957   *The Navajo Yearbook, Report No. 6.* Navajo Agency, Window Rock, Ariz.
    1961   *The Navajo Yearbook, Report No. 8, 1951–1961: A Decade of Progress.* Navajo Agency, Window Rock, Ariz.

Index

Acreage, 102–8; increase in, 106, 218, 305; reduction in, 106, 309
Adoption, 121, 232
Agriculture: commercial, 111, 125. *See also* Economy; Farming; Irrigation; Land; Market; Subsistence
Aholi, 42–43, 239
Aiyave, 93
Akchin field, 103
Allotment, 4, 34, 39, 53, 69, 80, 86, 100–101, 106, 111, 123, 127, 158, 303, 306; allottees, 119; chiefly, 63, 80, 294; in Colorado River Reservation, 182; of grazing land, 153; inheritance of, 87, 121; inheritance of, probation, 80, 114, 121–22, 154, 293, 296; Navajo, 103; "owner," 116; "ownership," 115, 118, 250; sanction of, 102; second project, 112. *See also* Land, right
Apples, 144; Tuba, 176
Arroyo, 18, 106, 127
Assimilation, 5, 23, 101, 306
Automobiles, 209, 298, 304, 310–11; purchase of, 207, 210; repair shop, 199
Awatobi, 3

Bacabi, 5, 11, 67, 96, 112, 195, 249, 284
Barter. *See* Trade, barter
Beaglehole: Earnest, 109, 139, 156, 168, 170; Pearl, 246–48, 254, 257, 259

Bean, 108, 124, 144; adaptability to sand dune farms, 146; dance, 196
Bear clan, 42–43, 99
BIA. *See* Bureau of Indian Affairs
Black Mesa, 16, 18, 21
Blue Canyon, 34, 36, 46–47, 198, 223
Boarding school, 4, 34, 36–37, 47, 49; Navajo, 106; off-reservation, 179, 187–88, 273, 303, 306; at Tuba City, 179, 184, 262, 268, 303
Boundary maintenance. *See* Tribal, identity
Brainard, Margaret, 203, 246–48, 254, 257–58
Brugge, David, 194
Bureau of Indian Affairs, xv, 2, 24, 36, 44, 57–58, 60–61, 66, 101–2, 111, 154, 171, 174–75, 181, 184, 188, 190, 194, 220, 247–48, 273, 290, 309; Phoenix Area Office, 83; trusteeship of land ownership, 100, 102, 111, 119. *See also* Government; Economics of trust management; Reservation, system
Business: Indian, 185, 297; private, 5, 185, 194, 204, 220, 289, 309, 311; small businessmen, 187

Capital: agricultural, 120; farm land, 119; land, 214; land, legal compartmentalization of, 219; land, reservation control of, 192, 211, 213, 296, 298–99, 313; money, 178; productive, investment in, 211, 298

327

Carrying capacity, 4, 56, 154, 160, 167, 306
Cash: demand for, 186, 201, 219, 306; disposal of, 314; economy, 2, 5, 37, 50, 83, 106, 111, 119–20, 143, 151, 153, 155, 192, 197, 211, 219, 244, 250, 304–6, 311–12, 315; economy, contact with, 120; economy, involvement in, 124; hoarding of, 210, 298; male control of, 203; transactions within community, 298. See also Economy; Income; Spending; Subsistence
Cattle, 69, 155–56, 158, 161, 165, 167, 174, 304, 310; beef, 159; business, 159. See also Grazing; Livestock
Cattlemen, 158, 164–69 passim, 173, 175; white, 176
Ceremony, 2, 292; coordination of, 12; cycle, articulation of, 12; exchange in, 144, 149, 175; lifecycle, 236–39; participation in, 93; and spending, 209–10; and wage work, 186
Charcos. See Rainwater catches
Chiefs: hereditary, 69; village, 7, 10, 38, 42–44, 57, 99, 109, 129; war, 9–10. See also Lower Moenkopi, chief; Moenkopi; Oraibi, chief
Christianity. See Missions
Clan, 2, 6, 9–10, 112, 117, 229–40, 245, 247–48; corporateness, 231; economic basis, 230; exogamy, 235–37, 239; head, 229; house, 14, 38, 214, 230, 244–45, 285–86; land, 99, 110, 112, 157, 229, 248–49; land, breakdown of, 243; legends, 1; matrilineal, 3, 8; membership, 229; mother, 14, 230; paternal, 235–36; and politics, 240; "reseeding," 232; segmentation of, 23–31; solidarity of, 230, 235; subclan, 230–31. See also Kinship; Lineage
Class: economic, 298, 314
Coal, 21, 48, 99–101, 207; mine, 21, 176–78; mining, 193
Coconino: County, 28, 291; National Forest, 21
Collier, John, 56, 101, 181, 296
Colonial setting, 23
Colony, 1, 13–15, 22, 32, 45, 100, 234, 270, 305, 314; ambiguous role of, 15
Colton, Harold S., xvii, 109, 223

Communal village garden. See Vegetables, garden
Community: agency, 29; apathy, 74, 293; Center, Navajo, 90; contact, 28; differentiation of, 13, 148; projects, 52; segmentation, 92, 96–97, 110; solidarity, 75; wealth, 83. See also Reservation, community
Compartmentalization, 65, 239, 298
Competition: individual, 95, 211; inter-village, 11; with the Mormons, 302; with the Navajo, 173, 222, 305; pattern of, 89–90
Connelly, John, 12, 244
"Conservatives": double standard of, 290; ideology, 97
Construction: work, 268; workers, 204, 297. See also Union, construction laborers'
Consumer durables, 207, 211, 311. See also Household, investment
Contracts. See Land, contractual relationship in
Cooperation, 88, 295: agricultural, 50, 250; ceremonial, 51; deterioration of, 72–73, 96, 307, 314; economic, 43, 137; in irrigation, 51, 83, 127; of kin, 123, 244, 300, 314; religious, 9. See also Irrigation, ditch repairing parties
Cooperative, agricultural, 296
Corn, 124–25, 128, 139, 144, 151, 176; blue, 145, 149, 152, 208, 297; grinding machine, 125, 211; husks, 140; sweet, 145, 147; white, 145, 149, 208, 297
Cotton, 143–44, 195
Craft: differentiation of, 12; goods, 197; goods, price of, 195–96; industry, 194; pottery, 21, 195
Credit: service of the government, 310; standing, 201; system of traders, 220; union, voluntary, 202. See also Loan, agencies
Crops: commercial, 148; rotation, 146; salability, 146; for sale, 149, 152
Culture: Hopi, 2; Pueblo, integration of, 3

Dances: exchange of, 67; puppet, 14; social, 38, 75, 293, 302; unmasked, 14. See also Kachina, dance; Snake, dance
Dawes Act. See General Allotment Act

Decision-making: and unanimity, 9; units, 63, 315
Demonstration effect, 212
Division of labor: absence of, 9; sexual, 124; traditional, 109, 125, 297. *See also* Specialization, of skills
Divorce, 259, 261, 263, 265, 269, 278–85 *passim*; and children, 284; factors of, 281–85; frequency of, 279–81. *See also* Marriage
Dozier, Edward P., 13, 136

Economic: activities, individualization of, 119; integration, 215, 220; opportunities, 61
Economics of trust management, 218
Economies: boundaries of, 120
Economy: areal, integration of, 213; capitalistic, 98; commercial, 119; "dual," 113, 120, 123, 148, 218; Indian, reorientation of, 181; national market, 251; national, integration to, 212, 311, 313; off-reservation, 207; peasant, 98; primitive, 98. *See also* Cash, economy; Subsistence, economy
Education. *See* Boarding school; Moenkopi, Day School; Schools
Eggan, Fred, xv–xvi, 13, 208, 233–34, 246–47, 270, 278, 280, 285
Electricity, 80, 185, 208, 211
Employment, 262; off-reservation, 187, 189, 214, 273, 308; on-reservation, 194, 220; part-time, 281; Service, State, 61, 189–90, 289, 311; tribal, 190. *See also* Government, employment; Unemployment; Wage work
Enclavement, 219, 221
Entrepreneur, 221–22, 299; incentives of, 297
Eototo, 43
Examiner of inheritance, 102
Extension: continuous, 257–61, 264; defined, 257; discontinuous, 259, 261–65, 286–87; lateral, avoidance of, 258. *See also* Household, group

Factional: dispute, 237, 307; segment, 6, 307
Factionalism, xiv, 2, 9–10, 49, 52, 92, 96, 110, 185, 294, 307, 312; colonial extension of, 294; defined, 50; pervasive, 92, 96; schismatic, 92, 96

Factions, 45, 53, 67, 78, 92, 221, 296; ambiguity in terms, 93; fluidity in membership, 94; loyalty, 94; recruitment, 92
Family: finance, 204, 208; migration in, 309; spending pattern of, 208. *See also* Household, nuclear family; Migration
Farm: distribution, 111, 121; dry, 103, 140; esthetic preference of, 139; land, inefficient employment of, 124, 296; land appropriation, mode of, 111; school, 39, 138, 176, 178, 180, 184, 186, 193, 215, 303; strategic significance of, 73. *See also* Acreage; Agriculture; Farming; Land; Subsistence
Farming, 297, 300, 304; and annual rainfall, 17; calendar, 129; decline of, 267, 310; dry, 18, 119, 137; flood-water, 18, 103, 106, 129, 137; nonirrigation, 137–41; productivity, 142; sand dune, 19, 139; technology, 125–43, 219; and wage work, 186, 189. *See also* Acreage; Agriculture; Farm; Irrigation; Land; Subsistence
Father's sister, 148, 236–38
FDL. *See* Letterbooks, Fort Defiance
Fertilizer, 140
First Mesa, 11–13, 55, 117, 173, 230
Flagstaff, xiv, xvii, 28, 32–33, 37, 65, 71, 115, 122, 153, 174, 176, 181, 186–87, 190, 193, 199, 201–2, 261–62, 290–91, 303–4, 307, 314; shopping in, 206–7
Food: crops, shortage of, 219; sales, 201
"Force account method," 190
Forde, Daryll, 109, 117, 120, 241, 248
Forest Fire Fighting Service, 194, 268, 308, 310
Freedom, individual, 92, 95
Freightage, 33, 178, 186, 193, 304
Freighter, 37, 50, 178
Friendship, 79, 150, 170
Fruit trees, 108, 144; in school farm, 176

Genealogy, 121, 229, 232, 242
General Allotment Act, 34, 100–101
Gossip, 75
Government: agencies, decentralization of, 61; employment, 41, 175,

179, 186; federal, 23, 154, 184, 202, 301–4, 306, 309–10; Indian employees in, 185–86; "issues," 138; monopsonic control by, 194, 221, 313; paternalistic, 4, 24, 304, 309; proliferation of agencies, 289; resource control by, 215; as social investor, 221–22, 313; state, 26–27, 202, 309, 315; tribal, 5, 58, 100, 307; "wards" of, 4, 24, 304; white employees in, 191. *See also* Bureau of Indian Affairs; Capital, land; Economics of trust management; Hopi, Tribal Council; Navajo, Tribal Council; Reservation, system; Self-determination

Grand Canyon, 8, 16, 261, 310
Graveyard, 55, 239, 310
Grazing: camp, 167–69, 173; committee, 58, 68, 101, 155, 288–89, 310; permits, 70, 153–57, 161, 168, 289. *See also* Herding; Livestock; Range
Gregory, Herbert E., 17, 19, 21, 36, 126, 144, 176, 223, 270

Hano, 3, 11, 13, 16
Harmony, 8, 52
Havasupai, 2, 197
Herders, 159, 161; Navajo, 173; Navajo and Hopi, competition between, 159
Herding: groups, 157, 166, 168, 170; practices, 157, 168–74 *passim*
Hopi: Agency, xv, 28–29, 34, 57, 63, 68, 79, 83, 91, 121, 130, 202, 225, 288, 291, 306, 310; Hearings, 61, 75; Reservation, xvii, 33, 46, 101, 112, 153, 173, 179, 181–82, 226, 288, 290, 306, 313; revolving funds, 202; Tribal Council, xiv, 52, 56–59, 61, 63, 288, 294, 296–97, 310, 312; Tribal Court, 307; Tribal Police, 75–77, 294, 307. *See also* Government; Tribal
Horses, 138, 158, 167, 277; for barter, 197
Hospital, 29, 182, 184, 189, 306; at Tuba City, 89, 238
Hotevilla, xiv, 5, 11–12, 16, 45, 54, 58, 67–68, 78, 87, 94, 115, 118, 157, 167. 173–74, 188, 203, 240, 245, 254, 257–58, 261–63, 278, 289
House: inheritance of, 266; site, 81

Household: bilateral family, 6, 255, 286; developmental cycle of, 257, 259–61, 265–68, 314; extended, 259; forms of, 255–65; group, definition of, 246–48; investment, 211–12, 220, 298; nuclear family, 6, 9, 94, 204, 245, 246–69 *passim*, 276, 299–300, 314–15; nuclear family, solidarity of, 251, 299, 312; nuclear family, predominance of, 256–57; size of, 251–55. *See also* Extension; Kinship; Lineage, household
Hunting, 99, 101

Income: cash, 202, 204, 214; distribution of, 217; individual control of, 218; surplus, 208; tax, 68. *See also* Wage, income
Indian: Reorganization Act, 5, 25, 55, 56, 61, 101, 153, 181, 202, 306, 308; Rights Association, 56; self-determination, 101, 306; special status of, 100
Innovation, 95–96
Installment purchase, 201–2, 207
Interaction: face-to-face, 2, 5, 60; inter-village, 12. *See also* Competition
IRA. *See* Indian, Reorganization Act
Irrigation, 19, 32, 103, 114, 125–37 *passim*, 143, 151, 181, 235, 303, 305–6; canal, 21, 63, 82–83, 125–32 *passim*, 178, 301; and clan, 136–37; contribution to farming, 137; culvert, 126; dam, 126–27, 131, 301; ditch repairing parties, 85, 132; flume, 131–32, 134; intake gate, 129, 133–34; lack of integration with the traditional farming, 126; maintenance, 130–32; from Moenkopi Wash, 119, 131–35; potential of, 142; from springs, 135, 303; strategic significance of, 73; system, 50, 103; system, decentralization of, 79, 83, 135, 137, 307; water, 51, 74, 84. *See also* Cooperation, in irrigation; Reservoir; Watermaster
Isolation, 5, 6, 24, 179, 212, 308; from kin, 283; from national economy, 212, 221; price for, 206. *See also* Marginal; Marginality

Job: hunters, 186, 197; hunting, 189, 192

INDEX 331

Kachina: cult, 225, 230, 245, 291; clowns, 76; dance, 38, 51, 63, 76, 91, 148, 210, 305; dolls, 196; initiation to, 14, 67, 149, 291-93; parade of, 54; society, 8, 14, 54, 67, 70, 292, 307, 309
Kalé:taqa. See Chiefs, war
KCL. See Letterbooks, Keams Canyon
Keams Canyon, 28–29, 34, 46, 60–61, 71, 121, 289, 290. See also Hopi, Agency
Kennard, Edward A., xiii, 167, 208–9, 212
Kikochomovi. See Oraibi, New
Ki:kya, 65, 245
Kinship, 2, 9, 79, 117, 119, 122, 135, 238, 241, 244, 281, 305; bilateral, 121, 125, 137; ceremony, 148–49, 230, 239; exchange, 145, 148, 175, 237, 239; and marriage stability, 285–87; matrilineal, 2, 6, 94, 112, 229, 300. See also Clan; Household; Lineage
Kiva, 3, 38, 50, 55, 63, 80, 292; differentiation of, 54; groups, 9
Kiya'a. See Father's sister

Labor: construction, 124, 204, 297, 310; contractual, 125; farming, recruitment in, 124; Indian, 184, 214; Negro, 4; recruitment, 123, 125; reservoir, 188, 297, 311, 314; semi-skilled, 189; sharing between brother households, 124; shortage in farming, 108, 123–24, 138, 219, 264, 282, 297; shortage in herding, 173, 175; shortage in unskilled, 181, 308; surplus, 215; unskilled, 297. See also Union, trade; Wage, labor
Land: accumulation of, 119; assignment, 102, 117, 118, 289, 303; bilateral division of, 267, 274; Board, 59, 101-2, 106, 113, 118, 250, 288–89, 310; contractual relationship in, 119; holdings, fragmentation of, 119, 219; and labor, 119, 122; management district, 25, 56, 153, 158, 160, 184; "ownership," 115, 118, 250; rent, relative, 142; "rent," 117, 119–20; right, flexibility in, 113; right, of individual disposal, 108–9, 112–13, 116, 117, 118, 119, 121, 307, 313; shortage, 124; tax, exempt, 100, 209; tenure, 99, 108–
9, 111, 119; tenure, "individual," 116, 235, 250, 286, 296. See also Allotment; Clan, land; Village, outland
Leaders, 87, 97; predicament of, 74
Leadership, 92–95 passim; collective, 68–69; monolithic, 69; traditional, 42–44. See also Chiefs; Lower Moenkopi, leadership; Moenkopi, chiefly position; Upper Moenkopi
Legal system: national, 23–24, 68, 193. See also Government, federal; Indian, special status of
Letterbooks: Fort Defiance, xvi; Keams Canyon, xvi; Tuba City, xvi
Levy, Jerrold E., 290n
Lineage, 6, 44, 229, 237, 241–47, 249, 251, 285, 314; chiefly, 81, 116, 128; defined, 241; differentiation of, 13, 244–46; household, 9, 229, 248–49, 255, 268, 285, 314; lack of solidarity, 94; land holding, 2, 250; marginal, 13, 41, 44, 244–45, 305; matrilineal, 112, 117, 229, 249, 279, 285, 286, 313; segments, 241–43; solidarity, 244, 250, 307. See also Clan; Household; Kinship
Little Colorado River, 32, 177, 179
Livestock, 153–74 passim; individual ownership of, 155; inheritance of, 155–56, 159; market demand for, 166–67; operation, 161, 167, 220, 305; ownership, exclusion of women from, 156, 161; sale of, 174–75. See also Grazing; Range
Living, standard of, 212, 299
Loan, 69; agencies, 201, 220, 311. See also Credit; Trading posts, territorial control of
Lololoma, 37–38, 71
Long Range Rehabilitation Program, 182, 187, 223, 309, 311
Lower Moenkopi, xv, 63, 65, 67–69, 71, 80, 88, 90, 94, 291–92, 294–95; chief, 69–70, 80, 87, 89–90, 122, 130, 209, 237, 294, 297; chiefly succession in, 70; leadership, 73–74, 78, 91. See also Moenkopi, chiefly position of
Lowie, Robert H., 241–42
Luxury goods, 221. See also Spending, luxury

Mail order houses, 207

Marau, 12, 14
Marginal: land, 4, 213, 214; role, 13. *See also* Isolation; Lineage, marginal
Marginality: of labor, land, and resources, 221, 298, 313. *See also* Isolation
Market: agricultural, 120; consumer, 206, 210, 212, 213, 215, 218, 221, 251, 291, 298, 307; labor, 194, 212; stock, 302; wage work, 188. *See also* Economy; Labor; Subsistence; Wage
Marriage, 112, 113, 228, 232, 249, 261, 269–78 *passim*, 286; brittleness of, 278, 285; inter-tribal, 270, 273, 282–83, 312; inter-village, 117, 270; prohibition, 235–37. *See also* Clan, exogamy; Divorce; Residence
Matrifocal family, 268–69, 284, 286
Matrilineage. *See* Lineage, matrilineal
Matrilineal descent. *See* Kinship, matrilineal
Medicine: man, 65, 69, 201; woman, 201
Mennonite, 47, 48; church, 45, 65–67, 176, 251, 293, 310; disruptive effects of, 49; Hopi attitude to, 65; Hopi converts, 65; mission, 47, 49. *See also* Missions
Migration, 97, 110, 225, 228; internal, 103, 106, 180, 223, 243, 269, 309; from off-reservation towns, 211; to off-reservation towns, 187, 218, 307–9. *See also* Moenkopi, population; Population; Residence
Military: draft, 58, 181; service, 57, 189, 220, 308–10
Mindeleff, Victor, 143, 223, 248
Mishongnovi, 11–12, 117, 234–35, 242, 247, 258, 262, 270
Missions, 5, 28, 202, 309–10; Christian, 49; control, 4; Protestant, 37, 47, 304. *See also* Mennonite; Mormon; Spanish
Missionaries, 24–25, 60, 66, 177, 180, 252, 307–8. *See also* Mennonite; Mormon; Spanish
Missionization, 3, 301. *See also* Mennonite; Mormon; Spanish
Mobility: social, 2; spatial, 2, 229, 277, 314. *See also* Migration; Residence
Modernization, 6–7, 311–12, 315; sources of, 24

Moenave, 19, 37, 47, 103, 112
Moenkopi: accomodative "stance" of, 215; boundary of two segments, 54, 62; charter of, 7; chiefly position of, 38–39, 42–44, 245; climate of, 16–17; colonial position of, 29, 112, 214, 221, 243, 277; colonists of, 100, 277; Day School, 48, 65–66, 89, 108, 179, 193, 200, 291, 306; division of, 63, 78; as ethnic enclave, 6; ethnic exclusiveness of, 47, 312; fairs, 60, 200, 304; fear of discrimination, 36, 191; geology of, 19; jurisdictional ambiguity of, 28, 315; minority status of, 29, 215, 288, 305, 315; Plateau, 16, 21, 160; population, 1, 53, 103, 106, 233–39, 248, 279, 291, 305; proximity to Tuba City, 28, 311; rainfall in, 17; reservation status of, 16; spring, 55, 87, 135; symbiotic relationship with Navajo, 47, 151; vegetation of, 21; Wash, 1, 18, 32, 34, 103, 127, 158–59, 176. *See also* Colony; Lower Moenkopi; Population; Upper Moenkopi
Money. *See* Cash
Mormon: church, 176, 252, 293, 310; colonization, 32, 301–2; commerce, 32, 102; crops, 32; irrigation farming, 103, 127; orchards, 37; period, 301–3; village, 182; withdrawal, 34, 102, 127, 144, 302. *See also* Missions
Mormons, 6–7, 24, 32, 36, 39, 47, 103, 111, 125, 135, 175, 180, 213, 302, 304
Mother's brother, 118, 251, 312
Mö:wi, 38, 53, 236–37
Museum of Northern Arizona, xv, 1, 233n; Research Center, xiv–xv, xvii

Nashileowi, 38–39, 41–43, 114–16, 245
Navajo: Agency, xvi, 6, 28; boarding school, 106; chapters, 60; conflicts with Mormons, 33; Reservation, 1, 143, 153, 169, 181–82, 184, 190, 202, 288, 306, 310, 313; Tribal Council, 21, 56, 63, 88–91, 97, 101–2, 154, 161, 184–85, 200, 220, 250, 288–89, 296, 310–11; Tribal Court, 76, 118, 288–89; Tribal Police, 59, 68, 76, 89, 187, 289, 294. *See also* Grazing, committee; Land,

Board; Tuba City, Agency; Western Navajo

Oasis, 19, 21, 185, 270, 315
Oraibi (Old), 1, 5–6, 11–14, 32, 37, 41–45, 50–51, 55, 73–76, 99–100, 112, 117–18, 123, 129, 148, 158–60, 180, 230–35, 243–49, 277–78, 293, 300–309, 313–14; authority of, 51, 294; chief, 42–43, 67, 239–40; disorganization of, 110; "Chief's Talk," 43; enclave, 6, 304–5; Friendlies, 45; Hostiles, 44–46; land basis of, 110; New, 5, 11, 45, 48, 62, 67, 78, 96, 195, 198, 261–62, 278, 292; outland, 101, 108; population increase in, 110; split, 38, 45, 96, 230, 240, 280; Wash, 110, 157. *See also* Village, outland
Orchards, 39, 180; Mormon, 37; school, 127, 144, 176, 184, 186, 193, 303
Outfit. *See* Herding, groups
Outland. *See* Oraibi (Old), outland; Village, outland
Ownership. *See* Allotment, "ownership"; Land, right; Village, residential lots
Page, Gordon B., 108, 110, 159–60, 168, 173
Paiute, 2, 37, 301
Parsons, Elsie C., 13, 241
Paternalism. *See* Government, paternalistic; White "patrons"
Patki clan, 99, 112, 118
Peasantry, 99, 221, 313
Phoenix, 174–76, 185, 207, 262, 263; Area Office, 83; Indian school, 46; Land Operations office, 83–84
Phratry, 229, 231–32, 235; exogamy, 235–37. *See also* Clan
PHS. *See* Public Health Service
Pi:kyas clan, 14, 38–44 *passim*, 69, 94, 234, 237, 239–40, 243–45. *See also* Aholi; Lower Moenkopi, chief; Moenkopi, chiefly position of; Water Coyote clan
Plantation, 4, 213, 215, 221, 313
Poaka, 44n
Polacca, 11, 29, 47, 96, 150
Policemen, 178, 193, 304; Hopi, 59; Navajo, 101. *See also* Hopi, Tribal Police; Navajo, Tribal Police; Tribal, police
Politicians, Indian, 289–90

Politics without confrontation, 82, 84, 88, 91–92. *See also* Factionalism
Population: fluid, 117; growth rate, 225–26; genealogical composition of, 112; "service," 226; "tribal," 226, 228. *See also* Moenkopi, population
Pottery. *See* Craft, pottery
Poverty, 298–99
Powamu, 12, 14, 69, 186, 245, 291–92, 305; society, 14, 67, 70
Power: colonial, 99; purchasing, 304; supernatural, 44n; traditional, 49, 57, 130. *See also* Chiefs; Lower Moenkopi, chief; Moenkopi, chiefly position of
Production: cost of, 142; factors of, 122; means of, 98; resources, sanction of, 100. *See also* Capital; Economy; Government; Land; Subsistence
"Progressives," 93, 222
Proletarianization, 190, 298–99, 311, 313
Property: communal, 92; individual, concept of, 296. *See also* Wealth
Public Health Service, 25, 61, 71, 78, 88, 184, 194, 288–89, 310; at Keams Canyon, 89; at Tuba City, 91, 291–92
Pueblos: Revolt, 3; Western, social organization of, 2, 3, 11

Radcliffe-Brown, Alfred R., 7, 229, 230
Rainwater catches, 153, 159
Range, 109, 153, 159–60, 167, 303, 310; boundaries of, 157; "customary use area," 154; disputes over, 159–60; flexible right in, 160; Hopi, 173; Navajo, 158; open, 153–54, 157, 175; resources, 153; for sheep, 157; usufruct, 155–56, 157, 158. *See also* Grazing; Herding; Livestock
Red Lake, 37, 103, 106, 137, 198, 261
Relatives. *See* Clan; Household; Kinship; Lineage
Relocation Program: in Colorado River Reservation, 182; Service, 186
Renting: of house, 276. *See also* Land, "rent"
Reservation, 4, 5, 103, 151, 202, 218, 226, 306–9, 314; community, 37,

129, 175, 178, 214–15; lands, 24, 101, 221, 306; system, 22–26 *passim*, 98, 100, 109–11, 121, 193, 214, 219, 296, 298, 303, 315. See also Bureau of Indian Affairs; Government, federal; Isolation; Marginality

Reservoir, 39, 62, 82–83, 85, 131, 135, 158, 301; headgate, 126, 129; headgate keys, 84, 130; irrigation, 126–27; at Tuba city, 176. See also Farming; Irrigation; Watermaster

Reservoir Canyon, 19, 32, 34, 39, 88, 100–103, 126–27, 129, 135, 158, 185

Residence, 94, 273, 281; dual, 277; instability of, 74, 277–78; matrilocal, 8, 10, 259, 261, 273, 297; neolocal, 257, 265, 273–77, 286, 299; patrilocal, 244, 261; post-marital, 117, 255; seasonal, 32, 248, 302. See also Divorce; Marriage; Village, residential lots

Retirement payment, 60, 202, 204

Right of individual disposal. See Allotment; Land, right

Rumor, 75

San Francisco Mountains, 8, 16, 21

Savings, 208, 210; bank, 69, 201. See also Cash; Spending

Schools, 29, 46, 67; government, 189; off-reservation, 186, 190, 210, 289; primary, 292; principal, 60; public, 61, 66, 182, 189, 190, 289; schooling, 25, 210, 309–11; shower room, 60, 66; Sunday, 48–49, 65; tuition, 209. See also Boarding school; Farm, school; Missions; Moenkopi, Day School; Orchards, school

Second Mesa, 11, 13, 90, 108, 111, 167, 209–10, 212, 221, 234, 257, 270, 277

Self-determination. See Indian; Tribal, self-government

Sewage system: of Upper Moenkopi, 72, 85–88, 108, 211–12; of Navajo, 88. See also Water-sewer, system

Shato Plateau, 16, 21

Sheep, 155, 161, 167–68; drovers, 304; herders, 57, 151, 157–58, 164, 168–70, 174; herding, 69, 117, 168. See also Grazing; Livestock; Range

Shichomovi, 11, 13, 15, 230

Shipaulovi, 11–13, 97, 230–31, 237, 242, 247, 257

Shongopavi, 11–13, 87, 93, 115, 230–31, 237, 263, 270, 293

Shonto, 101, 190, 208, 210, 212, 221, 229

Shrine, 14, 99

Siyamptewa, 48, 50, 52, 69–70, 115

Snake: ceremony, 230; dance, 12

Social control, 75–76, 82–83, 95, 293–94

Societies, religious, 8–9, 99

Soil: Conservation Service, 57, 110, 114, 119, 173; salinization of, 129

So'o, 238. See also Clan, mother

South Tuba, 71, 187, 192, 289

Soyal, 12–13, 38, 42, 69–70, 239, 293, 305, 307

Spanish: control, 3; mission, 28; period, 13, 46; policies, 3–4

Specialization: in agriculture, 125; of skills, 190, 298. See also Division of labor

Spending, 202, 298; contexts, 213–14, 311; family, 208; luxury, 208–10, 212; seasonal, 208. See also Cash; Credit; Loan; Savings

Spicer, Edward H., 23, 28, 221

Springs: contact, 126; irrigation from, 135, 303; sacred, 55, 87, 135

State. See Government, state

Steward, Julian H., xiii, 97, 232

Stock: overgrazing of, 153, 160; reduction, 5, 25, 56, 153–54, 160–61, 173, 181, 218, 306–7; water, 159. See also Livestock

Store: general, 49; off-reservation, 206. See also Village, store

"Studies of Cross-Cultural Regularities," xiii

Subclan. See Clan, subclan

Subsistence, 2, 4, 111, 120, 297, 302–3, 306; agriculture, 37, 39, 106, 123; crops, 125, 142–43, 144, 152, 208, 215; economy, 98–100, 108, 119–20, 122–23, 125, 153, 181, 192, 213, 214, 215, 219, 305, 311, 315; farming, 4, 6; needs, 122. See also Economy; Farming; Land

Suburbanization, 298, 311–15 *passim*

Sun Chief, 50, 125, 144, 148, 180, 186, 203, 207

Superintendent, 4, 46, 50, 60, 193, 198

Supermarkets, 81, 151, 160, 189, 206, 310

INDEX   335

Symbiosis. *See* Moenkopi, symbiotic relationship with Navajo

Tawaquaptewa, 45, 71
Tewa, 3, 198
TCL. *See* Letterbooks, Tuba City
Termination policy, 25
Third Mesa, 11, 13, 99–102, 109–11, 123, 168–69, 173, 231, 243, 249, 254, 270, 277, 292, 297, 308–9, 314
Thompson, Laura, 13, 49
Titiev, Mischa, 14, 94, 233–34, 237, 241–43, 246–47, 265, 270, 274, 278–80, 283, 285
Tourism, 16, 196, 198, 296, 310
Towns: agency, 28; off-reservation, 181, 187–89, 204, 211, 218, 220, 266, 276–78, 283, 297, 304; on-reservation, 228; railroad, 179. *See also* Reservation, community
Tractors, 138, 210–11
Trade: barter, 98, 150–51, 197, 305; inter-tribal, 197
Traders, 24, 149, 151, 157, 182, 185, 196
Trading posts, 37, 41, 132, 174, 176, 178, 181, 185, 198, 201–6, 215, 218, 304, 307–8, 310; territorial control of, 201, 220
"Traditionals," 71, 78, 87, 93, 188, 222, 240, 290, 296, 312. *See also* Faction; Factionalism
Tribal: council, 44n, 54–56, 59, 60, 62, 78, 94, 96, 289, 307, 310, 314; court, 101–2, 130; enterprise, incorporation of, 296; game regulations, 101; identity, 143, 149, 219, 293; lawyer, 59, 87; police, 77–78, 96, 101; self-government, 55, 61. *See also* Government, tribal; Indian; Hopi; Navajo
Tribalization, 60, 296
Tuba, 38
Tuba City, xv, xvii, 1, 6, 28–29, 32, 34, 37, 45, 47, 61, 76, 78, 88–89, 121, 152, 160, 174–76, 182, 185–86, 196, 198–99, 203, 206, 214, 220, 223, 228, 237, 260–62, 268, 278, 283, 292, 294–97, 299, 302, 305, 310, 314; Agency, xvi, 21, 47, 49, 57–58, 63, 79, 83, 106, 130, 156, 176–77, 179–81, 184, 187, 192, 199–200, 266, 303, 305–6; population in, 1, 289; Post Office, 81, 132, 182, 310. *See also* Western Navajo, Subagency

Unemployment, 124, 262, 283; compensation, 192; reaction to, 192; sources of, 192. *See also* Employment; Wage, work
Union: construction laborers', 71; trade, 190, 297, 311. *See also* "Force account method"; Labor; Wage, work
Unionism, 299
Unionization, 220
Upper Moenkopi, xiv, xv, 57, 88, 291–95 *passim;* Council, xv, 56, 62, 63, 66–95 *passim,* 199, 211, 225, 289, 293, 310, 312; district, 56, 62; governor, 68. *See also* Moenkopi
Uranium mill, 21, 185
Usufruct, 109, 118; inheritance of, 120; in the outland, aboriginality of, 109. *See also* Land, right; Range, usufruct
Utility, public, 207, 210–11

Valkenburgh, Richard van, xvii
Vegetables: garden, 99, 126, 135, 147, 176; melons, 147, 151–52; squash, 108, 144
Village: control over, 73; as a corporate group, 7; crier, 69, 127, 239; "friendly," 38; major, 11–13; "mother," 13–15, 37, 230–31, 249, 302; "outland," 8, 99–100, 108–10, 112, 121; plaza, 55, 63, 76, 91, 148; residential lots, 8, 53, 93, 228, 296; site, 50, 52, 81, 99, 114, 293; solidarity of, 10, 305; store, 198–200, 205, 215, 307; territory, 8, 99. *See also* Colony; Land, right
Village Council, 52, 55, 68, 130, 305
Vocational training, 188–89

Wage: income, 41, 188, 189, 192, 194, 203, 251, 299; labor, 39, 125, 180, 186, 197, 220, 303, 311; rate, 193-94; work, 41, 44, 97, 106, 108–9, 119–24 *passim,* 151, 179, 214, 218, 224, 250, 269, 305, 312–13; work, colony, 297; work, economy, 6, 167, 178, 180, 267, 276, 298–99; work, effect on herding, 173–75; work, nepotistic tendency in, 189; work, off-reservation, 180–81, 185–

86, 307–8; work, on-reservation, 218, 297; work, opportunities of, 123, 176, 178, 185, 188, 291; work, pattern of, 186; work, seasonality in, 124, 192; workers, 124, 131, 297, 299. *See also* Labor; Union
Wages: cash, 125; paid in checks, 202, 204. *See also* Cash
Walapai, 2; trading parties of, 197
Walpi, 11–13, 230–31, 262
Water Coyote clan, 39, 48, 51, 54, 69–70, 195, 240, 243–45; chiefly alliance of, 44. *See also* Pi:kyas clan
Watermaster, 62, 79, 84, 87, 130. *See also* Irrigation; Reservoir
Water-sewer: project, 71, 86; system, 63, 293, 310, 311. *See also* Sewage system
Watson, James B., 109, 156–57, 170
Wealth, 307, 310; community, 83; corporate, 50; display of, 298; social, 210, 220, 311; strategic, 68

Wedding, 149; ceremony, 236–37, 239
Welfare, 61, 68, 202, 268, 288, 291, 309–10; state, 28, 311
Western Navajo: Agency, 6; Reservation, 34, 36, 101, 158, 198, 303; Subagency, 1, 28, 121, 184, 288. *See also* Navajo; Tuba City, Agency
Wheat, 143–44, 176
White "patrons," 187, 189, 282
Windmills, 153–54, 159, 172–73
Window Rock, xv-xvi, 60, 71, 182, 289–90
World War: I, 5, 308; II, 5, 57, 181, 186, 218, 244, 270, 308
Wright, Barton A., xv, 233n
Wuwuchim, 12, 14, 51, 69, 70, 230, 293, 305

Yokioma, 45, 58, 68

Zuni, 2, 196, 262, 282